A Textbook of Science for Class IX

CBSE CONCISE CHEMISTRY

Part-2

In accordance with the latest syllabus prescribed by the Central Board of Secondary Education, New Delhi.

CBSE CONCISE CHEMISTRY

A Textbook of Science for Class IX

Part-2

Ravi Shankar Sharma
M.Sc., B.Ed., P.G.T. (Chemistry)
Mayo College
Ajmer, (Raj.)

Subha Raghavan
B.Sc., M.Sc.

E. Anna Purna
M.Sc., B.Ed.

OSWAL PUBLISHERS
1/12, Sahitya Kunj, M. G. Road, Agra-282 002

No Part of this book can be reproduced in any form or by any means without the prior written permission of the publisher.

Edition : 2019

ISBN : 978-93-87660-90-8

OSWAL PUBLISHERS

Head office	:	1/12, Sahitya Kunj, M.G. Road, Agra-282 002
Phone	:	(0562) 2527771-4, +91 75340 77222
E-mail	:	contact@oswalpublishers.com, sales@oswalpublishers.com
Website	:	www.oswalpublishers.com
Facebook link	:	https://www.facebook.com/oswalpublishersindia
Available at	:	amazon.in, Flipkart, snapdeal, paytm

PREFACE

We are deeply grateful in bringing out this book **CBSE CONCISE CHEMISTRY** for the students of Class IX as per the latest NCERT syllabus prescribed by the Central Board of Secondary Education (CBSE). The book has been primarily designed to equip students with guidance and prepare themselves for getting maximum marks. It covers all the problems faced by the students and is written in simple language and lucid style for the benefit of the students. We hope that the students and teachers will appreciate our effort.

The exclusive features of this book are as follows :

- Entire subject matter has been summarized in simplified manner in order to understand the chapter easily.
- Each topic is described in simple language with an array of examples which helps to understand the concepts better.
- Description and illustration of text and activities clearly in points with simple and well-labelled diagram.
- The text in the chapters is supported by intext questions in the form of Paper-Pen Test to make good revision of the studied topic.
- Compendium at the end of each chapter is useful for making a quick note on the chapter.
- Exercises are given at the end of each chapter for the practice of students.

Lastly, We wish to express our gratitude and sincere thanks to all our team who gave their valuable time for discussion and **Oswal Publishers**, for their full co-operation in bringing out this book to our entire satisfaction. We sincerely hope that this book will improve teaching learning process in chemistry to a great extent and will be appreciated by our learned colleagues and students. We will be glad to receive constructive suggestions for the further improvement of the book.

Authors

LATEST CBSE CURRICULUM, CLASS IX SCIENCE (CHEMISTRY)

Theme : Materials

UNIT I : MATTER – NATURE AND BEHAVIOUR

Matter in Our Surroundings : Definition of Matter; Solid, Liquid and Gas; Characteristics - Shape, Volume, Density; Change of State-Melting (Absorption of Heat), Freezing, Evaporation (Cooling by Evaporation), Condensation, Sublimation.

Is Matter Around us Pure : Elements, Compounds and Mixtures. Heterogeneous and Homogenous Mixtures, Colloids and Suspensions.

Atoms and Molecules : Particle Nature, Basic Units: Atoms and Molecules, Law of Constant Proportions, Atomic and Molecular Masses. Mole Concept : Relationship of Mole to Mass of the Particles and Numbers.

Structure of Atom : Electrons, Protons and Neutrons; Valency, Chemical Formula of Common Compounds. Isotopes and Isobars.

QUESTION PAPER DESIGN FOR SCIENCE
CLASS IX

Time : 3 Hours
Max. Marks : 80

S. No.	Typology of Questions	Very Short Answer (VSA) 1 Mark	Short Answer-I (SA-I) 2 Marks	Short Answer-II (SA-II) 3 Marks	Long Answer (LA) 5 Marks	Total Marks	% Weightage
1.	**Remembering** (Knowledge based simple recall questions, to know specific facts, terms, concepts, principles, or theories, Identify, define, or recite, information)	2	–	1	1	10	15%
2.	**Understanding** (Comprehension - to be familiar with meaning and to understand conceptually, interpret, compare, contrast, explain, paraphrase, or interpret information)	–	1	4	2	24	35%
3.	**Application** (Use abstract information in concrete situation, to apply knowledge to new situations, Use given content to interpret a situation, provide an example, or solve a problem)	–	1	2	2	18	26%
4.	**High order thinking skills** (Analysis & synthesis - Classify, compare, contrast, or differentiate between different pieces of information, Organize and/or integrate unique pieces of information from a variety of sources)	–	–	1	1	8	12%
5.	**Inferential and Evaluative** (Appraise, judge, and/or justify the value or worth of a decision or outcome, or to predict outcomes based on values)	–	1	2	–	8	12%
	Total (Theory Based Questions)	2 × 1 = 2	3 × 2 = 6	10 × 3 = 30	6 × 5 = 30	68 (21)	100%
	Practical Based Questions (PBQs)		6 × 2 = 12	–	–	12 (6)	
	Total	2 × 1 = 2	9 × 2 = 18	10 × 3 = 30	6 × 5 = 30	80 (27)	

1. Questions paper will consist of 27 questions.
2. All questions would be compulsory. However, an internal choice will be provided in three questions of 3 marks each and two questions of 5 marks each, two questions of 5 marks each and one question (for assessing the practical skills) of 2 marks.

CONTENTS

1. **MATTER IN OUR SURROUNDINGS** — 11–66

2. **IS MATTER AROUND US PURE** — 67–140

3. **ATOMS AND MOLECULES** — 141–209

4. **STRUCTURE OF ATOM** — 210–260

1 MATTER IN OUR SURROUNDINGS

CONTENTS

1.0 Introduction
1.1 Matter Is Made Up of Particles
1.2 Brownian Motion
1.3 Characteristics of particles of Matter
1.4 Classification of Matter
1.5 Solids and their Characteristics
1.6 Liquids and their Characteristics
1.7 Gases and their Characteristics
1.8 Diffusion
1.9 The Common and SI Unit of Temperature
1.10 Change of State of Matter
1.11 Effect of change of Temperature
1.12 Effect of change of Pressure
1.13 Evaporation
1.14 Other states of Matter

1.0 INTRODUCTION

We know that the universe is made up of matter and energy. Humans are constantly trying to discover the relationship between energy and matter and the interactions that occur between them in our day to day life. In order to understand this relationship, we need to know more about the matter. Matter existed on the earth even before the first man had appeared on it. Do you know that all substances present around us can be classified as matter? What this matter is? *Anything or everything which occupies space, possesses mass and offers resistance to any stress applied on it is called matter.* The air we breathe in, the food we eat, the clothes we wear, the house we live, the clouds, the stars and different planets, rocks, minerals etc., are all different kinds of matter. Ancient Indian philosophers postulated that all the matter was made up of five basic elements namely, air, earth, fire, water and sky.

The nature of matter can be ascertained by studying its properties and composition. Modern scientists, classified matter in two ways which are as follows :

(a) Based on Appearance

(b) Based on Composition

The classification based on appearance is known as physical properties. The classification based on composition is known as chemical properties.

In this chapter, we shall study the classification of matter based on its physical properties.

1.1 MATTER IS MADE UP OF PARTICLES

Every matter is made up of particles which differ in size, shape and nature. These particles are so small that we cannot see them even with a high power microscope. However, the number of particles in matter is very, very large.

Note

- Matter is not continuous but it is particulate in nature i.e., it is made up of particles.

For instance, if we hold a glass sheet in our hand, we can observe that sheet is a continuous one. But what happens when it falls accidentally? The glass sheet breaks into very small pieces. This shows that the sheet is made up of particles (Fig. 1.1).

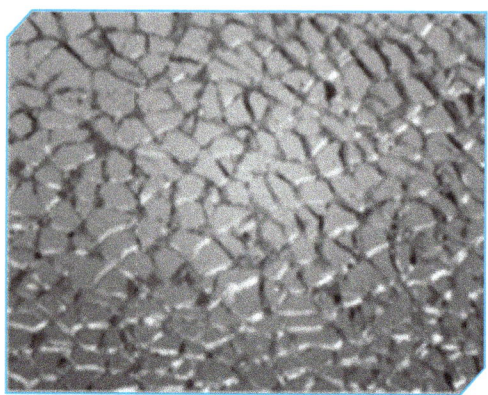

Fig. 1.1 : This figure shows that a glass sheet is made up of several tiny particles.

How Small are these Particles of Matter?

Once established that matter is made up of particles, the question raised was about the size of these particles?

The particles which makes up the matter are in constant motion. For instance, a small raindrop contains about 10^{21} particles of water in it (Fig. 1.2).

Fig. 1.2 : A small rain drop on a leaf contains about 10^{21} tiny particles of water in it.

Though, we cannot see these particles, we have certain evidences which tells us that all matter is made of tiny particles. Let us perform an experiment which clearly shows that the particles which make up the matter are constantly moving.

Note
- The particles which make up matter are atoms or molecules.

Evidences to Show that Particles are Found in Matter

Is matter continuous or particulate in nature? The existence of particles in matter and their motion can be clearly observed from the experiments of diffusion and Brownian movement. Let us look into few simple experiments by assuming that all matter is made up of tiny particles which are constantly moving.

(a) Dissolving a Solid in a Liquid : When a solid crystal of purple coloured potassium permanganate ($KMnO_4$) is placed in a beaker of water, the colour of the water turns into purple on its own without stirring. This is because of the spreading of purple coloured potassium permanganate ($KMnO_4$) as a whole in the water. (Fig. 1.3). However, the actual reason behind the spread of purple coloured potassium permanganate throughout the water is that, the particles of potassium permanganate get into the inter-particle spaces between the molecules of water thereby making the whole water look purple.

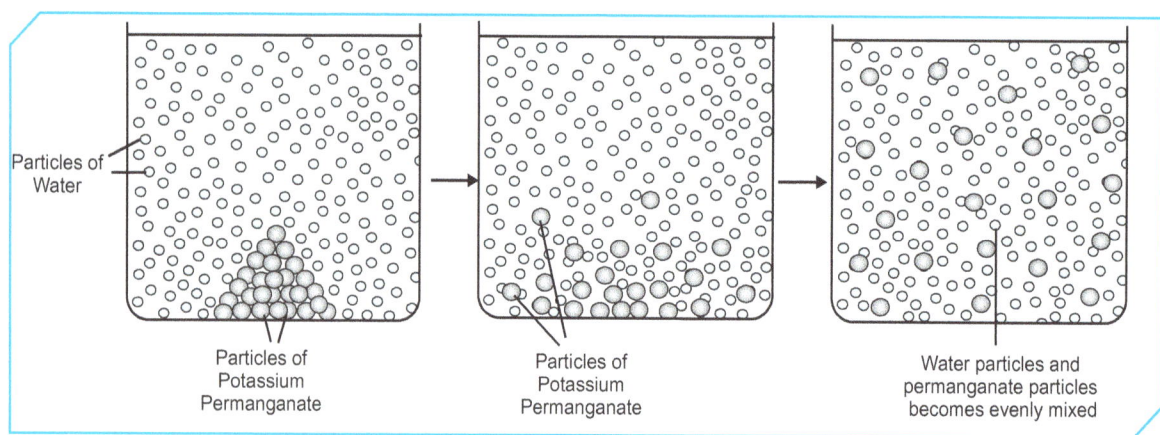

Fig. 1.3 : This figure shows the diffusion of potassium permanganate in water.

In this experiment, both potassium permanganate ($KMnO_4$) crystal and water are made up of tiny particles. The particles of potassium permanganate ($KMnO_4$) are purple in colour whereas the particles of water are colourless. These particles mixes on their own without any external stirring, turning the whole water into purple. It can be concluded from the experiment that the particles of water and potassium permanganate crystals are constantly in motion and this can be seen as the spreading of purple colour in the upward direction of the beaker, (Fig. 1.4).

Fig. 1.4 : This figure shows the diffusion of potassium permanganate in water

Similarly, when sugar is added to water, the sugar dissolves and disappears in water. But do you know how sugar dissolves and disappears in water or where does the sugar go? Let us explain. When sugar is mixed with water, the tiny particles in the sugar breaks and occupies the spaces between the particles of water and gets mixed with them. Thus, sugar dissolves in water and disappears (Fig. 1.5).

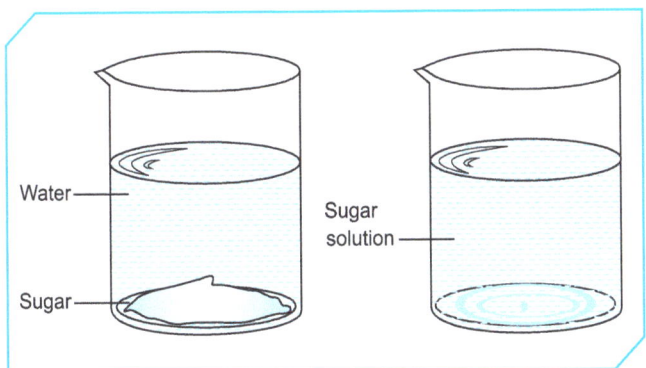

Fig. 1.5 : This figure shows the dissolution of sugar in water.

Note

- In this experiment, the sugar is dissolved in water by stirring to dissolve it quickly. Even if we do not stir, the sugar will dissolve very slowly in water.

Let us understand this by performing an activity to show that matter is made up of particles.

Activity 1.1 – To dissolve a solid in a liquid.

PROCEDURE

Step 1– Take a 100 mL beaker.

Step 2– Fill half the beaker with water and mark the level of water.

Step 3– Dissolve some salt or sugar by constantly stirring with the help of a glass rod.

Step 4– Observe any change in the water level.

Step 5– What do you think has happened to the salt?

Step 6– Where does it disappear?

Step 7– Does the level of water changes?

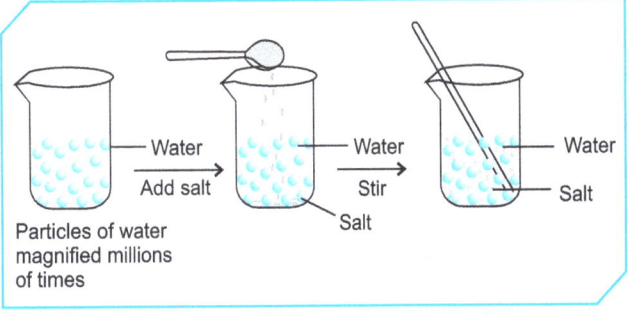

Fig. 1.6 : This figure shows the dissolution of salt in water.

OBSERVATION

The salt will dissolve in water. There will be no change in the level of the solution so formed.

CONCLUSION

This experiment indicates that there are some vacant spaces among the particles of water and the particles of salt occupies these spaces.

(b) Mixing of Two Gases : We know that air is a mixture of gases. An empty gas jar is filled with air. However, we cannot see the air in the gas jar, as air is colourless. Let us consider, a glass jar 2 containing air, placed inverted on another glass jar 1 containing a reddish brown gas i.e., bromine gas. The bromine gas being heavier than air gets spread from the lower gas jar into the upper gas jar containing air and makes both the gas jars completely filled with reddish-brown colour. This is because the moving particles of bromine gas and air collide with each other and spread in all directions getting uniformly mixed (Fig. 1.7).

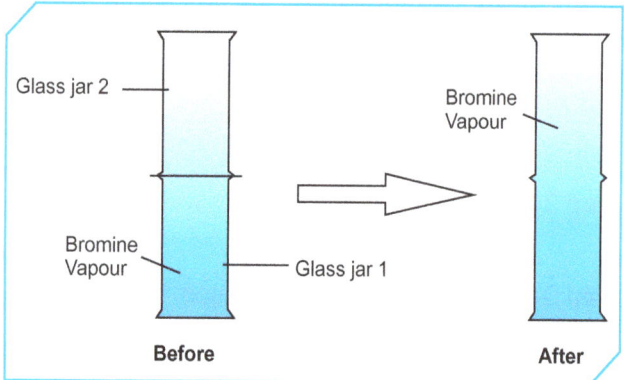

Fig. 1.7 : This figure shows the diffusion of the bromine gas into air.

Though bromine gas is heavier than air, it moves up and mixes with the air in the upper jar because its particles are moving with high speed, having sufficient kinetic energy to overcome the force of gravity. Similarly, the air also diffuses downwards into bromine gas in the lower glass jar but we cannot observe it since air is colourless. Thus, we can conclude the following points of nature of matter with respect to the process of diffusion :

(i) The particles of matter are constantly moving.

(ii) The matter is made up of tiny particles.

PAPER- PEN TEST : 1

1. Define matter.
2. How the nature of matter can be ascertained?
3. How scientists classified the matter in two ways?
4. What are physical and chemical properties?
5. What happens when a glass sheet accidently falls ?
6. Which phenomenon helps us to find out the existence of particles in matter and their motion ?
7. Perform an experiment to show that particles in matter are constantly in motion.
8. How does sugar dissolve and disappear in water?
9. Perform an activity to find out how to dissolve a solid in a liquid?
10. How do two gases get mixed?
11. What conclusion can you make with respect to the process of diffusion?

Let us now discuss the experiments involving Brownian motion to explain the existence of motion of in particles.

1.2 BROWNIAN MOTION

The best evidence for the existence and motion of particles in liquids was given by an English Botanist, **Robert Brown** in 1827. He observed a continuous and rapid zig-zag motion in colloidal solution under the microscope. He called this continuous and rapid zig-zag motion of the colloidal particles as *Brownian motion*. This motion is independent of the nature of the colloidal particles. It is more rapid when the size of the particles is small and the solution is less viscous. The Brownian motion is due to the bombardment of colloidal particles by molecules of dispersion medium. The intensity of motion depends upon the size of the particles and the viscosity of the dispersion medium (Fig. 1.8). The smaller the particles and the less viscous the dispersion medium, the more vigorous is the Brownian motion and vice versa.

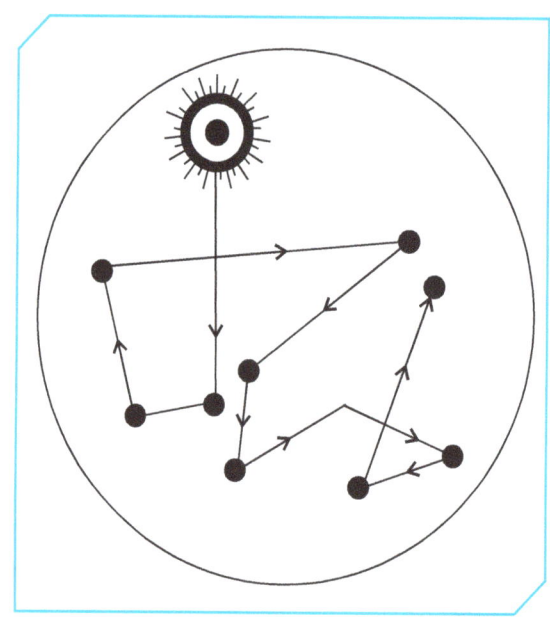

Fig.1.8 : This figure shows Brownian motion in colloidal solution as observed through the microscope.

Movement of Pollen Grains in Water

This phenomenon was observed first by Robert Brown when he observed the suspended small pollen grains in water through the microscope and found that the pollen grains were moving rapidly throughout the water in a zig-zag pattern (Fig.1.9). He also observed that warmer the water, faster the pollen grains moves on the surface of the water. He explained the reason of the movement of the pollen grains as follows : We know that water is made up of fast moving tiny particles which are invisible under the microscope. However, the effect of water particles on the pollen grains can be seen clearly by the random motion of the pollen grains. This random or zig-zag motion of pollen grains on the surface of water is due to the constant hitting by the fast moving water particles.

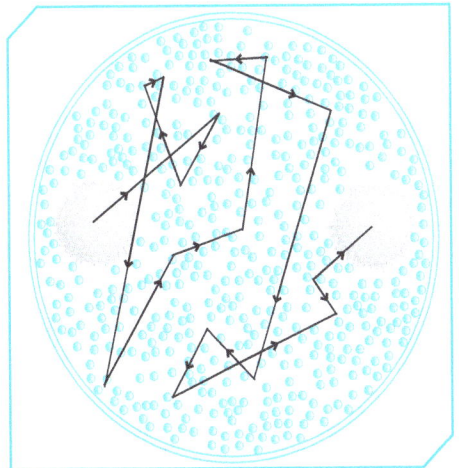

Fig. 1.9 : This figure shows the phenomenon of Brownian motion.

Have you ever noticed a beam of sunlight entering a dark room? What happens when a beam of sunlight enters a room?

We can see tiny dust particles suspended in air moving rapidly in a zig-zag pattern. Since, the tiny dust particles show rapid movement, they are constantly hit by the fast moving particles of air. Though we cannot see the particles or molecules of air we can see the effect produced by their continuous and fast motion. The tiny dust particles suspended in air shows that air is made up of particles and these particles of air are moving constantly. Thus, it is clear that Brownian motion can also be observed in gases (Fig. 1.10).

Fig. 1.10 : The figure shows the tiny dust particle suspended in air moving rapidly in a zig-zag motion.

Note

The existence of Brownian movement gives us two conclusions :

- The matter is made up of tiny particles.
- The particles of matter are constantly moving.

1.3 CHARACTERISTICS OF PARTICLES OF MATTER

The most important characteristics of particles of matter are the following :

(a) *The particles of matter attract each other.*

(b) *The particles of matter are very, very small.*

(c) *The particles of matter are constantly moving.*

(d) *The particles of matter have inter-particle spaces between them.*

Let us now perform some activities to understand the characteristics of particles of matter.

(a) **The Particles of Matter attract each other :** The particles of a substance have certain forces of attraction between them which keeps the particles together. The magnitude of the force of attraction depends on the nature of the particles which constitute a matter and the inter-particle spaces between them (Fig. 1.11). The force of attraction between the particles of the same substance is known as cohesion. The force of attraction is different in the particles of different kinds of matter.

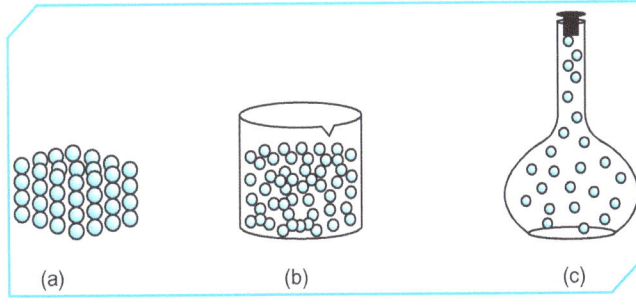

Fig. 1.11 : This figure shows the forces of attraction between the particles in (a) Solid (b) Liquid (c) Gas.

This will become clear from the following activities.

Activity 1.2 (a)- To show that the particles of matter attract each other.

PROCEDURE

Step 1– Play this game in the field — make four groups and form human chains as suggested:

Step 2– The first group should hold each other from the back and lock arms like Bihu dancers as shown in the figure below.

Step 3– The second group should hold hands to form a human chain.

Step 4– The third group should form a chain by touching each other with only their fingertips.

Step 5– Now, the fourth group of students should run around and try to break the three human chains one by one into as many small groups as possible.

Step 6– Which group was the easiest to break and why?

Step 7– If we consider each student as a particle of matter, then in which group should the particles be held with each other with the maximum force?

Fig. 1.12 : This figure shows the group of Bihu dancers holding each other from back forming a human chain.

OBSERVATION

The third group is easiest to break. This is because, in third group the students form chain by touching each other with only their fingertips. The group in which the particles hold each other with maximum force is First group.

CONCLUSION

This shows that particles of matter which are held with each other with maximum force show maximum force of attraction.

Let us perform another activity to show that the particles of matter attract each other.

Activity 1.2 (b) -To show that the particles of matter attract each other.

PROCEDURE

Step 1– Take an iron ball and a piece of chalk.

Step 2– Try to break them by hammering, cutting or stretching.

Step 3– In which of the above two substances do you think the particles are held together with greater force?

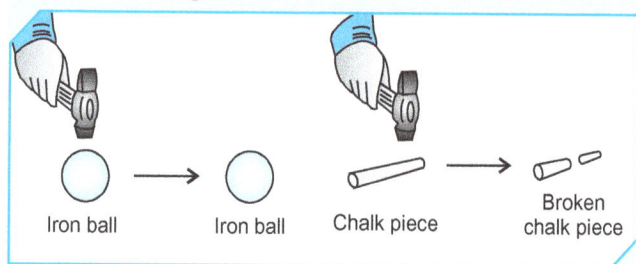

Fig. 1.13 : Experimental set-up to show that particles of matter attract each other.

OBSERVATION

It is very easy to break the piece of chalk into smaller particles. On the other hand, the iron ball does not break even with a large force.

CONCLUSION

This shows that the force of attraction between the particles of chalk is quite weak; whereas the force of attraction between the particles of iron ball is very, very strong.

Let us perform another activity to show that the particles of matter attract each other.

Activity 1.2 (c)–To show that the particles of matter attract each other.

PROCEDURE

Step 1– Open a water tap, try breaking the stream of water with your fingers.

Step 2– Were you able to cut the stream of water?

Step 3– What could be the reason behind the stream of water remaining together?

OBSERVATION

Yes. This shows that the inter-particle attraction between particles of water (liquid state) is not very strong. The stream of water remains together because the particles of matter attract each other to form uniform layers.

CONCLUSION

This shows that particles of water have force acting between them which keeps them together. However, the strength of this force is not very strong.

Thus, we can conclude from the above three activities [1.2 (a), (b) and (c)] that the particles of matter have force acting between them which keeps the particles together and the strength of this force of attraction varies from one kind of matter to another.

PAPER-PEN TEST : 2

1. When and who found the existence and motion of particles in liquids?
2. Define Brownian motion.
3. Name the factors on which the intensity of Brownian motion depends.
4. What is the cause of Brownian motion?
5. Who was the first to find the movement of pollen grains in water?
6. What happens when a beam of sunlight enters a dark room?
7. Mention the two conclusions regarding matter provided by the existence of Brownian motion.
8. What are the characteristics of particles of matter?
9. Define cohesion.
10. Perform an activity to understand the characteristics of particles of matter.
11. Name the factors on which the magnitude of the force of attraction depends.
12. Is the force of attraction different in the particles of different kinds of matter?
13. Comment: "It is very easy to break the piece of chalk into smaller particles but on the other hand an iron nail does not break even with a large force.

(b) **The Particles of Matter are very, very Small :** The particles differ from one matter to the other. Generally, the size of particles is very small, but they can vary from matter to matter. Let us demonstrate an activity to show that the particles of matter are very, very small using potassium permanganate and water.

Activity 1.3 – To show that the particles of matter are very, very small.

PROCEDURE

Step 1– Take 2-3 crystals of potassium permanganate.

Step 2– Dissolve them in a beaker containing 100 mL of water. A deep purple solution of potassium permanganate is obtained in second beaker.

Step 3– Take out approximately 10 mL of potassium permanganate solution from second beaker and put it into 90 mL of clear water present in third beaker. Stir the contents till you get a uniform mixture or solution.

Step 4– Now, take out 10 mL of the potassium permanganate solution from third beaker and put it into another 90 mL of clear water present in fourth beaker.

Step 5– Keep diluting the solution like this 5 to 8 times.

Step 6– Is the water still coloured?

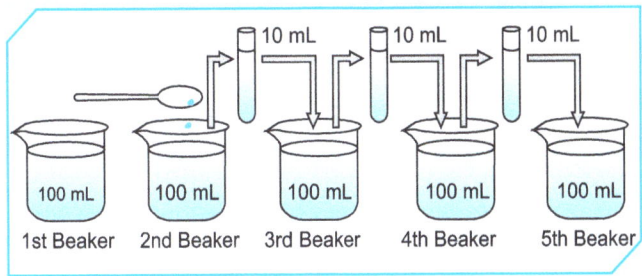

Fig. 1.14 : Experimental set-up to show that particles of matter are very, very small in size.

OBSERVATION

The dark purple colour of the potassium permanganate solution will somewhat decrease.

CONCLUSION

When this experiment is repeated 5 – 8 times, the purple colour of the potassium permanganate solution will not disappear completely. Some colour will always persist even when the solution is very dilute. This shows that there must be millions of tiny particles in just one crystal of potassium permanganate which keep on dividing themselves into smaller and smaller particles.

(c) **The Particles of Matter are Constantly Moving :** The process of diffusion and Brownian motion shows that the particles of matter are constantly moving. Let us describe few experiments involving diffusion of gases and diffusion in liquids which shows that the particles of matter are constantly moving.

Activity 1.4 – To show that the particles of matter are constantly moving by diffusion of liquids.

Step 1– Drop a crystal of potassium permanganate or copper sulphate into a beaker containing hot water and another containing cold water.

Step 2- Do not stir the solution.
Step 3- Allow the crystals to settle at the bottom.
Step 4- What happens as time passes?
Step 5- What does this suggest about the particles of solid and liquid?
Step 6- Does the rate of mixing changes with temperature. Why and How?

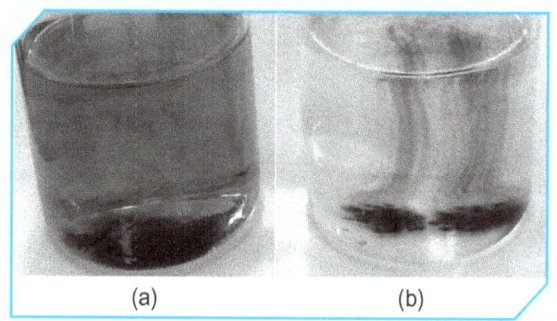

Fig. 1.15 : This figure shows the diffusion of potassium permanganate in (a) Hot water (b) Cold water.

OBSERVATION

As the time passes, the water turns into purple colour solution in both the beakers because the particles of water and potassium permanganate get evenly mixed by the process of diffusion. But the water contained in the hot beaker turns into a purple colour solution at a faster rate as compared to water contained in the cold beaker. Yes, the rate of mixing changes with temperature. This is because, in hot water the particles of water and that of potassium permanganate have more kinetic energy and therefore move faster. Hence, they mix with each other more quickly.

CONCLUSION

This shows that particles of matter are constantly moving and their rate of diffusion into liquid varies with temperature.

(d) The Particles of Matter have Inter-particle Spaces between them : The inter-particle spaces between the particles of matter can be shown by performing the following activity using water and sugar.

Activity 1.5 – To show that the particles of matter have inter-particle spaces between them.

PROCEDURE

Step 1- Take a 100 mL beaker.

Step 2- Fill half the beaker with water and mark the level of water.
Step 3- Dissolve some salt or sugar with the help of a glass rod.
Step 4- Observe any change in the water level.
Step 5- What do you think has happened to the salt?
Step 6- Where does it disappear?
Step 7- Does the level of water change?

Fig. 1.16 : Experimental set-up to show that matter has inter-particle spaces between them.

OBSERVATION

No, the level of water does not change. When sugar or salt is dissolved in water, its crystals separate into fine particles. These particles of sugar go into inter-particle spaces between various particles of water due to which there is no change in the volume of water on dissolving sugar or salt in it.

CONCLUSION

Since there is no change in the volume on dissolving sugar or salt in water, it shows that there are inter particle spaces between the particles of water.

PAPER-PEN TEST : 3

1. Demonstrate an activity to show that the particles of matter are very, very small using potassium permanganate and water.
2. Give an activity to show that the particles of matter are constantly moving by diffusion of liquids.
3. Explain an activity to show that the particles of matter have inter-particle spaces between them.
4. Does the diffusion of liquids change with temperature? Why and how?
5. Why does the stream of water remains together?

1.4 CLASSIFICATION OF MATTER

Based on the physical state, all the matter can be classified into three groups namely,

(a) Solids

(b) Liquids

(c) Gases

For example,

Solids : Wood, sugar, rocks, minerals, sand, iron, etc (Fig. 1.17 a and b).

Liquids : Water, milk, petrol, alcohol, etc. (Fig. 1.17 c and d).

Gases : Air, oxygen, carbon dioxide, steam etc. (Fig. 1.17 e).

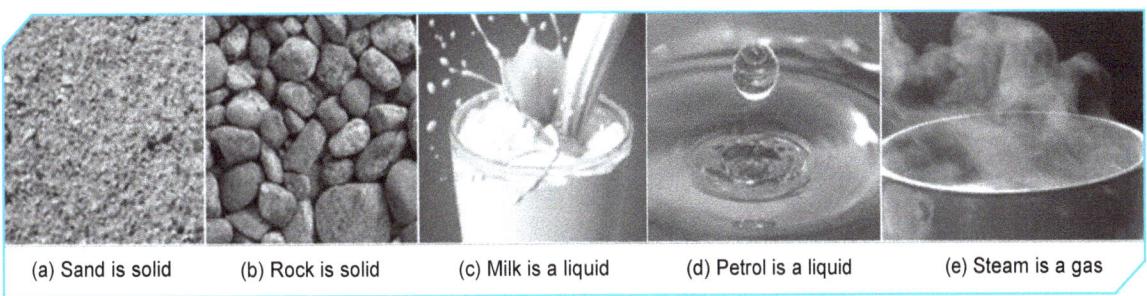

Fig. 1.17 : This figure shows some of the examples of Solids (a) and (b), Liquids (c) and (d) and Gases (e).

But how will you classify these matters as solids, liquids or gases? In order to find out this, we should know the characteristics of these States of Matter. The properties of these states are different from each other.

Reasons for Difference in the Properties of Solids, Liquids and Gases

Based on kinetic theory of matter, all the three states of matter i.e., solids, liquids and gases are made up of very small particles which are in continuous motion. This makes them possess kinetic energy. There are always forces of attraction, called inter-particle forces between the particles which holds the particles together giving maximum space. When the spaces between the particles of the matter increases, the force of attraction between them decreases and vice-versa. The motion of the particles can be changed by heating or cooling. Higher the temperature, greater is the movement of the particles.

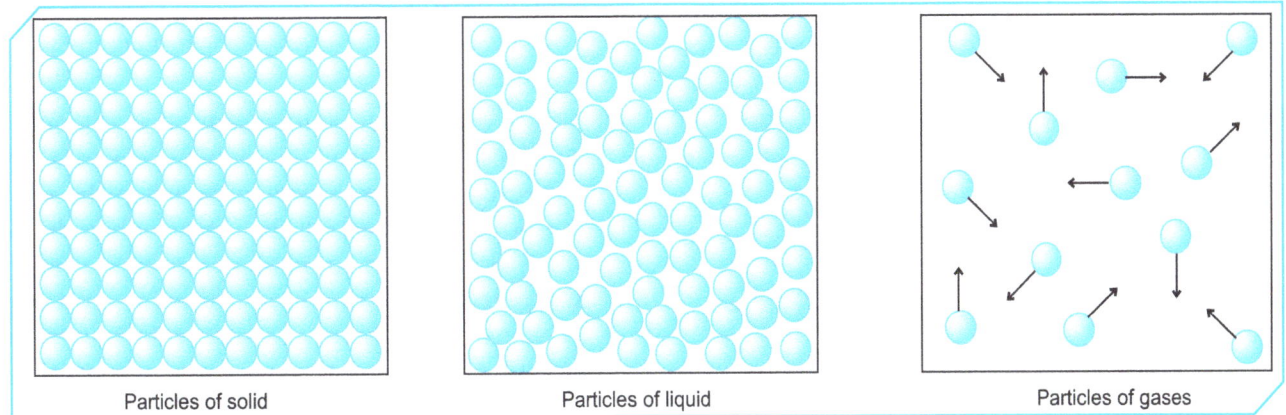

Fig. 1.18: This figure shows the arrangement of particles in solids, liquids and gases.

Now we need to find the answer for the following questions. How do the properties of particles determine the physical states of matter? Is there any specific property which determines the physical state of matter? Let us find out the answer.

The following properties of particles decide whether a given substance will exist as a solid, a liquid or a gas (Fig. 1.18).

(a) The forces of attraction between the particles. The forces of attraction between the particles are strongest in solids, less strong in liquids and negligible in gases.

(b) The inter-particle spaces between the particles. The inter-particle spaces or distances between the particles are minimum in solids, a little more in liquids and maximum in gases.

(c) **The movement of the particles.** The movement of particles is minimum in solids, more in liquids and maximum in gases.

PAPER-PEN TEST : 4

1. Classify matter based on their physical states.
2. Define inter-particle forces.
3. How can the motion of the particles be changed?
4. How does the movement of the particles get affected with the increase in temperature?
5. Give reasons for difference in the properties of solids, liquids and gases.
6. How do the properties of particles determine the physical states of matter?

Keeping the above properties in mind, we can further explain the structure of all the three states of matter and also the differences in their properties based on their structure.

1.5 SOLIDS AND THEIR CHARACTERISTICS

Solids

Generally, all solids have a definite shape, distinct boundaries and fixed volumes i.e., have negligible compressibility. Solids have a tendency to maintain their shape when subjected to outside force. This shows that they are rigid (Fig. 1.19). However, solids may break under force. Let us study the characteristics of solids in detail.

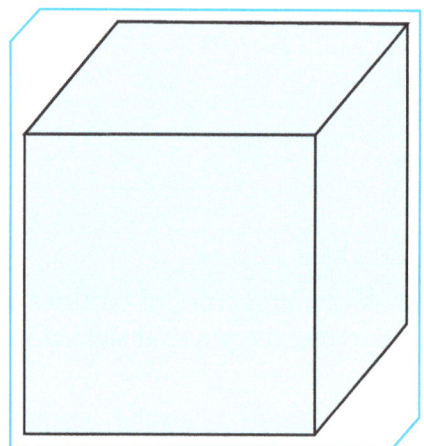

Fig. 1.19 : A solid is a rigid substance which has a definite shape and boundary.

Characteristics of Solids

In solids, the particles are closely packed i.e., there is a strong force of attraction between the particles of solid which hold them together in fixed positions. Hence, we can say that the position of the particles in a solid are fixed. However, the particles of a solid only vibrate about their fixed positions. When the solid is heated, its particles start to vibrate faster. This reduces the spaces between the particles of a solid and the kinetic energy becomes minimum. Thus, solids have the most ordered arrangement of particles.

(a) **Solids have a fixed shape :** Generally, solids have definite shapes and distinct boundaries at normal room temperature, without applying a force. This is because the particles of a solid are closely packed and their positions are fixed due to the strong forces of attraction between them (Fig. 1.20).

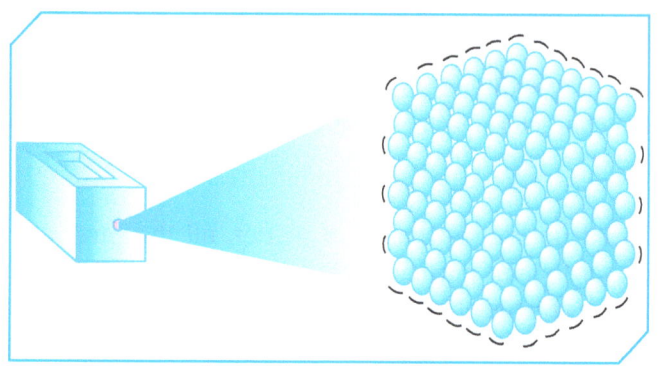

Fig. 1.20 : This figure shows the arrangement of particles in a solid brick.

(b) **Solids have a fixed volume :** A solid has fixed volume because the inter-particle spaces between its particles are fixed.

(c) **Solids cannot be compressed :** It is difficult to compress a solid even on applying pressure. This is because the constituent particles in the solids are so closely packed that they either do not come closer or do so when a very high pressure is applied. For example, we cannot press a piece of stone by applying pressure with our hands. On the other hand, a sponge made from rubber material can be easily compressed. We know that the sponge has very small pin size holes throughout the body. So, when the pressure is applied, the air from the hole is expelled out and the sponge gets compressed.

(d) **Solids have high densities :** The density of a solid may be defined as, *'Mass occupied by a solid per unit volume'*. Since, the constituent particles in the solids are so closely packed, the density will be maximum in the solid state of a substance. Thus, more closer the constituent particles; greater will be the density.

(e) **Solids have negligible kinetic energy of the particles :** The kinetic energy deals with the movement of the particles from one place to another. Since, the constituent particles in the solids are so closely packed, they have negligible kinetic energy. Hence, the solids do not flow.

(f) **Solids do not have the property of diffusion :** Since, the solids have negligible kinetic energy of the particles, there is hardly any diffusion due to the absence of vacant spaces between the constituent particles.

(g) **Solids do not fill the container completely :** A solid does not fill its container completely because its particles are held tightly by strong inter-particle forces and hence, cannot leave their positions to fill the whole container.

(h) **Solids do not flow :** A solid does not flow because its particles are held very strongly and are unable to leave their fixed positions.

There are some solids which do not have fixed shape. For instance, a rubber band changes its shape when stretched. But we call it a solid. Why? This is because a rubber band changes shape due to external force produced by stretching and when the force is removed, stretching is stopped i.e., the rubber band regains its original shape. Further, if rubber band is stretched with a large force, it breaks. Similarly, when salt and sugar are kept in jars of different shapes, they take the shape of the jars. Then why do we call them solids? This is because the salt and the sugar have very tiny crystals and so possess fixed shape even when put in jars of different shapes.

Examples of Solids : Stones, wood, metals like iron, copper, nickel, etc., ice, sand, rock etc.

Let us discuss an activity to understand the characteristics of solids.

Activity 1.6 – To understand the characteristics of solids.

PROCEDURE

Step 1– Collect the following articles : a pen, a book, a needle and a piece of thread.

Step 2– Sketch the shape of the above articles in your notebook by moving a pencil around them.

Step 3– Do all these articles have a definite shape, distinct boundaries and a fixed volume?

Step 4– What happens if they are hammered or dropped?

Step 5– Are they capable of diffusing into each other?

Step 6– Try compressing them by applying force. Are you able to compress them?

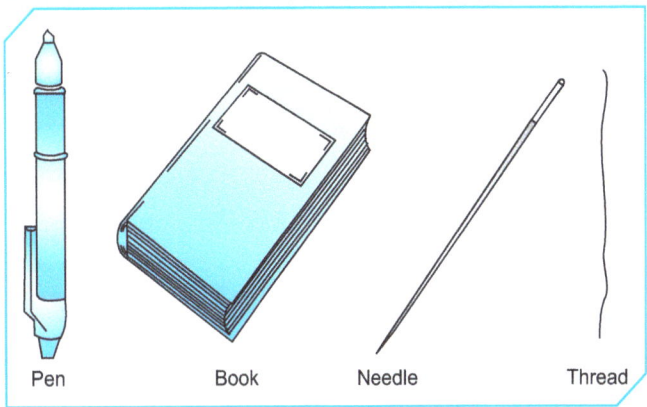

Fig. 1.21 : This figure shows the things required to understand the characteristics of solids.

OBSERVATION

Yes, all these articles have a definite shape, distinct boundaries and a fixed volume. Pen will break, there will be no effect on book and thread and after long time needle will break. No, the articles are not capable of diffusing into each other. No, the articles do not get compressed.

CONCLUSION

Thus, we can conclude that solid articles have a definite shape, distinct boundaries and a fixed volume. They are rigid and non-compressible i.e., they may break under force but their shape cannot be changed.

PAPER-PEN TEST : 5

1. Why the particles in solids are closely packed?
2. How do you say that solids have the most orderly arrangement of particles?
3. Comment: "Solids cannot be compressed".
4. Why solids have definite shapes and distinct boundaries at normal room temperature without applying a force?
5. Give a reason for a solid to have fixed volume.
6. Comment: "A sponge made from rubber material can be easily compressed".
7. Define density.
8. It is difficult to compress a solid even on applying pressure. Comment.
9. Why solids do not flow?
10. Explain why solids do not have the property of diffusion?

11. Give reason: A solid does not fill its container completely.
12. A rubber band can be called a solid. Why?
13. Give any three examples of solids.
14. Explain an activity to understand the characteristics of solids.

1.6 LIQUIDS AND THEIR CHARACTERISTICS

Liquids

In liquids, the particles are somewhat loosely packed. The spaces between the particles of a liquid are slightly more than that in a solid. Though, there is a quite strong force of attraction between the particles of a liquid which holds the particles together, but it is not strong enough to hold the particles in liquids in fixed positions. Hence, we can say that the particles of a liquid move from one position to another within the liquid. The particles of a liquid have more kinetic energy and so liquids have more disordered arrangement of particles (Fig. 1.22). When the liquid is heated, the particles of the liquid vibrate and begin to move. Let us now discuss the characteristics of liquids.

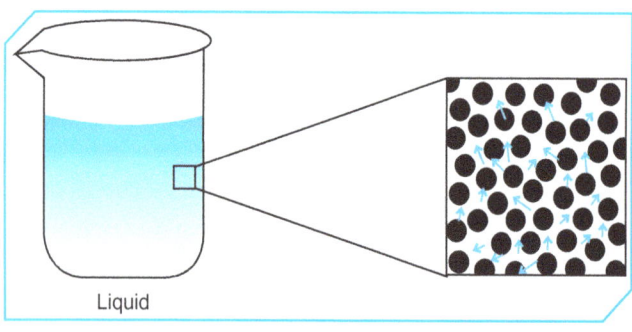

Fig. 1.22 : This figure shows the disordered arrangement of particles in liquids.

Characteristics of Liquids

(a) **Liquids do not have a fixed shape:** Liquids do not have a fixed shape because the position of the particles of a liquid are not fixed due to comparatively less strong forces of attraction between them. Hence, the liquids take the shape of the container and the particles can slide over one another easily (Fig. 1.23).

(b) **Liquids have a fixed volume :** Since, the inter-particle forces between the liquid particles are very strong; the pressure applied cannot overcome these forces. Therefore, liquids keep their volume.

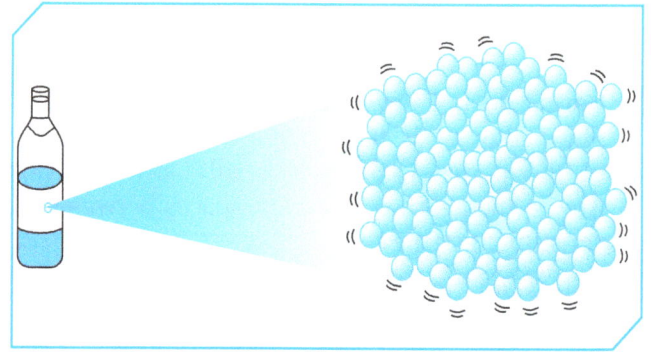

Fig. 1.23 : This figure shows the arrangement of particles in liquids.

(c) **Liquids cannot be compressed much :** This is because its particles are still close together and possess very small spaces between them.

(d) **Liquids do not fill their container completely :** This is because its particles are held fairly strong by the inter-particle forces and cannot leave the body of liquid to fill the whole container.

(e) **Liquids flow easily :** This is because its particles have the ability to slide over one another due to weaker inter-particle forces of attraction.

(f) **Liquids have moderate to high densities :** This is because its particles are close together.

(g) **The kinetic energy of the particles in the liquid is more than in solids :** Since, the particles in the liquid are less closely packed, the inter-particle forces are weaker. Hence, the kinetic energy of the particles in the liquid is more than in solids. However, it increases with increase in temperature.

(h) **The particles in the liquid get diffused easily :** Since, the particles in the liquid possess comparatively less inter-particle forces of attraction, it diffuses more readily. This property helps in intermixing of certain liquids. For example, alcohol and water can easily mix to form a liquid mixture or solution.

Examples of Liquids : Water, kerosene, petrol, alcohol, benzene, milk, etc.

Let us now perform an experiment to show that liquids do not have a fixed shape, but they have a fixed volume (Fig. 1.24).

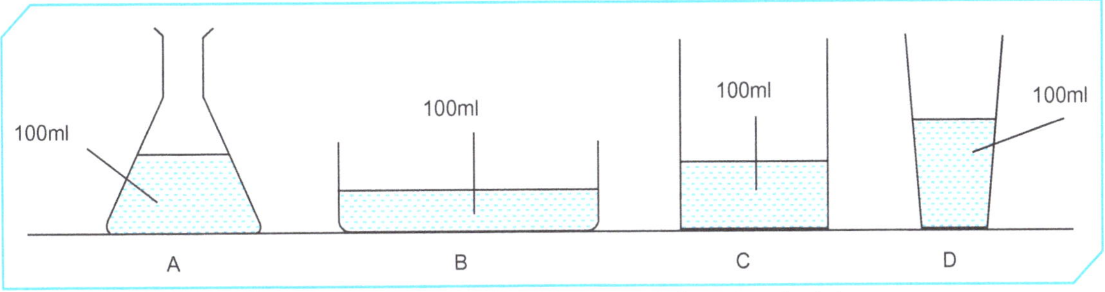

Fig. 1.24 : Experimental set-up to show that liquids do not have fixed shape.

Take some water in a beaker and mark the level of the water. We observe that water takes the shape of the beaker. Now, if we pour this water into the vessels or containers of different shapes, one by one, we will find that the same water takes the different shapes of vessels in which it is poured. This experiment shows that liquid has no fixed shape of its own; it takes the shape of the container in which it is poured. On the other hand, if we pour the same water into the beaker back, we can observe that there is no change in the volume of the water when it is poured into different containers. This shows that a liquid has a fixed volume.

Let us perform an activity to understand the characteristics of liquids.

Activity 1.7 – To understand the characteristics of liquids.

PROCEDURE

Step 1– Collect the following - water, cooking oil, milk, juice and a cold drink.

Step 2– Take containers of different shapes.

Step 3– Put a 50 mL mark on these containers using a measuring cylinder from the laboratory.

Step 4– What will happen if these liquids are spilt on the floor?

Step 5– Measure 50 mL of any one liquid and transfer it into different containers one by one.

Step 6– Does the volume remain the same?

Step 7– Does the shape of the liquid remain the same?

Step 8– When you pour the liquid from one container into another, does it flow easily?

OBSERVATION

The liquids will flow. But the rate of flow of different liquids will be different. Yes, the volume remains the same.

No, the volume of the liquid changes with the shape of the container.

Yes, the liquid flows easily.

CONCLUSION

Thus, we can conclude that liquids do not have a fixed shape but have a fixed volume. , i.e, they take up the shape of the container in which they are poured but their volume does not change on changing the shape of the container. Liquids flow and hence they can be called as fluids.

PAPER-PEN TEST : 6

1. How we can say that the particles of a liquid move from one position to another within the liquid?
2. What happens when a liquid is heated?
3. Why liquids do not have a fixed shape?
4. Why liquids take the shape of the container and the particles can slide over one another easily?
5. Comment: "Liquids keep their volume".
6. Give reason: "Liquids cannot be compressed much".
7. Why liquids do not fill their container completely?
8. Does the liquid flow, Why?
9. Compare the densities of solids and liquids.
10. Why is the kinetic energy of the particles in the liquid more than in solids?
11. Which property helps in intermixing of certain liquids?
12. Give any three examples of liquids.
13. Perform an experiment to show that liquids do not have a fixed shape, but they have a fixed volume.
14. Explain an activity to understand the characteristics of liquids.

1.7 GASES AND THEIR CHARACTERISTICS

Gases

Gases have neither a fixed shape nor a fixed volume. Hence, they do not have fixed boundaries. They can flow in all directions and can be easily compressed. In a given space, the number of particles in gases are less than that in solids and liquids. The constituent particles of gases have maximum kinetic energy because of the presence of large inter-particle spaces between them and therefore, they show a random motion by moving in all directions. Due to a large distance between the particles in gases, the forces of attraction between them is the lowest (Fig. 1.25).

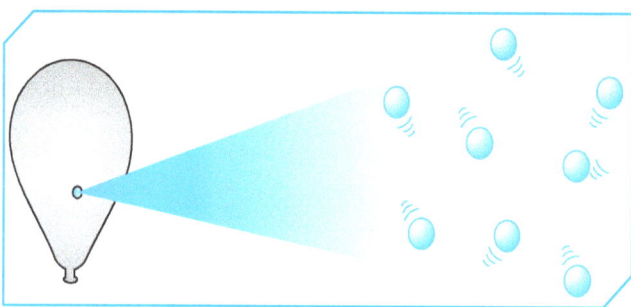

Fig. 1.25 : This figure shows that gaseous particles move randomly in all directions.

Characteristics of Gases

The following are the characteristics of gases on the basis of particle nature of matter:

(a) **Unlike solids and liquids, gases are highly compressible :** This is because the particles in the gas are far apart and there are large spaces between them. So, the gases can be compressed into very small volumes by applying large pressures. Due to this property of gas, a large volume of a gas can be put in a small metal cylinder by compression. Examples, the oxygen gas supplied to hospitals in cylinders, CNG (Compressed Natural Gas) is used to run vehicles and LPG (Liquefied Petroleum Gas) is used for cooking in our homes (Fig. 1.26).

Fig.1.26 : This figure shows oxygen gas cylinder used in hospitals.

(b) **They do not have any fixed shape :** Gases take the shape of the container in which they are present. This is because the positions of the particles in the gas are not fixed (Fig. 1.27).

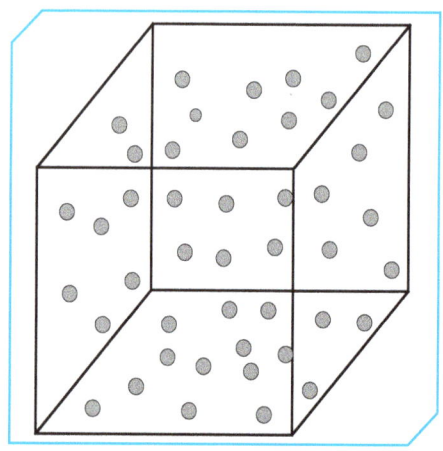

Fig. 1.27 : This figure shows the arrangement of gaseous particles.

(c) **They do not have a fixed volume :** In other words, gases have no fixed boundaries. This is because the spaces between the particles in the gas are not fixed and so the particles are free to move and hence, takes the shape of the container it is present in (Fig. 1.27).

(d) **They flow in all directions :** This is because, the particles in gas are completely free to move (Fig. 1.28).

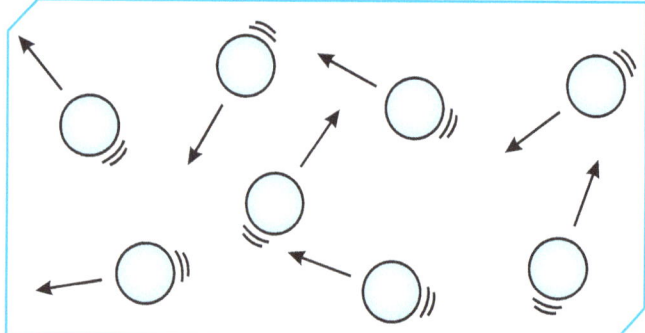

Fig. 1.28 : This figure shows the random movement of gaseous particles.

(e) **The rate of diffusion is very high in gases :** The rate of diffusion of gases is very high because the particles of gases travel with high speed. The rate of diffusion is highest in gases, much slower in liquids whereas in solids it is almost negligible.

(f) **They have lesser density than solids and liquids :** This is because the particles in the gas are very far apart from one another in comparison to solids and liquids.

(g) **Gases fill its container completely :** This is due to the presence of high kinetic energy and negligible forces of attraction. The particles of a gas can move with high speeds in all directions.

Example of Gases : Air, oxygen, carbon dioxide, steam etc.

Can you give an example of compressibility of gases? Liquefied Petroleum Gas cylinders or LPG, which is used in our homes for cooking, contains gases in the compressed state. Similarly, Compressed Natural Gas (CNG) is used as a fuel in vehicles. Large volumes of gases can be compressed and transported in small cylinders.

Let us perform an activity to understand the characteristics of gases.

Activity 1.8- To understand the characteristics of gases.

PROCEDURE

Step 1– Take three 100 mL syringes.

Step 2– Close their nozzles with rubber corks, as shown in the figure below.

Step 3– Remove the pistons from all the syringes.

Step 4– Leaving one syringe untouched, fill water in the second and pieces of chalk in the third.

Step 5– Insert the pistons back into the syringes.

Step 6– You may apply some vaseline on the pistons before inserting them into the syringes for their smooth movement.

Step 7– Now, try to compress the content by pushing the piston in each syringe.

Step 8– Note down your observations.

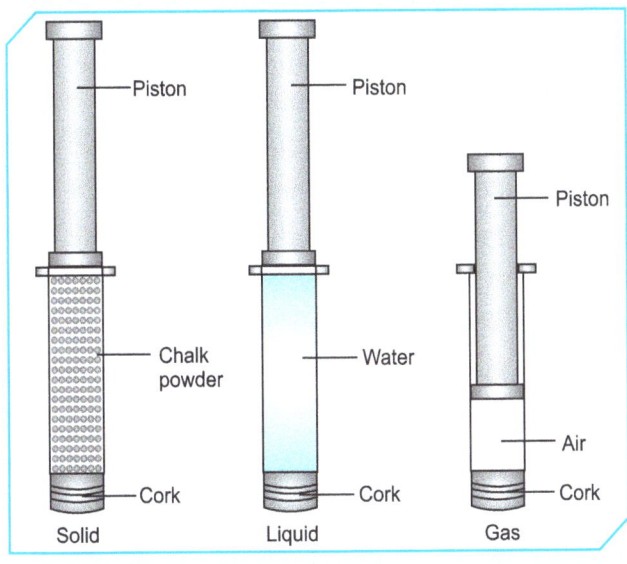

Fig. 1.29 : Experimental set-up to study the characteristics of gases.

OBSERVATION

The pistons of the syringes (containing chalk pieces and water) require a large amount of force, while the piston of the third syringe which contains air is comparatively easier to push.

CONCLUSION

Thus, we can conclude that a solid and a liquid does not get compressed on applying pressure, But a gas can be compressed easily by applying pressure.

PAPER–PEN TEST : 7

1. Why gases show a random motion by moving in all directions?
2. Compare the compressibility of solids, liquids and gases.
3. Gases take the shape of the container in which they are present. Comment.
4. Give reason: "Gases have no fixed boundaries".
5. Compare the densities of solids, liquids and gases.
6. Can you give an example of compressibility of gases?
7. Perform an activity to understand the characteristics of gases.

1.8 DIFFUSION

The phenomenon of spreading of a substance within another substance by the motion of the particles present in the substance is called diffusion. The phenomenon of diffusion of one substance into another substance goes on until a uniform mixture of the substance is formed. Let us explain the phenomenon of diffusion with an example.

Take a glass jar full of chlorine gas and invert another glass jar containing air over it. What do you think will happen after sometime? After sometime, you will observe that the greenish yellow gas of chlorine has spread into the upper glass jar containing air. Thus, the upper glass jar which contains colourless air turns greenish yellow. This is due to the diffusion of chlorine gas in air. The rate of diffusion increases with increase in the temperature of the substance. This is because when the temperature of a substance is increased by heating, the particles present in it gains kinetic energy and moves faster which increases the rate of diffusion (Fig. 1.30).

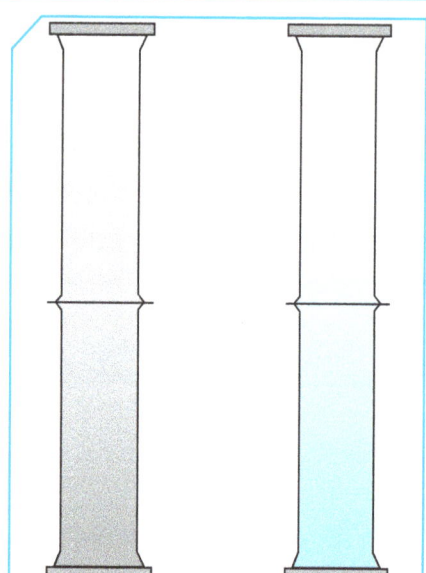

Fig. 1.30 : This figure shows the diffusion of chlorine gas.

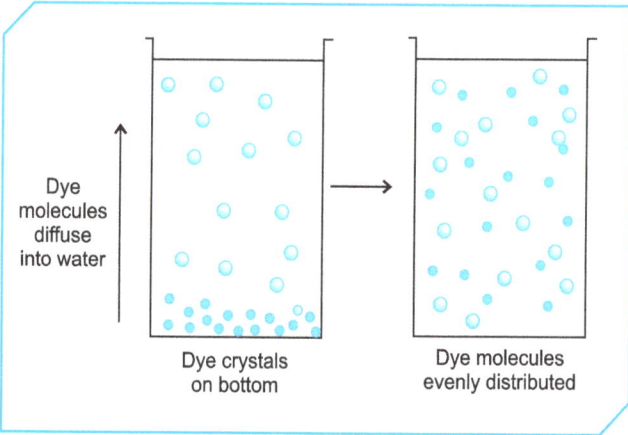

Fig. 1.31: This figure shows the process of diffusion in liquids.

Diffusion in Solids

Many people think that diffusion does not take place in solids. But, the process of diffusion takes place very, slowly in solids because the particles in solids do not move from their fixed positions. However, the constituent particles in solids vibrate about their fixed positions.

We can explain this with few examples.

Example 1 : When two metal blocks are bound together tightly and kept undisturbed for a few years, then the particles of one metal have been found to diffuse into the other metal.

Example 2 : When we write on a blackboard using chalk and leave it uncleaned for a considerable period of time, we will find it difficult to clean the blackboard later. This is because some of the particles of chalk have diffused into the surface of the blackboard.

Diffusion in Liquids

The process of diffusion takes place slower than that in gases. This is because the constituent particles in liquids move slowly compared to the particles in gases. We can explain this with few examples.

Example 1 : The spreading of purple colour of potassium permanganate into water on its own.

Example 2 : The spreading of blue colour of copper sulphate into water on its own.

Example 3 : The spreading of ink or dye into water on its own (Fig. 1.31).

Let us look into the activity for the process of diffusion in liquids.

Activity 1.9 – To show that diffusion takes place in liquids.

PROCEDURE

Step 1– Take two glasses or beakers filled with water.

Step 2– Put a drop of blue or red ink slowly and carefully along the sides of the first beaker and honey in the same way in the second beaker.

Step 3– Leave them undisturbed in your house or in a corner in the class.

Step 4– Record your observations.

Step 5– What do you observe immediately after adding the ink drop?

Step 6– What do you observe immediately after adding a drop of honey?

Step 7– How many hours or days does it take for the colour of ink to spread evenly throughout the water?

Fig. 1.32 : Figure shows the process of diffusion in liquids.

OBSERVATION

The colour of the blue or red ink spreads throughout the water in the beaker immediately. The drop of honey also spreads but takes much more time than ink. The total time taken by the drop of ink to spread evenly throughout the water is much move less than that of honey.

CONCLUSION

Thus, we can conclude that particles of liquid diffuse on its own because they are constantly in motion. However, the rate of diffusion of two different liquid particles may vary.

Diffusion in Gases

The process of diffusion in gases takes place very fast. This is because the particles in gases move very quickly in all directions. The rate of diffusion of a gas depends on its density i.e., lighter gases diffuse faster than heavy gases. The gases from the atmosphere diffuse and dissolve in water. These gases, especially oxygen and carbon dioxide, are essential for the survival of aquatic animals and plants. All living creatures need to breathe for survival. The aquatic animals can breathe under water due to the presence of dissolved oxygen in water. Thus, we may conclude that solids, liquids and gases can diffuse into liquids. The rate of diffusion of liquids is higher than that of solids. This is due to the fact that in the liquid state, particles move freely and have greater space between each other as compared to particles in the solid state.

We shall explain this phenomenon with few examples.

Example 1 : The smell of hot food reaches us even when we are at a considerable distance. But to get the smell of cold food, we need to go close to it. This is because the rate of diffusion of hot gases released by the hot food is much faster than the rate of diffusion of cold gases released by the cold food (Fig. 1.33 a).

Example 2 : When we open a perfume bottle in one corner of a room, the smell spreads to whole room very quickly. This can be explained as follows: When the bottle of the perfume is opened, the liquid perfume quickly changes into vapour or gas which moves in all directions mixing with air particles (Fig. 1.33b).

Example 3 : The leakage of cooking gas (LPG) in our homes is detected due to the diffusion of a strong smelling substance (Ethyl mercaptan) present in the cooking gas into air (Fig. 1.33 c).

Fig. 1.33 : (a) We can smell the hot food being cooked even at a distance by the process of diffusion.

(b) We can smell perfume because its vapours spread into the air by the process of diffusion.

(c) We can smell leakage of cooking gas from gas cylinders because of the diffusion of strong smelling gas ethyl mercaptan into the air.

Let us now perform an activity for diffusion in gases.

Activity 1.10 - To show that the particles of matter are constantly moving by diffusion of gases.

PROCEDURE

Step 1– Put an unlit incense stick in a corner of your class.

Step 2– How close do you have to go near it so as to get its smell?

Step 3– Now light the incense stick. What happens?

Step 4- Do you get the smell sitting at a distance?

Step 5- Record your observations.

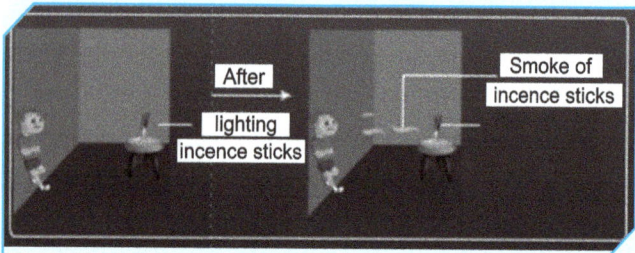

Fig. 1.34 : Experimental set-up to show the process of diffusion in gases.

OBSERVATION

In order to feel the smell of incense stick, we need to go near them. When the incense stick is lighted, the fragrance will immediately spread. Yes we will get the smell sitting at a distance.

CONCLUSION

It can be concluded that particles of matter are always in motion. The movement of the particles is slow in case of unburnt incense stick. On the other hand, the movement of particles of matter is fast when you supply heat energy by burning the incense stick.

PAPER-PEN TEST : 8

1. Define diffusion.
2. Explain the phenomenon of diffusion with an example.
3. How does the rate of diffusion increase with increase in the temperature of a substance?
4. Why does the process of diffusion take place very, very slowly in solids?
5. When we write on a blackboard using chalk and leave it uncleaned for a considerable period of time, we will find it difficult to clean the blackboard later. Why?
6. Give reason : The process of diffusion takes place slower in liquids than in gases.
7. Explain the diffusion in liquids with two examples.
8. Perform an activity to understand the diffusion in liquids.
9. Why does the process of diffusion in gases take place very fast?
10. Can the solids, liquids and gases diffuse into liquids?
11. Why is the rate of diffusion of liquids higher than that of solids?
12. Explain the phenomenon of diffusion in gases with a few examples.
13. Explain an activity to show that the particles of matter are constantly moving by diffusion of gases.

Till now we have studied and discussed about the characteristics of the three states of matter and have come to a conclusion that the difference in them is of inter-particle spaces and forces. Let us tabulate and compare the important characteristics associated with these three states of matter.

Comparison of the Characteristics of Three States of Matter

S. No	Characteristics	Solids	Liquids	Gases
1.	Inter-molecular spaces	Very small	Comparatively large	Very large
2.	Arrangement of particles	Closely packed	Loosely packed	Very loosely packed
3.	Nature	Hard and rigid	Fluid	Highly fluid
4.	Compressibility	Negligible	Very small	Highly compressible
5.	Inter-particle forces	Very strong	Weak	Very weak
6.	Shape and volume	Fixed shape and volume	Indefinite shape and fixed volume	Indefinite shape and volume
7.	Density	High	Less than the density of the solid	Very low density
8.	Kinetic Energy	Low	Comparatively high	Very high
9.	Diffusion	Negligible	Slow	Very fast

1.9 THE COMMON AND SI UNIT OF TEMPERATURE

The Celsius scale of temperature is used for measuring temperature in our everyday life. Thus, the common unit for measuring temperatures such as melting points, boiling points etc., is *'degrees Celsius'* written in short form as °C. Even the laboratory thermometers and the clinical thermometers are calibrated in degrees Celsius. It was **Anders Celsius** who invented Celsius scale of temperature (Fig. 1.35).

Note
- The melting point of ice on Celsius scale of temperature is 0°C i.e., zero degree Celsius.
- The boiling point of water on Celsius scale is 100°C.

There is another scale of temperature called *Kelvin* scale of temperature, used mainly for research work. The SI unit for measuring temperature is *Kelvin* which is denoted by the symbol 'K'. It was **Lord William Thomson Kelvin** who discovered Kelvin scale of temperature (Fig. 1.36). The main advantage of Kelvin scale is that all the temperatures on this scale are positive.

Note
- The melting point of ice on Kelvin scale is 273 K.
- The boiling point of water on Kelvin scale is 373 K.

Fig. 1.35 : Anders Celsius.   Fig. 1.36 : Lord William Thomson Kelvin.

Thus, from above discussion we can say that the temperature of 0°Celsius scale is equal to 273 on Kelvin scale. Hence,

$$0°C = 273 \text{ K}$$

The relationship between Kelvin scale and Celsius scale of temperature will be :

Temperature on Kelvin scale = Temperature on Celsius scale + 273

The above relation can be used to solve the numerical problems for the conversion of Celsius temperature into Kelvin temperature or a Kelvin temperature into Celsius temperature.

Note
- To convert a temperature on Kelvin scale to Celsius scale, subtract 273 from the Kelvin temperature.
- To convert a temperature on Celsius scale to Kelvin scale, add 273 to the Celsius temperature.

Solved Sample Problems

Formulae Used :

Temperature on Kelvin scale = Temperature on Celsius scale + 273

Sample Problem 1 : Convert the temperature of 35°C to the Kelvin scale.

Solution : Temperature on Celsius scale = 35°C

Substituting the value of Temperature on Celsius scale in the formula, we get

Temperature on Kelvin scale = Temperature on Celsius scale + 273

Temperature on Kelvin scale = 35 + 273 = 308 K

Thus, a temperature of 35°C on Celsius scale is equal to 298 K on the Kelvin scale.

Sample Problem 2 : Convert the temperature 310 K to the Celsius scale.

Solution : Temperature on Kelvin scale = 310 K

Substituting the value of Temperature on Kelvin scale in the formula, we get

Temperature on Kelvin scale = Temperature on Celsius scale + 273

Temperature on Celsius scale = 310 − 273 = 37°C

Thus, a temperature of 310 K is equal to 37°C on Celsius scale.

Try Yourself

1. Convert the following temperatures to the Kelvin scale.
   (a) 28°C
   (b) 18°C
   (c) 38°C

2. Convert the following temperatures to the Celsius scale.
   (a) 430 K
   (b) 300 K
   (c) 274 K

PAPER-PEN TEST : 9

1. Compare solids, liquids and gases with respect to (a) arrangement of particles (b) inter-molecular space (c) density.
2. Name the scale of temperature used for measuring temperature in our everyday life.
3. The laboratory thermometers and the clinical thermometers are calibrated in ------------------
4. What is the melting point of ice on Celsius scale?
5. What is the boiling point of water on Celsius scale?
6. Name the scale of temperature used mainly for research work.
7. Who invented Celsius scale of temperature?
8. What is the SI unit for measuring temperature?
9. Who discovered Kelvin scale of temperature?
10. What is the main advantage in using Kelvin scale?
11. What is the melting point of ice on Kelvin scale?
12. What is the boiling point of water on Kelvin scale?
13. 0°C = ----------- K
14. How do you convert a temperature on Kelvin scale to Celsius scale?
15. How do you convert a temperature on Celsius scale to Kelvin scale?

1.10 CHANGE OF STATE OF MATTER

We have already studied that matter can exist in three physical states namely solid state, liquid state and gaseous state or vapour state. We should remember that solid, liquid and gas are not substances but are three states of the same substance which differ in inter-particle spaces. For example, water exists as a solid in the form of ice, as a liquid in the form of water and as a gas in the form of steam.

Do you think the three states can be interchanged or not? Yes, these three states can be interchanged. If we keep some ice in a container, it starts to melt and becomes water. When this water is heated, it produces water vapours. Here, the ice is a solid, water is a liquid and the water vapour is a gas (Fig. 1.37).

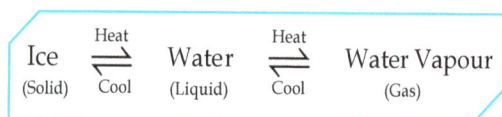

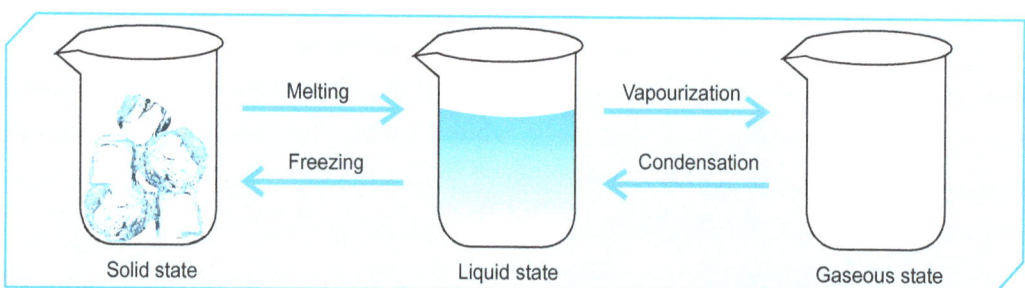

Fig. 1.37 : This figure shows the conversion in the physical states of matter.

Now, the question arises, what happens inside the matter during this change of state? What happens to the particles of matter during the change of states? But how can we interchange the states? We can change the physical state of matter in two ways as follows :

(a) By changing the temperature

(b) By changing the pressure

We have learnt that the three states of matter differ with respect to the inter-particle spaces. The inter-particle space is maximum in gaseous state and minimum in solid state.

Let us study the effect of pressure and temperature in the inter-conversion of states of matter.

1.11 EFFECT OF CHANGE OF TEMPERATURE

Temperature is a major factor responsible for causing a change in the state of matter. The changes in the states of matter with increasing or decreasing temperature can be shown in the form of the figure shown below. On heating a solid substance, the kinetic energy of its constituent particles increases. As a result, the particles start vibrating with greater speed. This extra energy helps the particles to overcome the inter-particle forces of attraction. Soon, they leave their positions and start moving more freely. Consequently, the substance melts and converts into liquid state.

It has been observed that temperature remains constant until all solid melts into liquid. The heat supplied is used for changing the solid state into liquid state by overcoming the inter-particle attraction force. Thus the solid substance absorbs heat energy without showing any rise in temperature.

Similarly, when the liquid substance is heated, the kinetic energy of its constituent particles increases and due to this the particles start vibrating with greater speed. This extra energy helps the particles to overcome the inter-particle forces of attraction. Soon they start to move more freely. Consequently, the liquid state gets converted into gaseous state (Fig. 1.38).

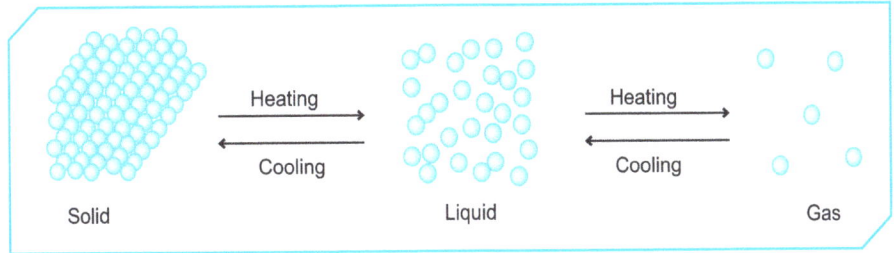

Fig. 1.38 : This figure shows the conversion in the particle arrangement of matter by the effect of change in temperature.

Let us perform an activity to find out the effect of change in temperature.

Activity 1.11 - To find out the effect of change in temperature.

PROCEDURE

Step 1– Take about 150 g of ice in a beaker.
Step 2– Suspend a laboratory thermometer so that its bulb is in contact with the ice as shown in the figure given below.
Step 3– Start heating the beaker on a low flame.
Step 4– Note the temperature when the ice starts melting.
Step 5– Note the temperature when all the ice gets converted into water.
Step 6– Record your observations for this conversion of solid to liquid state.
Step 7– Put a glass rod in the beaker and stir it till the water starts boiling.
Step 8– Keep a careful eye on the thermometer reading till most of the water has vapourised.
Step 9– Record your observations for the conversion of water in the liquid state to the gaseous state.

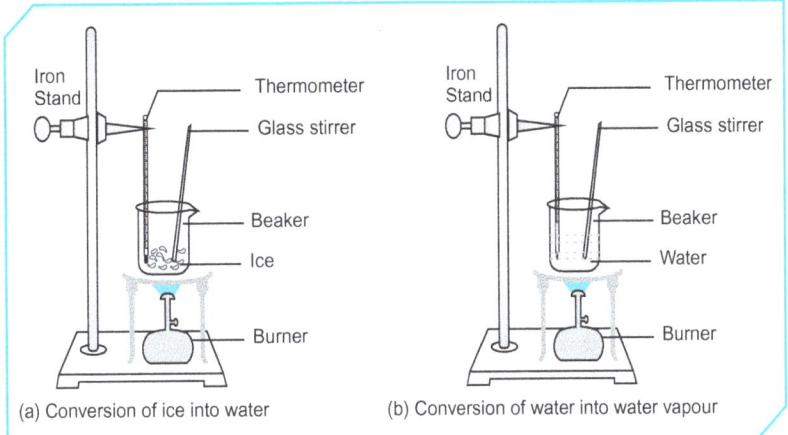

Fig. 1.39: Experimental set-up to show the effect of change in temperature

OBSERVATION

On increasing the temperature of solids, the kinetic energy of the particles increases. Due to the increase in kinetic energy, the particles start vibrating with greater speed.

CONCLUSION

The energy supplied by heat overcomes the forces of attraction between the particles. The particles leave their fixed positions and start moving more freely. A stage is reached when the solid melts and is converted in a liquid. This stage is called as the melting point of the solid.

Change of State from Solid to Gas (Directly) : Sublimation

When a solid changes its state to a gas and vice versa without passing through the liquid state, it is called sublimation. Certain solids undergo the process of sublimation as they possess high vapour pressures. Examples are iodine, solid carbon dioxide, camphor, ammonium chloride, Napthalene etc.

$$\text{Solid} \underset{\text{Cooling}}{\overset{\text{Heating}}{\rightleftharpoons}} \text{Vapour}$$

We have discussed the change of solid state into liquid state and then liquid state into the gaseous state when the temperature is increased. But, the change of state can also be reversed when the temperature is decreased. Certain solids such as iodine, camphor, naphthalene and ammonium chloride change directly into gaseous state on heating without passing through the liquid state. This process is called **sublimation.** The solid substance which undergoes sublimation is known as *sublime* whereas the substance obtained on cooling the vapours of solid is known as *sublimate*. Thus, sublimation may be defined as,

'The process of changing of solid directly into the gaseous state without passing through the liquid state on heating' is known as sublimation

Let us perform an activity to understand the process of sublimation.

Activity 1.12 - To understand the process of sublimation.

PROCEDURE

Step 1– Take some camphor or ammonium chloride.

Step 2– Crush it and put it in a china dish.

Step 3– Put an inverted funnel over the china dish.

Step 4– Put a cotton plug on the stem of the funnel in order to prevent the escape of ammonium chloride vapours into the atmosphere, as shown in the figure below.

Step 5– Now, heat the china dish slowly with the help of a burner and observe. What do you infer from the activity?

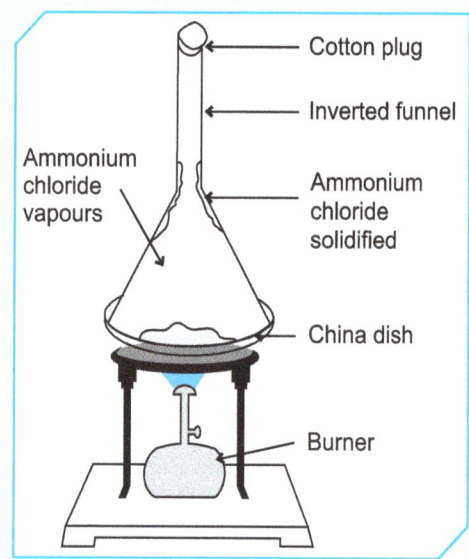

Fig. 1.40 : Experimental set-up for the sublimation of ammonium chloride.

OBSERVATION

The solid ammonium chloride does not melt on heating. It is directly converted into vapours and gets deposited on the inner wall of the funnel as crystalline solid on coming in contact with the cold inner walls of the funnel.

CONCLUSION

A change of state directly from solid to gas without changing into liquid state or vice versa is called sublimation.

Significance of Sublimation

The process of sublimation can be used to purify the impure samples of substances. The non-volatile impurities which are present in the impure sample will not change into vapours and remains in the dish. While the pure solid substance sublimes on heating which can be later recovered by cooling.

PAPER–PEN TEST : 10

1. What are the three physical states of matter?
2. Will the three states be interchanged or not?
3. How we can change the physical state of matter?

4. What is the effect of temperature in the inter-conversion of states of matter?

5. Which is a major factor responsible for causing a change in the various states of matter?

6. How does the liquid state get converted into gaseous state?

7. How would you perform an activity to find out the effect of change in temperature?

8. Define sublimation.

9. What is meant by sublime?

10. What do you understand by the term 'sublimate'?

11. How would you perform an activity to understand the process of sublimation?

12. Give the significance of sublimation process.

Change of Solid State into Liquid State : Melting

In order to bring about the change, the substance matter must be heated or cooled. When we heat ice, it changes into water i.e., the solid substance changes into a liquid. This process is called melting or fusion of ice. The melting of a solid substance takes place at a fixed temperature. Thus, we can define melting as-

'The temperature at which a solid substance melts and changes into a liquid at atmospheric pressure is known as melting point of the solid.'

Since ice melts at zero degree Celsius, the melting point of ice is 0°C i.e., ice melts at the temperature of 0°C and changes its state from solid to liquid. For ice, the latent heat of fusion is 334kJkg^{-1}. This means that 334 kJ of heat is required to convert 1 kg of ice at 0°C into 1 kg of water at 0°C. Conversely, 334 kJ of heat is released when 1 kg of water freezes at 0°C to give 1 kg of ice at 0°C (Fig. 1.41).

Fig. 1.41: This figure shows the melting of ice.

However, different solids have different melting points. Thus, we can say that the melting point of a solid is a measure of the force of attraction between its particles. When the melting point of a substance is high, the force of attraction between its particles will be greater. For example, the melting point of iron is very high and so, the force of attraction between the particles of iron is very strong.

Let us describe how a solid changes into a liquid on heating.

When a solid is heated, the heat energy makes the particles in it to vibrate more vigorously. At the melting point, the particles in the solid have sufficient energy to overcome the strong force of attraction holding the particles in fixed positions and so break it to form small group particles thereby forming a liquid (Fig. 1.42).

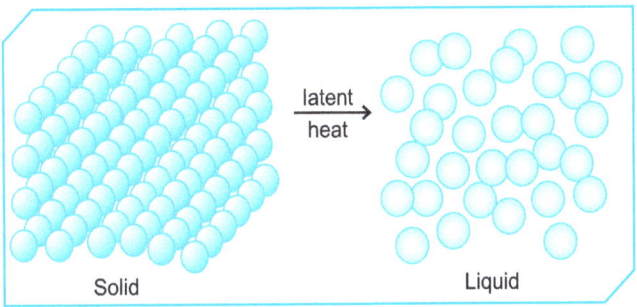

Fig. 1.42 : This figure shows the conversion in the particle arrangement from solid state to liquid state.

The heat energy absorbed by ice is the latent heat which is in hidden form and is called latent heat of fusion.

Latent Heat of Fusion or Melting

The process of conversion of a solid into a liquid form is called fusion. Hence we can define latent heat of fusion as,

'The quantity of heat required to convert one unit of mass of solid into liquid at atmospheric pressure at its melting point (0°C) without any change in the temperature is called latent heat of fusion.'

In other words, *'The amount of heat energy required to convert one kg of a solid into a liquid at its melting point without any rise in temperature under atmospheric pressure.'*

The SI unit of latent heat of fusion is joules per kilogram (J/Kg).

Latent Heat of Fusion of Ice

The latent heat of fusion of ice can be defined as,

'The quantity of heat required to convert one unit of mass of ice into water at atmospheric pressure, at its melting point (0°C) without any change in the temperature is called latent heat of fusion of ice.'

The value of latent heat of fusion of ice is 3.35 x 10⁵ J/Kg. It means that 3.35 x 10⁵ J of heat is required to change 1 kilogram of ice at its melting point of 0°C into water at the same temperature of 0°C. Hence, the energy of 1kg of water at 0°C is 3.35 x 10⁵ J/kg more than that of ice at the same temperature.

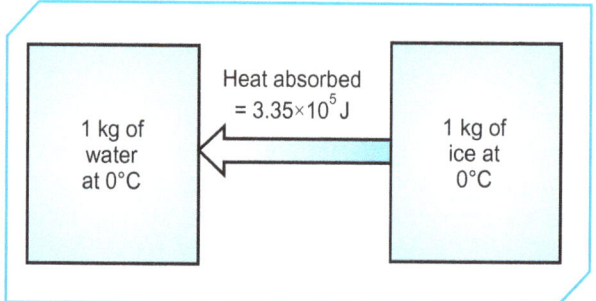

The heat absorbed during the conversion of 1 kg of ice to water at 0°C is 3.35 x 10⁵ J/kg. This absorbed heat is called as the latent heat of fusion.

Melting Point

The melting point temperature of a solid is the same as the freezing point temperature of its liquid state i.e., the melting point of ice is the same as the freezing point of water.

Generally, the temperature is recorded by a thermometer in which mercury is used. There are three scales for measuring the temperature namely *Celsius*, *Kelvin* and *Fahrenheit*. We have already studied Celsius and Kelvin. The thermometers with Fahrenheit scale are calibrated from 32°F to 212°F. The relation between Fahrenheit scale and Celsius scale is,

$$^0F = \frac{9}{5}(^0C) + 32^0$$

Note

- The melting point of a solid is an indication of the strength of the force of attraction between its particles.

The freezing point as well as the boiling point of water on the three scales is shown (Fig. 1.43) below :

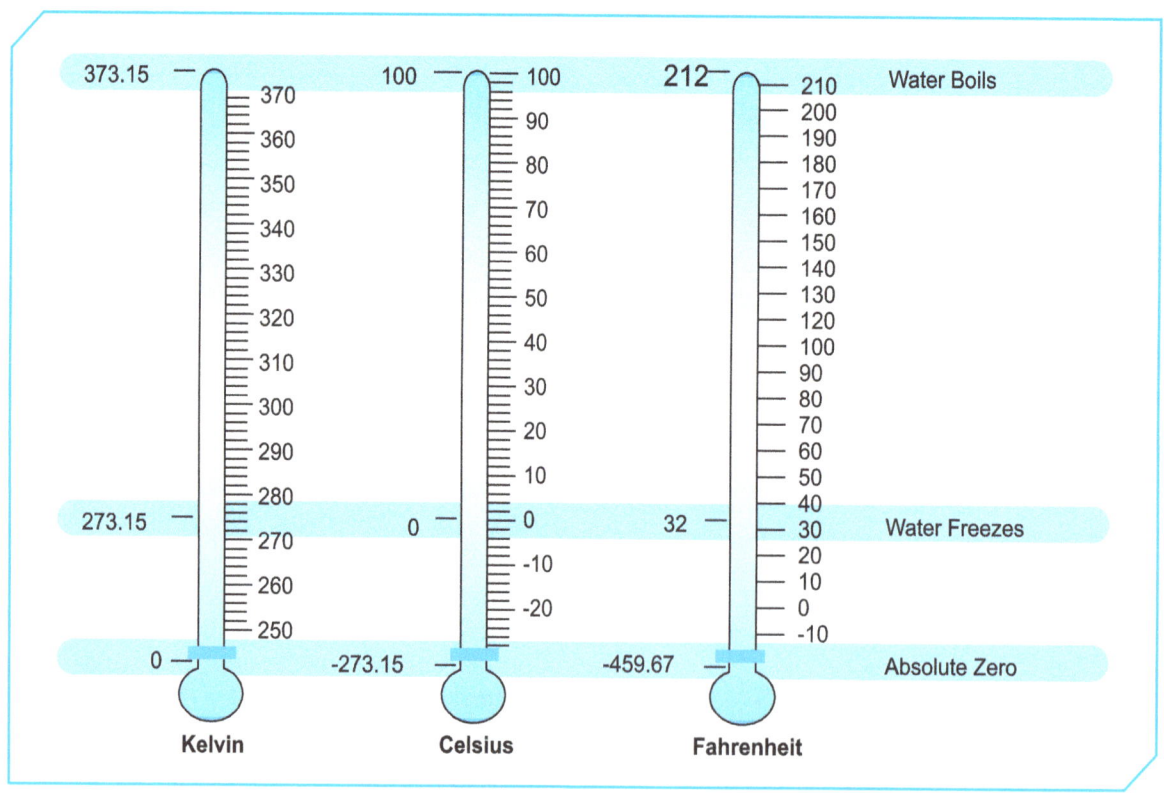

Fig. 1.43 : This figure shows the freezing point and boiling point of water on Kelvin, Celsius and Fahrenheit scale.

Note

- At zero temperature on the Kelvin scale or at –273°C, the molecular motion completely stops i.e., the particles in any state are at rest. This temperature is called absolute zero or 0 K.

MATTER IN OUR SURROUNDINGS

Significance of Melting Point

The melting point of a substance helps to predict the magnitude of inter-particle forces of attraction between its particles. In other words, greater the melting point, more will be the magnitude of inter particle forces of attraction of the substance.

Let us work out a few sample problems based on temperature.

Solved Sample Problems

Formulae Used :

(a) $^0F = \dfrac{9}{5}(^0C) + 32^0$

(b) Temperature on Kelvin scale = Temperature on Celsius scale + 273

Sample Problem 1 : The room temperature of Celsius scale is 35°C. Convert it into the other two scales of measurements.

Solution : Given :
Temperature on Celsius scale = 35°C
Temperature on Kelvin scale = 273 + 35 = 308 K
Temperature on Fahrenheit scale = $\dfrac{9}{5}(35) + 32^0 = 95^0 F$

Hence, the temperature on kelvin scale and fahrenheit scale is 308K and 95°F respectivley.

Sample Problem 2 : The body temperature of a normal and healthy person is 98.4°F. What is the temperature on the Celsius scale?

Solution : Given :
Temperature on Fahrenheit scale = 98.4°F
Temperature on Fahrenheit scale = $^0F = \dfrac{9}{5}(^0C) + 32^0$

Substituting the value in Fahrenheit scale, we get

$\dfrac{9}{5}(^0C) = {^0F} - 32^0$

$\dfrac{9}{5}(^0C) = (98.4 - 32) = 66.4^0$

$^0C = 66.4 \times \dfrac{5}{9} = 36.89\,^0C$

Hence, the temperature on celsius scale is 36.89°C

Try Yourself

1. The body temperature of a normal and healthy animal is 88.4°F. What is the temperature on the Celsius scale?

2. The temperature in Celsius scale is 45°C. Convert it into the other two scales of temperature.

3. The body temperature of a normal and healthy animal is 78.4°F. What is the temperature on the Celsius scale?

4. The temperature in Celsius scale is 55°C. Convert it into the other two scales of temperature.

PAPER -PEN TEST: 11

1. Define melting point of a substance.
2. Define latent heat of fusion.
3. What is the latent heat of fusion of ice?
4. What is the value of latent heat of fusion of ice?
5. What does the statement "The value of latent heat of fusion of ice is 3.35 x 10^5 J/Kg" refers to?
6. What happens to the force of attraction when the melting point of a substance is high?
7. Describe how a solid changes into a liquid on heating.
8. Why the energy of 1kg of water at 0°C is 3.35 x 10^5 J/kg more than that of ice at the same temperature?
9. The temperature is recorded by -------------------------.
10. The thermometers with Fahrenheit scale are calibrated from ------------------.
11. Give the relation between Fahrenheit scale and Celsius scale.
12. Mention the significance of melting point.

Change of Liquid State into Gaseous State : Boiling or Vapourisation

Different liquids have different boiling points. When water is heated, it starts boiling and changes into steam, a gaseous state (Fig. 1.44). This process is called boiling. It may be defined as,

'The process in which a liquid substance changes into gas rapidly on heating.'

The boiling of a liquid takes place at a fixed temperature. Thus, when water is heated to a temperature of 100°C, it boils rapidly to form steam and so the boiling point of water is 100°C. We can say that the boiling point of a liquid is a measure of the force of attraction between its particles. So, when the boiling point of a liquid is higher, the force of attraction between its particles will be greater.

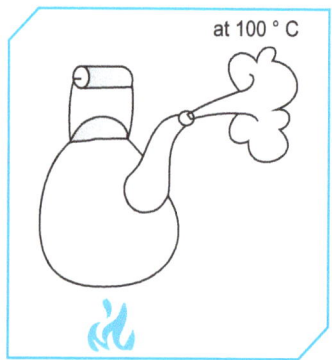

Fig. 1.44 : This figure shows the Steam coming out of a Kettle

'*The temperature, at which a liquid boils and changes rapidly into a gas at atmospheric pressure, is called boiling point of the liquid.*'

Let us describe how the change of state from a liquid to gas takes place.

When a liquid is heated, the heat energy makes its particles move even faster. This is because, at boiling point the particles of a liquid possess sufficient energy to overcome the force of attraction holding them together and separate the particles to form a gas. At the boiling point, the liquid starts boiling but its temperature does not change although it is still being heated. This heat energy which is used to bring about a change from liquid state to gaseous state is known as *latent heat of vapourisation* (Fig. 1.46).

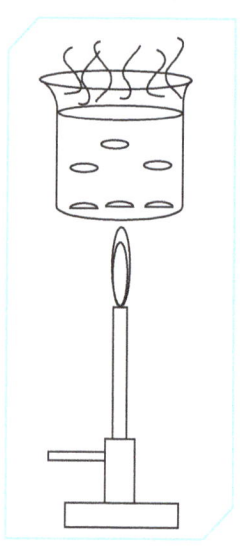

Fig. 1.45 : This figure shows the presence of water vapours inside the bubbles

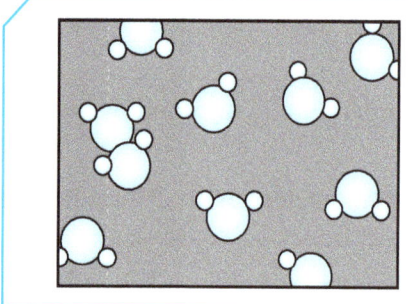 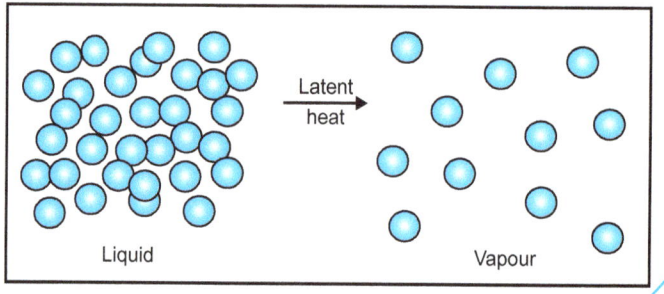

Fig. 1.46: This figure shows the molecular arrangement of water particles in liquid and vapour state.

Latent Heat of Vapourisation or Boiling

The process of change of a liquid into a vapour is known as vapourisation. Hence, we can define latent heat of vapourisation as,

'*The quantity of heat energy required to change unit mass of a liquid into vapour at atmospheric pressure at its boiling point without any change in temperature is known as latent heat of vapourisation.*'

In other words,

'*The amount of heat energy required to convert one kg of a liquid at its boiling point into its gaseous state without any rise in temperature.*'

The SI unit of latent heat of fusion is J/Kg.

Latent Heat of Vapourisation of Water

The latent heat of vapourisation of water may be defined as,

'*The amount of heat energy required to change unit mass of water into vapour at boiling point of water under the atmospheric pressure without any change in the temperature.*'

The value of latent heat of vapourisation of water is 22.6×10^5 J/kg. It means that 22.6×10^5 J of heat is required to change 1 kilogram of water at its boiling point of 100°C into steam at the same temperature of 100°C. Hence, the energy of 1kg of steam at 100°C is

22.6×10^5 J/kg more than that of water at the same temperature.

Note

- The heat required to convert the liquid state into gaseous or vapour state is called as the latent heat of vapourisation.
- The heat required to convert the solid state into liquid state is called as the latent heat of fusion or latent heat of melting.

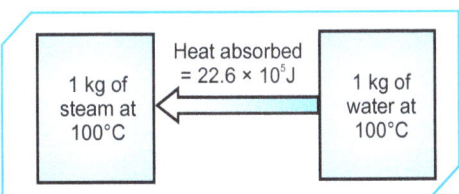

The heat absorbed during the conversion of 1 kg of water to steam at 100°C is 22.6×10^5 J/kg. This absorbed heat is called as the latent heat of vapourisation.

Significance of Boiling Point

The boiling point of the liquids helps to compare the magnitude or strength of the inter-particle forces of attraction present in them. When the forces of attraction are greater, the boiling point of the liquid will be more. Thus, the low boiling liquids are called volatile liquids.

Thus we can conclude that,

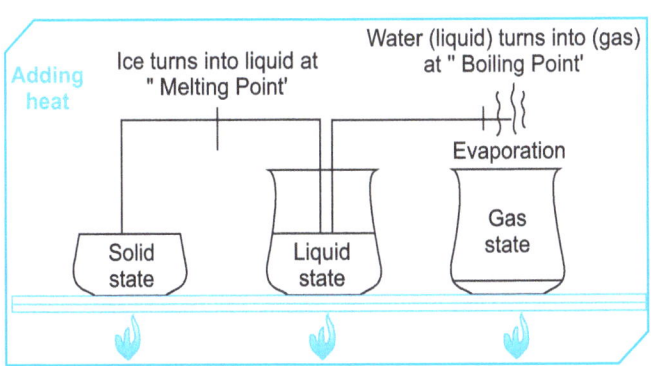

Fig. 1.47 : This figure shows the change in the physical state of matter (Solid, liquid and gas).

PAPER-PEN TEST: 12

1. Define boiling point of the liquid.
2. Describe how the change of state from a liquid to gas takes place?
3. Define latent heat of vapourisation.
4. What is the SI unit of latent heat of fusion?
5. What is the value of latent heat of vapourisation of water?
6. What do you understand by the statement 'The value of latent heat of vapourisation of water is 22.6×10^5 J/kg'?
7. Why are the low boiling liquids called volatile liquids?
8. What is the significance of boiling point?

Change of Gaseous State into Liquid State : Condensation

When the water vapour or steam is cooled by lowering its temperature, it gets converted into liquid water. This process is called condensation. It may be defined as,

'The process of changing of a gas into a liquid by cooling.'

Let us describe how the process of condensation takes place.

When a gas is cooled enough by lowering its temperature, its particles lose kinetic energy and move slowly until they come closer and get attracted to each other to form a liquid.

Note

- The process of condensation is the reverse of boiling or vaporisation.

Change of Liquid State into Solid State : Freezing or Solidification

When water is cooled by lowering its temperature, it changes into solid ice. Thus, when water freezes to form ice, there is a change from liquid state to solid state. The freezing point of a liquid is the same as the melting point of its solid form. Thus, the freezing may be defined as,

'The process of changing a liquid into a solid by cooling.'

Let us describe how the process of freezing takes place.

When a liquid is cooled enough by lowering its temperature, each of its particles loses energy due to which the particles stops moving and vibrate about a fixed position and become a solid (Fig. 1.48).

Note

- The process of freezing is the reverse of melting.

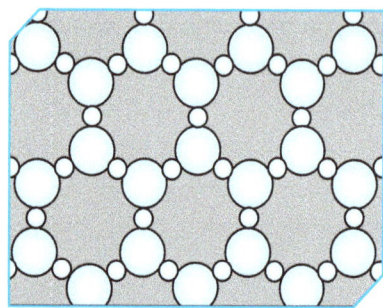

Fig. 1.48 : Molecular arrangement of water in frozen or solid state.

We can summarize the inter-conversion of states as follows (Fig. 1.49) :

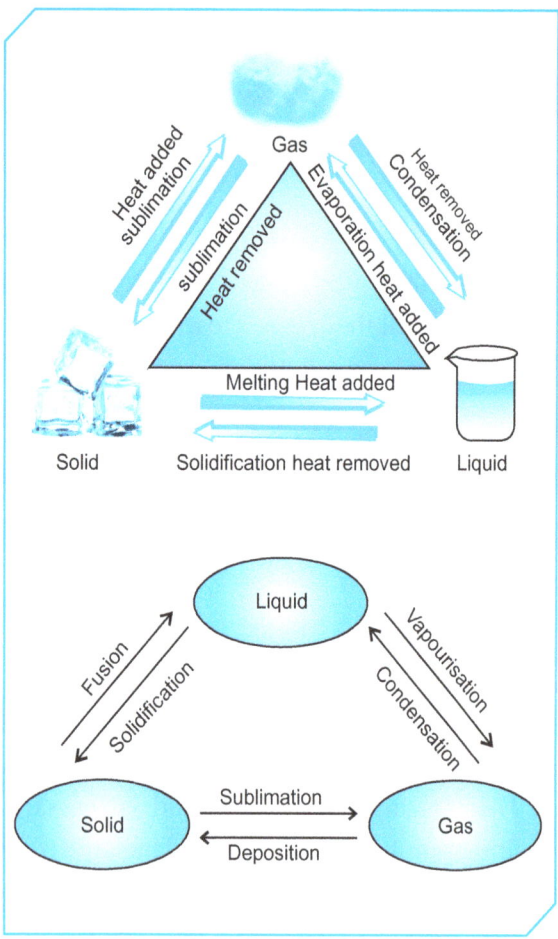

Fig. 1.49: This figure shows the inter-conversion of three states of matter

1.12 EFFECT OF CHANGE OF PRESSURE

We have already discussed the effect of temperature in bringing about the change in state. However, the physical state of matter can also be changed by increasing or decreasing the pressure. The gases can be changed into liquids by increasing the pressure accompanying with the low temperature and solids can be changed into gases by decreasing the pressure.

Let us now discuss about the effect of pressure on the change of state.

The increase in pressure brings the particles of the substance closer and reduces the inter-particle spaces leading to change in the physical state. We can observe the effect of pressure in our day to day life activities while cooking. The cooking of food generally takes place in a pressure cooker. This is because the pressure inside the cooker is high due to which the boiling point of water is increased and cooking becomes quicker and effective. Similarly, the effect of pressure can be seen in inflating tyres of automobiles. If the pressure of air in the tyres is less, it will get punctured and sometimes the tyres will burst also.

Gases can be liquefied by applying Pressure and Lowering Temperature

The change in pressure can also lead to a change in the physical state. A gas is taken in a container (Fig. 1.50 a). When pressure is applied on the piston, the gas particles present in container come closer to each other. This reduces the kinetic energy of the particles. However, the particles are still quite far away from each other, and are still in the gaseous state (Fig. 1.50 b). When pressure is increased further, the gas particles come so close together that they start attracting each other, and consequently, the gas liquefies (Fig. 1.50 c).

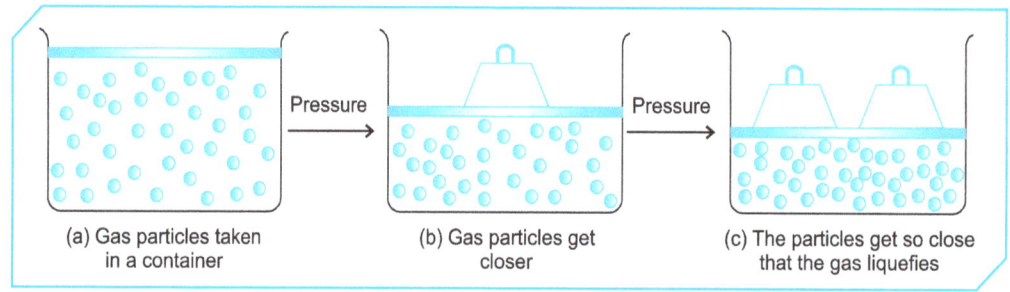

Fig. 1.50 : This figure shows the effect of change in pressure on the physical state of matter.

Hence, it can be concluded that a change in pressure can cause a change in the state of matter.

On the other hand, when a gas is compressed too much, then heat is produced. Thus, while applying pressure to liquefy gas, it is necessary to cool them to remove the heat produced during compression. The lowering of temperature by cooling helps in liquefying the gas during compression. In other words, high pressure together with low temperature is generally used to liquefy gases. Thus, we can conclude that gases can be liquefied by applying pressure and lowering temperature.

Note

- Care must be taken while opening aerated soda water bottles in summer. If proper care is not taken to cool them under tap water, they will burst.

Let us discuss some of the examples of gases which are liquefied by changing the pressure and the temperature

(a) **Oxygen can be liquefied :** Oxygen can be liquefied by applying high pressure and lowering the temperature. Liquid oxygen is blue in colour.

(b) **Solid carbon dioxide (or Dry ice) can be liquefied :** Solid carbon dioxide is a white solid called dry ice. When a slab of solid carbon dioxide is exposed to air, then the pressure on it is reduced to normal atmospheric pressure, i.e., 1 atmosphere, its temperature rises and it starts getting converted into carbon dioxide gas. Thus, the conversion of solid carbon dioxide into carbon dioxide gas is a change of state from solid to gas caused by decreasing the pressure and increasing the temperature. We can say that solid carbon dioxide can be stored under high pressure because on decreasing the pressure, it gets converted directly into carbon dioxide gas (Fig. 1.51).

(c) **Ammonia can be liquefied :** Ammonia can be liquefied by applying high pressure and lowering the temperature. In other words, ammonia can be liquefied by compression and cooling (Fig. 1.52).

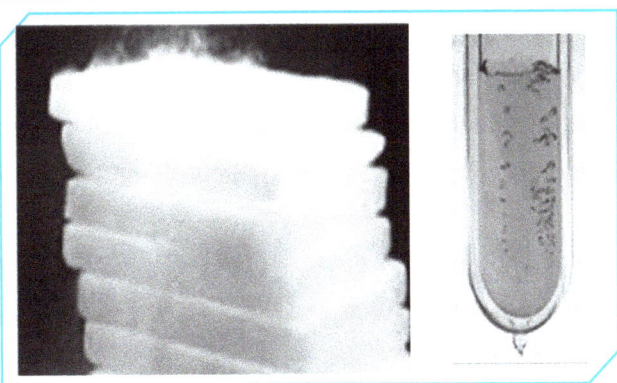

Fig. 1.51 : Solid Carbon dioxide.   Fig. 1.52 : Liquid Ammonia.

Note

- The pressure at sea level is one atmosphere and is called normal atmospheric pressure.
- The atmospheric pressure is maximum at sea level.
- The pressure is normally expressed in atmospheres.

    1 atmosphere = 76 cm = 760 mm

- The pressure is also measured in Pascal (Pa)

    1 atmosphere = 1.01×10^5 Pa

- The pressure is measured with the help of barometer.

Simultaneous Effect of Temperature and Pressure on the Physical State of a Substance

When both temperature and pressure are applied simultaneously on a substance, they give opposing effects. The decrease in temperature or increase in pressure brings the particles of a substance closer. Hence, at low temperature and high pressure, a gas can be liquefied easily. It is not possible for a gas to be liquefied at high temperature and low pressure. There is certain temperature above which the gases cannot be liquefied, but at high pressure it can be liquefied. This temperature is called *critical temperature* and the pressure is called *critical pressure*. The critical temperature of carbon dioxide (CO_2) is 304.15 K and its critical pressure is 73.9 atm. This means that carbon dioxide cannot be liquefied above 304.15 K temperature.

Note

- Carbon dioxide can be liquefied or even solidified at very low temperature accompanied by high pressure. Solid carbondioxide is called dry ice, because the gas on solidifying gives an appearance similar to that of ice. If the pressure on the solid carbon dioxide is reduced to one atmosphere, it directly changes into vapour state. This change resembles sublimation.

PAPER-PEN TEST : 13

1. Define condensation.
2. How does the process of condensation take place?
3. The process of condensation is the reverse of --------------------------.
4. Define freezing.
5. Describe how the process of freezing take place?
6. The process of freezing is the reverse of ------------------------.
7. Explain the effect of pressure on the change of state.
8. Can the physical state of matter be changed by increasing or decreasing the pressure? How?
9. Give the effect of pressure in our day to day life activities while cooking?
10. How can gases be liquefied by applying pressure and lowering temperature?
11. What is dry ice?
12. How can solid carbon dioxide can be stored under high pressure?
13. How is the conversion of solid carbon dioxide into carbon dioxide gas considered to be a change of state from solid to gas?
14. What is meant by normal atmospheric pressure?
15. The pressure is --------------------- at sea level.
16. Define critical pressure.
17. What is critical temperature?
18. What is the critical temperature of carbon dioxide?
19. What is the critical pressure of carbon dioxide?

1.13 EVAPORATION

We have studied how a liquid changes to gaseous state by increasing the temperature. Now let us see how a liquid changes into vapour on its own? When a liquid is left exposed to air, its volume decreases gradually due to the process of evaporation (Fig. 1.53). The evaporation of a liquid can take place even at room temperature, though it is faster at higher temperatures. The evaporation may be defined as,

'The process of change of liquid state into vapour state even below its boiling point'

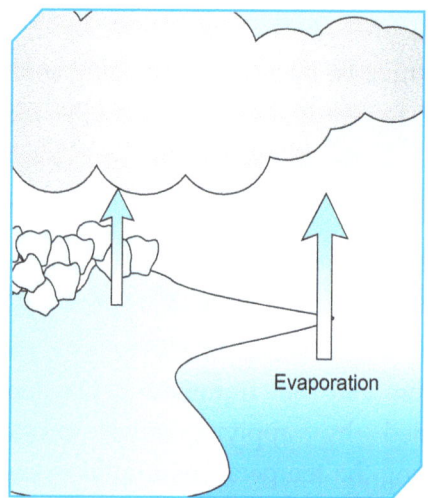

Fig.1.53 : This figure shows the process of evaporation.

Let us describe how the process of evaporation takes place.

The process of evaporation is a surface phenomena which means that only those particles of the liquid change into vapours which are present on its surface. Some particles in a liquid always have more kinetic energy than the others. This energy is enough to break the forces of attraction between the particles and escape from the surface of the liquid in the form of water vapour. Thus, the fast moving particles of a liquid constantly escape from the liquid to form vapours.

Consider two molecules of water, molecule 1 is present on the surface of water, while molecule 2 is present deep inside it. We can say that molecule 2 is surrounded by other water molecules from all sides. All these molecules exert forces of attraction on molecule 2. On the other hand, molecule 1 experiences such force only from one side. The other side is occupied by air. Therefore, molecule 1 experiences lesser force of attraction than molecule 2. Also, molecule 1, being present on the surface of water, absorbs more heat from its surroundings. Hence, it possesses higher kinetic energy than molecule 2. This allows molecule 1 to escape and get converted into vapours. This evaporated molecule mixes with the gases present in the air (Fig. 1.54 a and b).

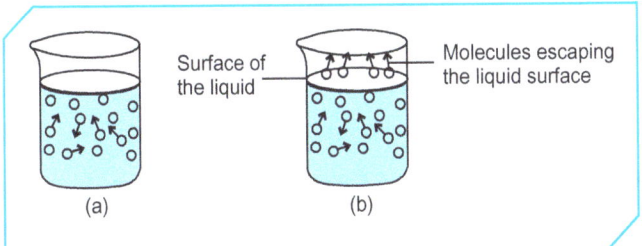

Fig. 1.54 : This figure shows the process of evaportion in a beaker

Note

- Evaporation of a liquid is always accompanied by decrease in temperature or cooling. This is because the liquid uses energy while changing into gaseous state.

Evaporation Causes Cooling

We know that whenever a liquid evaporates, it must be supplied with the latent heat of vapourisation. This is because when a liquid evaporates, it takes the latent heat from anything which it touches and when it loses heat, it gets cooled.

Let us now illustrate evaporation with few examples.

Example 1 : In summer, we feel comfortable under a fan. This is because the air from a fan causes quick evaporation of sweat from the body and hence, the body temperature gets lowered and we feel relief.

Example 2 : In remote villages, people generally keep drinking water either in earthen pots or in earthen pitchers, commonly called as *matka*, to keep the water cool during summer. Do you know how the water is cooled? There are fine holes in the earthen pots which allow water to percolate to the outer surface of the pot. This water evaporates from the outer surface of the pot. The energy required to bring about change in the state is supplied by the water present in the pot. Hence, the temperature gets lowered slowly and the water becomes cold (Fig. 1.55).

Fig. 1.55 : This figure shows the example of the process of evaporation

Example 3 : During a hot sunny day, some people sprinkle water on the roof or on the ground to sleep comfortably during the night. This is because, the water from the ground or roof evaporates by taking heat from the ground or roof and hence causes cooling effect.

Example 4 : We prefer cotton clothes during summer. This is because cotton is porous in nature and is a good absorbent of water coming out of the skin pores as sweat. As the sweat evaporates, it absorbs energy from the body due to its contact with our skin, the temperature gets lowered and we feel more comfortable (Fig. 1.56).

Fig. 1.56 : Cotton clothes

Example 5 : During summer, a desert cooler is used. This is because the hot and dry air passes through the wet pads of wood-shaving. The water start to evaporate and temperature inside the cooler gets lowered and so, the air from the cooler is very cool. The fan inside the cooler speeds up the process of evaporation of water (Fig. 1.57).

Fig. 1.57 : Desert cooler

Note

- Surgeons perform minor surgeries on the part of skin by spraying ether. This is because, ether has low boiling point of 308 K and hence evaporates at faster rate from the skin resulting in numbness in that part.

PAPER-PEN TEST : 14

1. Define evaporation.
2. How does a liquid change into vapour on its own?
3. Describe how the process of evaporation takes place.
4. Evaporation of a liquid is always accompanied by ------------------------in temperature or cooling.
5. Why evaporation of a liquid is always accompanied by decrease in temperature or cooling?
6. Whenever a liquid evaporates, it must be supplied with the latent heat of vapourisation. Why?
7. Give reasons :
   (a) In summer, we feel comfortable under a fan.
   (b) In remote villages, people generally keep drinking water in earthen pots to keep the water cool during summer.
   (c) During a hot sunny day, some people sprinkle water on the roof or on the ground to sleep comfortably during the night.
   (d) We prefer cotton clothes during summer.
   (e) During summer, a desert cooler is used.
8. Surgeons spray ether to perform minor surgeries. Why?

Factors Affecting Evaporation

The rate of transformation of a liquid into vapour depends on various factors as follows :

(a) *Humidity of air*

(b) *Temperature*

(c) *Surface area of the liquid*

(d) *Speed of wind*

(e) *Nature of the liquid*

We shall discuss these factors in detail one by one.

(a) Humidity of Air : The degree of 'dampness' of air tells us the humidity of air. In other words, *the amount of water vapours present in air is called humidity.* When the amount of water vapours present in air is small, the air appears to be 'dry' and when the amount of water vapour present in air is large, the air appears to be 'damp'.

When the humidity of air is low, then the rate of evaporation is high and water evaporates more readily. During such conditions, the sweat from our body evaporates readily and we feel comfortable. So, the wet clothes dry quickly under the conditions of low humidity of air.

When the humidity of air is high, then the rate of evaporation is low and water evaporates very slowly. During such conditions, the sweat from our body evaporates slowly and we become uncomfortable. So, the wet clothes take long time to dry. This type of weather is experienced during cloudy days in rainy season.

To Show the Presence of Water Vapour in Air

The amount of water vapour in air keeps on changing. The water vapour comes into air by the process of evaporation of water from ponds, lakes, rivers etc. The plants also give out water vapour by the process of transpiration. Similarly, the animals also give out water vapour when they breathe out air. Do you know that land also gives water vapour on being warmed by the sun? This entire water vapour enter the air around us.

Let us now demonstrate an activity to show the presence of water vapour in air.

Activity 1.13 - To show the presence of water vapour in air.

PROCEDURE

Step 1– Take a steel tumbler.

Step 2– Put some well crushed ice into it.

Step 3– Dry the tumbler from outside by wiping it with a piece of clean and dry cloth.

Step 4– Leave the tumbler with ice undisturbed for about five minutes.

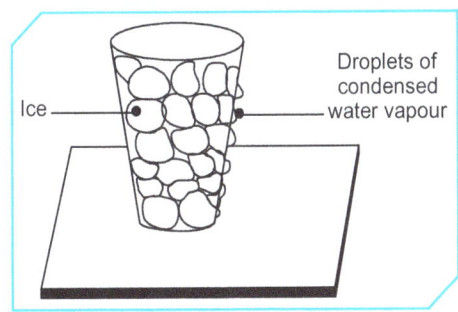

Fig. 1.58 : Experimental set-up to show the presence of water vapour in air.

OBSERVATION

A large number of tiny drops of water appear on the outer surface of the tumbler.

CONCLUSION

The drops of water on the outer surface of tumbler containing crushed ice appear after five minutes. This is because, the air around the tumbler contains water vapour in it. When these water vapours come in contact with cold tumbler containing ice, they condense to form tiny drops of liquid water.

(b) Temperature : The rate of evaporation of a liquid increases with the increase in temperature. When the liquid is heated by increasing the temperature, the particles of the liquid get enough kinetic energy to go into gaseous state, thereby increasing the rate of evaporation. The rate of evaporation becomes maximum at its boiling point.

(c) Surface Area of the Liquid : Since evaporation is a surface phenomena, when the surface area of the liquid is larger the rate of evaporation will be more. Have you ever thought what happens to the rate of evaporation when a liquid is kept in the test tube and the same liquid in the china dish? The liquid kept in the china dish will evaporate more rapidly because of its larger surface area as compared to the liquid in the test tube. We can observe this process in our everyday life as follows :

(i) When we spread wet clothes to dry them in air, there is an increase in surface area available for the evaporation of water to take place and hence the clothes get dried faster (Fig. 1.59).

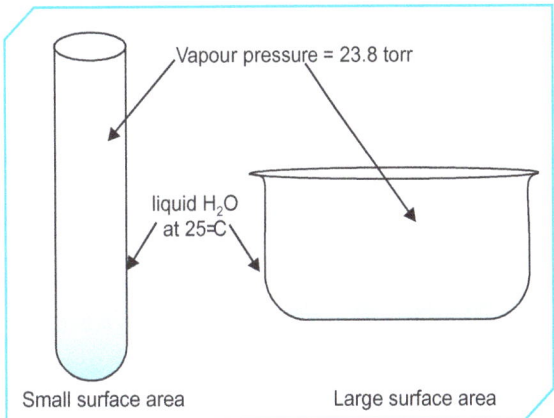

Fig. 1.59 : Experiment to show that surface area increases the rate of evaporation

(ii) After rain, the wet roads dry quickly because the rain water is spread over a large area of road which gives the particles of water more surface area to evaporate faster.

(iii) When we are in hurry, we often pour hot tea, milk or coffee in a saucer in order to reduce the temperature of it. This is because of the surface area of the saucer is greater than the surface area of the cup. Pouring the hot liquid in the saucer increases the rate of evaporation and cools it more quickly (Fig. 1.60)

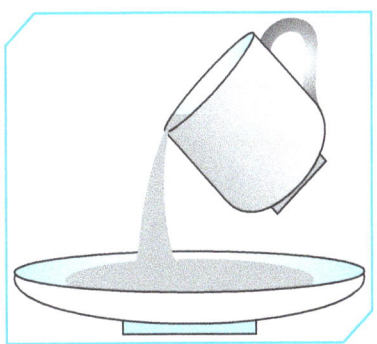

Fig.1.60 : This figure shows that the rate of evaporation increase with the increase in surface area.

(d) Speed of Wind : The rate of evaporation of a liquid increases with increase in the speed of the wind. This is because when the speed of the wind increases, the particles of water vapour move away with the wind, which decreases the amount of water vapour in the surrounding, thereby increasing the rate of evaporation of water. We can notice this when the wet clothes dry fast on a windy day.

(e) Nature of the Liquid : The nature of the liquid is important for the rate of evaporation to take place. Alcohol evaporates at a faster rate than water. This is because, the boiling point of alcohol is less than that of water. This shows that the inter-particle forces of attraction in alcohol is less than that in water. Hence, lesser the boiling point of a liquid, more will be its tendency to change into vapour.

Let us perform an activity to find out the factors affecting evaporation.

Activity 1.14–To understand the factors affecting evaporation.

PROCEDURE

Step 1- Take 5 mL of water in a test tube (see fig a).
Step 2- Keep it near a window or under a fan.
Step 3- Take 5 mL of water in an open china dish (see fig b).
Step 4- Keep it near a window or under a fan.
Step 5- Take 5 mL of water in an open china dish.
Step 6- Keep it inside a cupboard or on a shelf in your class (see fig c).
Step 7- Record the room temperature.
Step 8- Record the time or days taken for the evaporation process in the above cases.
Step 9- Repeat the above three steps of activity on a rainy day and record your observations. What do you infer about the effect of temperature, surface area and wind velocity (speed) on evaporation?

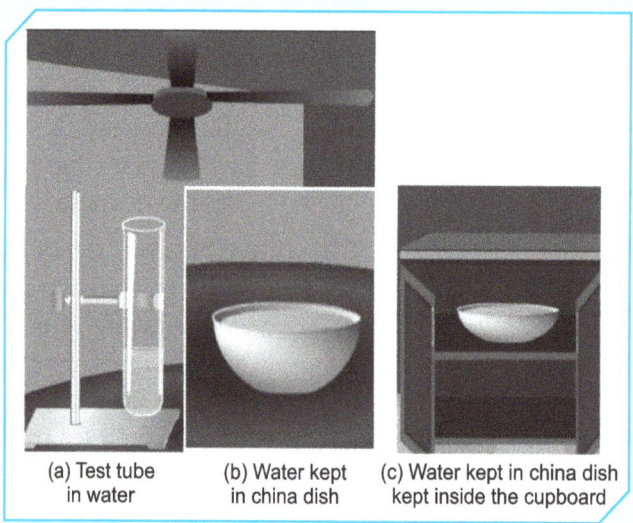

(a) Test tube in water　(b) Water kept in china dish　(c) Water kept in china dish kept inside the cupboard

Fig.1.61 : Experimental set-up to show the factors that effects the process of evaporation.

OBSERVATION

The water kept in an open china dish evaporates faster than the water kept in a test tube. The water kept inside the cupboard will take more time to evaporate than in other places mentioned above.

On a rainy day, when the humidity of air is high, the rate of evaporation will be low and water evaporates very slowly.

CONCLUSION

Evaporation is a surface phenomena and so, when the surface area of the liquid is greater, the rate of evaporation will be more. The rate of evaporation of a liquid decreases with increase in the humidity of air and it increases with increase in the speed of the wind.

Let us now differentiate evaporation and boiling.

Differences between Evaporation and Boiling

S. No	Evaporation	Boiling
1.	It is a surface phenomena and hence occurs only from the surface of the water.	It is a bulk phenomena and hence occurs from the surface as well as from below the surface of the water.
2.	It takes place at all temperatures.	It takes place at specific temperature known as boiling point of the liquid.
3.	The evaporation of a liquid takes place on its own.	Boiling of a liquid can take place only on heating.
4.	It results in cooling.	It does not result in cooling.
5.	It is a slow process.	It is a fast process.
6.	It takes place at all temperatures.	It takes place at a particular temperature.

1.14 OTHER STATES OF MATTER

There are two more states of matter namely,

(a) Plasma

(b) Bose – Einstein Condensate

(a) Plasma : Plasma is a mixture of free electrons and ions which occurs naturally in the stars. The plasma is created in stars because of very high temperature. The sun and the stars glow because of the presence of plasma in them. Plasma can be formed on the earth by passing electricity through gases at very low pressures in a glass tube or discharge tube. The fluorescent tube and neon sign bulbs consist of plasma. Inside a neon sign bulb, there is neon gas, and inside a fluorescent tube, there is helium gas or some other gas. The gas gets ionised, i.e., gets charged, when electrical energy flows through it. This charging up creates a plasma glowing inside the tube or bulb. The plasma glows with a special colour depending on the nature of gas (Fig. 1.62).

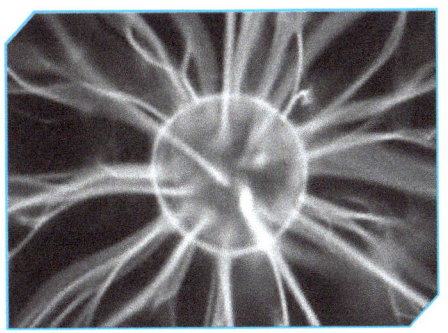

Fig. 1.62 : Plasma.

(b) Bose – Einstein Condensate : In 1920, Indian physicist **Satyendra Nath Bose** had done some calculations for the fifth state of matter. Based on his calculations, **Albert Einstein** predicted a new state of matter called the Bose-Einstein Condensate (BEC). The BEC is formed by cooling a gas of extremely low density, about one-hundred-thousand the density of normal air, to super low temperatures (Fig. 1.63).

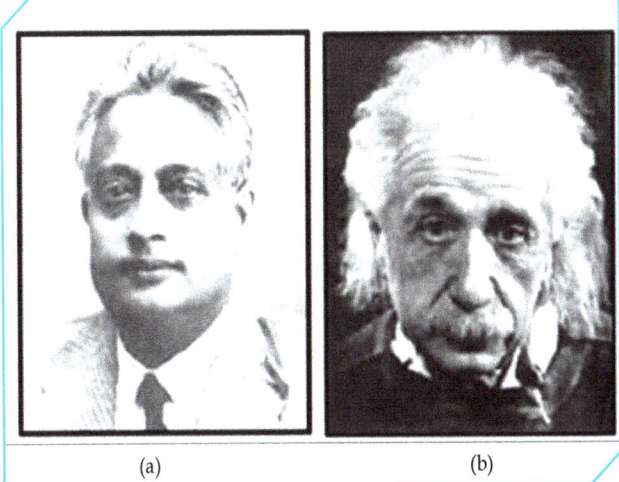

Fig. 1.63 : The two famous scientists, (a) S.N. Bose, and (b) Albert Einstein.

Note

- In 2001, Eric A. Cornell, Wolfgang Ketterle and Carl E. Wieman of USA received the Nobel prize in physics for achieving 'Bose-Einstein condensation'.

PAPER-PEN TEST : 15

1. What are the factors affecting evaporation?
2. Define humidity.
3. What is degree of dampness?
4. Why do the wet clothes dry quickly under the conditions of low humidity of air?
5. Why do the wet clothes take long time to dry when the humidity in air is high?
6. It is easier to sip hot tea or milk faster from a saucer than from a tumbler or a cup. Why?
7. How will you perform an experiment to show the presence of water vapour in air?
8. The rate of evaporation becomes maximum at its boiling point. Why?
9. What happens to the rate of evaporation when a liquid is kept in the test tube and the same liquid in the china dish?
10. Justify : "Evaporation is a surface phenomena".
11. Give reason: After rain, the wet roads dry quickly.
12. Why do the wet clothes dry fast on a windy day?
13. Why is the boiling point of alcohol less than that of water?
14. The boiling point of alcohol is --------------------.
15. The boiling point of water is --------------------.

COMPENDIUM

- Anything that occupies space and has mass is known as matter.
- Matter is not continuous but rather consists of large number of particles.
- Characteristics of Particle
    (a) Large number of particles constitutes matter.
    (b) Particles of matter are very small in size.
    (c) Particles of matter have spaces between them.
    (d) Particles of matter are continuously moving.
- Solids have definite shape, distinct boundaries and fixed volume.
- Liquids have fixed volume but no fixed shape.
- Gases neither have fixed shape nor volume.
- Solids possess least compressibility.
- Liquids possess higher compressibility than solids.
- Gases possess highest compressibility as compared to solids and liquids.
- Diffusion is the process in which the movement of particles from higher concentration to that of lower concentration takes place.
- The process in which a solid changes to liquid state by absorbing heat at constant temperature is called fusion or melting.
- The temperature at which a solid melts to become a liquid at the atmospheric pressure is called as melting point.
- The SI unit of temperature is Kelvin.
- The formula for finding the temperature T in Kelvin. $(K) = T(°C) + 273$
- The hidden heat which breaks the force of attraction between the molecules during change of state is called latent heat.
- The latent heat of fusion is the amount of heat energy required to change 1kg of solid into liquid at its melting point.
- The melting point of a solid is an indication of the strength of the force of attraction between its particles.
- The temperature at which a liquid changes to solid by giving out heat at atmospheric pressure is called freezing point.
- The temperature at which a liquid starts boiling at the atmospheric pressure is known as boiling point.
- The latent heat of vapourisation is the heat energy required to change 1kg of liquid to gas at atmospheric pressure at its boiling point.
- When a solid changes its state to a gas and vice versa without passing through the liquid state, it is called sublimation.
- Boiling is a bulk phenomena.
- The phenomenon of change of a liquid into its gaseous state at any temperature below its boiling point is known as evaporation.

- In evaporation, the conversion of liquid to gaseous state occurs at a much slower rate, compared to boiling.
- Evaporation takes place only at the surface of the liquid while boiling takes place in all parts of the liquid.
- Evaporation is a surface phenomenon and therefore, it increases with an increase in surface area.
- Evaporation causes cooling.
- The rate of evaporation is affected by the surface area exposed to atmosphere, temperature, humidity and wind speed.
- Evaporation increases with an increase in temperature.
- Evaporation decreases with an increase in humidity.
- Evaporation increases with the increase in wind speed.
- The process in which a gas changes into liquid state by giving out heat at constant temperature is called condensation.
- The amount of water vapour present in the air is called humidity.

EXERCISES (SOLVED)

NCERT INTEXT QUESTIONS

1. Which of the following is matter? Chair, air, love, smell, hate, almonds, thought, cold, cold-drink, smell of perfume.

Ans : Chair, air, smell, almonds, smell of perfume and cold-drink are the examples of matter. Things that occupy space and have some mass are called matter. All the above occupy some space and have some mass, so these are matter.

2. Give reasons for the following observation: The smell of hot sizzling food reaches you several meters away, but to get the smell from cold food you have to go close.

Ans : Smell of anything comes because of gases emanating from the given thing and it reaches to us because of diffusion of gas. The rate of diffusion increases with increase in temperature. This happens because of higher kinetic energy due to higher temperature. That is why smell of hot sizzling food reaches to us from several feet. On the other hand, the kinetic energy of gases emanating from cold food is low because of lower temperature. Due to this, we have to go close to a cold food to take its smell.

3. A diver is able to cut through water in a swimming pool. Which property of matter does this observation show?

Ans : Water is also a matter. We know that particles of matter have space between them. In case of fluids, the space between particles is large enough and due to this it becomes easier for a diver to cut through water in a swimming pool.

4. What are the characteristics of the particles of matter?

Ans : The characteristics of the particles of matter are as follows :

(a) The particles of matter are very small.

(b) The particles of matter have inter-particle spaces between them.

(c) The particles of matter are moving constantly.

(d) The particles of matter attract one another.

5. The mass per unit volume of a substance is called density. (Density = mass/volume) Arrange the following in order of increasing density : air, exhaust from chimneys, honey, water, chalk, cotton and iron.

Ans : Air < Exhaust from chimneys < Cotton < Water < Honey < Chalk < Iron. Air is the mixture of gases and hence has the lowest density. Chimney exhaust is also a mixture of gases; along with some heavier particles, such as ash. This makes the density of chimney exhaust more than air. Cotton is a porous solid and has lot of air trapped within pores. This makes its volume more than water. Therefore, it is less dense than water. Water is a liquid which has closely packed particles and so its density is higher than the cotton. Honey is a thick liquid having closely packed heavy particles and so its density is higher than that of water. Chalk is porous solid which has less closely packed particles but has higher density than honey. Iron is highly compact solid and hence it has density higher than that of chalk.

6. Tabulate the differences in the characteristics of states of matter.

Ans :

S. No	Characteristics	Solids	Liquids	Gases
1.	Inter-particle spaces	Very small	Comparatively large	Very large
2.	Arrangement of particles	Closely packed	Loosely packed	Very loosely packed
3.	Nature	Hard and rigid	Fluid	Highly fluid
4.	Compressibility	Negligible	Very small	Highly compressible
5.	Inter-particle forces	Very strong	Weak	Very weak
6.	Shape and volume	Fixed shape and volume	Indefinite shape and fixed volume	Indefinite shape and volume
7.	Density	High	Less than the density of the solid	Very low density
8.	Kinetic energy	Low	Comparatively high	Very high
9.	Diffusion	Negligible	Slow	Very fast
10.	Flow	Cannot flow	Flow	Flow

7. Comment upon the following: in relation to properties of states of matter-solid, liquid, gas : rigidity, compressibility, fluidity, filling a gas container, shape, kinetic energy and density

Ans : **(a) Rigidity :** The greatest force of attraction between particles and close packing of particles make solids rigid. Rigidity is one of the unique properties of solids. Because of rigidity, a solid has definite shape and volume and can resist itself from getting distorted. On the other hand, rigidity is negligible in fluid and gas.

(b) Compressibility : Compressibility is one of the most important characteristics of gas. Because of lot of space between particles, a gas can be compressed to a great extent. Liquid and solid cannot be compressed because of less space between their particles.

(c) Fluidity : The ability to flow is called fluidity. The less force of attraction and more space between particles make liquid and gas to flow. That's why liquid and gas are called fluid.

(d) Filling of a gas container : Liquids do not fill a gas container completely, while gases fill the gas container completely in which it is kept. This is because the particles of gas can move in all the directions.

(e) Shape : Solids have fixed shape. Liquid and gas take the shape of the container in which they are kept. This happens because of less force of attraction and more kinetic energy between particles of liquids and negligible force of attraction and highest kinetic energy between particles of gas.

(f) Kinetic energy : The kinetic energy of particles of solid is the minimum. They only vibrate at their fixed position. The kinetic energy of particles of liquid is more than that of solid. But they can slide above one another. The kinetic energy of particles of gas is the maximum.

(g) Density : The mass per unit volume of a substance is called density. The density of solid is highest, of liquid is less than solid and of gas is minimum.

8. Give reasons :

(a) A gas fills completely the vessel in which it is kept.

(b) A gas exerts pressure on the walls of the container.

(c) A wooden table should be called a solid.

(d) We can easily move our hand in air but to do the same through a solid block of wood we need a *karate* expert.

MATTER IN OUR SURROUNDINGS

Ans : (a) The force of attraction between particles of gas is negligible. Because of this, particles of gas move in all directions. Thus, a gas fills the vessel completely in which it is kept.

(b) Because of negligible force of attraction between particles of gas, the particles of gas have the highest kinetic energy. These properties enable the particles of gas to move in all directions and hit the walls of the container from all sides. Because of this, a gas exerts pressure on the walls of the container in which it is kept.

(c) A wooden table has fixed shape and fixed volume, which are the main characteristics of a solid. Thus, a wooden table should be called a solid.

(d) Since, air is gas, so its particles are loosely packed and there is negligible force of attraction between its particles. Because of that, we can easily move our hand in air. But wood is a solid, so the force of attraction between its particles is greatest. Also, the particles of wooden block are closely packed. That's why we cannot move our hand through a solid block of wood. However, a karate expert can exert required pressure to break the great force of attraction between the particles of a solid wooden block.

9. Liquids generally have lower density as compared to solids. But you must have observed that ice floats on water. Find out why.

Ans : This is because of a property called anomalous expansion of water or ice. Water has its lowest density at 4°C which means that when water is heated from 4°C, its density decreases. Also when water is cooled below 4°C, its density decreases. So ice at 0°C or less temperature has a lower density than water at a slightly higher temperature. So ice floats on water. Trapped air could also contribute to this phenomenon. This is the reason why the surface of a lake may be frozen but the lower layers could have liquid water. This property ensures the survival of aquatic animals..

10. Convert the following temperatures to Celsius scale : (a) 300 K (b) 573 K

Ans : (a) Temperature on Kelvin scale = Temperature on Celsius scale + 273

Therefore,
Temperature on Celsius scale = Temperature on Kelvin scale – 273

Hence,
Temperature on Celsius scale = 300K – 273
= 27°C

(b) Temperature on Kelvin scale = Temperature on Celsius scale + 273

Therefore, temperature on Celsius scale = Temperature on Kelvin scale – 273

Hence, temperature on Celsius scale = 573K – 273 = 300°C

11. What is the physical state of water at : (a) 250°C (b) 100°C

Ans : (a) Since, water boils at 100°C, thus it is in gaseous state at 250°C.

(b) Since, water boils at 100°C, thus at 100°C water is in transition phase, i.e. in both liquid and gaseous states.

12. For any substance why does the temperature remain constant during the change of state?

Ans : During the change of state of any substance, the heat supplied or released is utilized in phase change. This heat is called latent heat. So, the temperature of any substance remains constant during the change of state.

13. Suggest a method to liquefy a gas.

Ans : A gas is liquefied by increasing pressure and decreasing temperature.

14. Why does a desert cooler cool better on a hot dry day?

Ans : Desert cooler works on the basis of evaporation. In hot and dry days the moisture level is very low in atmosphere which increases the rate of evaporation. Because of faster evaporation, cooler works well. That's why desert cooler cools better on a hot dry day.

15. How does the water kept in an earthen pot *(matka)* become cool during summer?

Ans : Water from porous walls of earthen pot evaporates continuously, which lowers the temperature of water kept in the earthen pot. In summer, moisture level is very low in the atmosphere, which increases the rate of evaporation, as evaporation is inversely proportional to the moisture level in atmosphere. That is why, in summer water kept in earthen pot becomes cool.

16. Why does our palm feel cold when we put some acetone or petrol or perfume on it?

Ans : When acetone, petrol or perfume is poured

over the palm, it evaporates quickly as these are volatile liquids. The evaporation lowers the temperature of palm and our palm feels cold.

17. **Why are we able to sip hot tea or milk faster from a saucer rather than a cup?**

Ans : When hot tea or milk is powred in a saucer, the liquid is exposed over a larger surface area as compared to the liquid being kept in a cup. The larger surface area enables faster cooling. That's why we are able to sip hot tea or milk faster from a saucer rather than from a cup.

18. **What type of clothes should we wear in summer?**

Ans : We should wear cotton clothes in summer because cotton clothes are good absorbent and they absorb sweat excreted in summer. Because of evaporation of sweat from the surface of cotton cloth, we feel cool and comfortable.

NCERT EXERCISE QUESTIONS

1. Convert the following temperatures to the Celsius scale : (a) 293 K (b) 470 K

Ans : (a) Temperature in Celsius scale = Temperature in Kelvin scale − 273

$\Rightarrow$ 293 K = 293 K − 273
= 20°C

(b) Temperature in Celsius scale = Temperature in Kelvin scale − 273

$\Rightarrow$ 470 K = 470 K − 273
= 197°C

2. Convert the following temperatures to the Kelvin scale : (a) 25°C (b) 373°C

Ans : (a) Temperature in Kelvin scale = Temperature in Celsius scale + 273
= 25°C + 273 = 298 K

(b) Temperature in Kelvin scale = Temperature in Celsius scale + 273
= 373°C + 273 = 646 K

3. Give reason for the following observations.

(a) Naphthalene balls disappear with time without leaving any solid.

(b) We can get the smell of perfume sitting several meters away.

Ans : (a) Naphthalene ball is a sublimate and a sublimate turns into vapour without changing into liquid. Thus, naphthalene balls disappear with time without leaving any solid.

(b) Perfume turns into gas at room temperature. The vapour of perfume travels up to several meters because of diffusion. That's why we can get the smell of perfume sitting several meters away.

4. Arrange the following substances in increasing order of forces of attraction between the particles − Water, Sugar, Oxygen.

Ans : Oxygen < Water < Sugar. Oxygen is a gas, thus force of attraction is negligible between particles. Water is a liquid, thus force of attraction between particles is more than liquid and less than solid. Sugar is a solid, thus force of attraction between particles is greatest.

5. What is the physical state of water at : (a) 25°C (b) 0°C (c) 100°C

Ans : (a) At 25°C : Water is in liquid state.

(b) At 0°C : Water is in transition state, i.e. in solid and liquid both.

(c) At 100°C : water is in transition state, i.e. in liquid and gas both.

6. Give two reasons to justify.

(a) Water at room temperature is a liquid.

(b) An iron almirah is a solid at room temperature.

Ans : (a) Water at room temperature is a liquid because :

(i) It has definite volume, but not definite shape as it takes the shape of the container in which it is kept.

(ii) It flows at room temperature.

(b) An iron almirah is a solid at room temperature because:

(i) It has definite shape.

(ii) It has definite volume.

7. Why is ice at 273K more effective in cooling than water at the same temperature?

Ans : At 273K, ice requires latent heat to melt into water, while water at 273K requires less heat to come to the room temperature. So, ice at 273 K is more effective in cooling than water at the same temperature.

8. What produces more severe burns, boiling water or steam?

Ans : Steam produces more severe burns than boiling water because steam has more latent heat than boiling water.

9. Name A, B, C, D, E and F in the following diagram showing change in its state.

Ans : A : Heating : Melting, B : Heating : Vapourisation, C : Cooling : Condensation : Liquefaction, D : Cooling : Freezing, E : Sublimation and F : Solidification

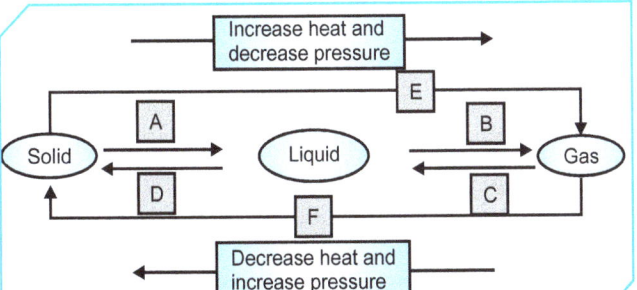

NCERT EXAMPLAR QUESTIONS

1. Which one of the following sets of phenomena would increase on raising the temperature?

    (a) Diffusion, evaporation, compression of gases

    (b) Evaporation, compression of gases, solubility

    (c) Evaporation, diffusion, expansion of gases

    (d) Evaporation, solubility, diffusion, compression of gases

2. Seema visited a Natural Gas Compressing Unit and found that the gas can be liquefied under specific conditions of temperature and pressure. While sharing her experience with friends she got confused. Help her to identify the correct set of conditions :

    (a) Low temperature, low pressure

    (b) High temperature, low pressure

    (c) Low temperature, high pressure

    (d) High temperature, high pressure

3. The property to flow is unique in fluids. Which one of the following statement is correct?

    (a) Only gases behave like fluids

    (b) Gases and solids behave like fluids

    (c) Gases and liquids behave like fluids

    (d) Only liquids are fluids

4. During summer, water kept in an earthen pot becomes cool because of the phenomenon of :

    (a) Diffusion

    (b) Transpiration

    (c) Osmosis

    (d) Evaporation

5. A few substances are arranged in the increasing order of 'forces of attraction' between their particles. Which one of the following represents a correct arrangement?

    (a) Water, air, wind

    (b) Air, sugar, oil

    (c) Oxygen, water, sugar

    (d) Salt, juice, air

6. On converting 25°C, 38°C and 66°C to Kelvin scale, the correct sequence of temperature will be :

    (a) 298 K, 311 K and 339 K

    (b) 298 K, 300 K and 338 K

    (c) 273 K, 278 K and 543 K

    (d) 298 K, 310 K and 338 K

7. Choose the correct statement of the following :

    (a) Conversion of solid into vapours without passing through the liquid state is called vaporization.

    (b) Conversion of solid into vapours without passing through the liquid state is called sublimation.

    (c) Conversion of vapours into solid without passing through the liquid state is called freezing.

    (d) Conversion of solid into liquid is called sublimation.

8. The boiling points of diethyl ether, acetone and n-butyl alcohol are 35°C, 56°C and 118°C respectively. Which one of the following correctly represents their boiling points in Kelvin scale?

    (a) 306 K, 329 K, 391 K

    (b) 308 K, 329 K, 392 K

    (c) 308 K, 329 K, 391 K

    (d) 329 K, 392 K, 308 K

9. Which condition out of the following will increase the evaporation of water?

    (a) Increase in temperature of water

(b) Decrease in temperature of water

(c) Less exposed surface area of water

(d) Adding common salt to water

10. In which of the following conditions, the distance between the molecules of hydrogen gas would increase?

(a) Increasing pressure on hydrogen contained in a closed container

(b) Some hydrogen gas leaking out of the container

(c) Increasing the volume of the container of hydrogen gas

(d) Adding more hydrogen gas to the container without increasing the volume of the container

(i) (a) and (c)

(ii) (a) and (d)

(iii) (b) and (c)

(iv) (b) and (d)

Ans : 1. (c), 2. (c), 3. (c), 4. (d), 5. (c), 6. (a), 7. (b), 8. (c) 9. (a), 10. (c).

11. A sample of water under study was found to boil at 102°C at normal temperature and pressure. Is the water pure? Will this water freeze at 0°C? Comment.

Ans : The boiling point of pure water is 100°C. Soluble impurities increase the boiling point of a liquid. As the sample of water boils at 102°C, hence it is not pure. Impurities effect both boiling and melting points, The presence of impurities lowers (depresses) the freezing point of a liquid. That is why sea water freezes at –2°C instead of normal 0°C.

12. A student heats a beaker containing ice and water. He measures the temperature of the content of the beaker as a function of time. Which of the following graph would correctly represent the result? Justify your choice.

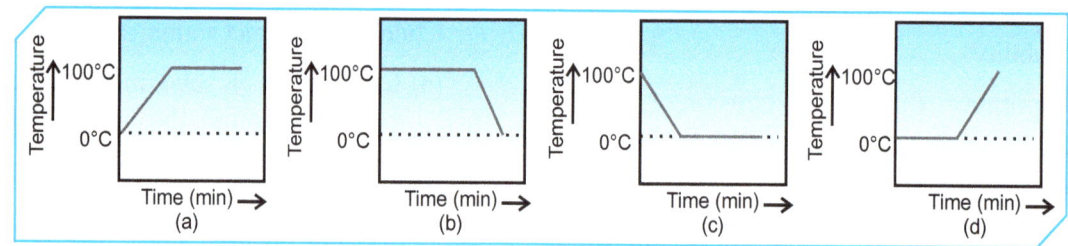

Ans : Since ice and water are in equilibrium, the temperature would be zero. When we heat the mixture, energy supplied is utilized in melting the ice and the temperature does not change till all the ice melts because of latent heat of fusion. On further heating, the temperature of the water would increase. Therefore, the correct option is (d).

13. Fill in the blanks :

(a) Evaporation of a liquid at room temperature leads to a ----------------- effect.

(b) At room temperature the forces of attraction between the particles of solid substances are -----------------than those which exist in the gaseous state.

(c) The arrangement of particles is less ordered in the ----------------- state. However, there is no order in the ----------------- state.

(d) ----------------- is the change of solid state directly to gaseous state without going through the ----------------- state.

(e) The phenomenon of change of a liquid into the gaseous state at any temperature below its boiling point is called -----------------.

Ans : (a) Cooling (b) Stronger (c) Liquid, gaseous (d) Sublimation, liquid (e) Evaporation

14. Match the physical quantities given in column A to their SI units given in column B :

(A)	(B)
(a) Pressure	(i) cubic metre
(b) Temperature	(ii) kilogram
(c) Density	(iii) pascal
(d) Mass	(iv) kelvin
(e) Volume	(v) kilogram per cubic metre

Ans : (a) – (iii), (b) – (iv), (c) – (v), (d) – (ii), (e) – (i)

15. The non SI and SI units of some physical quantities are given in column A and column B respectively. Match the units belonging to the same physical quantity :

(A)	(B)
(a) Degree celsius	(i) kilogram
(b) Centimetre	(ii) pascal
(c) Gram per centimetre cube	(iii) metre
(d) Bar	(iv) kelvin
(e) Milligram	(v) kilogram per metre cube

Ans : (a) – (iv), (b) – (iii), (c) – (v), (d) – (ii), (e) – (i)

16. 'Osmosis is a special kind of diffusion'. Comment.

Ans : Yes, this is true. In both the phenomena, there is movement of particles from region of higher concentration to that of lower concentration. However, in the case of osmosis the movement of solvent is through a semi-permeable membrane which is permeable only to water molecules.

17. Classify the following into osmosis or diffusion
    (a) Swelling up of a raisin on keeping in water.
    (b) Spreading of virus on sneezing.
    (c) Earthworm die on coming in contact with common salt.
    (d) Shrinking of grapes kept in thick sugar syrup.
    (e) Preserving pickles in salt.
    (f) Spreading of smell of cake being baked throughout the house.
    (g) Aquatic animals using oxygen dissolved in water during respiration.

Ans : (a) Osmosis (b) Diffusion (c) Osmosis
      (d) Osmosis (e) Osmosis   (f) Diffusion
      (g) Diffusion

18. Water as ice has a cooling effect, whereas water as steam may cause severe burns. Explain these observations.

Ans : In case of ice, the water molecules have low energy while in the case of steam the water molecules have high energy. The high energy of water molecules in steam is transformed as heat and may cause burns. On the other hand, in case of ice, the water molecules take energy from the body and thus give it a cooling effect.

19. Alka was making tea in a kettle. Suddenly she felt intense heat from the puff of steam gushing out of the spout of the kettle. She wondered whether the temperature of the steam was higher than that of the water boiling in the kettle. Comment.

Ans : The temperature of both boiling water and steam is 100°C, but steam has more energy because of latent heat of vapourisation. That's why she felt intense heat from the puff of steam gushing out of the spout of the kettle.

20. A glass tumbler containing hot water is kept in the freezer compartment of a refrigerator (temperature < 0°C). If you could measure the temperature of the content of the tumbler, which of the following graphs would correctly represent the change in its temperature as a function of time.

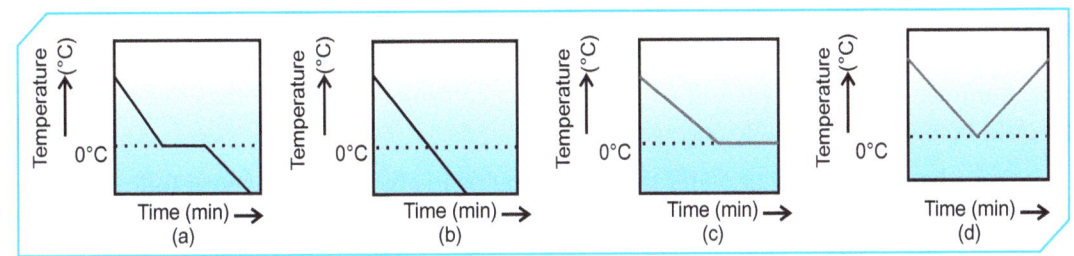

Ans : The correct option is (a) The water will cool initially till it reaches 0°C, the freezing point. At this stage the temperature will remain constant till all the water freezes. After this, the temperature will fall again.

21. Look at figure given on the next page and suggest in which of the vessels A, B, C or D the rate of evaporation will be the highest? Explain.

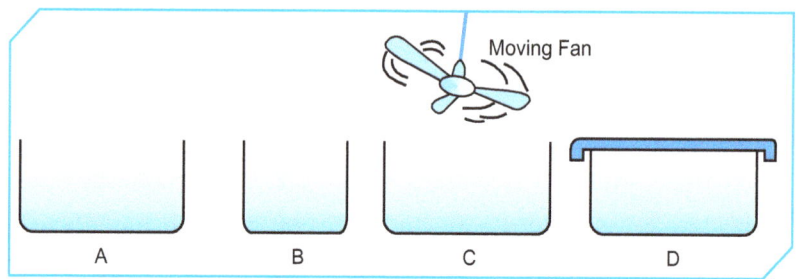

Ans : The correct option is (c) The rate of evaporation increases with increase in surface area because evaporation is a surface phenomena. Also, with the increase in air speed, the particles of water vapour will move away with the air, which will increase the rate of evaporation.

22. (a) Conversion of solid to vapour is called sublimation. Name the term used to denote the conversion of vapour to solid.

(b) Conversion of solid state to liquid state is called fusion; what is meant by latent heat of fusion?

Ans : (a) Solidification.

(b) The amount of heat required to convert 1 kg of solid into liquid at one atmosphere pressure at its melting point is known as its latent heat of fusion.

23. You are provided with a mixture of naphthalene and ammonium chloride by your teacher. Suggest an activity to separate them with well labelled diagram.

Ans : Naphthalene is insoluble in water but soluble in ether, an organic solvent. It is volatile at room temperature. Ammonium chloride is soluble in water and volatile at higher temperature. It decomposes on heating into two colourless gases, ammonia and hydrogen chloride. It is an example of sublimation.

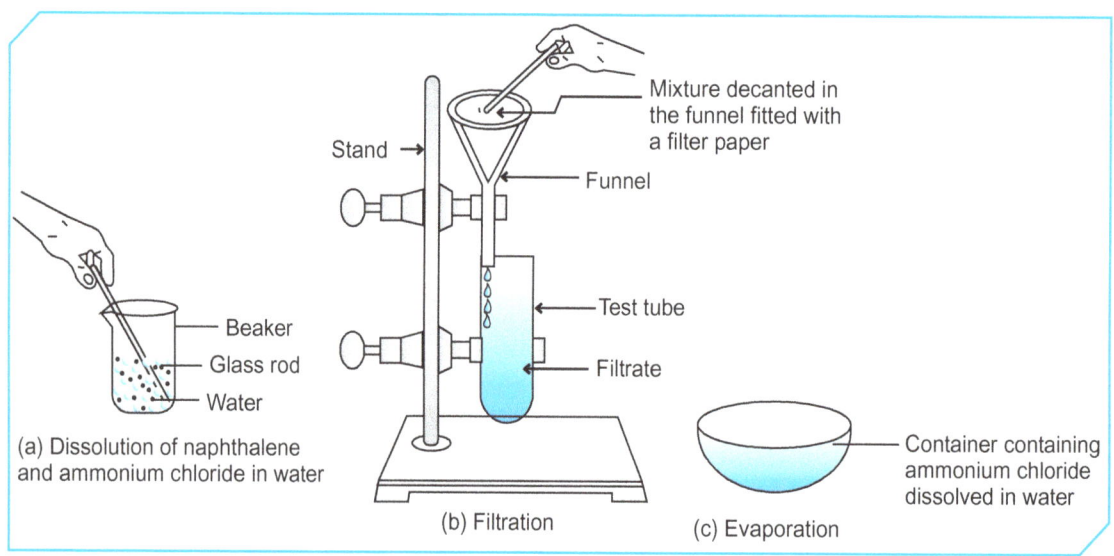

24. It is a hot summer day, Priyanshi and Ali are wearing cotton and nylon clothes respectively. Who do you think would be more comfortable and why?

Ans : Cotton being a better absorber of water than nylon helps in absorption of sweat followed by evaporation which leads to cooling. So, Priyanshi would be more comfortable as compared to Ali.

25. You want to wear your favourite shirt to a party, but the problem is that it is still wet after the wash. What steps would you take to dry it faster?

Ans : Conditions that can increase the rate of evaporation of water are :

(a) An increase of surface area by spreading the shirt.

(b) An increase in temperature by putting the shirt under the sun.

(c) Increase the wind speed by spreading it under the fan.

26. Comment on the following statements:
    (a) Evaporation produces cooling.
    (b) Rate of evaporation of an aqueous solution decreases with increase in humidity.
    (c) Sponge though compressible is a solid.

Ans : (a) Evaporation produces cooling because the particles at the surface of the liquid gain energy from the surroundings and change into vapour thereby producing a cooling effect.

(b) Air around us cannot hold more than a definite amount of water vapour at a given temperature which is known as humidity. So, if the air is already rich in water vapour, it will not take up more water therefore, the rate of evaporation of water will decrease.

(c) A sponge has minute holes in which air is trapped. Also the material is not rigid. So, when we press it the air inside it is expelled out and we are able to compress it.

27. Why does the temperature of a substance remain constant during its melting point or boiling point?

Ans : The temperature of a substance remains constant at its melting and boiling points until all the substance melts or boils because, the heat supplied is continuously used up in changing the state of the substance by overcoming the forces of attraction between the particles. This heat energy absorbed without showing any rise in temperature is given the name–latent heat of fusion or latent heat of vapourisation.

HIGHER ORDER THINKING SKILL QUESTIONS (HOTS)

1. Kala has four cups made of four different materials, A, B, C and D. The cups are of the same size and thickness. She put an equal amount of ice cubes into each cup. Then, she placed all the cups into a plastic container of hot water as shown below:

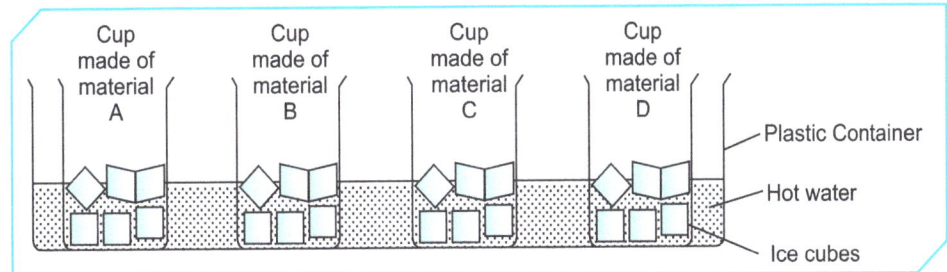

She recorded the time taken for the ice cubes to melt completely in each cup in the graph alongside :

Her friend saw the results of the experiment and wanted to choose one of the materials to make a pot for cooking. Which material should her friend choose?

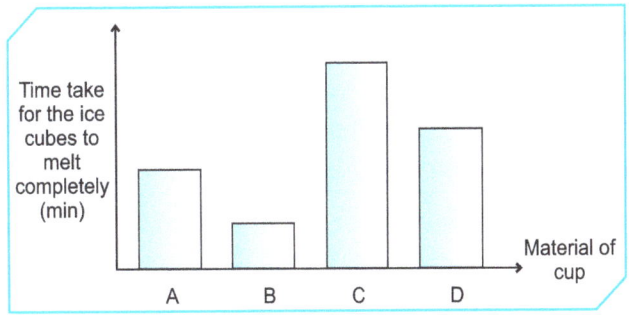

Ans : B. This is because, the time taken by the cup B to melt the ice is lesser. This indicates that material B is a good conductor of heat. Hence her friend should choose material B to make the pot for cooking.

2. Mala was told that in countries where it snowed during winter, salt was sprinkled on roads to prevent water from melted snow to turn into ice again, causing danger to motorists. She conducted an experiment to find out the effect of salt on ice cubes as shown in the set-up given alongside. Mala placed 3 ice cubes in each of the 4 beakers. She added different amounts of salt into each beaker and placed all the beakers near a window. Mala recorded his observations in a table as shown below :

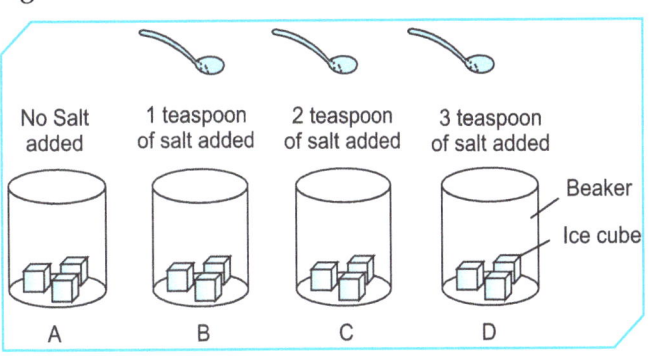

S. No	Beaker	Time taken for ice cubes to turn into liquid (minutes)
1.	A	48
2.	B	40
3.	C	35
4.	D	22

What could Mala conclude from her experiment?

OBSERVATION

Ans : The more the salt that is added to the ice cubes, higher is the rate of melting.

CONCLUSION

(1) Adding salt to water increases the rate of melting.

(2) Higher the amount of salt, faster the ice melts.

3. Tom carried out an experiment to find out the rate of evaporation of water in different containers. An equal amount of water was poured into each container. All containers were left under the hot sun until all the water dried up completely. He obtained the result as shown in the table below :

S. No	Container	A	B	C	D
1.	Exposed surface area of water in the container (cm^2)	10	15	25	30
2.	Time taken for all water in the container to dry up completely (in hours)	3	2.5	1.5	1

(a) Suggest the time needed for the same amount of water in a container with an exposed water surface area of $20 cm^2$ to evaporate completely?

(b) State the relationship between the exposed surface area of water in the container and the time taken for the water in it to dry up completely.

(c) Name two other factors that will affect the rate of evaporation of water.

Ans : (a) Greater than 1.5 hr but less than 2.5hr.

(b) As the exposed surface area of the water in the container increases the time taken for water to dry up or evaporate increases.

(c) Temperature of surroundings and amount of water vapour in the air (humidity).

4. A student of class IX carried out an experiment using two beakers of ice as shown below. Beaker A and B contained the same amount of ice. A thermometer was put into each beaker. Then some salt was added to the ice in Beaker B. The temperatures of both beakers were observed and recorded at regular intervals.

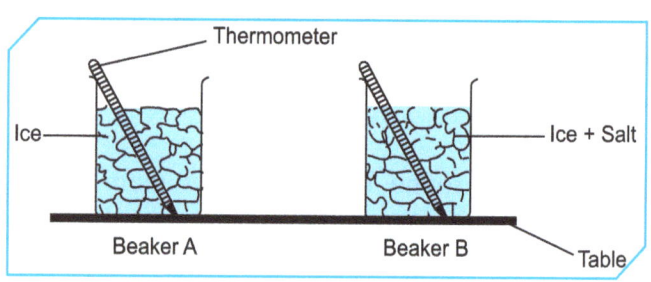

Draw a graph showing the changes in the temperature in both beakers over time.

Ans :

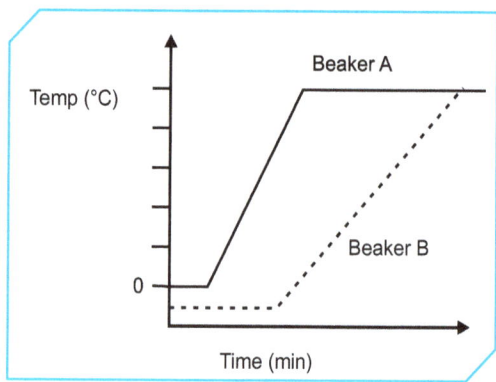

5. Mira wants to store $100 cm^3$ of oxygen gas in a container.

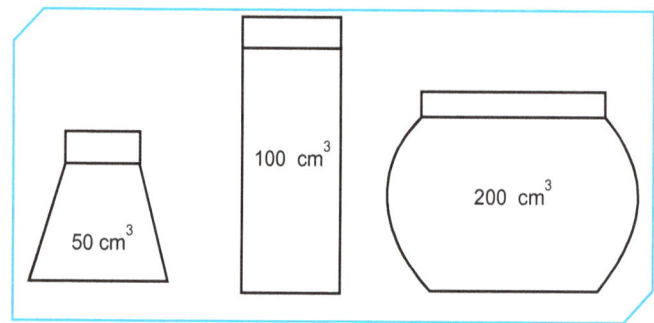

Which of these containers can be used to store the gas completely?

Ans : Oxygen gas can be stored in $200 cm^3$ vessel. This is because the oxygen gas occupies much space. The gas can be stored in any of the vessels provided the facility to compress it exists. gases are compressible. The pressure of the gas and temperature when it occupies 100 cm³ volume can give an idea if the gas can be stored in the 50 cm³ vessel also.

6. Two syringes, A and B, contained the same amount of matter X and Y, at room temperature respectively. On one end each syringe was sealed. The plunger in syringe A could NOT be pushed in while the plunger in syringe B could be pushed in slightly as shown in the diagram given alongside :

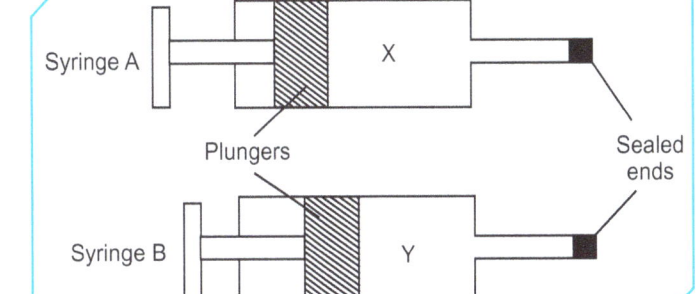

(a) Why plunger in syringe B could be pushed in slightly?
(b) Suggest the state of matter for matter X.
(c) Give an example of matter X.

Ans : (a) Because the matter Y in syringe B could be compressed.

(b) The matter X is in solid state.

(c) Sand, salt, ice, clay etc.

7. A beaker of ice cubes was heated till the boiling point of water was reached as shown in the figure below :

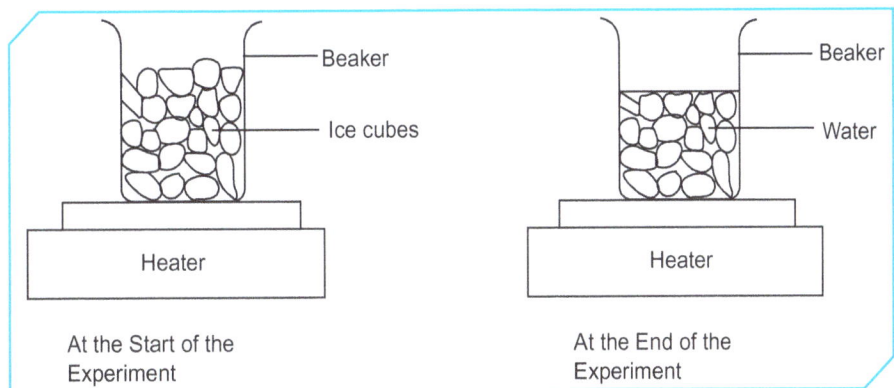

Draw the graph showing the change in temperature of the content in the beaker correctly?

Ans :

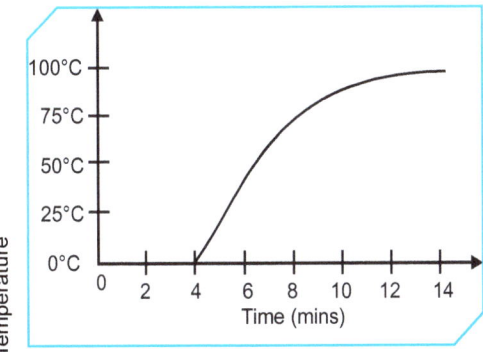

8. A teacher asked the class IX to observe the 'clouds' formed at the mouth of a boiling kettle. What were these white 'clouds'?

Ans : The white 'clouds' formed at the mouth of boiling kettle were water vapour droplets.

9. Priya placed a glass jar containing air in the inverted position over a glass jar full of red-brown bromine vapours. She observed that the red-brown colour spread upwards into the jar containing air. She concluded that it is only the bromine vapour which moves up and diffuse into air in the upper jar, the air from the upper jar does not move down by diffusion into the lower jar containing bromine vapours. What do you say about the conclusion of Priya?

Ans : No, her conclusion is wrong. This is because the air from upper glass jar also diffuses down into the lower glass jar containing bromine vapour. Since air is colourless, it cannot be noticed by her.

10. When water is heated to a temperature A, it gets converted into steam at the same temperature by a process called B. When steam at the same

temperature is cooled, it gets reconverted into water by a process called C. Identify A, B and C.

Ans : A – 373 K, B – Boiling or Vapourisation, C – Condensation.

MULTIPLE CHOICE QUESTIONS (MCQs)

1. Gases have :
   (a) Definite volume, definite shape and are not compressible.
   (b) Definite volume, no definite shape and are highly compressible.
   (c) Definite volume, no definite shape and are slightly compressible.
   (d) No definite volume, no definite shape and are highly compressible.

2. Solids have :
   (a) Definite volume, definite shape and are not compressible.
   (b) Definite volume, no definite shape and are highly compressible.
   (c) Definite volume, no definite shape and are slightly compressible.
   (d) No definite volume, no definite shape and are highly compressible.

3. Liquids have :
   (a) Definite volume, definite shape and are not compressible.
   (b) Definite volume, not definite shape and are highly compressible.
   (c) Definite volume, no definite shape and are slightly compressible.
   (d) No definite volume, no definite shape and are highly compressible.

4. Inter-particle space is maximum in :
   (a) Solids   (b) Liquids
   (c) Gases   (d) All the above

5. Inter-particle force of attraction is maximum in :
   (a) Solids   (b) Liquids
   (c) Gases   (d) All the above

6. Which is not a matter?
   (a) Air   (b) Bread
   (c) Cold   (d) Doll

7. Particles of matter :
   (a) Have space between them
   (b) Have force of attraction between them
   (c) Are continuously moving
   (d) All the above

8. The matter which are called fluids :
   (a) Solids   (b) Liquids
   (c) Gases   (d) Liquid and gases

9. We can scratch a :
   (a) Solid   (b) Liquid
   (c) Gases   (d) All the above

10. Matter which are highly compressible :
    (a) Solids   (b) Liquids
    (c) Gases   (d) All the above

11. Matter which have no definite shape but have definite volume :
    (a) Solids   (b) Liquids
    (c) Gases   (d) All the above

12. Matter which have no definite shape and volume.
    (a) Solids   (b) Liquids
    (c) Gases   (d) All the above

13. CNG is used now a days in :
    (a) Hospitals   (b) Vehicles
    (c) Cooking   (d) Drinks

14. The boiling point of water is :
    (a) 0°C   (b) 273 K
    (c) 373 K   (d) 3730°C

15. Changing of a solid directly into gaseous state is called :
    (a) Melting   (b) Boiling
    (c) Evaporation   (d) Sublimation

16. Which among the following is a sublime substance?
    (a) Ammonium chloride
    (b) Naphthalene
    (c) Camphor
    (d) All the above

17. Dry ice is :
    (a) Ice without water
    (b) Solid carbon monoxide
    (c) Solid carbon dioxide
    (d) All the above

18. For liquefaction of gas :
    (a) Temperature and pressure should be high.
    (b) Temperature should be low and pressure should be high.
    (c) Temperature and pressure should be low.
    (d) Temperature should be high and pressure should be low.

19. Steam of 100°C causes more severe burns than boiling water, because :
    (a) Kinetic energy of steam is lesser than water.
    (b) Steam has latent heat of vaporization.
    (c) Steam has water vapour in it.
    (d) All the above.

20. Evaporation is the process of a liquid changing into vapour :
    (a) At 100°C
    (b) Only at its boiling point
    (c) Below its boiling point
    (d) Only at room temperature

21. Evaporation always causes :
    (a) Thermal expansion
    (b) Liquefaction
    (c) Cooling down
    (d) All the above

22. The arrangement of particles is most ordered in :
    (a) Liquids   (b) Solids
    (c) Gases   (d) All of the above

23. One small crystal of potassium permanganate may contain particles of :
    (a) More than 10^3 (b) More than 10^4
    (c) More than 10^5 (d) More than 10^6

24. The fluorescent tubes and neon sign bulbs glow because :
    (a) Presence of charged particles
    (b) High density of gases
    (c) High temperature
    (d) High applied voltage

25. Which is not the characteristic of matter?
    (a) Particles of a matter are continuously moving
    (b) Particles of matter move faster on increasing temperature
    (c) Particles of matter intermix with each other on their own
    (d) Particles of all maters have same kinetic energy

26. Which of the following is the simplest form of matter?
    (a) Element   (b) Mixture
    (c) Compound   (d) None of these

27. Gases are liquefied under :
    (a) High pressure and high temperature
    (b) High pressure and low temperature
    (c) Low pressure and high temperature
    (d) Low pressure and low temperature

28. The compressibility of which state of matter is high :
    (a) Solid   (b) Liquid
    (c) Gas   (d) All the above

29. The temperature at which the solid melts to become liquid at the atmospheric pressure is called :
    (a) Melting point   (b) Boiling point
    (c) Freezing point   (d) None of the above

30. Which of the following statements is not correct?
    (a) The density of ice is less than the density of water.
    (b) To convert a temperature on the Kelvin scale to Celsius scale, subtract 273 from the given temperature.
    (c) To convert a temperature on the Celsius scale to Kelvin scale, add 273 to the given temperature.
    (d) Vaporization of a liquid causes cooling.

31. When we add sugar in water, particles of sugar disappear because they :
    (a) Are very small
    (b) Get into the spaces between water particles
    (c) Are moving
    (d) All the above

32. Which of the following pairs will not exhibit diffusion?
    (a) Hydrogen and oxygen
    (b) Oxygen and water
    (c) Salt and sand
    (d) Sugar and water

33. Zig-zag movement of the solute particles in a solution is known as :
    (a) Linear motion   (b) Circular motion
    (c) Brownian motion   (d) Curved motion
34. Density of a substance is defined as :
    (a) Ratio of mass and volume
    (b) Product of mass and volume
    (c) Ratio of mass and temperature
    (d) Product of mass and temperature
35. Which of the following is not matter?
    (a) Blood   (b) Humidity
    (c) Electron   (d) Moon rock
36. Which of the following is NOT a property of particles of a matter?
    (a) The particles of matter are extremely small
    (b) The particles of matter have spaces between them.
    (c) The particles of matter are in stationary state.
    (d) The particles of matter attract each other.
37. The heat absorbed when 1 kg of liquid is converted to its vapour at its boiling point is called :
    (a) Evaporation
    (b) Latent heat of vaporization
    (c) Latent heat of fusion
    (d) Latent heat of sublimation
38. The rate of evaporation decreases with increase in :
    (a) Surface area   (b) Temperature
    (c) Humidity   (d) Wind speed
39. When we put some crystals of potassium permanganate in a beaker containing water, we see that whole water has turned pink after some time. This is because :
    (a) Diffusion
    (b) Boiling
    (c) Sublimation of crystals
    (d) Melting of $KMnO_4$
40. The state of matter which have fixed volume but lack definite shape is :
    (a) Solid   (b) Liquid
    (c) Gas   (d) Plasma

ANSWERS

1. (d), 2. (a), 3. (c), 4. (c), 5. (a), 6. (c), 7. (d), 8. (d), 9. (a), 10. (c), 11. (b), 12. (c), 13. (b), 14. (c), 15. (d), 16. (d), 17. (c), 18. (b), 19. (b), 20. (c), 21. (c), 22. (b), 23. (d), 24. (a), 25. (d), 26. (a), 27. (b), 28. (c), 29. (a), 30. (d), 31. (d), 32. (c), 33. (c), 34. (a), 35. (b), 36. (c), 37. (b), 38. (c), 39. (a), 40. (b).

VERY SHORT ANSWER TYPE QUESTIONS

1. What happens to the heat energy supplied to the solid once it starts melting?
2. What do you expect when you open a bottle of perfume?
3. Convert the following temperatures to other scale :
   (a) 280 K
   (b) – 23°C
4. How do you relate the melting point of a substance with the strength of its intermolecular forces of attraction?
5. (a) Is rubber band, a solid or not?
   (b) Justify your answer.
6. Why do the water molecules have more energy compared to the molecules of ice at same temperature?
7. Why is a wooden chair solid at room temperature? Give reasons.
8. Though sponge is a solid, we are able to compress it. Why?
9. Mention any two properties of matter.
10. Evaporation is called surface phenomena. Comment.
11. Which substance in its gaseous state is called vapour?
12. Give reason: "Water droplets are formed on the outer surface of a glass containing ice cold water".
13. What are the two processes which show that the particles of a gas move continuously?
14. Name the phenomena of changing of liquid into its vapour at temperature below its boiling point.
15. What happens to the dry ice stored under high pressure when it is reduced to atmosphere ?
16. Which characteristic of particles of matter is illustrated when the fragrance of an incense stick lighted in one corner of a room spreads in the whole room quickly?

17. Which characteristic of particles of matter is illustrated when a piece of chalk is broken into small particles by hammer while a piece of iron cannot be broken?
18. Which characteristic of particles of matter is illustrated when crystals of potassium permanganate impart colour to a very large volume of water?
19. Name the term used to describe the mixing of copper sulphate and water kept in a beaker on its own.
20. Which characteristic of particles of matter is illustrated when sugar is dissolved in water without increase in the volume of water?
21. Name the particles which make up matter.
22. Give one property of gas and liquid which shows that their molecules are moving constantly.
23. Name two gases supplied in homes and hospitals in compressed form.
24. Expand : (a) CNG (b) LPG
25. What is the chemical name of dry ice? Why is it called dry ice ?
26. Give the relation between Celsius scale and Kelvin scale of temperature.
27. Mention a condition necessary to liquefy gases.
28. Define latent heat.
29. Define melting point of a substance.
30. Define boiling point of a substance.

SHORT ANSWER TYPE-I QUESTIONS

1. Compare the compressibility of liquids and gases.
2. Give reasons : "We are able to sip hot milk faster from a saucer than from a cup".
3. All the water of the earth does not get evaporated during hot summer days. Why?
4. Why naphthalene balls kept in stored clothes in our homes disappear over a period of time?
5. Can ammonia gas be liquefied? How?
6. Why does steam cause more severe burns than boiling water?
7. Why heat energy is required to melt a solid?
8. How does perspiration help to keep our body cool on a hot day?
9. Why does the temperature remain constant during the boiling of water even though heat is supplied continuously?
10. Why does a desert cooler cool better on a hot, dry day?
11. What are the two characteristics of matter demonstrated by :
    (a) Brownian movement
    (b) Diffusion
12. Why honey is more viscous than water?
13. Give reasons :
    (a) Air is used to inflate tyres.
    (b) Steel is used to make railway lines.
14. Does diffusion occur more quickly in a gas than in a liquid? Why?
15. Explain how bromine vapour diffuses into air.
16. Why does our palm feel cold when we put some perfume on it?
17. How does the water kept in the earthen pot become cold during summer?
18. Define the following term :
    (a) Freezing   (b) Condensation.
19. How we would cool a bucket of water more quickly : by placing it on ice or by placing ice in it?
20. Give reasons :
    (a) Solids, liquids and gases differ in shape and volume.
    (b) Gases have neither a fixed shape nor a fixed volume.

SHORT ANSWER TYPE-II QUESTIONS

1. (a) Define diffusion.
   (b) Why gases diffuse very fast?
   (c) Name two gases which dissolve in water by diffusion.
2. Give reasons :
   (a) When a bottle of perfume is opened in a room, we can smell it even from a considerable distance.
   (b) Diffusion occurs more quickly in a gas than in a liquid.
3. Draw diagram to show the movement of a particle during Brownian movement.

4. Mention the characteristics of matter.
5. Can a small volume of water in a kettle fill a kitchen with steam? Justify.
6. How will you demonstrate that water vapour is present in air?
7. (a) Give the diagrammatic sketch to show interconversion of states of matter.
   (b) What are the two ways in which the physical states of matter can be changed?
8. Why there is no increase in temperature of a substance when it undergoes a change of state even though heat is supplied continuously?
9. Explain briefly how gases can be liquefied?
10. Compare the properties of solids, liquids and gases.

LONG ANSWER TYPE QUESTIONS

1. State the various factors affecting evaporation.
2. Draw a labelled diagram of the experimental set up to demonstrate the sublimation of ammonium chloride.
3. Explain latent heat of vapourisation of water.
4. Explain the latent heat of fusion of ice.
5. Explain an activity to show the effect of change of temperature on the solid.
6. Explain an activity to show the factors affecting evaporation.

EXERCISES (UNSOLVED)

VIVA VOCE QUESTIONS

1. What is the physical state of water at 25°C?
2. Which physical state does not have a surface?
3. Which physical state has the maximum inter-particle space?
4. Give a method to liquefy atmospheric gases.
5. At what temperature does the solid ice and liquid water co-exist together?
6. What is dry ice?
7. In which states of matter the arrangement of particles is in most ordered form?
8. Which form of water is highly compressible?
9. Is melting exothermic or endothermic process?
10. Under what condition, we can boil water at room temperature?

NAME THE FOLLOWING

1. The substance obtained by cooling the vapours.
2. A bulk phenomenon.
3. A change of state directly from solid to gas without changing into liquid state.
4. A surface phenomenon.
5. One property shown by ammonium chloride.
6. The process by which a drop of ink spreads in a beaker of water.
7. The scientist who studied the movement of pollen grains suspended in water through a microscope.
8. A gas in air which dissolve in water by diffusion.
9. The common name of solid carbon dioxide.
10. The liquids which are easily vapourisable.

FILL IN THE BLANKS

1. Matter is made up of small --------------------.
2. Matter occupies space and has ----------------.
3. The particles of matter have kinetic energy as they are in continuous --------------------.
4. In gases, the force of attraction between molecules is -------------------.
5. The rate of mixing of solid particles is --------------------- in hot water.
6. On heating a substance, the kinetic energy is ----------------------.
7. Evaporation causes -------------------.
8. Latent heat is used to --------------------- the force of attraction between the particles.
9. On heating, the intermolecular space between the molecules ----------------------.
10. For liquefaction of gas, temperature should be ---------------- and pressure should be --------.

DIAGRAM BASED QUESTIONS

1. A, B, C and D are processes involved in interchanging the states of a matter as shown below :

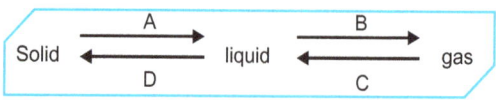

Which of these processes, A, B, C or D involve (s) heat loss?

2. In the cycle given below, name the processes taking place at X and Y.

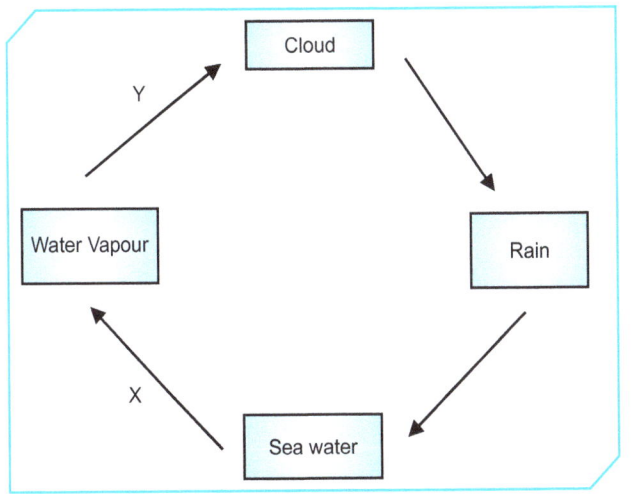

3. In the flow chart, given below identify X, Y and Z.

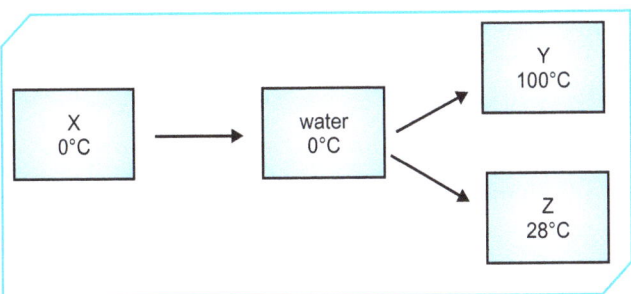

4. Identify X, Y and Z in the flow chart given below.

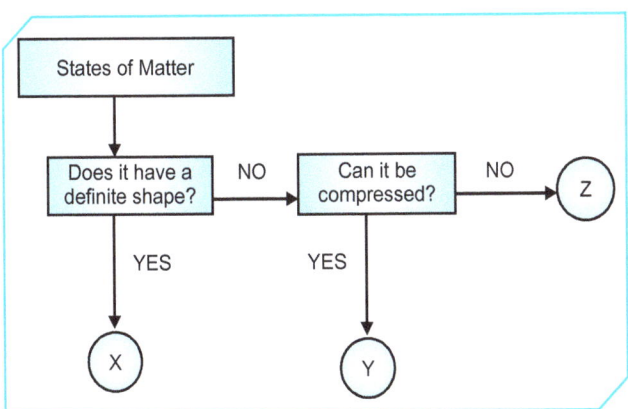

5. Identify the two processes taking place in the diagram shown below.

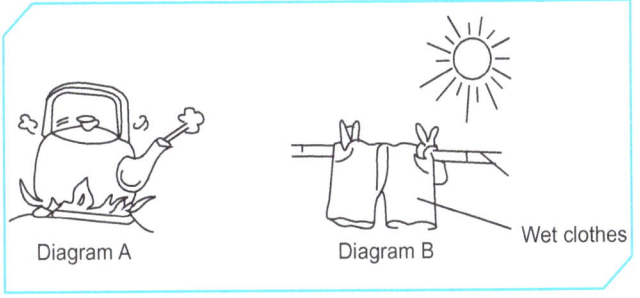

TRUE OR FALSE

1. The term 'vapour' represents the gaseous state of a substance that exists as a liquid or solid.
2. By applying high pressure and reducing temperature, gases can be liquefied easily.
3. The heat which can be seen easily is called latent heat.
4. The particles of liquids vibrate around their mean position only.
5. Solids cannot flow from one place to another.
6. The intermolecular force is the force of attraction between the constituent particles in any form of matter.
7. An absolute temperature scale is the Celsius scale.
8. -273 K $= 0°$C.
9. $-273°$C $= 0$ K.
10. The process of conversion of vapours into solid without passing through the liquid state is called condensation.

SYMPOSIUM

Split the students into two groups based on the number of students in the class and give them some topics to be prepared of their choice with the help of few examples.

Topic 1 : Various factors which influence the evaporation of a liquid.

Discussion points :

(a) Introduction to evaporation. (b) Illustrations.
(c) Explanations.
(d) Factors which influence the evaporation of a liquid.
(e) Conclusion.

Topic 2 : Experiments based on diffusion and osmosis.

Discussion points :

(a) Introduction to diffusion and osmosis.
(b) Illustrations.
(c) Explanations.
(d) Experiments based on diffusion.
(e) Experiments based on osmosis.
(f) Difference between diffusion and osmosis.

GROUP DISCUSSION

Split the students into two groups based on the number of students in the class and give them some topics to be prepared of their choice with the help of few examples.

Discussion 1 : Inter-conversion of states of matter.

Developing Ideas :

(a) Introduction to states of matter.
(b) Different types of states of matter.
(c) Conversion of states of matter.
(d) Conclusion.

Discussion 2 : Various states of matter based on kinetic theory of matter.

Developing Ideas :

(a) Introduction to kinetic theory of matter.
(b) Different states of matter based on kinetic theory of matter.
(c) Explaining different states with examples.
(d) Conclusion.

Discussion 3 : Particulate nature of matter and its role in our everyday life.

Developing Ideas :

(a) Introduction to the matter.
(b) Characteristics of matter.
(c) Explaining only about the particulate nature of matter.
(d) Illustration.
(e) Explaining the role of particulate nature of matter in our everyday life with an activity.

MATCH THE FOLLOWING

1. Match the Following :

S. No	Column 1	Column 2	Correct Match
1.	Melting point of ice	Maximum fluidity	
2.	Solid state	373 K	
3.	Boiling	273 K	
4.	Gaseous state	Maximum rigidity	
5.	Boiling point of water	Bulk phenomena	

2. Match the Following :

S. No	Column 1	Column 2	Correct Match
1.	Latent heat of vapourisation	22.6×10^5 J/kg	
2.	Evaporation	Both gaseous and liquid	
3.	Physical state of water at 273 K	Surface phenomena	
4.	Latent heat of fusion of ice	Both solid and liquid	
5.	Physical state of water at 373 K	3.34×10^5 J/kg	

ANSWERS

VIVA VOCE QUESTIONS

1. Liquid state.
2. Gaseous state.
3. Gaseous state.
4. By increasing pressure and decreasing temperature.
5. 0°C i.e., at the melting point of ice or at 273 K.
6. Solid carbon dioxide.
7. Solid state.
8. Gaseous form.
9. Endothermic process.
10. Under low pressure.

NAME THE FOLLOWING

1. Sublimate.
2. Boiling.
3. Sublimation.
4. Evaporation.
5. Undergo sublimation.
6. Diffusion.
7. Robert Brown.
8. Hydrogen, Oxygen.
9. Dry ice.
10. Volatile liquids.

FILL IN THE BLANKS

1. Particles.
2. Mass.

3. Motion.
4. Minimum.
5. Faster.
6. Increased.
7. Cooling.
8. Overcome.
9. Increases.
10. Low; high.

DIAGRAM BASED QUESTIONS

1. C and D.
2. X – Evaporation ; Y – Condensation
3. X– Solid, Z – Liquid/ice, and Y – Liquid/Gas
4. X – Solid, Y – Gas, and Z – Liquid
5. Diagram 'A' is showing the process of boiling while diagram 'B' is showing the process of evaporation.

TRUE OR FALSE

1. True.
2. True.
3. False.
4. False.
5. True.
6. True.
7. False.
8. False.
9. True.
10. False.

MATCH THE FOLLOWING

1.

S. No	Column 1	Column 2	Correct Match
1.	Melting point of ice	Maximum fluidity	4
2.	Solid state	373 K	5
3.	Vapourisation	273 K	1
4.	Gaseous state	Maximum rigidity	2
5.	Boiling point of water	Bulk phenomenon	3

2.

S. No.	Column 1	Column 2	Correct Match
1.	Latent heat of vapourisation	22.6×10^5 J/kg	1
2.	Evaporation	Both gaseous and liquid	5
3.	Physical state of water at 273 K	Surface phenomenon	2
4.	Latent heat of fusion of ice	Both solid and liquid	3
5.	Physical state of water at 373 K	3.34×10^5 J/kg	4

MOCK TEST–1

Time : 2 Hours

Max. Marks : 30

General Instructions :

- All questions are compulsory.
- There is no overall choice.
- Questions 1 to 3 are one mark questions. These are to be answered in one word or in one sentence.
- Questions 4 to 7 are two marks questions. These are to be answered in about 30 words each.
- Questions 8 to 10 are three marks questions. These are to be answered in about 50 words each.
- Questions 11 to 12 are five marks questions. These are to be answered in about 70 words each.

1. Which among the three physical states of matter has the maximum intermolecular force?
2. What is the melting point of ice?
3. What is latent heat of melting?
4. What is the boiling point of water?

5. Define sublimation.
6. Why rate of evaporation is low in rainy season?
7. Why do the clothes dry faster in summer?
8. What are the factors responsible for bringing a change in the physical state of a substance?
9. List four characteristics of particle nature of matter.
10. How does the interconversion of three states of matter takes place in terms of force of attraction and kinetic energy of the molecules?
11. With the help of an activity show that the rate of evaporation increases with increase in surface area.
12. Describe an activity to show that the particles of matter are very small.

MOCK TEST-2

Time : 2 Hours   Max. Marks : 30

General Instructions :
- All questions are compulsory.
- There is no overall choice.
- Questions 1 to 3 are one mark questions. These are to be answered in one word or in one sentence.
- Questions 4 to 7 are two marks questions. These are to be answered in about 30 words each.
- Questions 8 to 10 are three marks questions. These are to be answered in about 50 words each.
- Questions 11 to 12 are five marks questions. These are to be answered in about 70 words each.

1. Define evaporation.
2. Is osmosis a special kind of diffusion?
3. Which among the three physical states of matter do not have a surface?
4. What happens when you pour some acetone on your palm?
5. Differentiate between evaporation and boiling.
6. The molecules of water have more energy compared to the molecules of ice at the same temperature. Justify.
7. Why are gases highly compressible while solids are incompressible?
8. Why a wooden table should be called a solid?
9. Justify: "Melting of wax is a physical change".
10. Give reason: "A liquid generally flows easily".
11. Describe an activity to determine the melting point of ice with diagram.
12. With the help of an activity, how will you separate naphthalene from a mixture of naphthalene and sodium chloride?

2

IS MATTER AROUND US PURE

CONTENTS

2.0 Introduction
2.1 Pure and Impure Substances
2.2 Elements
2.3 Metals
2.4 Non-Metals
2.5 Metalloids or Semi-Metals
2.6 Compounds
2.7 Mixtures
2.8 Solutions, Suspensions and Colloids
2.9 Concentration of a Solution
2.10 Solubility
2.11 Separation of the Components of a Mixture
2.12 Separation of Solid-Solid Mixtures
2.13 Separation of Solid-Liquid Mixtures
2.14 Separation of Liquid-Liquid Mixtures
2.15 Separation of Solid-Gas Mixtures
2.16 Physical change and Chemical change

2.0 INTRODUCTION

In the previous chapter, we have discussed the physical nature of matter. In this chapter, we will discuss about the chemical nature of matter. We have studied that anything that has mass and occupies space is called matter. The matter is made up of one or more components called substances. These substances cannot be separated into any other types of matter by physical means. When a substance has only one component, it is called a pure substance. But it is difficult to get a pure substance. Because most of the substances are mixed with one another, they are called mixtures and are impure.

For example, when we place some sugar and soil on two different sheets of paper and observe it with a magnifying glass, we can find that the colour, shape and size of all the particles of sugar are almost the same, whereas the soil contains particles of different colours, shapes and sizes. Hence, we can say that sugar which contains particles of only one kind, is a pure substance, where as soil which contains particles of different kinds is a mixture or an impure substance (Fig. 2.1 and 2.2).

From this, we can conclude that all matter around us is not pure. We can thus, classify matter into two types namely,

(a) Pure substances

(b) Impure substances

Fig. 2.1 : Soil – An impure Substance.

Fig. 2.2 : Sugar – A pure Substance.

2.1 PURE AND IMPURE SUBSTANCES

Pure Substances

When a substance is made up of only one kind of particles, it is called a pure substance. These particles may be atoms or molecules. Hence, we can define a pure substance as :

"The substance which is made up of only one kind of atoms or one kind of molecules"

For example, the elements such as oxygen (O), nitrogen (N), hydrogen (H), chlorine (Cl), bromine (Br), iodine (I), carbon (C), sulphur (S), iron (Fe), copper (Cu), silicon (Si) etc., are all pure substances because they contain only one kind of particles. Similarly, compounds such as water (H_2O) in the form of ice and steam, carbon dioxide (CO_2), sodium chloride (NaCl), copper sulphate ($CuSO_4$), calcium oxide (CaO), sodium hydroxide (NaOH), hydrochloric acid (HCl), sulphuric acid (H_2SO_4), sand, camphor etc., are pure substances (Fig. 2.3).

Thus, we can say that a pure substance is homogeneous throughout its mass. It cannot be separated into other kinds of matter by any physical means. It has a fixed composition as well as a fixed melting and boiling point.

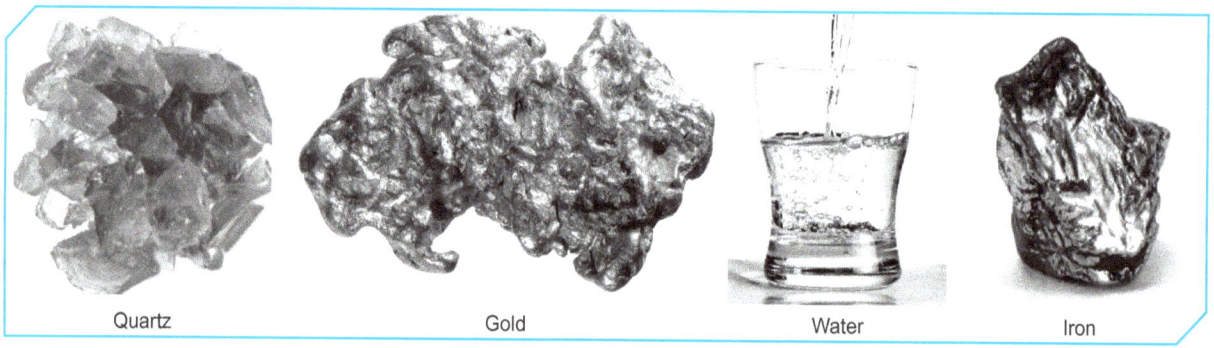

Fig. 2.3 : This figure shows some examples of pure substances.

Impure Substances or Mixtures

Most of the matter around us exists as mixture of two or more pure substances. Impure substance contains more than one kind of particles. Hence, we can define it as-

"The substance which contains two or more different kinds of particles"

Thus, we can say that all the mixtures are impure substances because they contain more than one kind of particles. In other words, mixing together of two or more pure substance gives a mixture. Some of the common examples of mixtures are salt solution (salt and water), sugar solution (sugar and water), milk (water, fat and proteins), sea water (mixture of different types of salt in water), air (mixture of gases), soft drinks, rocks, petroleum, LPG (Liquefied Petroleum Gas), tea, coffee, paint etc (Fig. 2.4). A mixture may be homogeneous or heterogeneous. It can be separated into other kinds of matter by physical means. It does not have a fixed composition or a fixed melting and boiling point.

IS MATTER AROUND US PURE

Salt Solution   Milk   Sea Water   Soft drinks   Rocks

Fig. 2.4 : This figure shows some examples of impure substance.

Thus, based on the above discussion, we can conclude that all the matter can be classified as follows and can be schematically represented as (Fig. 2.5).

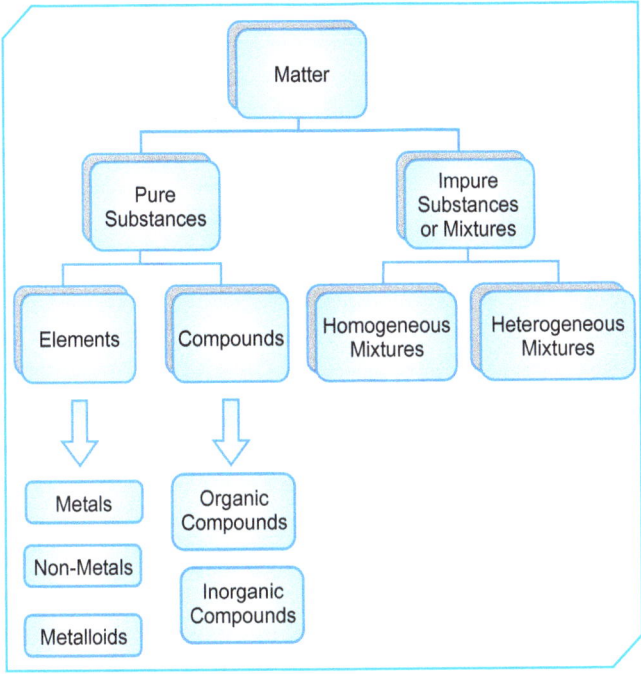

Fig. 2.5 : This figure shows the classification of matter

We shall now discuss the three types of matter i.e., elements, mixtures and compounds in detail.

2.2 ELEMENTS

The term "element" was first introduced by a French chemist, **Antoine Lavoisier** (Fig. 2.6). According to him, *'An element is the simplest form of a pure substance which cannot be broken by any physical or chemical method'*. Later, **John Dalton** (Fig. 2.7) found that the simplest form of matter is the atom. He defined element as,

Fig. 2.6 : Antoine Lavoisier- a scientist who first introduced the term "element."

'A pure substance which is made up of only one kind of atom'.

All living things in nature are made up of a few common elements such as Hydrogen (H), Carbon (C), Oxygen (O), Nitrogen (N), Calcium (Ca), Phosphorus (P) etc. Hence, we can say that the elements are the building blocks of universe. Though there are 118 major elements known to us, the universe is made up of two major elements namely, Hydrogen (H) 92% and Helium (He) 7% and 1% rest of the elements.

Fig. 2.7 : John Dalton, a scientist who proposed that the simplest form of matter is atom.

Before we proceed to next topic, try to solve the following questions.

PAPER-PEN TEST : 1

1. Define matter.
2. What is meant by substances?
3. Define mixture.
4. What is a pure substance?
5. How can you say sugar is a pure substance?
6. How can you say soil is a mixture?
7. Differentiate between pure and impure substances with examples.
8. Schematically represent the classification of matter.
9. Who introduced the term 'element'?
10. Who showed that the simplest form of matter is atom?
11. Define element according to Lavoisier.
12. --------------- are the building blocks of universe.

Classification of Elements

All the elements can be classified into three types :

(a) Based on their physical states.

(b) Based on their characteristics.

Let us discuss these classifications of elements in detail.

(a) Types of Elements Based On Their Physical States

The elements are classified into three types based on their physical states, namely :

(i) *Solid elements*

(ii) *Liquid elements*

(iii) *Gaseous elements*

(i) **Solid Elements :** Most of the elements exist as solids at room temperature. For example, potassium (K), lithium (Li), copper (Cu), sodium (Na), magnesium (Mg), gold (Au), silver (Ag), iodine (I), phosphorus (P), carbon in the form of diamond and graphite etc. (Fig. 2.8).

Fig. 2.8 : This figure shows some of the elements which exist as solid at room temperature.

(ii) **Liquid Elements :** Only bromine and mercury exist as liquids at room temperature. Gallium (Ga) becomes liquid at 302 K while caesium (Cs) becomes liquid at 303 K. Thus, the elements gallium and caesium exist as liquids at slightly higher temperature than the room temperature of 298 K (Fig. 2.9).

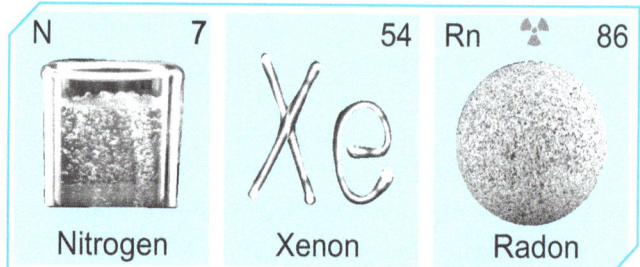

Fig. 2.10 : This figure shows some of the elements which exist as gas at room temperature.

(b) Types of Elements Based On Their Characteristics

The elements are classified into three types based on their characteristics, namely :

(i) *Metals*

(ii) *Non – metals*

(iii) *Metalloids or semi-metals*

Let us discuss the characteristics of these types in detail.

2.3 METALS

More than 115 different chemical elements are known at present out of which 80% of elements are metals.

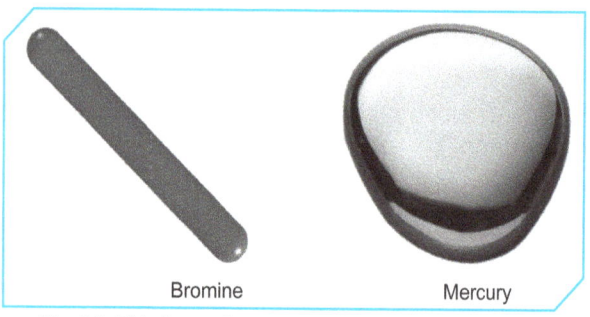

Fig. 2.9 : This figure shows some of the elements which are liquid at room temperature

(iii) **Gaseous Elements :** There are 11 elements which exists as gas at room temperature. These include oxygen (O), hydrogen (H), nitrogen (N), fluorine (F), chlorine (Cl), helium (He), neon (Ne), argon (Ar), krypton (Kr), xenon (Xe) and radon (Rn) (Fig. 2.10).

Do you know that metals are very important for the National economy of every country? The most abundant metal in the earth's crust is aluminium (Al), which constitutes about 8% of the earth's crust. The second most abundant metal in the earth's crust is Iron (Fe), which constitutes about 5% of the earth's crust. The other metals found in the earth's crust in the descending order are calcium (Ca), sodium (Na), potassium (K) and magnesium (Mg) (Fig. 2.11).

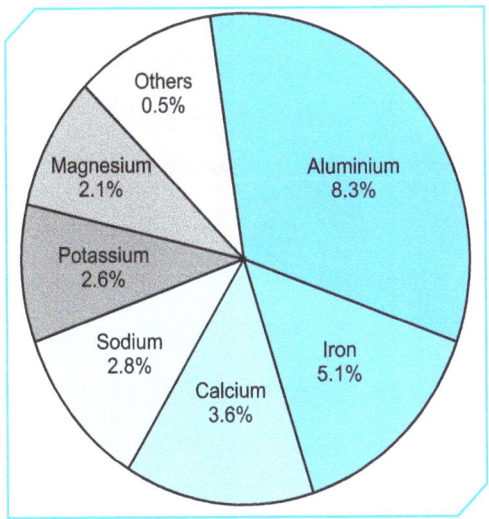

Fig. 2.11 : This figure shows the relative percentage of metals in Earth's crust.

The general physical properties of metals include its lustre, malleability, ductility, hardness, sonorosity and conduction. Metals include sodium (Na), potassium (K), magnesium (Mg), calcium (Ca), barium (Ba), aluminium (Al), copper (Cu), gold (Au), silver (Ag), platinum (Pt), nickel (Ni) etc. *The mixtures of metals are called alloys.* Based on the reactivity, metals can form positive ions or cations by losing electrons. Thus, we can define metals as :

"The elements which forms positive elements due to their ability to form positive ions by losing or donating electrons"

In other words, we may say that metals are electropositive elements due to their ability to form positive ions by losing electrons. We shall now discuss the physical properties of metals in detail.

Physical Properties of Metals

(a) **Metals are Malleable :** The word 'malleable' means—*can be beaten with hammer to form thin sheets.* Most of the metals are malleable; hence, malleability is an important characteristic property of metals. Though, most of the metals are malleable, silver and gold are said to be most malleable metals. The metals such as aluminium and copper are also said to be highly malleable metals as they can be converted into thin sheets of aluminium foils and copper respectively. The thin sheet of aluminium foils are used for making cooking utensils and for packing food items like medicines, chocolates, biscuits etc. Similarly, copper sheets are also used for making cooking utensils. All these metals can be hammered into thin foils due to their high malleability (Fig. 2.12).

Fig. 2.12 : This figure shows the uses of some common metals.

(b) **Metals are Ductile :** The word 'ductile' means—*can be drawn into thin wires.* Most of the metals are ductile, hence ductility is another important characteristic property of metals. But, all the metals are not equally ductile. We can observe that some metals are more ductile than the others. The most ductile metals are gold and silver. The other ductile metals include copper, aluminium, magnesium, iron and tungsten. All these metals can be drawn into thin wires due to their high ductility (Fig. 2.13).

Fig. 2.13 : This figure shows thin wires of metals such as gold and silver.

(c) **Metals are Lustrous :** The word 'lustrous' refers to *shiny surface*. Metals such as gold and silver in their pure state possess a shining surface and hence are used in making jewellery, ornaments and decorative items (Fig. 2.14).

Fig. 2.14 : This figure shows the lustrous property of metals.

(d) **Metals are Hard :** Most of the metals are strong i.e, *hard*. However, the hardness varies from metal to metal. There are some hard metals which can hold heavy weights without breaking like iron, copper, aluminium etc. However, sodium and potassium are soft metals because they can be easily cut with a knife (Fig. 2.15).

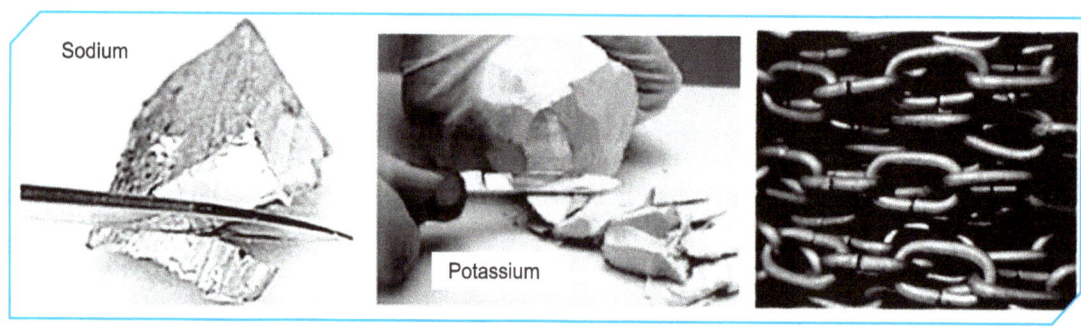

Fig. 2.15 : This figure shows the property of metals; i.e., hardness.

(e) **Metals are Good Conductors of Heat :** The word 'good conductors of heat' refers to the fact that — *the metals allow heat to pass through them easily*. In other words, we can say that metals get heated faster. But do you know how a metal conducts heat? Let us explain that clearly.

When a metal is heated, the atoms in the metal gain energy and vibrate more vigourously. This energy is then transferred to the electrons present in the atoms and move through the metal. When these energetic electrons move through the metal, they transfer the energy to other electrons and atoms of the metal. We call this as heat or thermal conductivity, which is also a characteristic property of metals. This shows that heat can be conducted from one end of the metal to its other end. Silver metal is the best conductor of heat because it has the highest thermal conductivity. The cooking utensils that we use in our homes are usually made up of copper or aluminium metals because they are also very good conductors of heat and electricity. The metals which are poor conductors of heat are lead (Pb) and mercury (Hg) (Fig. 2.16).

Copper Vessels used for cooking | Aluminium vessels used for boiling water

Fig. 2.16 : This figure shows the use of metals like copper and aluminium.

(f) Metals are Good Conductors of Electricity: The word 'good conductors of electricity' refers to the fact that— *the metals allow electric current to pass through them easily.* The metals offer very little resistance to the flow of electric current and hence shows high electrical conductivity. Do you know why metals conduct electricity? Metals are good conductors of electricity due to the presence of free electrons. These free electrons move easily through the metal and allow the metal to conduct electric current. For this reason, copper and aluminium metals are used in making electric wires. Silver is the best conductor of electricity. There are some metals like iron (Fe) and mercury (Hg) which offer comparatively greater resistance to the flow of current and hence, have lower electrical conductivity (Fig. 2.17).

Fig. 2.17 : This figure shows the use of copper metal in making electric wires.

(g) Metals are Sonorous : The word 'sonorous' means— *capable of producing a sound.* When metal strikes a hard surface, it produces sound. It is due to the sonorous property of metals, that they are used in making bells, strings of musical instruments like violin and sitar (Fig. 2.18).

Fig. 2.18 : This figure shows the sonorous property of metals

(h) Metals have High Melting Point and Boiling Point : Most of the metals have high melting point and boiling point. For example, iron metal has a high melting point of 1535°C [Fig 2.19 (a)]. Copper metal also has a, high melting point of 1083°C. But there are some metals such as sodium and potassium which possess low melting point of 98°C and 64°C respectively. Other metals such as gallium and caesium also have low melting point of 30°C and 28°C respectively and therefore, they start melting in the hand (Fig. 2.19)

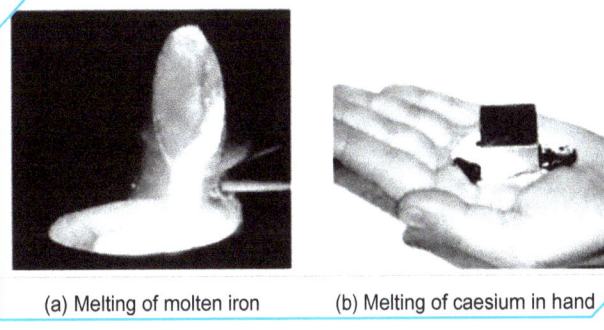

(a) Melting of molten iron   (b) Melting of caesium in hand

Fig. 2.19 : This figure shows the melting of iron and caesium metals.

Note
- The metals which are good conductors of heat and electricity offer very low resistance to the flow of electric current and hence possess high melting point.
- The metals which are poor conductors of heat and electricity offers very high resistance to the flow of electric current and hence possess low melting point.

(i) Metals have High Densities : The word 'high density' refers to *heavy substance.* Though most of the metals have high densities, there are some metals which have low densities. For example, the density of iron is quite high i.e.,

7.8 g/cm³, while the density of sodium is 0.97 g/cm³ and that of potassium is 0.86 g/cm³ which is quite low. Thus, we can say that heavy metals have high density whereas light elements have low density.

(j) **Metals are Solids at Room Temperature :** Though most of the metals are solids at room temperature, there is only one metal which is present in liquid state at room temperature. Metals such as iron (Fe), copper (Cu), aluminium (Al), silver (Ag) and gold (Au) are present in solid state at room temperature whereas mercury (Hg) exists in liquid state at room temperature (Fig. 2.20).

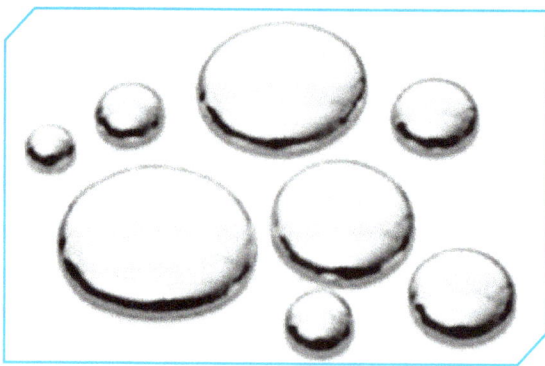

Fig.2.20 : This figure shows that mercury metal exists in liquid state at room temperature.

Before we proceed to next topic, try to solve the following questions.

PAPER-PEN TEST : 2

1. How are elements classified?
2. Classify elements based on their physical states.
3. Name a few metals which exist as solids at room temperature.
4. At what temperature gallium becomes liquid?
5. Name a metal which exist as liquid at room temperature.
6. Name the 11 elements which exist as gas at room temperature.
7. Classify the elements based on their characteristics.
8. Which is the most abundant metal in the earth's crust?
9. Which is the second most abundant metal in the earth's crust?
10. Mention the general properties of metals.
11. The mixtures of metals are called --------------.
12. Comment: "metals are electropositive elements".
13. Define metals.
14. What does the word 'malleable' refers to?
15. Name two most malleable metals.
16. What does the word 'ductile' refer to?
17. Name two most ductile metals.
18. What does the word 'lustrous' refers to?
19. Name two lustrous metals.
20. Name three metals which can hold heavy weights without breaking.
21. Name two soft metals.
22. Why metals get heated faster?
23. Which metal is the best conductor of heat? Why?
24. Why metal conducts electricity?
25. Which metal is the good conductor of electricity?
26. Name two metals which are bad conductors of electricity.
27. Comment: "Metals show high electrical conductivity".
28. What does the word 'sonorous' refers to?
29. Name two metals which possess low melting point.
30. Name two metals which possess low density.

2.4 NON-METALS

There are 22 non-metals known at present. Though non-metals are less in number compared to metals, they play an important role is our everyday life. The most important non-metal is carbon. This is because all the life on this earth is based on carbon compounds. The carbon compounds such as proteins, fats, carbohydrates, vitamins, enzymes etc. are important for the growth and development of living organisms. There is another important non-metal, oxygen which is essential for breathing to maintain life, for burning fuels etc. Nitrogen and Sulphur are also non-metals which are essential in our everyday life. Sulphur is present in plants, animals, garlic, onion, hair, wool, etc. Nitrogen, on the other hand, helps to reduce the rate of combustion and makes the burning safe.

The most abundant non-metal in the earth's crust is oxygen which constitutes about 50% of the earth's crust. The second most abundant non-metal in the earth's crust is silicon, which constitutes about 26% of earth's crust. The other non-metals included in the earth's crust are phosphorus and sulphur. The non-metals are the major constituents of earth, air and seas (Fig. 2.21).

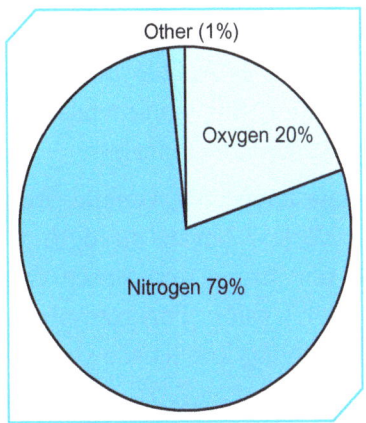

Fig. 2.21 : This figure shows the percentage of non-metals in earth's crust

Based on the reactivity, non-metals can form negative ions or anions by gaining electrons. Thus, we can define non-metals as,

'The elements which form negative ions by gaining or accepting electrons'

In other words, we can say that non-metals are electronegative elements due to their ability to form negative ions by gaining electrons. The general physical properties of non-metals include brittleness, non-lustrous, low strength, soft, low density, non-conductance of heat and electricity and non–sonorous. We shall now discuss the physical properties of non-metals in detail.

Physical Properties of Non-Metals

(a) **Non-Metals are Brittle :** The word 'brittle' refers to being *easily breakable*. In other words, non-metals can be broken into pieces when hammered or stretched. This shows that non-metals cannot be beaten with a hammer to form thin sheets and cannot be stretched to form thin wires. Thus, it is obvious that solid non-metals can neither be hammered into thin sheets nor drawn into thin wires. Hence, the characteristic property of brittleness is applicable only to solid non-metals and not for liquid or gaseous non-metals (Fig. 2.22).

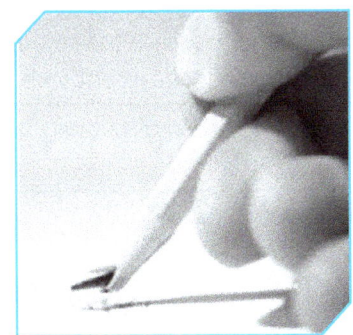

Fig.2.22: This figure shows the property of brittleness in non metals.

(b) **Non-Metals are Non-lustrous or Dull in Appearance :** The word 'dull' refers to the fact that *non-metals do not have lustre* which means non–metals do not have a shining surface. The solid non-metals such as sulphur (S) and phosphorus (P) do not have a shining surface and so appears to be dull (Fig. 2.23 a). However, iodine (I) is a non-metal having lustrous i.e., shiny surface (Fig. 2.23 b).

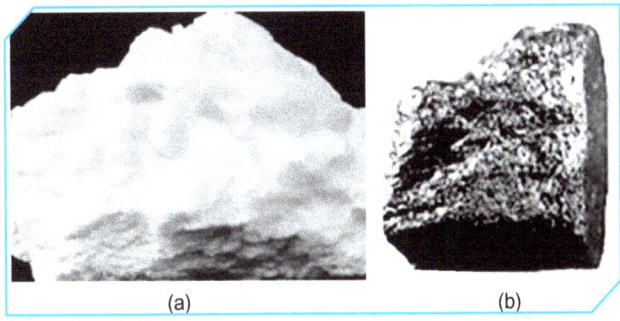

Fig. 2.23 : This figure shows the lustrous property of non-metals (a) solid sulphur is non-lustrous (b) iodine is lustrous.

(c) **Non-Metals are Soft :** Most of the non-metals are soft which means they can be easily cut with a knife. For example, Non-metals such as sulphur (S) and phosphorus (P) are soft. But, carbon (C) in the form of diamond, an allotrope, is the hardest substance known (Fig. 2.24).

Fig. 2.24 : Diamond, an allotrope of carbon is the hardest substance.

(d) **Non-Metals are Poor Conductors of Heat and Electricity :** Non-metals do not have free electrons like metals and hence they do not conduct heat and electricity. They are therefore, often referred to as insulators. However, carbon which is a non-metal is exception as it is good conductor of heat and electricity in the form of graphite. Thus, graphite which is an allotropic form of carbon is used for making electrodes (Fig. 2.25).

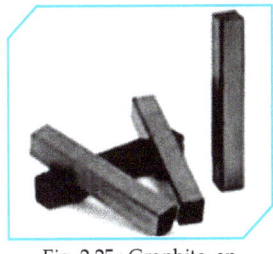

Fig. 2.25 : Graphite, an allotrope of carbon

(e) Non-Metals are Non-Sonorous : The word 'non-sonorous' means *incapable of producing a sound*. Thus, non-metals do not produce sound when hit by an object.

(f) Non-Metals have Low Melting Point and Boiling Point : Most of the non-metals have low melting point and boiling point. For example, the melting point of sulphur is quite low i.e., 115°C But diamond is an exception as it possesses very high melting point and boiling point. The melting point of diamond is more than 3500°C.

(g) Non-Metals have Low Densities : The word 'low densities' refers to *light weight*. Most of the non-metals are light substances. For example, the density of sulphur is 2g/cm^3. However, iodine which is a non-metal is an exception as it possesses high density.

(h) Non-Metals at Room Temperature : Though most of the non-metals are solids at room temperature, there are non-metals which are liquids and gases at room temperature. The solid non-metals include carbon, sulphur, phosphorus and iodine; the liquid non-metal includes bromine and the gaseous non-metals include hydrogen, oxygen and chlorine (Fig. 2.26).

(i) Non–Metals have Different Colours : Some non-metals have different colours. For example, white phosphorus and red phosphorus, sulphur is yellow, an allotrope form of carbon i.e., graphite is black in colour, chlorine gas is yellowish-green in colour. But, non-metals such as hydrogen and oxygen are colourless.

(j) Non-Metals have Low Tensile Strength : Non-metals have low tensile strength which means they are not strong and hence can be broken easily under tension. For example, graphite is a non-metal having low tensile strength.

2.5 METALLOIDS OR SEMI-METALS

Elements having both the characteristics of metals and non-metals are called *semi-metals or metalloids*. Only few elements are metalloids such as germanium (Ge), silicon (Si), arsenic (As), antimony (Sb), and tellurium (Te). Since they are neither metals nor non-metals their properties are also intermediate between the properties of metals. For example, they are semiconductors and they appear like metals but they are brittle like non-metals (Fig. 2.27).

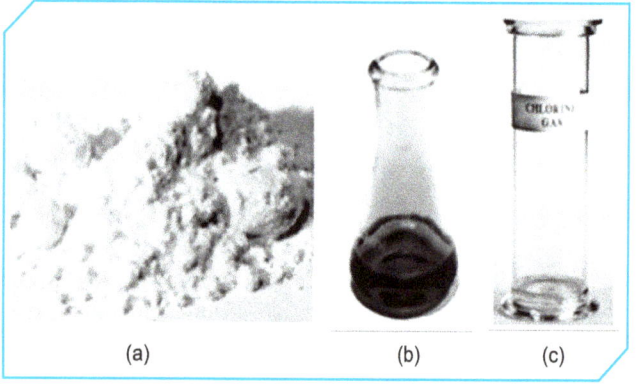

(a) (b) (c)

Fig. 2.26 : This figure shows that non-metals exist in solid, liquid and gaseous state at room temperature.

Germanium Silicon Antimony

Fig. 2.27 : This figure shows some examples of semi-metals or metalloids.

Let us now sum up the physical properties of metals and non-metals for comparison.

Comparison of Physical Properties of Metals and Non-metals

S.No.	Property	Metals	Non-Metals
1.	Lustre	They possess lustre and can be polished.	They do not possess lustre and cannot be polished except iodine.
2.	Hardness	All metals are hard except sodium and potassium.	All non-metals are soft except diamond.
3.	Malleability and Ductility	Metals are malleable and ductile.	Non-metals are brittle and are neither malleable nor ductile.
4.	Conductivity	Metals are good conductors of heat and electricity.	Non-metals are poor conductors of heat and electricity except graphite.

5.	Sonorosity	Metals are sonorous.	Non-metals are non-sonorous.
6.	Density	Metals have high density.	Non-metals have low density.
7.	Melting and Boiling Point	Metals have high melting and boiling point except mercury and gallium.	Non-metals have low melting and boiling point except carbon in the form of diamond.
8.	Tensile Strength	Metals have high tensile strength.	Non-metals have low tensile strength.
9.	Physical States	Metals are generally solids except mercury and gallium at room temperature.	Non-metals are generally either solids or gases except bromine which is liquid at room temperature.

Before we proceed to next topic, try to solve the following questions.

PAPER-PEN TEST : 3

1. Define non-metals.
2. Which is the most important non-metal? Why?
3. Mention the use of following non-metal.
   (a) Oxygen.   (b) Nitrogen.
4. Which is the most abundant non-metal in the earth's crust?
5. Which is the second most abundant non-metal in the earth's crust?
6. Comment: "Non-metals are electronegative elements."
7. Mention the physical properties of non-metals.
8. What does the word 'brittle' refers to?
9. What does the word 'dull' refers to?
10. Name a non-metal which is lustrous.
11. Name two non-metals which are non-lustrous.
12. Name an allotrope of carbon which is among the hardest substances known.
13. Name an allotrope of carbon which conducts electricity.
14. Why non-metals are called insulators?
15. Name a non-metal which possess high melting and boiling point.
16. Name a solid, liquid and gaseous non-metal.
17. Name two gaseous non-metals which are colourless.
18. Name some non-metals possessing different colours.
19. What are metalloids? Give examples.
20. Compare the physical properties of metals and non-metals.

2.6 COMPOUNDS

A compound is also a pure substance which is made up of two or more elements chemically combined in a fixed proportion by mass. For example, water is represented as H_2O in which hydrogen and oxygen are present in the fixed proportion of 1 : 8 by mass i.e., the atomic mass of H = 1u, O = 16u. Therefore,

Water has the formula H_2O

Hence, 2u : 16u = 1 : 8

Other examples include limestone, glucose, lime, starch, cane sugar, chalk, Baking soda, slaked lime, iron sulphide, potassium nitrate etc.

Classification of Compounds

(a) *The compounds are classified into three types based on their properties.*

(b) *The compounds are classified into two types based on the source or constituent elements.*

(a) Classification of Compounds Based on Their Properties

Compounds can be divided into three classes based on their properties namely,

(i) *Acids*

(ii) *Bases*

(iii) *Salts*

Sulphuric acid (H_2SO_4), hydrochloric acid (HCl) and nitric acid (HNO_3) are three common acids (Fig. 2.28). Sodium hydroxide (NaOH), potassium hydroxide (KOH) and calcium hydroxide ($Ca(OH)_2$) are common bases (Fig. 2.29).

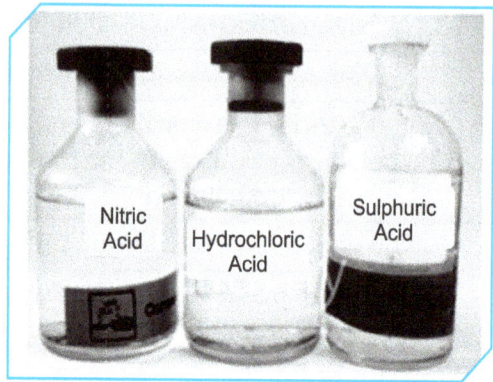

Fig. 2.28 : This figure shows some of the common acids.

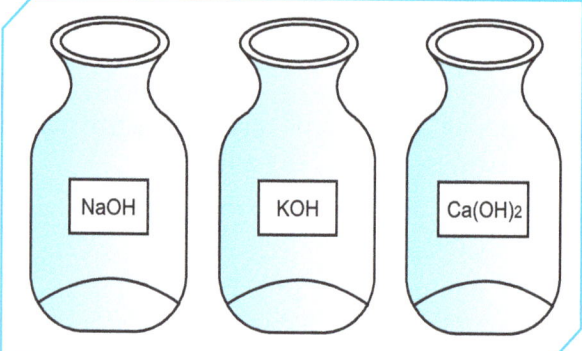

Fig. 2.29 : This figure shows some of the common bases.

Sodium chloride (NaCl), calcium nitrate (Ca(NO$_3$)$_2$), zinc sulphate (ZnSO$_4$) are common salts. These salts are formed by the chemical combination of acids and bases dissolved in water. For example, when hydrochloric acid dissolved in water is treated with sodium hydroxide, sodium chloride salt and water is formed (Fig. 2.30).

$$\underset{\text{Hydrochloric acid}}{\text{HCl}} + \underset{\text{Sodium hydroxide}}{\text{NaOH}} \rightarrow \underset{\text{Sodium chloride}}{\text{NaCl}} + \underset{\text{Water}}{\text{H}_2\text{O}}$$

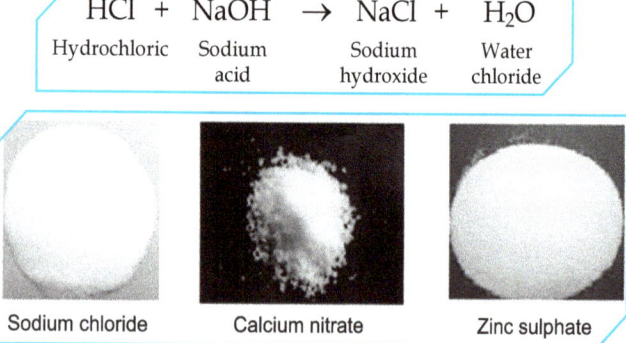

Fig. 2.30 : This figure shows some of the examples of common salts.

(b) Classification of Compounds Based on The Source

Generally, compounds can be classified into two types based on the source namely,

(i) Organic compounds

(ii) Inorganic compounds

The compounds which are obtained from living beings such as plants and animals are called *organic compounds.* All organic compounds contain carbon as their essential constituent. Thus, these compounds are also called carbon compounds. They include methane (CH$_4$), ethane (C$_2$H$_6$), propane (C$_3$H$_8$), acetic acid, proteins, alcohol, fats, oils etc.

On the other hand, the compounds which are obtained from non-living sources such as rocks and minerals are called *inorganic compounds.* They include common salt, marble, carbon dioxide, ammonia, sulphuric acid, washing soda, baking soda etc.

Characteristics of Compounds

(a) **A pure compound is made up of same elements combined in a fixed ratio by mass :** In carbon dioxide (CO$_2$), carbon and oxygen are present in the ratio of 3 : 8 by mass. The ratio will always remain the same.

(b) **A pure compound is homogeneous in nature :** A pure compound is a single substance made up of certain elements which cannot be seen even with the help of a powerful microscope. For example, in water, hydrogen and oxygen cannot be identified by physical means. This shows that a pure compound is homogeneous in nature.

(c) **A pure compound is formed by the chemical reaction between two elements :** A pure compound is formed by combining the elements due to chemical reaction. For example, carbon dioxide (CO$_2$) is formed by burning coke (C) in air (Fig. 2.31).

Fig. 2.31 : This figure shows the burning of coke.

(d) **The properties of a pure compound are different from its constituent elements :** We know that a compound is formed due to chemical reaction and so its properties are different from the elements from which it is formed. In other words, the constituting elements lose their identity in the compound. For instance, water is formed due to the chemical reaction of hydrogen and oxygen. Hydrogen is combustible while Oxygen is the supporter of combustion. But water is neither combustible nor a supporter of combustion.

(e) The constituents in a compound cannot be separated by physical or mechanical means : Since a compound is formed due to a chemical reaction, its constituent elements can only be separated chemically. For example, the constituents of water i.e., hydrogen and oxygen can be separated by passing electric current by a process called as the electrolysis of water (Fig. 2.32).

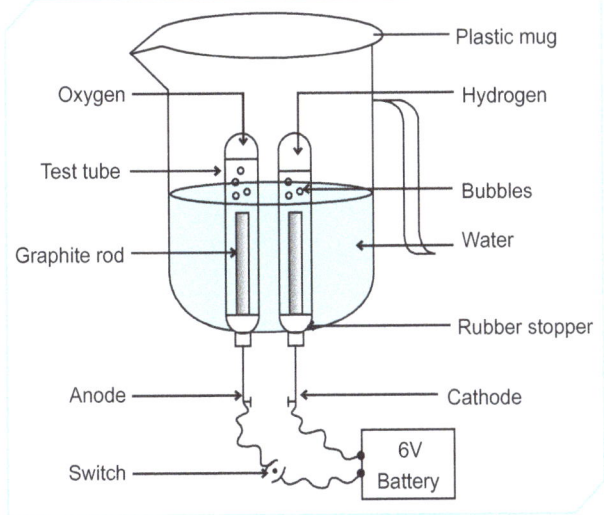

Fig. 2.32 : This figure shows the electrolysis of water.

(f) The energy changes helps in the formation or decomposition of compounds : The energy in the form of heat, light or electricity is either absorbed or evolved during the formation of a compound. For example, hydrogen and chlorine gas combine to form hydrogen chloride gas in the presence of energy in the form of sunlight. Thus, we can conclude that a large amount of energy in the form of heat from the sunlight is absorbed during the formation of hydrogen chloride compound.

Formation of compound :

$$H_2(g) + Cl_2(g) \xrightarrow{sunlight} HCl(g)$$
Hydrogen   Chlorine   Hydrogen chloride

Decomposition of compound :

$$HCl(g) \xrightarrow{sunlight} H_2(g) + Cl_2(g)$$
Hydrogen chloride   Hydrogen   Chlorine

Before we proceed to next topic, try to solve the following questions.

PAPER-PEN TEST : 4

1. Define compound.
2. How compounds are classified?
3. Classify the compounds based on their properties.
4. Name three common bases, salts and acids.
5. Classify the compounds based on their sources.
6. Differentiate between organic and inorganic compounds.
7. Name a few carbon compounds.
8. Mention the properties of compounds.
9. Comment: "The constituents in a compound cannot be separated by physical or mechanical means".
10. Comment: "The energy changes help in the formation or decomposition of compounds".

2.7 MIXTURES

'The substance having two or more elements or compounds which combine physically and not chemically are called mixtures'. The various substances present in the mixture are known as the constituents or components of the mixture. For example, Brine is a mixture of common salt in water. Thus, common salt is one of the components of the brine solution or mixture. Other examples include air (a mixture of gases like oxygen (O), nitrogen (N), argon (Ar), carbon dioxide (CO_2), water vapour); gun powder (a mixture of potassium nitrate (KNO_3), sulphur and charcoal); brass (a mixture of copper and zinc); sugar solution, salt solution, milk, sea water, ink, petrol, coal, soil, starch solution, blood, wood, butter, cheese, smoke, fog and mist, dyes etc. There are different ways by which mixtures are formed. Generally, substances exist in combination with each other to form a mixture. In a mixture the constituents or components may be present in any proportion (Fig. 2.33).

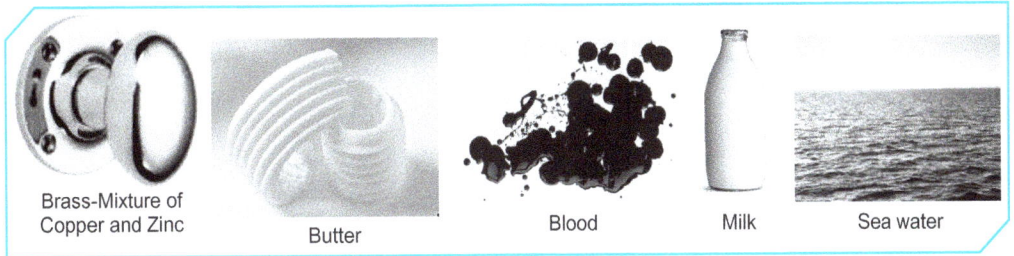

Fig. 2.33 : This figure shows some of the examples of mixtures.

Types of Mixtures

There are two types of mixtures namely,

(a) Homogeneous mixtures

(b) Heterogeneous mixtures

Let us discuss these two types of mixtures with examples.

(a) Homogeneous Mixtures : *Those mixtures in which the substances are uniformly mixed without any clear boundary of separation are called homogeneous mixture.* A homogeneous mixture has a uniform composition throughout its mass. In this type of mixture the constituent particles cannot be seen with naked eye. Let us discuss homogeneous mixture with examples :

Example 1 : A mixture of sugar or salt in water is a homogeneous mixture. This is because, the different constituents are uniformly mixed without any boundary of separation.

Example 2 : A mixture of two or more miscible liquids such as ethanol in water, acetone, benzene etc.

Example 3 : Air is a homogeneous mixture of oxygen (O), nitrogen (N), argon (Ar), carbon dioxide (CO_2) etc. This is because the gases present in it are uniformly mixed without any boundary of separation.

Example 4 : Other examples include soda water, soft drinks, alcohol and water mixture, vinegar, kerosene and petrol mixture, sea water, petrol, brass etc.

Example 5 : Only solutions and alloys are homogeneous mixtures (Fig. 2.34).

Fig. 2.34 : This figure shows some of the examples of Homogeneous mixtures.

(b) Heterogeneous Mixtures : *Those mixtures in which the substances have uniform composition and also have visible boundaries of separation between the constituents are called heterogeneous mixtures.* In heterogeneous mixtures, the constituent particles can be seen easily with naked eye. Let us discuss heterogeneous mixture with few examples :

Example 1 : The mixture of sugar and sand is heterogeneous mixture. This is because different parts of this mixture will have different compositions of the constituents and therefore, there is a visible boundary of separation between sugar and sand particles.

Example 2 : The suspensions of solids in liquids are heterogeneous mixture. For example, suspensions of chalk (a solid) in water (a liquid).

Example 3 : A mixture of two or more immiscible liquids is also a heterogeneous mixture. A mixture of two immiscible liquid i.e., petrol and water is an example of heterogeneous mixture.

Example 4 : Other examples include flour in water, salt and sand mixture, sugar and sand mixture, paint, glass, coal, milk, ink, butter, cheese, blood, starch solution, soap solution, etc.

Example 5 : All suspension and colloids are heterogeneous mixtures (Fig. 2.35).

Fig. 2.35 : This figure shows some of the examples of Heterogeneous mixtures.

Let us perform an experiment to illustrate homogeneous and heterogeneous mixtures.

Activity 2.1 – To illustrate homogeneous and heterogeneous mixtures.

PROCEDURE

Step 1– Let us divide the class into groups A, B, C and D.

Step 2– Group A takes a beaker containing 50 mL of water and one spatula full of copper sulphate powder.

Step 3– Group B takes 50 mL of water and two spatulas full of copper sulphate powder in a beaker.

Step 4– Groups C and D can take different amounts of copper sulphate and potassium permanganate or common salt (sodium chloride) and mix the given components to form a mixture.

Step 5– Report the observations based on the uniformity in colour and texture.

Step 6– Compare the colour of the solutions of the two groups.

OBSERVATION

Groups A and B have obtained a mixture which has a uniform composition throughout. Such mixtures are called homogeneous mixtures or solutions. Though both the groups, i.e., A and B have obtained copper sulphate solution but the intensity of colour of the solutions is different. This shows that a homogeneous mixture can have a variable composition. Groups C and D have obtained mixtures, which contain physically distinct parts and have non-uniform compositions. Such mixtures are called heterogeneous mixtures.

CONCLUSION

A mixture which has a uniform composition throughout. Such mixtures are called homogeneous mixtures or solutions. A mixture which has variable composition throughout. Such mixtures are called heterogeneous mixtures or solutions.

Let us now discuss the properties of mixtures.

Characteristics of Mixtures

The characteristics of mixtures which help us to differentiate it from a compound are as follows :

(a) It is not a pure substance.
(b) It may be homogeneous or heterogeneous.
(c) Two or more elements mix to form mixtures.
(d) The elements are not present in fixed ratio.
(e) The constituents in mixtures do not lose their identities.
(f) It does not have fixed melting and boiling points.
(g) The constituents in mixtures can be separated by physical methods.
(h) There is no change in the energy observed during the formation of mixtures.

Let us now try to differentiate compounds and mixtures.

Difference between Compounds and Mixtures

S. No	Compounds	Mixtures
1.	It is a pure substance.	It is not a pure substance.
2.	Two or more elements combine chemically to form a compound.	Two or more elements mix to form mixtures.
3.	The constituent elements are present in fixed ratio by mass. It means that the composition of a compound is fixed.	The constituent elements are not present in fixed ratio by mass, i.e., the composition of mixture may vary.
4.	It is always homogeneous.	It may be homogeneous or heterogeneous.
5.	The constituents in compounds lose their identities.	The constituents in mixtures do not lose their identities.
6.	It has fixed melting and boiling points.	It does not have fixed melting and boiling points.

| 7. | Change in energy in the form of heat, electricity or light is observed during the formation of a compound. | There is no change in the energy observed during the formation of mixtures. |
| 8. | The constituents in compounds cannot be separated by physical methods. They can only be separated by chemical means. | The constituents in mixtures can be separated by physical methods. |

Now that we have studied about compounds and mixtures, do you know how to identify a substance as compound or mixture?

Let us perform an activity to differentiate a mixture and a compound.

Activity 2.2–To differentiate a mixture and a compound.

PROCEDURE

Step 1– Divide the class into two groups.

Step 2– Give 5 g of iron filings and 3 g of sulphur powder in a china dish to both the groups.

Step 3– Let group 1 mix the crush iron filings and sulphur powder.

Step 4– Let group 2 mix the crush iron filings and sulphur powder and heat the mixture strongly till red hot.

Step 5– Remove the mixture from flame and allow it to cool.

Step 6– Check for magnetism in the material obtained by bringing a magnet near it.

Step 7– Compare the texture and colour of the material obtained by the groups.

Step 8– Add carbon disulphide to one part of the material obtained. Stir well and filter.

Step 9– Add dilute sulphuric acid or dilute hydrochloric acid to the other part of the material obtained.

Step 10– Perform all the above steps with both the elements (iron and sulphur) separately.

Step 11– Note down your observations.

Step 12– Did the material obtained by the two groups look the same?

Step 13– Which group has obtained a material with magnetic properties?

Step 14– Can we separate the components of the material obtained?

Step 15– On adding dilute sulphuric acid or dilute hydrochloric acid, did both the groups obtain a gas?

Step 16– Did the gas in both the cases smell the same or different?

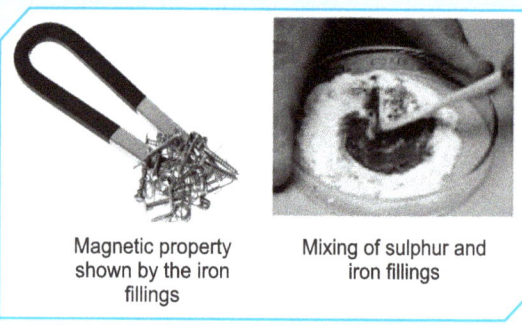

Magnetic property shown by the iron fillings

Mixing of sulphur and iron fillings

Fig. 2.36 : Experimental set-up to differentiate between Compounds and Mixtures.

OBSERVATION

The material obtained by group 1 is a mixture of the two substances i.e., iron and sulphur. The material obtained by group 2 is a compound. The properties of the mixture are the same as that of its constituents. We can also observe that the texture and the colour of the compound is the same throughout. A black substance is formed and it does not get attracted to the magnet any more. Hence, group 1 obtained a material with magnetic properties. The gas obtained by group 1 is hydrogen gas. It is colourless, odourless and combustible gas. So, it is not advised to do the combustion test for hydrogen in the class. The gas obtained by group 2 is hydrogen sulphide. It is a colourless gas with the smell of rotten eggs. Though the starting materials were same but the products obtained by both the groups showed different properties. The group 1 has carried out the activity involving a physical change whereas in group 2, a chemical change has taken place.

CONCLUSION

Heat is not needed for the formation of mixture but it is needed for the formation of the compound.

Though a compound is always homogeneous, a mixture can be homogeneous or heterogeneous. Thus, in order to find out whether a given substance is a mixture or compound, the following points are considered :

(a) If the substance can be separated into its constituents by physical process, then the substance is a mixture. If the substance cannot be separated into its constituents by physical process, then the substance is a compound.

(b) If the substance does not have fixed melting point, boiling point etc, then the substance is a mixture. If the substance has a fixed melting and boiling point, then the substance is a compound.

(c) If the substance is prepared or formed without absorption or release of energy in the form of heat and light, then the substance is a mixture. If the substance is prepared with absorption or release of energy in the form of heat and light, then the substance is a compound.

(d) If the substance shows the properties of its constituents, then the substance is a mixture. If the substance shows the properties different from its constituents, then the substance is a compound.

(e) If the composition of the substance is variable, then the substance is a mixture. If the composition of the substance is fixed, then the substance is a compound.

Before we proceed to next topic, try to solve the following questions.

PAPER-PEN TEST : 5

1. Define mixtures.
2. What is meant by constituents of mixture?
3. What are the components present in gun powder?
4. What are the different types of mixtures?
5. Differentiate between the different types of mixtures with example.
6. Illustrate the different types of mixtures with an experiment.
7. Mention the properties of mixtures.
8. Differentiate between compounds and mixtures.
9. Perform an activity to differentiate a mixture and a compound.
10. How would you differentiate whether a given substance is a mixture or a compound?

2.8 SOLUTIONS, SUSPENSIONS AND COLLOIDS

Solutions are of great importance in everyday life. Human being takes in food in the form of solution. Blood and lymph are in the form of solution to decide the physiological activity of human beings. A solution is a homogeneous mixture of two or more substances. All solutions exist in homogeneous form. The word 'homogeneous' refers to the state in which two or more substances are uniformly present in a given mixture (Fig. 2.37). If a solution contains two components, then it is called as a binary solution. For instance, salt solution containing common salt in water is a binary solution. Some common examples of solutions are salt solution, sugar solution, vinegar, alloys, air, sea water, copper sulphate solution, mixture of alcohol and water, mixture of petrol and oil, soft drinks etc.

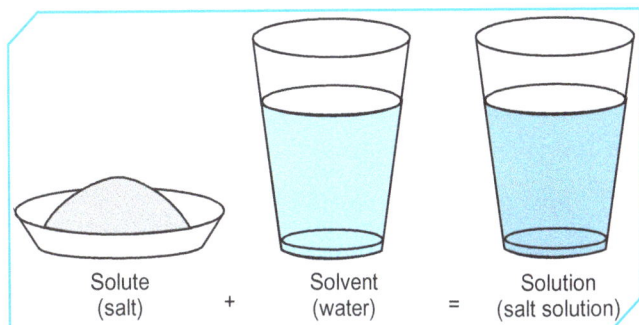

Fig. 2.37 : A solution is a homogeneous mixture of solute and solvent.

In a solution, the component present in lesser amount by weight is called *solute* and the component present in a larger amount by weight is called *solvent*. For instance, in a salt solution, the 'salt' is the 'solute' and 'water' is the 'solvent'. A solvent is a dissolving medium that surrounds the particles of solute to form a solution. In other words, the substance present in lesser amount in a solution is considered as solute and the substance present in greater amount in a solution is considered as solvent. Thus, a solution can be represented as :

$$\text{Solute + Solvent} \rightarrow \text{Solution}$$

Types of Solutions

Solutions are classified as follows :

(a) Based on the type of solvent

(b) Based on the amount of solute in the given solution

(c) Based on the physical state of solute and solvent

(d) Based on the particle size

(a) Based on the Type of Solvent

Based on the type of solvent, the solutions are classified into two types namely,

(i) Aqueous solutions

(ii) Non-aqueous solutions

(i) **Aqueous solution :** The solutions in which water acts as a solvent, is called aqueous solution. For example, sugar solution.

(iii) **Non-aqueous solution :** The solution in which any liquid other than water acts as a solvent is called non-aqueous solution. For example, solution of sulphur in carbon disulphide (CS_2), benzene, ether, etc

(b) Based on the Amount of Solute in the given Solution

Based on the amount of solute in the given amount of solvent, solutions are classified into the three types namely,

(i) Unsaturated solutions

(ii) Saturated solutions

(iii) Super saturated solutions

(i) **Unsaturated solution :** A solution in which the solute is in lesser amount in comparison with the solvent is called unsaturated solution. Here, the addition of more solute is possible till the solution reaches the point of saturation. For example, adding 5g, 10g or 20g of sodium chloride (NaCl) in 100g water.

(ii) **Saturated solution :** A solution in which no more solute can be dissolved in a definite amount of solvent at a given temperature is called a saturated solution. For example, 36g of sodium chloride (NaCl) dissolved in 100g of water at room temperature forms a saturated solution. This means a saturated solution contains 36 g of sodium chloride dissolved in 100 g of water. Similarly, 32 g of potassium nitrate dissolved in 100 g of water refers to a saturated solution containing 32 g of potassium nitrate dissolved in 100 g of water. To test a solution for saturated or unsaturated solution, add more solute to the solution and stir by keeping the temperature constant. If more solute does not dissolve in the given solution, then it will be a saturated solution. But, if more solute gets dissolved, then it will be an unsaturated solution.

However, a solution will be saturated only at a particular temperature. So, when a saturated solution is heated to a higher temperature, it becomes unsaturated. This is because the solubility of the solute increases on heating and more solute can be dissolved in the solution. On the other hand, when a saturated solution at a particular temperature is cooled to lower temperature, then some of its dissolved solute will get separated out in the form of solid crystals.

(iii) **Supersaturated solution :** A solution which has more of solute at a given temperature than that of saturated solution is called supersaturated solution. For example, carbonated water which contains more carbon dioxide dissolved in water.

(c) Based on the Physical State of the Solute and the Solvent

On the basis of the physical states of the constituents (solute and solvent), a solution can be of the following six types namely,

(i) **Type : Solid in Solid**

Solute : Solid

Solvent : Solid

Homogeneous solution

Examples : Alloys such as Brass (Zinc + Copper) and Bronze (Zinc + Tin +Copper)

Heterogeneous solution

Examples : Sand + Common salt, Iron + Sulphur and Charcoal + sulphur (Fig. 2.38)

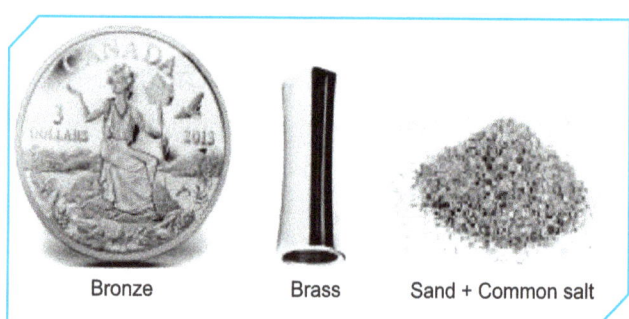

Fig. 2.38: This figure shows the examples of solid in solid type of solutions.

(ii) Type : Solid in Liquid

Solute : Solid

Solvent : Liquid

Homogeneous solution

Examples : Salt + water and Sugar + water

Heterogeneous solution

Examples : Chalk + water and Sand + water (Fig. 2.39)

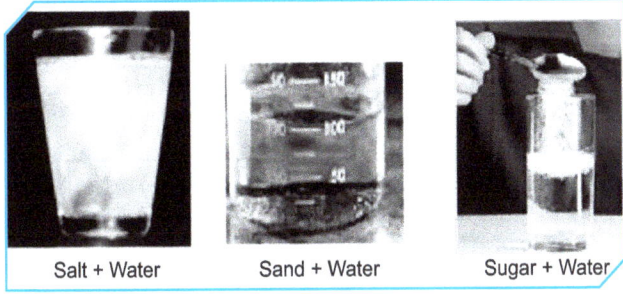

Fig. 2.39 : This figure shows the examples of solid in liquid type of solutions.

(iii) Type : Liquid in Solid

Solute : Liquid

Solvent: Solid

Homogeneous solution

Examples: Amalgamated zinc [Mercury +Zinc] (Fig. 2.40)

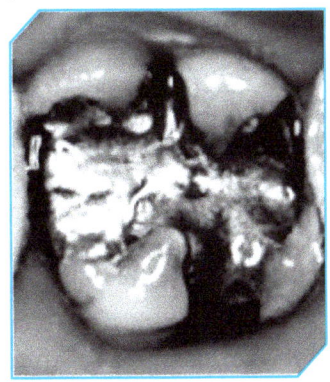

Fig. 2.40 : This figure shows amalgamated zinc.

(iv) Type : Liquid in Liquid

Solute : Liquid

Solvent : Liquid

Homogeneous solution

Examples : Alcohol + water and Diesel + petrol

Heterogeneous solution

Examples : Water + oil and Petrol + water (Fig. 2.41)

Fig. 2.41 : This figure shows the examples of liquid in liquid type of solutions.

(v) Type : Gas in Liquid

Solute : Gas

Solvent : Liquid

Homogeneous solution

Examples : Carbon dioxide + water and Ammonia + water (Fig. 2.42)

Fig. 2.42: This figure shows aerated drinks.

(vi) Type : Gas in Gas

Solute : Gas

Solvent : Gas

Homogeneous solution

Examples : Air (a solution of gases like carbon dioxide, argon, oxygen, water vapour etc in nitrogen gas).

Let us summarize the six types of solutions based on the physical state of the constituents.

Types of Solution

Type	Solute/Solvent	Homogeneous/ Heterogeneous solution	Examples
Solid in Solid	Solute : Solid Solvent : Solid	Homogeneous	Alloys such as Brass (Zinc + Copper) and Bronze (Zinc + Tin +Copper)
	Solute: Solid Solvent: Solid	Heterogeneous	Sand + Common salt; Iron + Sulphur; Charcoal + sulphur

Solid in Liquid	Solute : Solid Solvent : Liquid	Homogeneous	Salt + water; sugar + water
	Solute : Solid Solvent : Liquid	Heterogeneous	Chalk + water; sand + water
Liquid in Solid	Solute : Liquid Solvent : Solid	Homogeneous	Amalgamated zinc which is a mixture of mercury in zinc.
Liquid in Liquid	Solute : Liquid Solvent : Liquid	Homogeneous	Alcohol + water; diesel + petrol
	Solute : Liquid Solvent : Liquid	Heterogeneous	Water + oil; petrol + water
Gas in Liquid	Solute : Gas Solvent : Liquid	Homogeneous	Carbon dioxide + water; Ammonia + water
Gas in Gas	Solute : Gas Solvent : Gas	Homogeneous	Air

Before we proceed to next topic, try to solve the following questions.

PAPER-PEN TEST : 6

1. Define solutions.
2. What is a binary solution?
3. Define a solvent and a solute.
4. Classify solutions.
5. Classify solutions based on the type of solvent.
6. Classify solutions based on the amount of solute in the given amount of solvent.
7. Classify solutions based on the physical state of the solute and the solvent.
8. Differentiate between aqueous and non-aqueous solutions.
9. Differentiate between saturated and unsaturated solutions.
10. What is meant by supersaturated solutions?

(d) Based on the Particle Size

Based on the particle size of the solute, the solutions are divided into three types namely,

(i) True solutions

(ii) Colloidal solutions

(iii) Suspensions

(i) **True Solutions :** It is a homogeneous mixture that contains small solute particles that are dissolved throughout the solvent. In a true solu-tion, the solute particles are mixed so well that we cannot distinguish one from the other. A true solution is also known as molecular solution because the size of dissolved particles in such solution is same as that of a molecule.

Examples

- A solution of sugar in water is a solid in liquid solution. In this solution, sugar is the solute and water is the solvent.
- A solution of iodine in alcohol known as 'tincture of iodine' has iodine (solid) as the solute and alcohol (liquid) as the solvent.
- Aerated drinks like soda water, soft drinks etc., are gas in liquid solutions. These contain carbon dioxide (gas) as solute and water (liquid) as solvent.
- Air is a mixture of gas in gas. Air is a homogeneous mixture of a number of gases. Its two main constituents are: oxygen (21%) and nitrogen (78%). The other gases are present in very small quantities.

Properties of True Solutions

The following are the important characteristic properties of true solutions:

- A true solution is a homogeneous mixture.
- The particle size of a true solution is smaller than 1 nm i.e., 10^{-9} metre in diameter. Therefore, they cannot be seen by the naked eye or even with a microscope.
- Because of very small particle size, they do not scatter a beam of light passing through the solution. So, the path of light is not visible in a solution (Fig. 2.43).

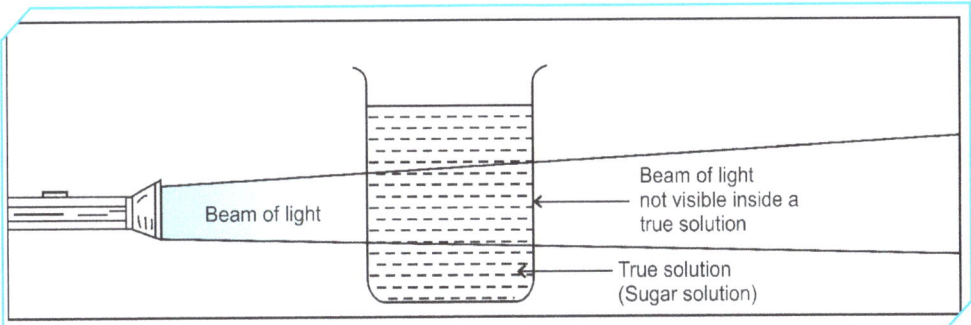

Fig. 2.43 : The path of light is not visible in a true solution as it does not scatter a beam of light passing through it.

- The solute particles do not settle down when left undisturbed i.e., the solution is stable.
- The particles of a true solution pass through the filter paper. So, the solute particles cannot be separated from the mixture by the process of filtration.

(ii) **Colloidal Solutions :** It is a heterogeneous mixture made up of two phases namely, dispersed phase and dispersion medium. The substance distributed as particles is called *dispersed phase*. The continuous phase in which the colloidal particles are dispersed is called *dispersion medium*. The mixture of milk powder containing fat, vitamin, protein and water forms a colloid. Thus, it can be represented as :

| Dispersed + Dispersion → Colloidal |
| phase medium solution |

The components of a colloidal solution are the dispersed phase and the dispersion medium. The solute-like component or the dispersed particles in a colloid form the dispersed phase, and the component in which the dispersed phase is suspended is known as the dispersing medium.

Lyophobic and Lyophilic Colloids : Colloidal solutions in which the dispersed phase has very little affinity for the dispersion medium are termed as lyophobic (solvent hating) colloids. Colloidal solutions of metals which have negligible affinity for solvents and sulphur in water are examples of this type. Colloidal solutions in which the dispersed phase has considerable affinity for the dispersion medium are called lyophilic (solvent loving) colloids. It includes gelatin, protein and starch.

Properties of Colloidal Solutions

The following are the important characteristic properties of colloidal solutions :

- A colloid is a heterogeneous mixture.
- The size of particles in a colloid ranges between 1nm and 100nm in diameter which is bigger than those in a true solution but smaller than those in a suspension.
- The size of particles is too small to be individually seen by naked eyes. They cannot be seen even with the microscope.
- The particles of colloid are big enough to scatter a beam of light passing through it and thus, make its path visible (Fig. 2.52).

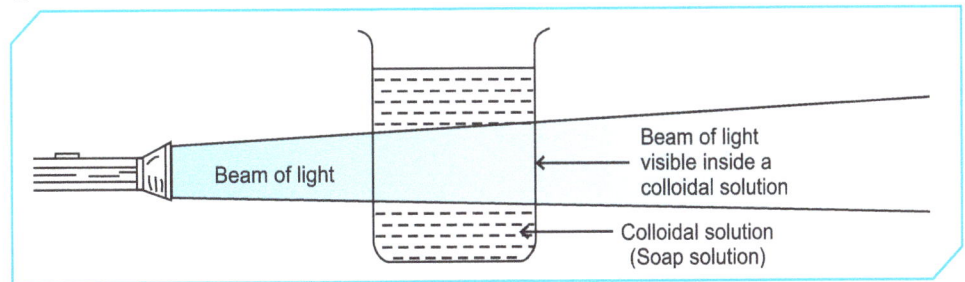

Fig. 2.44 : The path of light is visible in a colloidal solution as it scatters the beam of light passing through it.

- The particles of colloid do not settle down when left undisturbed, i.e., colloids are quite stable.
- The particles of colloid cannot be separated from the mixture by the process of filtration because they easily pass through a filter paper. However, a special technique of separation known as centrifugation can be used to separate the colloidal particles.

Types of Colloids

Colloids are classified into eight types according to the state (solid, liquid or gas) of the dispersing medium and the dispersed phase.

- *Sol*
- *Solid sol*
- *Aerosol*
- *Liquid aerosol*
- *Gel*
- *Emulsion*
- *Foam*
- *Solid foam*

Let us describe these different types of colloids in detail with examples.

Sol : It is a colloid in which tiny solid particles are dispersed in liquid medium.

Dispersed phase : Solid

Dispersed medium : Liquid

Examples : Milk of magnesia, mud (Fig. 2.45)

Fig. 2.45 : This figure shows examples of sols.

Solid Sol : It is a colloid in which solid particles are dispersed in solid medium.

Dispersed phase : Solid

Dispersed medium : Solid

Examples : Coloured gemstones, milky glass (Fig. 2.46)

Fig. 2.46 : This figure shows examples of solid sols.

Aerosol : It is a colloid in which solid or liquid-particles are dispersed in gaseous medium.

Dispersed phase: Solid or liquid

Dispersed medium: Gas

Examples : Smoke, automobile exhausts, hair spray (Fig. 2.47)

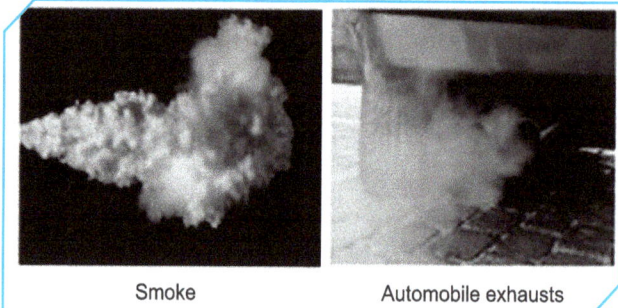

Fig. 2.47 : This figure shows examples of aerosols.

Fig. 2.48 : This figure shows examples of gels.

Gel : It is a semi-solid colloid in which there is continuous network of solid particles dispersed in a liquid.

Dispersed phase : Liquid

Dispersed medium: Solid

Examples : Cheese, butter, jellies (Fig. 2.48)

Emulsion : It is a colloid in which tiny liquid particles are dispersed in another liquid medium which is not miscible.

Dispersed phase : Liquid

Dispersed medium : Liquid

Examples: Face cream, milk (Fig. 2.49)

Liquid aerosol : It is a colloid in which liquid particles are dispersed in gaseous medium.

Dispersed Phase : Liquid

Dispersed medium : Gas

Examples: Mist, clouds, fog (Fig. 2.50)

Fig. 2.49 : This figure shows examples of emulsions.

Fig. 2.50 : This figure shows examples of liquid aerosol.

Solid foam : It is a colloid in which gas is dispersed in a solid medium.

Dispersed Phase: Gas

Dispersed medium: Solid

Examples : Cork, pumice stone, sponge (Fig. 2.51)

Foam : It is a colloid in which gas is dispersed in a liquid medium.

Dispersed Phase : Gas

Dispersed medium : Liquid

Examples : Soap bubbles, beer foam, shaving cream (Fig. 2.52)

Fig. 2.51 : This figure shows examples of solid foam.

Fig. 2.52: This figure shows examples of foam.

Let us summarize these different types of colloids in tabular form as follows:

Types of Colloids

S. No	Type	Dispersed Phase	Dispersed Medium	Examples
1.	Sol	Solid	Liquid	Milk of magnesia and Mud
2.	Solid Sol	Solid	Solid	Coloured gemstones and Milky glass
3.	Aerosol	Solid	Gas	Smoke and Automobile exhausts
4.	Gel	Liquid	Solid	Cheese, Butter and Jellies
5.	Emulsion	Liquid	Liquid	Face cream and Milk
6.	Liquid aerosol	Liquid	Gas	Mist, Clouds and Fog
7.	Solid foam	Gas	Solid	Cork, Pumice stone and Sponge
8.	Foam	Gas	Liquid	Soap bubbles, Beer foam and Shaving cream

Tyndall Effect

The particles of a colloid are uniformly spread throughout the solution. Due to the relatively smaller size of particles, as compared to that of a suspension, the mixture appears to be homogeneous. But actually, if a colloidal solution is observed under a high power microscope, we can see colloidal particles floating in a solution. This shows that a colloidal solution is a heterogeneous mixture. For example, milk, blood, ink, soap solution, starch solution, synthetic detergents etc. Because of the small size of colloidal particles, we cannot see them with naked eyes. But, these particles can easily scatter a beam of visible light passing through them. This scattering of a beam of light is called the Tyndall effect and is named after the name of an Irish scientist, **John Tyndall** who discovered this effect.

Tyndall effect can also be observed when a fine beam of light enters a dark room through a small hole. This happens due to the scattering of light by the particles of dust and smoke in the air. Tyndall effect can be observed when sunlight passes through the canopy of a dense forest. In the forest, mist contains tiny droplets of water, which act as particles of colloid dispersed in air (Fig. 2.53).

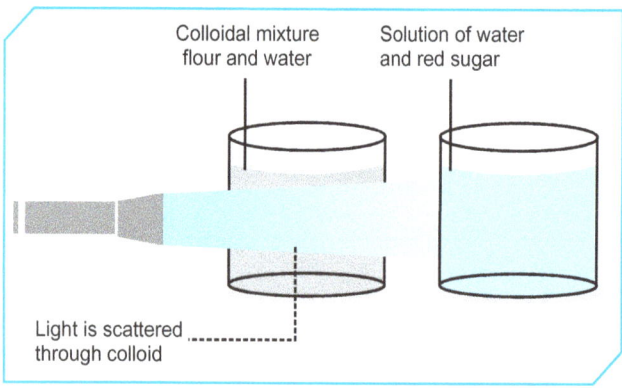

Fig. 2.53 : This figure shows the phenomenon of Tyndall effect.

Before we proceed to next topic, try to solve the following questions.

PAPER-PEN TEST : 7

1. Classify solutions based on the particle size of the solute.
2. Mention the properties of true solutions.
3. Define true solutions.
4. What is meant by dispersed phase and dispersed medium?
5. Define colloidal solution.
6. Classify colloids based on the state of the dispersing phase and dispersing medium.
7. Name a colloid in which tiny solid particles are dispersed in liquid medium. Give an example.
8. Name a colloid in which solid particles are dispersed in solid medium. Give an example.
9. Name a colloid in which solid particles are dispersed in gaseous medium. Give an example.
10. Name a semi-solid colloid in which there is continuous network of solid particles dispersed in a liquid. Give an example.
11. Name a colloid in which tiny liquid particles are dispersed in another liquid medium which is not miscible. Give an example.
12. Name a colloid in which liquid particles are dispersed in gaseous medium. Give an example.
13. Name a colloid in which gas is dispersed in a solid medium. Give an example.
14. Name a colloid in which gas is dispersed in a liquid medium. Give an example.
15. What are the components of a colloidal solution?
16. Differentiate between lyophilic and lyophobic colloids with an example each.
17. Mention the properties of colloidal solutions.
18. Explain Tyndall effect with an example.
19. What do you observe when a fine beam of light enters a dark room through a small hole?
20. What do you observe when sunlight passes through the canopy of a dense forest?

(iii) Suspensions : Suspension is a heterogeneous mixture in which the solute particles do not dissolve but remain suspended throughout the bulk of the medium. It is a heterogeneous mixture of small insoluble particles in a solvent. Here, the particles of solid stay in clusters that could be seen. The particles of a suspension are visible to the naked eye. For example, chalk powder in water, soil particles in water, flour in water, magnesium in water (Milk of Magnesia) etc (Fig. 2.54).

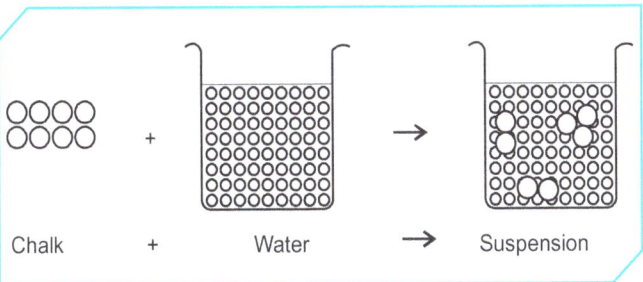

Fig. 2.54 : Chalk-water mixture is a suspension of chalk particles in water.

Properties of Suspensions

The following are the important characteristic properties of suspensions :

- A suspension is a heterogeneous mixture.
- The size of particles in a suspension is larger than 100nm in diameter and they can be easily seen by the naked eye.
- The particles of a suspension scatter a beam of light passing through it and make its path visible.
- The solute particles of a suspension settle down when it is left undisturbed, i.e., a suspension is unstable.
- The suspension particles can be separated from the mixture by the process of filtration because its particles do not pass through a filter paper. However, when the particles settle down, the suspension breaks and it does not scatter light any more.

Let us perform an activity to illustrate the characteristics of solutions, suspensions and colloids.

Activity 2.3 – To illustrate the characteristics of solutions, suspensions and colloids.

PROCEDURE

Step 1– Let us divide the class into four groups – A, B, C and D.

Step 2– Distribute few crystals of copper sulphate to group A.

Step 3– Give one spatula full of copper sulphate to group B.

Step 4– Give chalk powder or wheat flour to group C.

Step 5– Give few drops of milk or ink to group D.

Step 6– Each group should add the given sample in a beaker containing water and stir properly using a glass rod.

Step 7– Are the particles in the mixture visible?

Step 8– Direct a beam of light from a torch through the beaker containing the mixture.

Step 9– Observe from the front.

Step 10– Was the path of the beam of light visible?

Step 11– Leave the mixtures undisturbed for a few minutes.

Step 12– Is the mixture stable or do the particles begin to settle after some time?

Step 13– Filter the mixture.

Step 14– Is there any residue on the filter paper?

Step 15– Discuss the results and form an opinion.

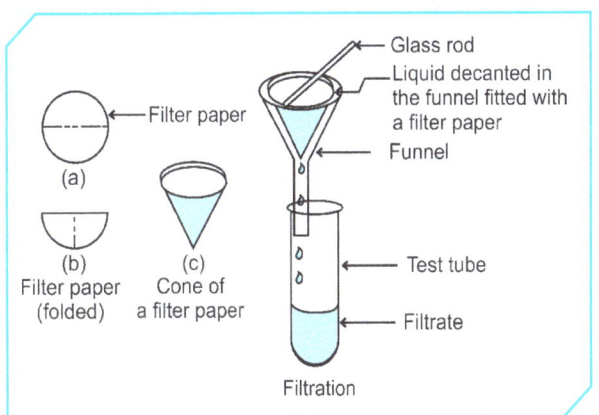

Fig. 2.55 : Experimental set-up to study the characteristics of solutions, suspensions and colloids.

OBSERVATION

The particles in case of group A and B will not be visible whereas in group C and D it would be visible. In case of group A and B, the particles will not show path of the beam of light whereas in group C and D the particles will show the path of beam of light. The mixture is stable only in case of group A and B, as it does not settle down when kept for sometime. On filtering the mixture, residue is left on the filter paper in case of group C and D.

CONCLUSION

Groups A and B have got a solution. Group C has got a suspension. Group D has got a colloidal solution.

Comparison of the Properties of True solution, Colloidal solution and Suspension

Property	True solution	Colloidal solution	Suspension
Particle size in nm (1nm = 10^{-9} metre)	< 1nm	1nm-100nm	> 100nm
Appearance	Transparent	Translucent	Opaque
Visibility	Not visible even under ultra-microscope	Visible under ultra-microscope	Visible to naked eye
Nature	Homogeneous	Heterogeneous	Heterogeneous
Diffusion of Particles	Diffuses rapidly	Diffuses slowly	Diffusion does not occur
Scattering Effect	Does not scatter light	Scatters light	Scatters light

Before we proceed to next topic, try to solve the following questions.

PAPER-PEN TEST : 8

1. Define suspensions.
2. Mention the properties of suspension.
3. Can we see the particles of suspension by our naked eyes? If Yes, why?
4. Differentiate between suspension and colloidal solution with an example each.
5. Perform an activity to illustrate the characteristics of solutions, suspensions and colloids.
6. Compare the properties of true solution, colloidal solutions and suspension.

2.9 CONCENTRATION OF A SOLUTION

Generally a solution may have a small amount of solute dissolved in it or may have a large amount of solute dissolved in it. The solution having a small amount of solute is said to have a low concentration while the solution having a large amount of solute is said to have a high concentration. This means that the solution can be diluted or concentrated based on the amount of solute present in it. Thus, the concentration of a solution may be defined as—'*The amount of solute present in a given quantity of the solution*'

$$\text{Concentration of solution} = \frac{\text{Amount of solute}}{\text{Amount of solution}}$$

Mass of Solution = Mass of Solute + Mass of Solvent

The mass of solution is equal to the mass of solute and the mass of solvent,

There are number of ways by which the concentration of a solution can be expressed. But, the most common method of expressing the concentration of a solution is the percentage method. In the percentage method, the percentage of solute present in the solution can be calculated by mass or by volume. Let us discuss these in detail with examples.

Mass Percent of a Solution

The concentration of a solution by mass percent may be defined as -'*The number of parts by mass of solute per 100 parts by mass of solution*'. Thus, concentration of solution can be calculated by this method using the following formula :

$$\%\ \text{Strength by Mass} = \frac{\text{Mass of solute}}{\text{Mass of solution}} \times 100$$

For example, if 10 percent salt solution is prepared by dissolving 10.0 g of salt in 90.0g of water, then the total mass of the solution will be,

Mass of the solute (salt) = 10 g

Mass of the solvent (water) = 90 g

So, Mass of solution = Mass of the solute + Mass of the solvent = 10 + 90 = 100 g

Now, substituting the values in the percent strength by mass formula, we get

$$\text{Concentration of Solution (by Mass)} = \frac{10}{100} \times 100 = 10\%$$

Thus, the concentration of solution of common salt is 10% by mass.

Volume Percentage of a Solution

The concentration of solution by volume percent may be defined as '*The number of parts by volume of solute per 100 parts by volume of solution*'. Thus, concentration of solution can be calculated by this method using the following formula :

$$\% \text{ Strength by Volume} = \frac{\text{Volume of solute}}{\text{Volume of solution}} \times 100$$

For example, if 20% of alcohol solution by volume is prepared by diluting 20.0 mL of alcohol to a volume of 80.0 mL by adding water, then the total volume of solution will be :

Volume of solute (alcohol) = 20 mL

Volume of solvent (water) = 80 mL

So, Volume of solution = Volume of solute + Volume of solvent = 20 + 80 = 100 mL

Now, substituting the values in the percent strength by volume formula, we get

$$\text{Concentration of Solution (by Volume)} = \frac{20}{100} \times 100$$

$$= 20\%$$

Thus, the concentration of alcohol solution is 20% by volume.

Let us perform an activity to understand the concentration of the solution.

Activity 2.4- To find out the concentration of the solution.

PROCEDURE

Step 1- Take approximately 50 mL of water each in two separate beakers.

Step 2- Add salt in one beaker and sugar or barium chloride in the second beaker with continuous stirring.

Step 3- When no more solute can be dissolved, heat the contents of the beaker to raise the temperature by about 5°C.

Step 4- Start adding the solute again.

Step 5- Is the amount of salt and sugar or barium chloride that can be dissolved in water at a given temperature, the same?

OBSERVATION

When no more solute can be dissolved in a solution at a given temperature, it is called a saturated solution. So, at any particular temperature, a solution that has dissolved as much solute as it is capable of dissolving is said to be a saturated solution.

No, the amount of salt and sugar or barium chloride that can be dissolved in water at a given temperature is not the same.

CONCLUSION

The amount of the solute present in the saturated solution at the given temperature is called its solubility. We can infer from the activity that different substances in a given solvent have different solubilities at the same temperature.

Let us try to solve few numericals based on the calculation of concentration of solution.

Solved Sample Problems

Formulae Used –

(a)

$$\text{Mass Percentage of Solution} = \frac{\text{Mass of solute}}{\text{Mass of solution}} \times 100$$

(b)

$$\% \text{ Strength by Volume} = \frac{\text{Volume of solute}}{\text{Volume of solution}} \times 100$$

(c)

$$\text{Concentration of Solution} = \frac{\text{Amount of solute}}{\text{Amount of solution}}$$

Sample Problem 1 : A solution contains 40 g of common salt in 320 g of water. Calculate the concentration in terms of mass percentage of the solution by mass.

Solution : Given :

Mass of solute (salt) = 40 g

Mass of solvent (water) = 320 g

We know,

Mass of solution = Mass of solute + Mass of solvent

= 40 g + 320 g = 360 g

Substituting the values in the formula, we get

$$\text{Mass Percentage of Solution} = \frac{\text{Mass of solute}}{\text{Mass of solution}} \times 100$$

$$\text{Mass Percentage of Solution} = \frac{40}{360} \times 100 = 11.1\%$$

Thus, the concentration of this solution is 11.1% by mass.

Sample Problem 2 : A solution contains 25 mL of alcohol mixed with 75 mL of water. Calculate the concentration of this solution.

Solution : Given :

Volume of solute (alcohol) = 25 mL

Volume of solvent (water) = 75 mL

So, Volume of solution = Volume of solute + Volume of solvent = 25 + 75 = 100 mL

Now, substituting the values in the percent strength, we get,

$$\text{Concentration of Solution (by Volume)} = \frac{25}{100} \times 100$$

$$= 25\%$$

Thus, the concentration of this solution is 25 % by volume.

Try Yourself

1. Calculate the concentration of the solution, if 2 mL of acetone is present in 45 mL of its aqueous solution. **[4.4%]**

2. How would you prepare 500 g of aqueous solution containing 15% by mass of sucrose?
[75 g of sucrose in 425 g of water]

3. Calculate the concentration of the solution, if 110 g of copper sulphate is present in 550 g of solution. **[20%]**

4. How would you prepare 250 mL of 60% by volume aqueous solution of rubbing alcohol?

5. Calculate the concentration of the solution, if a solution contains 30 g of sugar dissolved in 370 g of water. **[7.5%]**

2.10 SOLUBILITY

Solubility of a solute in a given solvent at a particular temperature is defined as the number of grams of solute necessary to saturate 100g of the solvent at that temperature. For instance, the solubility of $CuSO_4$ in H_2O is 20.7g at 20°C. The solubility of some ionic compounds at 20°C per 100 grams of water is given in the table below :

Solubility of some Ionic Compounds at 20°C /100 g of Water

Substance	Copper sulphate ($CuSO_4$)	Potassium nitrate (KNO_3)	Potassium chloride (KCl)	Sodium chloride (NaCl)	Ammonium chloride (NH_4Cl)	Sodium nitrate ($NaNO_3$)	Sodium bromide (NaBr)	Sodium iodide (NaI)	Sugar ($C_{12}H_{22}O_{11}$)
Solubility in water (at 20°C)	21 g	32 g	34 g	36 g	37 g	92 g	95 g	184 g	204 g

Thus, we can define solubility as, '*The maximum amount of a solute which can be dissolved in 100 g of a solvent at a specified temperature*'. The solubility is always stated as 'mass of solute per 100g of water or any other solvent'. Thus, we can say that solubility of a substance refers to its saturated solution.

Factors Affecting Solubility

The factors that affect the solubility of the substance are :

(a) Temperature

(b) Nature of solute (or) *solvent*

(c) Pressure

(a) Effect of temperature : In endothermic process (a reaction in which heat is absorbed), solubility increases with increase in temperature. For example, the solubility of potassium nitrate (KNO_3) increases with the increase in temperature. On the other hand, in exothermic process (a reaction in which heat is given off), the solubility decreases with increase in temperature. For example, the solubility of calcium oxide (CaO) decreases with increase in temperature.

(b) Nature of solute and solvent : The solubility of a solute in a solvent also depends on the nature of solute and solvent. A polar compound dissolves in a polar solvent. For example, common salt dissolves in water. However, a polar compound is less soluble or insoluble in a non-polar solvent (e.q. acetone).

(c) Effect of pressure : The effect of pressure is observed only in gases. An increase in pressure increases the solubility of a gas in a liquid and decreases on decreasing the pressure. For example, carbon dioxide (CO_2) gas is filled in soft drinks to make them fizzy by increasing its pressure. However, the solubility of solids in liquids remains unaffected by change in pressure (Fig. 2.56).

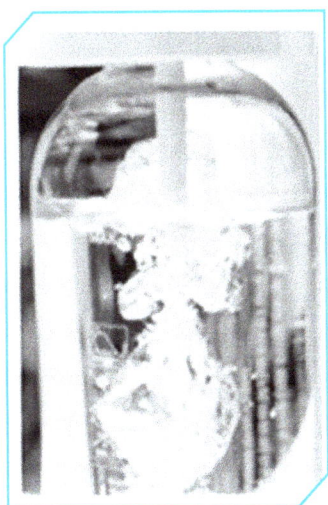

Fig. 2.56 : This figure shows pure carbon dioxide when added to water under pressure.

Let us now try to solve some numerical problems based on solubility.

Solved Sample Problems

Sample Problem 1 : Manu determined the solubility of four substances such as potassium nitrate, sodium chloride, potassium chloride and ammonium chloride in water at 100°C, 200°C, 400°C, 600°C and 800°C. He obtained the following data :

Substances taken	Solubility at different temperatures				
	100°C	200°C	400°C	600°C	800°C
Potassium nitrate	21 g	32 g	62 g	106 g	167 g
Sodium chloride	36 g	36 g	36 g	37 g	37 g
Potassium chloride	35 g	35 g	40 g	46 g	54 g
Ammonium chloride	24 g	37 g	41g	55 g	66 g

(a) What is the effect of change in temperature on the solubility of the salt as shown in the data above?
(b) Which salt has the highest solubility at 200°C?
(c) What is the solubility of each salt at 200°C?
(d) What happens if a saturated solution of potassium chloride at 800°C is left to cool at room temperature?
(e) What mass of potassium nitrate would be needed to make a saturated solution of potassium nitrate in 50 g of water at 400°C?

Solution :
(a) The solubility of salt increases with increase in temperature.
(b) Ammonium chloride.
(c)

Substances	Solubility at 200°C
Potassium nitrate	32 g
Sodium chloride	36 g
Potassium chloride	35 g
Ammonium chloride	37 g

(d) The solid potassium chloride or the crystals of potassium chloride will slowly get separated from the solution. In other words, the solubility decreases on cooling.
(e) The solubility of potassium nitrate at 400°C is 62g. If 62 g of potassium nitrate is required to make a saturated solution of potassium nitrate in 100 g of water at 400°C, then 50 g of water will require, half of 62 g of potassium nitrate, i.e.,

$$\frac{62}{2} = 31 g$$

Hence, 31 g of potassium nitrate is required to make a saturated solution of potassium nitrate in 50 g of water at 400°C.

Sample Problem 2 : If 12 g of potassium sulphate dissolves in 75 g of water at 400°C, then what is its solubility in water at 400°C?

Solution : 75 g of water dissolves = 12 g of potassium sulphate

So, 100 g of water dissolves = $\frac{12}{75} \times 100 = 16g$

Thus, the solubility of potassium sulphate in water is 16 g at 400°C.

Try Yourself

1. If 21.5 g of potassium chloride dissolves in 60 g of water at 400°C. Calculate the solubility of potassium chloride in water at that temperature.

[35.8 g]

2. If 9.72 g of sodium chloride dissolves in 30 g of water at 600°C. Calculate the solubility of sodium chloride in water at that temperature.]

[32.4 g]

Before we proceed to next topic, try to solve the following questions.

PAPER-PEN TEST : 9

1. Define the concentration of a solution.
2. Which is the common method of expressing the concentration of a solution?
3. What is the mass of a solution?
4. Define mass percent of a solution.
5. If 10 percent salt solution is prepared by dissolving 10.0 g of salt in 90.0g of water, then what is the total mass of the solution?
6. Define volume percent of a solution.
7. Explain an activity to find out the concentration of a solution.
8. Define solubility.
9. What are the factors affecting the solubility?
10. A solution contains 40 g of common salt in 320 g of water. Calculate the concentration in terms of mass percentage of the solution by mass.

2.11 SEPARATING THE COMPONENTS OF A MIXTURE

We have learnt that most of the natural substances are not chemically pure. Many materials around us are mixtures. Hence, different methods of separation are used to get individual components from a mixture. The separation makes it possible to study and use the individual components of a mixture. Heterogeneous mixtures can be separated into their respective constituents by physical methods like handpicking, sieving, filtration that we use in our day-to-day life. However, the methods of separation used depend upon the type of mixture and the properties of the constituents. Each constituent present in the mixture have different boiling points, volatility, solubility, density etc. These physical properties can be used to separate them from a mixture. In some cases, special techniques such as chromatography, centrifugation, distillation, fractional distillation etc; are use for the separation of the components of a mixture. In order to separate the constituents from a mixture, let us consider three cases as follows :

(a) Solid - Solid Mixtures
(b) Solid – Liquid Mixtures
(c) Liquid – Liquid Mixtures
(d) Solid-Gas Mixtures

Let us discuss the different methods involved in separating the constituents from a mixture by different physical means.

2.12 SEPARATION OF SOLID - SOLID MIXTURES

When the mixture is made up of two solid substances, any one of the following methods can be used to separate the constituents :

(a) By hand picking
(b) By using magnet
(c) By the process of sublimation
(d) By using suitable solvent
(e) By fractional crystallization

Let us discuss these methods in detail with examples.

(a) **Separation by Hand Picking**

The process of separating the constituent particles in the mixture based on the difference in its size or colour using hand is called hand picking.

Principle

This method of separation is possible when there is a clear difference in the size or colour of the constituent particles.

Process

When the components of the mixture are sufficiently large in size, they may be separated by simple hand picking method (Fig. 2.57). In other words, large sized impurities like the pieces of dirt, stone and husk can be removed from wheat, rice or pulses by this method. To remove the impurities from the grains or pulses, spread the grain on a sheet of paper. Now, remove with your hands the pieces of stone, husks, broken grain and particles of any other grains from it. This method is convenient only when the quantity of such impurities is usually not very large.

Fig. 2.57 : This figure shows the method of hand picking.

Examples

(i) Black stones can be picked by hand when mixed with rice grains.

(ii) Mixture of two pulses can be separated by hand-picking method.

(b) Separation by a Magnet

The process of separating the solid-solid mixture by using a magnet is called magnetic separation. This method of separation is possible only when one of the constituents in the mixture is magnetic in nature.

Principle

The mixture containing magnetic and non-magnetic components are spread over a piece of paper. Then, the magnet is moved over the piece of paper, close to the components of the mixture. On doing this, the magnetic components get attracted to the magnet and get separated whereas, non-magnetic component do not get attracted and therefore, remains behind.

Process

A mixture of iron filings and sulphur can be separated by this method. Take a mixture of iron filings and sulphur in a flat vessel. Now bring a strong magnet close to the mixture repeatedly. Since iron is magnetic in nature, it gets attracted to the bar magnet. The iron filings clinging to the magnet can be removed from the surface using a piece of card board. The sulphur being non-magnetic in nature remains behind in the vessel. On the other hand, we can also separate the iron filings from sulphur by spreading a thin layer of the mixture of iron filings and sulphur over a sheet of paper. Now, a strong magnet is passed over the sheet of paper repeatedly till all the magnetic particles of iron filings are separated. The sulphur remains in the spreaded paper (Fig. 2.58).

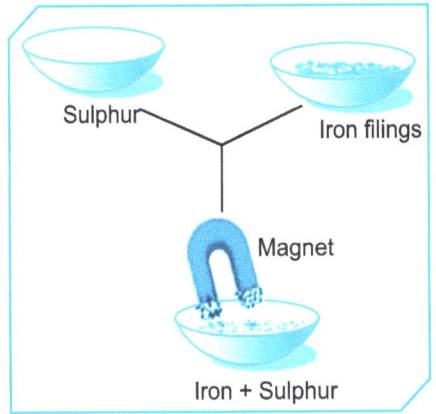

Fig. 2.58 : This picture shows the separation of iron fillings from a mixture of sulphur and iron filings by using magnet.

Examples

(i) A mixture of sulphur and iron filings.

(ii) A mixture of sand and iron filings.

(iii) A mixture of iron filings and saw dust.

(c) Separation by Sublimation

The process of conversion of a solid substance directly into its vapours on heating and vapour into solid on cooling is called sublimation. This method of separation is possible only when one of the constituents sublimes on heating and the other substance is left behind as the non-sublimable substance. The solid substance obtained by cooling the vapours is known as *sublimate* and the vapours are called as *sublime*.

Principle

The crude mixture of substance is heated in an evaporating dish covered with a perforated sheet on which an inverted funnel is placed. On heating, the vapour of the sublimable substance rises up and gets condensed on the cooler walls of the funnel. One of the constituent substance which does not sublime remains as a residue in the evaporating dish. The condensed vapours may be scrapped off from the inner walls of the funnel.

Process

A mixture of salt and ammonium chloride can be separated by the process of sublimation. The crude mixture of sublimate is heated in an evaporating dish covered with a perforated sheet on which an inverted funnel is placed as shown in the figure. A cotton wool plug is put at the open end of the funnel to prevent the fumes from escaping into the air. The ammonium chloride being sublimable substance rises up as vapours and gets condensed into pure solid ammonium chloride on the cooler walls of the funnel. The other non-sublimable constituent i.e., the salt does not sublime and so remain as a residue in the evaporating dish. The pure ammonium chloride thus obtained in the form of a sublimate may be scrapped off from the inner walls of the funnel (Fig. 2.59).

Examples

(i) A mixture of non-sublimable sand or salt (sodium chloride) and sublimable ammonium chloride.

(ii) A mixture of non-sublimable sand or salt (sodium chloride) and sublimable iodine.

(iii) A mixture of non-sublimable sand or salt (sodium chloride) and sublimable camphor.

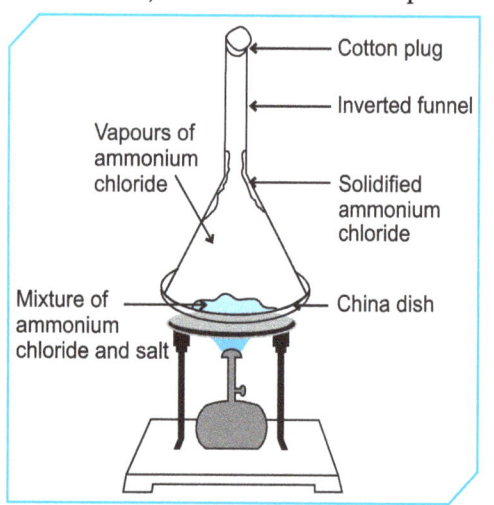

Fig. 2.59 : This figure shows the separation of a mixture of common salt and ammonium chloride by the process of sublimation.

(d) Separation by a Suitable Solvent

This method is feasible when one of the constituent is soluble in a suitable solvent and the other remains insoluble in that solvent. Generally, water is a universal solvent in which most of the common substances dissolve. Some of the common substances and solvents in which they dissolve have been tabulated below for your reference.

List of Some Common Substance and the Solvents in which they Dissolve.

S. No	Common substances	Dissolving solvent
1.	Sulphur, Phosphorus	Carbon disulphide
2.	Paint, Paraffin wax	Turpentine oil
3.	Rust	Oxalic acid
4.	Rubber	Benzene
5.	Nail polish	Acetone
6.	Iodine	Ethanol
7.	Grease	Petrol
8.	Sodium chloride, Potassium nitrate, Sugar etc.	Water
9.	Sugar	Alcohol

Principle

This method involves the use of a solvent in which only one of the solid present in the mixture dissolves. The undissolved solid is removed by the process of filtration. The filtrate thus obtained, is evaporated to dryness in order to recover the soluble solid.

Process

A mixture of common salt or sodium chloride and sand can be separated by using water as a solvent. Take a mixture of sodium chloride and sand in a beaker. Add an appropriate amount of water to the beaker containing the mixture. Stir the mixture slowly with the help of a glass rod. The soluble solid, i.e., sodium chloride gets dissolved in water while the sand remain undissolved and gets collected at the bottom of the beaker. The sand can be removed from the salt solution by the process of filtration. On pouring the salt solution containing sand over a filter paper kept in funnel, the sand remains as a residue on the filter while the salt solution is obtained as a filtrate in a beaker kept below the funnel. The filtrate contains the dissolved salt. Now, take the filtrate in a china dish and place it on a tripod stand for heating. The water in the filtrate gets evaporated leaving behind the pure crystals of common salt in the china dish (Fig. 2.60).

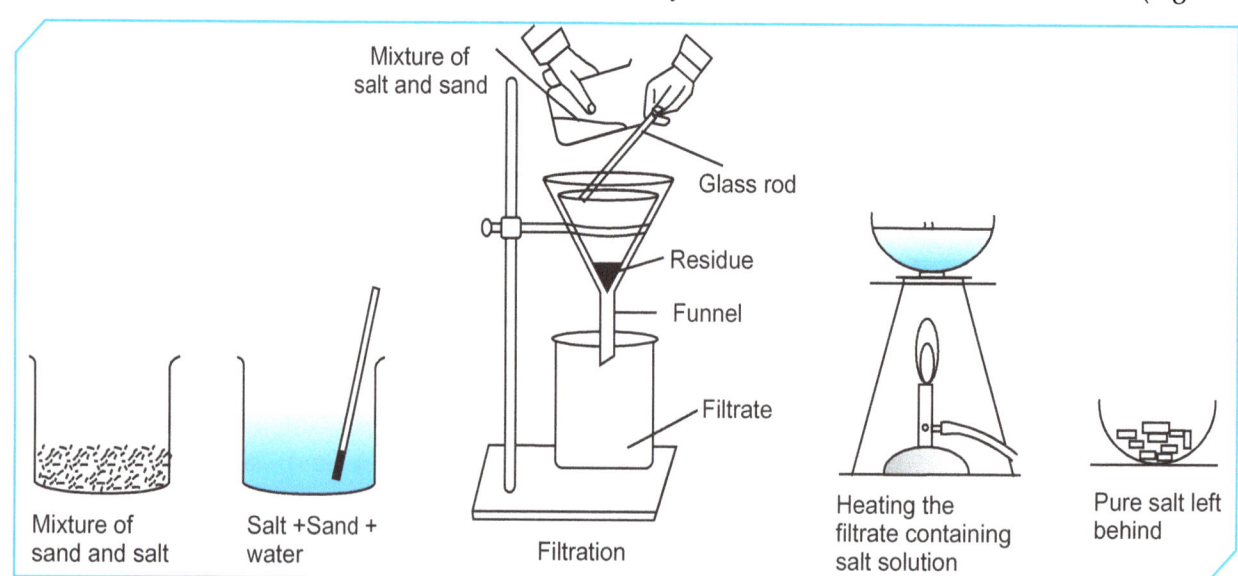

Fig. 2.60 : This figure shows the process of separation of a common salt and sand mixture by using suitable solvent, i.e, water.

Examples

(i) A mixture of common salt or sodium chloride and sand can be separated by using water as a solvent in which common salt gets dissolved in water. The dissolved salt can be obtained by evaporating the filtrate containing the salt solution.

(ii) A mixture of sugar and sand can be separated by using water as a solvent in which sugar gets dissolved in water. The dissolved sugar can be obtained by evaporating the filtrate containing the sugar solution.

(iii) A mixture of sulphur and sand can be separated using carbon disulphide as solvent in which sulphur gets dissolved in carbon disulphide. The dissolved sulphur can be obtained by evaporating the filtrate containing the carbon disulphide solvent.

(iv) A mixture of sugar and salt can be separated by using alcohol as solvent in which sugar gets dissolved in alcohol. The dissolved sugar can be obtained by evaporating the filtrate containing the alcohol solution.

(e) Separation by Fractional Crystallization

The process of separating two or more crystalline solids based on the difference in their solubilities in the same solvent is called fractional crystallization. In other words, this method is employed in some cases where both or all the constituents of the mixture are soluble in the same solvent but in different degrees. This method is feasible only if the solubility of two crystalline solids, in a particular solvent differ widely. In such cases, the solid having lower solubility crystallizes out first from the solution and gets separated.

Principle

The mixture of crystalline solids is dissolved in a common solvent at a temperature higher than room temperature. When this mixture is cooled to room temperature, the less soluble constituent crystallizes out first whereas the more soluble constituent crystallizes out separately, later on. When this process is repeated many times in minimum amount of hot solvent, the two solids can be ultimately separated.

Process

A saturated solution is prepared by dissolving mixture of potassium chloride and sodium nitrate in water as solvent at a temperature higher than room temperature. When the solution is allowed to cool, potassium chloride being less soluble in water crystallizes out first and sodium nitrate is crystallized later by the process of boiling and cooling (Fig. 2.61).

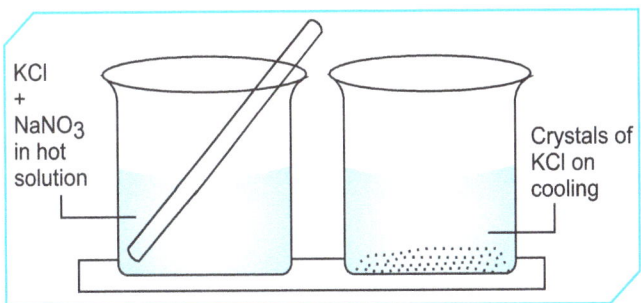

Fig. 2.61 : This figure shows the separation of KCl and $NaNO_3$ by the process of fractional distillation.

Examples

(i) Sodium chloride being less soluble crystallizes out first from a saturated solution of mixture of potassium nitrate (KNO_3) and sodium chloride (NaCl).

(ii) Similarly, potassium chloride being less soluble, crystallizes out first from a saturated solution of mixture of potassium chloride (KCl) and sodium nitrate ($NaNO_3$).

Before we proceed to next topic, try to solve the following questions.

PAPER-PEN TEST : 10

1. What are the different methods involved in separating solid–solid mixtures?
2. Mention the principle of hand picking method.
3. Define magnetic separation.
4. Explain the principle of magnetic separation.
5. Define sublimation.
6. What is meant by sublimate?
7. Explain the principle of sublimation.
8. How can a mixture of sugar and sand be separated?
9. Define fractional crystallization.
10. What is the basis of fractional crystallization?

2.13 SEPARATION OF SOLID-LIQUID MIXTURES

When the mixture contains one solid substance and a liquid, then any one of the following methods can be used to separate the constituents:

(a) *Filtration*
(b) *Sedimentation and decantation*
(c) *Evaporation*
(d) *Distillation*
(e) *Centrifugation*
(f) *Chromatography*
(g) *Crystallization*

Let us discuss these methods in detail with examples.

(a) Separation by Filtration

The process of separating suspended solid matter from a liquid, by causing the latter to pass through the pores of a filter is called filtration.

Folding of Filter Paper into Filter Paper Cone

A filter paper is folded twice and then opened out in the form of a cone and is fitted into a glass funnel. This cone is moistened a little to enable it to stick to the surface of the glass funnel (Fig. 2.62).

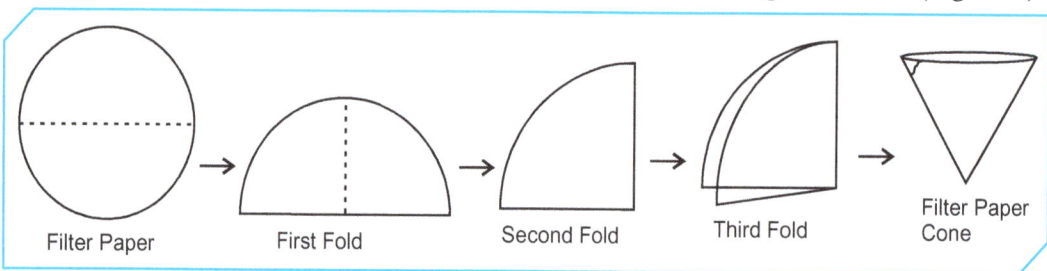

Fig. 2.62 : This figure shows the folding of a filter paper to form a cone.

Principle

An insoluble light solid substance can be separated from a liquid by this method. In filtration, particles of one of the components of the mixture can pass through the filter paper while the other cannot. For example, in a mixture of water and chalk powder, water particles can pass through the pores of a filter paper while chalk particles cannot. The fitration medium is selected based on the properties of the mixture. For example, filtering out fine particles might require a different type of filtration medium. Similarly, liquids at high temperature might require a different type of filtration medium. The glass funnel fitted to the stand is placed above a beaker or a flask. The filter paper cone is placed on the glass funnel. The mixture mixed along with water is poured on to the cone with the help of a glass rod. The clear liquid passes through the filter paper and collects in the beaker or a flask placed below. This clear liquid is called the *filtrate*. The insoluble substance which left behind in the filter paper is called *residue*. (Fig. 2.63).

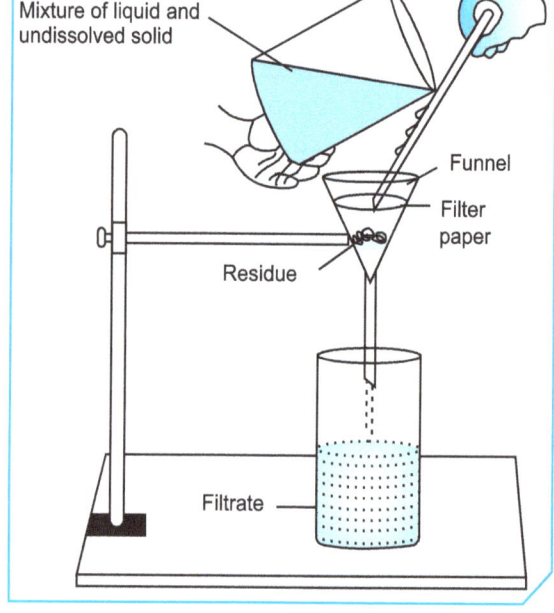

Fig. 2.63 : Separation of a mixture by filtration.

Process

In everyday life, we use this process of filtration while making tea. In order to prepare tea, we need to add tea leaves to hot boiling milk. Now, to separate the used tea leaves, we pour the prepared tea over a tea strainer. The tea strainer contains a wire mesh which acts as a filter. The liquid tea passes through the tea strainer and is collected in the cup placed below, while the tea leaves remain behind as the residue on the wire mesh of tea strainer (Fig. 2.64).

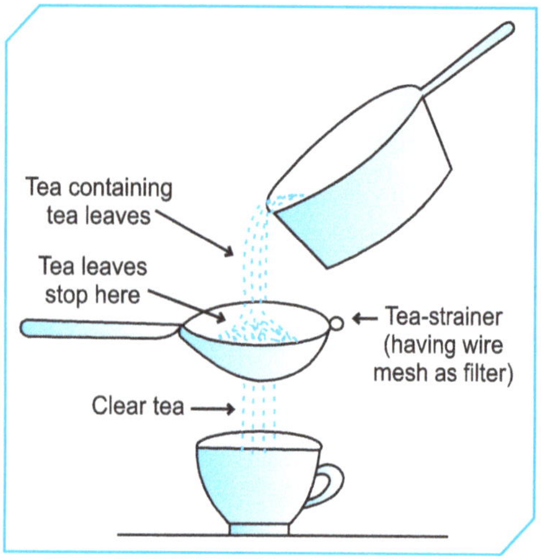

Examples

(i) A precipitate of barium sulphate or silver chloride can be separated from water by the process of filtration.

Fig. 2.64 : This figure shows the separation of used tea-leaves from prepared tea by the process of filtration.

(ii) Purification of river water for drinking purpose is carried out by filtration through sand beds.

(iii) A mixture of saw dust and water, charcoal and water, zinc dust and water can be separated by the process of filtration.

(iv) Used tea leaves can be separated from prepared tea by the process of filtration.

(v) A mixture of chalk and water can be separated by the process of filtration.

Application of Filtration

Supply of Drinking Water in a City

We know that the source of water supply in a city is either a nearby river or a lake. Generally, the water from river or lake collected in a reservoir which contains suspended impurities and so it must be purified before supplying to cities. This is done at a place called water works situated near the bank of the river or a lake.

Principle

The supply water is purified by sedimentation, decantation, loading, filtration and chlorination process to remove the suspended impurities and to kill the germs present in the water.

Process

The purification of water from a lake or a river is done in step by step process as follows :

(i) **Sedimentation Tank :** The water from the river is pumped into the reservoir by the pumping station into a sedimentation tank. The water is allowed to stand for sometime, so that the insoluble substances present in the water settles down at the bottom of the sedimentation tank.

(ii) **Loading Tank :** The water from sedimentation tank is sent to loading tank. Now, alum is added to the water. The suspended clay particles present in the water gets dissolved in the alum. Due to this, alum becomes heavy and settles down at the bottom of the loading tank.

(iii) **Filtration Tank :** The water is then passed to filtration tank which has three layers namely,
- Fine sand top layer
- Coarse sand middle layer
- Gravel bottom layer

The fine sand top layer acts as filters. When water passes through these layers, even the small suspended particles present in the water get removed and the water becomes clear.

(iv) **Chlorination Tank :** The clear water is then passed to chlorination tank where a measured quantity of chlorine is added to water to kill the germs present in the water. This process is called disinfecting the water or sterilization of water. Now, the disinfected water can be used for drinking purpose.

(v) **High storage Tank :** The disinfected water is then pumped into high storage tank from where the water is supplied to homes and factories in the city through pipes (Fig. 2.65).

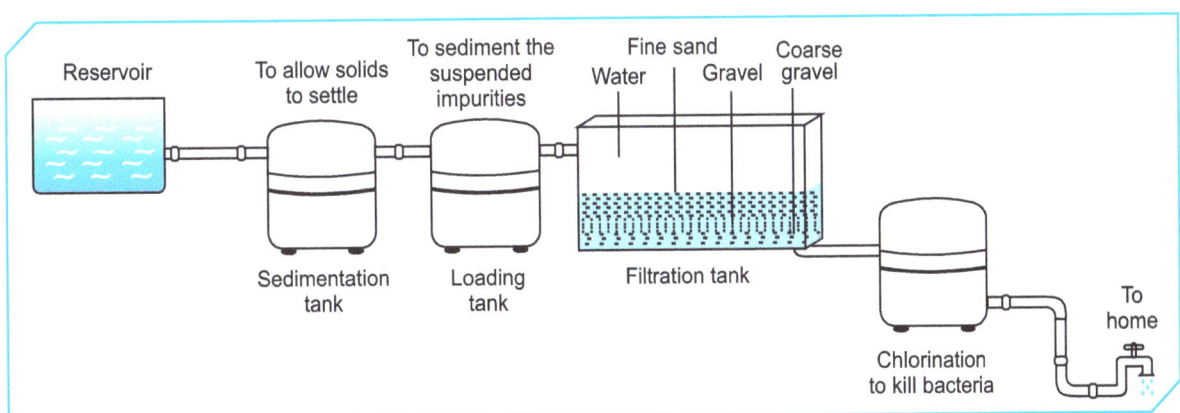

Fig. 2.65 : This figure shows the water purification system in water works.

(b) Separation by Sedimentation and Decantation

The process of settling down of heavy insoluble particles in a mixture of water is called sedimentation. The process of transferring clear liquid after sedimentation, without disturbing the sediment (insoluble heavy particle) is called decantation. This method is adopted to separate heavy insoluble solid substances from a liquid.

Principle

A suspension of an insoluble solid substance in a liquid is allowed to stand for some time in a beaker. The suspended particles settle at the bottom of the beaker leaving the clear liquid at the top. The heavy settled particles are called *sediment* while the clear liquid at the top is called *supernatant liquid*. Later, the supernatant liquid is transferred into another beaker without disturbing the sediment.

Process

Take a suspension of mud and water in a beaker and allow it to stand for some time in a beaker. The mud particles settle at the bottom of the beaker leaving clear water at the top. The clear water is transferred into another beaker without disturbing the mud particles (Fig. 2.66).

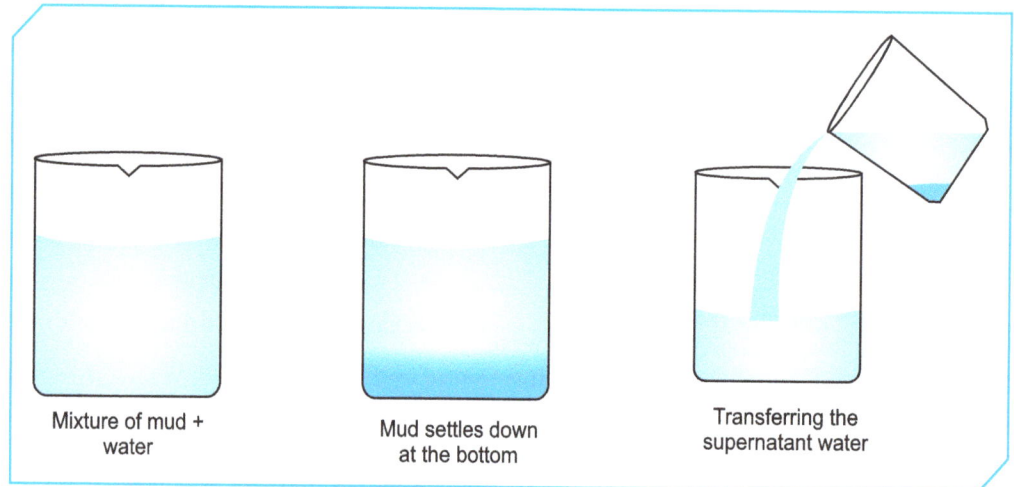

Fig. 2.66 : Separation of a mixture of mud and water by the process of sedimentation and decantation.

Examples

A mixture of pulses and water, a mixture of mud and water and a mixture of sand and water can be easily separated by this method.

(c) Separation by Evaporation

In this method, a non-volatile soluble solid can be separated from its liquid component. *The process of obtaining a non-volatile soluble solid from its solution by allowing the liquid component to vaporize is called evaporation.*

Principle

The solution of a non-volatile soluble solid in a liquid is heated gently on a sand bath or on a water bath in an evaporating dish. The solution escapes as vapour, leaving behind the solid salt in the dish as residue. Slow evaporation takes place at all temperatures even at room temperature. However, increase in temperature i.e., heating causes evaporation to occur rapidly.

Process

Common salt dissolved in water can be recovered from the mixture by the process of evaporation. In this process, the solution of common salt and water is taken in an evaporating dish and heated gently to dryness by using burner to allow evaporation. When all the water in the salt solution gets evaporated, the common salt is left behind as a residue in the evaporating dish (Fig. 2.67).

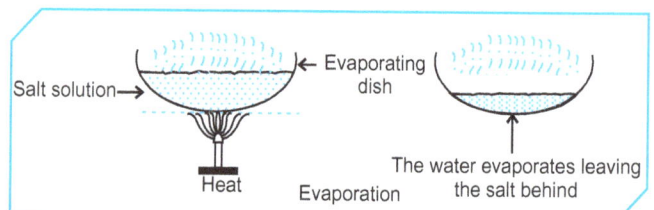

Fig. 2.67 : This figure shows the separation of common salt dissolved in water by the process of evaporation.

Examples

(i) Sugar can be separated from sugar solution.

(ii) The coloured component or 'dye' from black or blue ink can be separated from its liquid mixture.

(iii) Sulphur dissolved in carbon disulphide can be recovered.

(iv) Substances like copper sulphate, potassium nitrate and potash alum can be separated from their aqueous solution.

Note

- In the evaporation process, only dissolved solid component can be recovered from liquid, but the liquid cannot be recovered as it gets vapourized into the air.

Let us perform an activity to obtain coloured component or dye from blue or black ink by the process of evaporation.

Activity 2.5 – To obtain coloured component (dye) from blue or black ink.

PROCEDURE

Step 1- Fill half a beaker with water.

Step 2- Put a watch glass on the mouth of the beaker as shown in the figure below.

Step 3- Put few drops of ink on the watch glass.

Step 4- Now start heating the beaker.

Step 5- Continue heating as the evaporation goes on and stop heating when you do not see any further change on the watch glass.

Step 6- Observe carefully and record your observations.

Step 7- What do you think has got evaporated from the watch glass?

Step 8- Is there a residue on the watch glass? What is your interpretation?

Step 9- Is ink a single substance (pure) or is it a mixture?

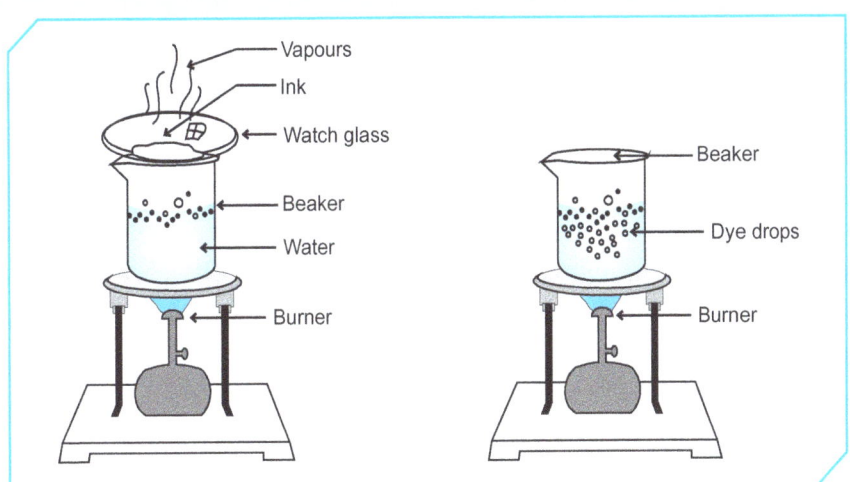

Fig. 2.68 : Experimental set-up for the separation of dye from ink by the process of evaporation.

OBSERVATION

The liquid present in the watch glass evaporates on heating. A residue will be left on the watch glass in a dry state. We can separate the volatile component (solvent) from its non-volatile solute by the method of evaporation. Ink is a mixture of a dye in water.

CONCLUSION

From this activity we can conclude that ink is not a single substance, but is a mixture of dye and water.

Applications of Evaporation

Separation of Common salt from Sea water

The common salt which we use daily in our cooking is obtained from the sea water. On large scale, the process of evaporation is used to recover common salt from the sea water which contains a large amount of common salt and salts of other metals dissolved in it. The sea water is collected into shallow ponds (commonly called salt pits) and allowed to evaporate in the sun. The heat from the sun increases the rate of evaporation and water changes into water vapour whereas the insoluble impurities such as sand, clay and slightly soluble impurities such as calcium carbonate settle to the bottom. The sea water is then pumped or moved by gravity flow to another pond where calcium sulphate settles out as evaporation continues. The remaining sea water is moved to another pond where the salt settles out as evaporation proceeds. The sea water is again moved one more time before evaporation is complete to prevent highly soluble impurities such as magnesium chloride, magnesium sulphate, potassium chloride, and magnesium bromide from settling out with the salt. The salt and other substances so obtained may be collected separately for commercial use (Fig. 2.69).

Fig. 2.69 : This figure shows the separation of common salt from sea water

(d) Separation by Distillation

In this method, both the non-volatile solid and the volatile liquid are recovered from a mixture. *The process of heating a liquid to form vapour and then cooling the vapour to get the liquid again is called distillation.* The method of distillation can be used to separate the mixture of two miscible liquids provided, the liquid components of the mixture boil without decomposition and have atleast or more than 25°C difference in their boiling points.

Principle

When the mixture is heated, the liquid component of the mixture evaporates while the solid component is left behind in the distillation flask. The vapours of the liquid are cooled or condensed to give back the pure liquid. The recovered liquid component is called the *distillate* while the solid is called the *residue*.

Process

The mixture of common salt and water is taken in a distillation flask with a thermometer and a water condenser (also called as Liebig's condenser). The distillation flask is a round bottomed flask having an inclined side tube at its neck. The side tube is connected to a water condenser which consists of a long glass tube surrounded by glass jacket through which cold water is circulated by means of inlet and outlet tubes. The distillation flask is heated and cold water is circulated through the water condenser. The water in the distillation flask is heated to produce vapours which is condensed by passing through the water condenser to give pure water which collects in the receiver. The common salt dissolved in a small quantity of water is left behind in the distillation flask. This left over semi-liquid matter is then transferred into an evaporating dish and the liquid is evaporated to recover the solid component, common salt. (Fig. 2.70).

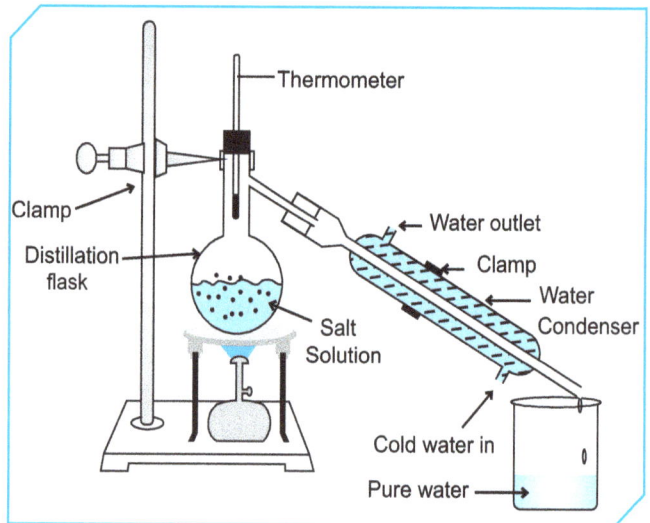

Fig. 2.70 : This figure shows the experimental set-up for carrying out the process of distillation.

Examples

(i) A mixture of salt and water (salt solution) can be separated into salt and water by the process of distillation.

(ii) Tap water which is a mixture of some impurities and dissolved salts can be converted into pure or distilled water by the process of distillation.

Let us perform an activity to separate miscible liquids by the process of distillation.

Activity 2.6 – To separate acetone and water from their mixture by the process of distillation.

PROCEDURE

Step 1– Take the mixture in a distillation flask.

Step 2– Fit it with a thermometer.

Step 3– Arrange the apparatus as shown in the figure.

Step 4– Heat the mixture slowly keeping a close watch at the thermometer.

Step 5– What do you observe as you start heating the mixture?

Step 6– At what temperature does the thermometer reading becomes constant for some time ?

Step 7– What is the boiling point of acetone ?

Step 8– Why do the two components separate ?

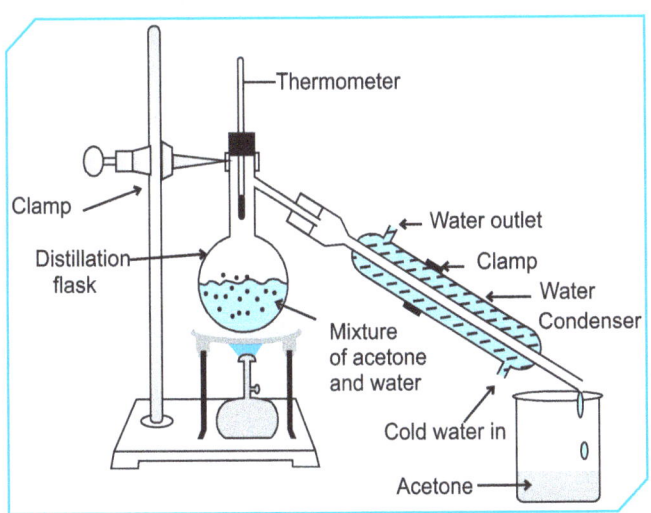

Fig. 2.71 : Experimental set-up for the separation of two miscible liquids by distillation.

OBSERVATION

The thermometer shows an increase in the temperature. At 56.5°C, the thermometer reading becomes constant for some time. At this temperature, acetone vapourizes, condenses and can be collected from the condenser outlet. Water is left behind in the distillation flask. Acetone boils at 56.5°C while water boils at 100°C. The two components of the mixture separate because acetone is more volatile than water.

CONCLUSION

The distillation process is used for the separation of components of a mixture containing two miscible liquids that boil without decomposition and have sufficient difference in their boiling points.

From the above activity we can conclude that distillation process can also be used to separate the components of mixture containing two miscible liquids having sufficient difference in their boiling points.

Note
- For complete separation of the components of mixture containing two miscible liquids, the process of fractional distillation is used.

Before we proceed to next topic, try to solve the following questions.

PAPER -PEN TEST : 11

1. How heterogeneous mixtures are separated?
2. Name the methods used to separate solid–liquid mixtures.
3. Define filtration.
4. How filter paper is made into filter paper cone?
5. Define filtrate.
6. What is meant by residue?
7. Explain the principle of the filtration process.
8. How tea leaves are separated from prepared tea by the process of filtration?
9. Give any three examples in which filtration process is used.
10. Explain the principle behind the supply of drinking water in a city.
11. Differentiate between sedimentation and decantation.
12. What do you understand by the term 'supernatant liquid'?
13. Give two examples for which the sedimentation and decantation processes are used.
14. Define evaporation.
15. Explain the principle of evaporation process.
16. Give any two examples for which evaporation is used.
17. Perform an activity to obtain coloured component or dye from blue or black dye by the process of evaporation.
18. Define distillation.
19. Explain the principle of distillation.

(e) Separation by Centrifugation

'The process of separating the suspended particles of a substance from a liquid in a mixture by churning it at high speed is called centrifugation'

Sometimes the solid suspended particles in a liquid are very small and can be separated by using a filter paper through the process of filtration. However, this process takes place very slowly. In order to separate the suspended particles of a substance in a liquid quickly, the method of centrifugation is used. In laboratories, centrifuge machine is used to carry out this process of centrifugation (Fig. 2.72).

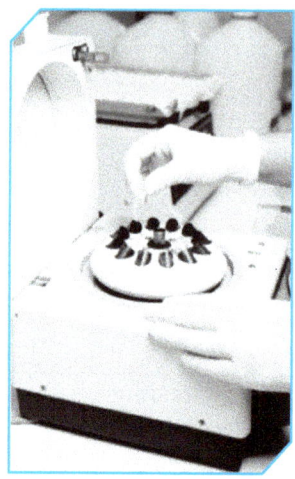

Fig. 2.72 : The centrifuge machine.

Principle

In this method, the mixture of fine suspended particles in a liquid is taken in centrifuge tube and placed in a centrifuge machine which is rotated rapidly at high speed for some time. Due to rapid rotation, the machine creates a force that acts on the heavier suspended particles and bring them to the bottom of the test tube. The clear liquid, being lighter remains at the top of the test tube. After centrifugation, both the layers can be separated by the process of decantation (Fig. 2.73).

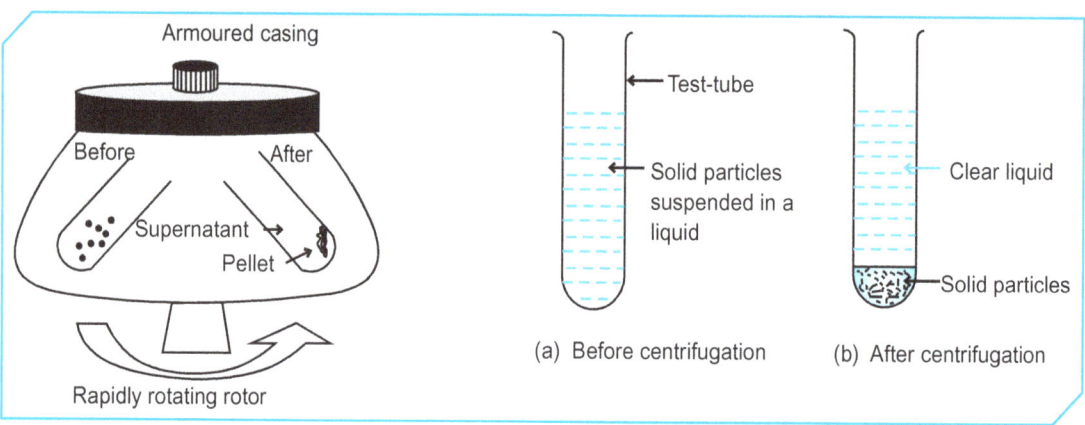

Fig. 2.73 : This figure shows the rotation of test-tubes containing suspension in a centrifuge machine.

Process

Blood can be separated into blood cells and plasma by the process of centrifugation. The sample blood is taken in a centrifuge tube and placed in a centrifuge machine. The tube is then rotated rapidly at high speed for some time in the machine. Due to this rapid rotation, the machine creates a force that acts on the blood and separates it into blood cells and plasma. They are then separated by the process of decantation (Fig. 2.74).

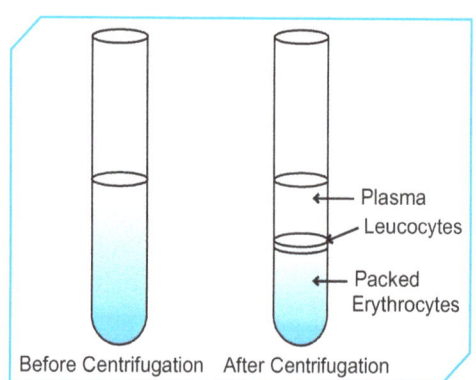

Fig. 2.74 : The centrifuge tubes in the figure shows the blood samples before and after centrifugation.

Examples

(i) Blood can be separated into blood cells and plasma.

(ii) Cream can be separated from milk.

(iii) Butter can be separated from curd.

Let us perform an activity to separate the cream from milk by the process of centrifugation.

Activity 2.7 - To separate cream from milk by the process of centrifugation.

PROCEDURE

Step 1– Take some full-cream milk in a test tube.

Step 2– Centrifuge it by using a centrifuging machine for two minutes.

Step 3– If a centrifuging machine is not available, you can use a milk churner.

Step 4– What do you observe on churning the milk?

Step 5- How cream is separated from milk?

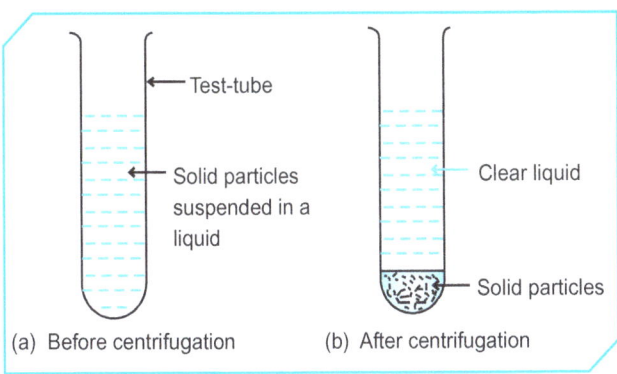

Fig. 2.75 : The centrifuge tubes in the figure shows the milk sample before and after centrifugation.

OBSERVATION

The number of soluble fats present in the milk collides with one another at high speed to form bigger particles in the form of cream. The cream formed is removed and leaves behind the fat free milk. Centrifugation works on the principle that the denser particles are forced to move to the bottom and the lighter particles stays at the top of the test tube when spin rapidly.

CONCLUSION

Cream can be separated from milk by the process of centrifugation.

(f) Separation by Chromatography

This technique was introduced by **M. S. Tsvet**, a Russian botanist in 1906. It is a method based on the difference in the rate of adsorption of various components of a mixture on a suitable adsorbent. There are four types of chromatography namely,

(i) Paper chromatography

(ii) Column chromatography

(iii) Thin layer chromatography

(iv) Gas chromatography

We shall discuss the last three types of chromatography in higher classes.

Note

- Adsorption is the process of accumulation of substances on the surface of a solid medium. A common adsorbent is a strip of filter paper of good quality.

- The different varieties of milk i.e, full-cream toned, single toned and double toned milk that are available in the market contain different amount of cream in milk. The process of centrifugation is used in dairies to separate cream from milk.

Paper Chromatography

Process

A base line is drawn at about one – third the distance from the edge of the filter paper. A spot of ink is placed at the centre of the line. The spot is dried and then the paper is suspended in a glass jar with its lower end immersed in the solvent. As the solvent rises through the filter paper and comes in contact with the spot, it gets dissolved and carries them along the paper. When the solvent is dried, the different spots of the colour appear at different intervals based on the rate of adsorption. The spotted paper after development with a suitable solvent is called *chromatogram*.

Principle

The principle of paper chromatography is based on the continuous differential partitioning of components of a mixture between stationary and mobile phases. In this process, the mixture of substances is applied onto a stationary phase which may be a solid or a liquid. A pure solvent, a mixture of solvents or a gas is allowed to move slowly over the stationary phase. The components of the mixture get gradually separated from one another. The moving phase is called the *mobile phase*.

Procedure

Green ink which is a mixture of various coloured components or dyes can be separated by paper chromatography. Take a thin and long strip of filter paper. Draw a base line at the bottom of the filter paper say 3 cm away from the base end. Now, put a drop of small green ink at the centre of the base line. After the ink dries, suspend the filter paper into a tall glass jar containing some amount of solvent i.e., a mixture of ethyl alcohol and water. Place the base line facing at the bottom without touching the solvent. The water gradually rises up the filter paper along with the dyes present in the ink. The blue dye which is more soluble in the solvent dissolves first and produces coloured spot on the filter paper at higher position. The yellow dye which is less soluble in the solvent rises slowly and forms coloured spots at lower heights. Thus, both blue and yellow dyes present in the green ink are separated (Fig. 2.76).

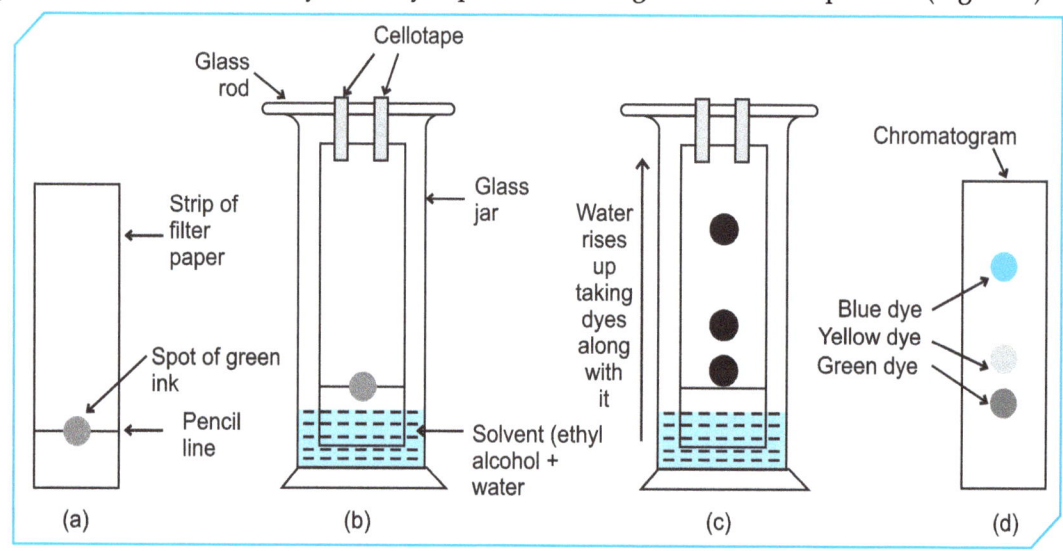

Fig. 2.76 : Separation of the colored components or dyes in green ink by paper chromatography.

Note

- The lower end of the filter paper strip should dip in water but the pencil line having the ink spot should remain above the water level in the glass jar.

Examples

(i) Separation of coloured samples from mixtures such as ink, dyes, pigments of flower etc.

(ii) Separation of small amounts of products in chemical reactions.

(iii) To detect the trace amount of substances in a given sample.

Applications of Chromatography

Chromatography has the following uses in the field of science.

(i) Separation of coloured samples from mixtures such as ink, dyes, pigments of flower etc.

(ii) Separation of small amounts of products in chemical reactions.

(iii) It is used in forensic science to detect the trace amount of substances like poison in the gall bladder or stomach.

Let us perform an activity to obtain coloured components or dyes from black ink by the gall process of chromatography.

Activity 2.8 To separate dyes in black ink using chromatography.

PROCEDURE

Step 1– Take a thin strip of filter paper.

Step 2– Draw a line on it using a pencil, approximately 3 cm above the lower edge as shown in the figure 2.77 (a).

Step 3– Put a small drop of ink (water soluble, that is, from a sketch pen or fountain pen) at the centre of the line.

Step 4– Allow it to dry.

Step 5– Put the filter paper into a jar, glass, beaker or test tube containing water so that the drop of ink on the paper is just above the water level, as shown in the figure (b).

Step 6– Leave it undisturbed.

Step 7– Watch carefully, as the water rises up on the filter paper.

Step 8– What do you observe on the filter paper as the water rises on it ?

Step 9– Do you obtain different colours on the filter paper strip ?

Step 10– What according to you can be the reason for the rise of the coloured spot on the paper strip ?

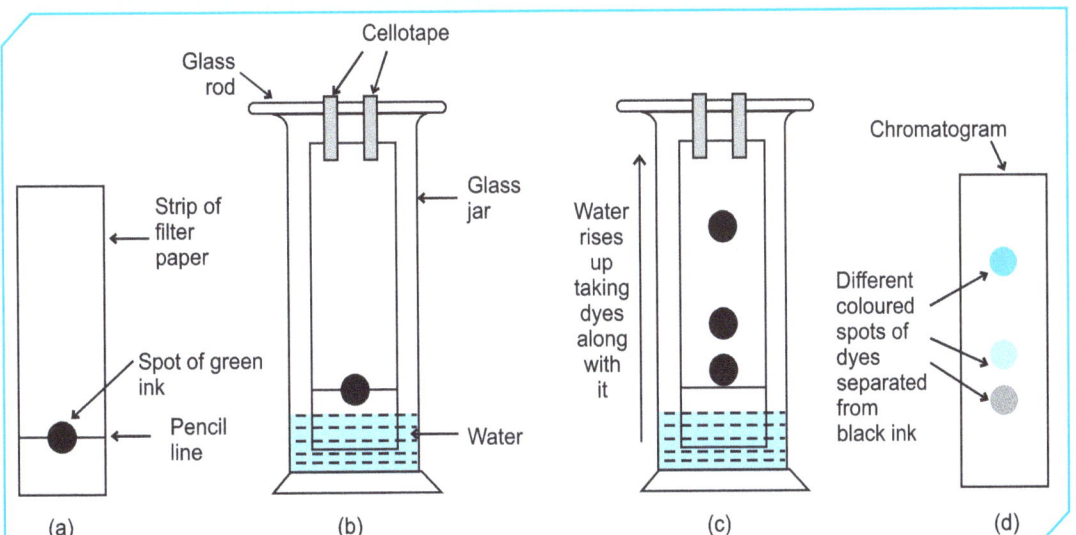

Fig. 2.77 : Experimental set-up showing the separation of coloured components or dyes from black ink by paper chromatography.

OBSERVATION

The ink that we use has water as the solvent and the dye is soluble in it and so when the water rises on the filter paper it takes along with it the dye particles. Yes, different coloured spots of dyes are obtained because a dye is a mixture of two or more colours. The coloured component is more soluble in water; therefore it rises faster on the paper strip.

CONCLUSION

Thus, coloured components can be separated from different mixtures by using chromatography.

(g) Purification by Crystallisation

This is one of the most commonly used techniques for the purification of solid organic compounds. If the compound is highly soluble in one solvent and very little soluble in another solvent, crystallisation can be satisfactorily carried out in a mixture of these solvents taken in appropriate proportions. Thus,

"The process of cooling a hot, concentrated solution of a substance to obtain crystals is called crystallisation".

Principle

It is based on the difference in the solubilities of the compound and the impurities in a suitable solvent. The impure solid compound is dissolved in a solvent in which it is sparingly soluble at room temperature but appreciably soluble at higher temperature. The solution is then concentrated by heating gently on a water bath to get a nearly saturated solution. Now, on cooling the hot saturated solution, the crystals of the pure solid compound is obtained. Crystals of pure compound so obtained are removed by filtration. The filtrate (mother liquor) contains dissolved impurities and a small quantity of the compound. Repeated crystallisation becomes necessary for the purification of compounds containing impurities of comparable solubilities.

Process

Pure alum crystals can be obtained from the sample of impure alum by the process of crystallisation. The impure alum is dissolved in water to form a solution. The solution is filtered to remove insoluble impurities. The clear solution is heated gently on a water bath till a concentrated solution is obtained. Then, the hot saturated solution is allowed to cool slowly. The crystals of pure alum are formed whereas the impurities remain dissolved in solution. The crystals of pure alum were separated by filtration and then dried (Fig. 2.78).

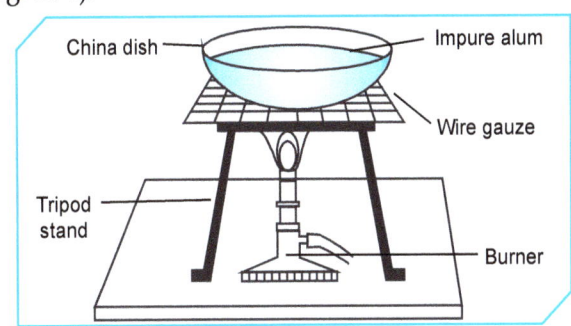

Fig. 2.78: Heating of impure alum to obtain pure crystals of alum by the process of crystallisation.

Examples

(i) Crystals of pure copper sulphate can be obtained from impure sample of copper sulphate.

(ii) Pure salt can be obtained from sea water on large scale.
(iii) Pure drugs can be obtained from an impure mixture.
(iv) Purification of impure sample of alum.

Let us perform an activity to obtain pure sample of copper sulphate from impure sample by the process of crystallization.

Activity 2.9 - To obtain pure copper sulphate from an impure sample by the process of crystallization.

PROCEDURE

Step 1– Take approximately 5 g impure sample of copper sulphate in a china dish.
Step 2– Dissolve it in a minimum amount of water.
Step 3– Filter the impurities out.
Step 4– Evaporate water from the copper sulphate solution by heating it on a water bath to get a saturated solution.
Step 5– Cover the solution with a filter paper and leave it undisturbed at room temperature to cool slowly for a day.
Step 6– What do you observe in the china dish?
Step 7– Do the crystals look alike?
Step 8– How will you separate the crystals from the liquid in the china dish?

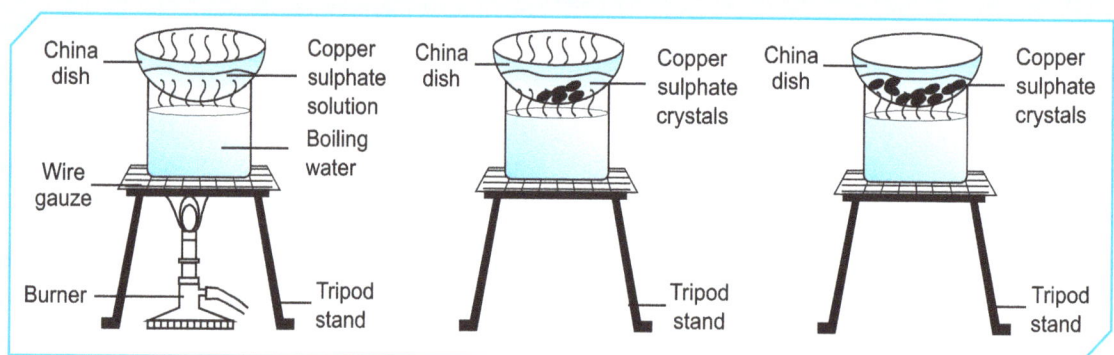

Fig. 2.79 : Experimental set-up for the purification of impure copper sulphate by crystallisation.

OBSERVATION

The crystals of pure copper sulphate in the china dish are observed. No the crystals are not alike. The pure crystals can be separated from the liquid in the china dish by filtration.

CONCLUSION

Thus, pure crystals of copper sulphate can be obtained from impure sample by the process of crystallisation.

Before we proceed to next topic, try to solve the following questions.

PAPER – PEN TEST : 12

1. Define centrifugation.
2. What is the advantage of using centrifugation method?
3. Explain the principle of centrifugation method.
4. Perform an activity to separate the cream from milk by the process of centrifugation.
5. Who introduced chromatography?
6. What are the different types of chromatography?
7. What is the basis of chromatography?

8. Explain the principle of chromatography.
9. Define chromatogram.
10. Perform an activity to obtain coloured component or dye from black ink by the process of chromatography.
11. Define crystallization.
12. Explain the principle of crystallization.
13. Perform an activity to obtain pure sample of copper sulphate from impure sample by the process of crystallisation.
14. Give examples of separation of solid-liquid mixtures.

2.14 SEPARATION OF LIQUID-LIQUID MIXTURE

Before we discuss the separation of mixtures containing two or more liquids, we should know about miscible and immiscible liquids. *Those liquids which mix together in all proportions and form a single layer are called miscible liquids.* For example, alcohol and water are miscible liquids as they mix together in all proportions. *Those liquids which do not mix together in all proportions and form separate layers are called immiscible liquids.* For example, oil and water are immiscible liquids as they do not mix together in all proportions. The miscible liquids can be separated by the process of fractional distillation while the immiscible liquids can be separated by using separating funnel. Thus, we can conclude that, when the mixture is made up of two liquid substances, anyone of the following methods can be used to separate the constituents :

(a) By using a separating funnel
(b) By fractional distillation

(a) Separation by a Separating Funnel

A mixture of two immiscible liquids which on intermixing form two distinct layers can be separated by using an apparatus called the *separating funnel*. The liquid mixture to be separated is taken in a separating funnel which has a stop-cock in its stem to allow or stop the flow of the lower layer of liquid from it. Thus, the liquids which do not mix easily i.e., immiscible liquids can be separated based on their density.

Principle

The principle involved in this method for the separation of two immiscible liquids is based on the difference in the densities of the liquids in the mixture. The two immiscible liquids are taken in separating funnel and are allowed to stand for some time. Based on the difference in the densities of liquid components, the lighter liquid forms the upper layer while the denser liquid forms the lower layer in the separating funnel. The stop-cock of the funnel is then opened slowly to collect the lower layer i.e., the heavier liquid from the separating funnel. When the lower layer completely runs down into a receiver placed below the funnel, the stop-cock is then closed. Later, the lighter liquid i.e., oil in the upper layer is removed by opening the stop-cock again and is collected in a separate receiver (Fig. 2.80).

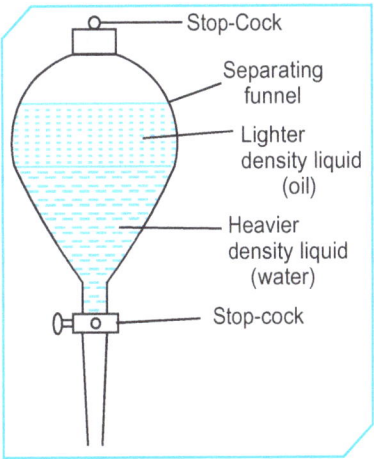

Fig. 2.80 : Separation of a mixture of two immiscible liquids by separating funnel based on the difference in their densities.

Process

Mix oil and water to form heterogeneous mixture. Pour the mixture in the separating funnel and allow it to stand for sometime. Due to the difference in the densities, mixture of oil and water always separates into two layers. The more dense liquid i.e., water will settle at the bottom of the separating funnel. It is removed by opening the stop-cock of the funnel and collected in a separate receiver. When the lower layer is removed completely, the stop-cock is closed. Later, the lighter liquid i.e., oil in the upper layer is removed by opening the stop-cock again and is collected in a separate receiver (Fig. 2.81).

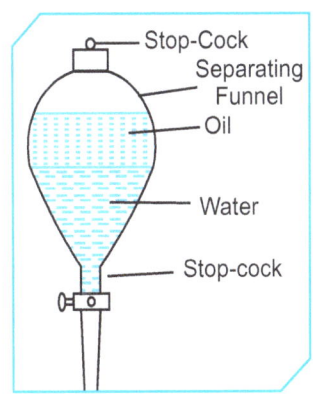

Fig. 2.81 : Separation of two immiscible liquids such as water and oil by using separating funnel.

Examples :

Following samples can be separated using the separating funnel.

(i) A mixture of groundnut oil and water.

(ii) A mixture of water and mustard oil.

(iii) A mixture of petrol and water.

(iv) A mixture of carbon disulphide and water.

(v) A mixture of mercury and water.

(vi) A mixture of chloroform and water.

(vii) A mixture of benzene and water.

(viii) A mixture of ether and water.

(ix) A mixture of mercury, water and benzene.

Note

- Mercury, chloroform and carbon disulphide are heavier than water and so are collected first. Benzene and ether are lighter than water and so are collected second.

Let us perform an activity to separate two immiscible liquids.

Activity 2.10 – To separate kerosene oil from water using a separating funnel.

PROCEDURE

Step 1– Pour the mixture of kerosene oil and water in a separating funnel as shown in the figure 2.82.

Step 2– Let it stand undisturbed for sometime. What do you observe?

Step 3– Open the stop-cock of the separating funnel.

Step 4– Pour out the lower layer of mixture carefully.

Step 5– Close the stopcock of the separating funnel as the oil reaches the stop-cock.

Step 6– What do you think is the principle behind this process?

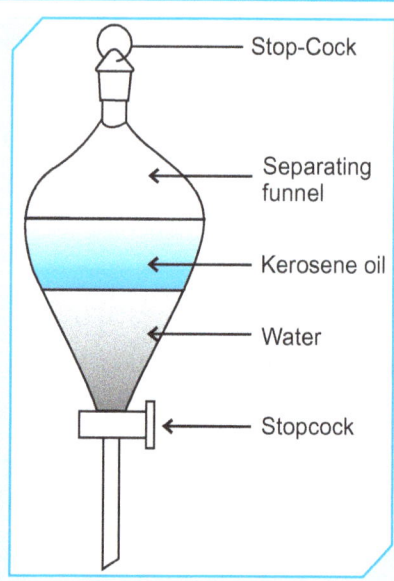

Fig. 2.82: Experimental set-up for the separation of immiscible liquids by using separating funnel.

OBSERVATION

Two distinct layers of kerosene oil and water are formed when separating funnel is left undisturbed for some time. This process is based on the principle that immiscible liquids separate out in layers depending on their densities.

CONCLUSION

A separating funnel helps in separating two immiscible liquids.

(b) Separation by Fractional Distillation

The process of separation of two or more miscible liquids with difference in their boiling points close to each other into individual components by distillation is called fractional distillation. In other words, fractional distillation method is used to separate mixtures of completely miscible liquids based on the difference in their boiling point temperatures. This method is applied when the mixture of liquids are miscible and have difference in their boiling points of the liquid less than 25°C under a pressure of one atmosphere.

Fractionating Column Apparatus

The fractions of liquids in a mixture are separated from each other by using an apparatus called *fractionating column*. A fractionating column is a long, vertical glass tube packed with glass beads. This provides a large surface area for hot vapours to cool and condense. Generally, a fractionating column is regarded as an arrangement to provide different temperature zones inside it with the highest temperature at the bottom of the column and the lowest at the top. There are various types of fractionating columns serving different purposes. The fractionating column is fitted to the neck of the distillation flask containing the mixture of liquids to be separated (Fig. 2.83).

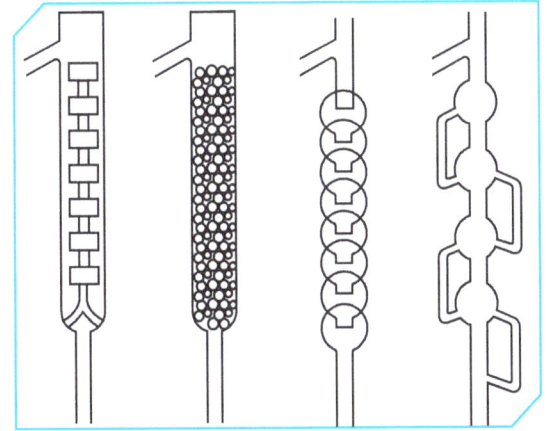

Fig. 2.83: Various fractionating columns used for fractional distillation.

Principle

The mixture of miscible liquid is heated in a distillation flask fitted with a fractionating column. Both the liquids produce vapours which rise up in the fractionating column. When the temperature at the top of the fractionating column reaches the boiling point of one liquid, the vapours of the liquid passes into condenser, gets cooled and is collected in a beaker kept at the other end of the condenser as distillate (Fig. 2.84).

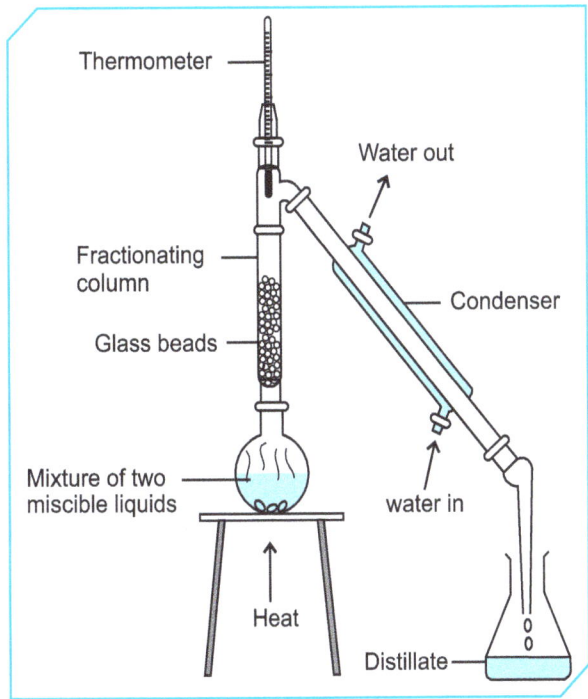

Fig. 2.84 : Experimental set-up showing the separation of two miscible liquids by fractional distillation.

Process

A mixture of ethanol and water is taken in a distillation flask fitted with a fractionating column. The mixture is heated to about 78°C i.e., the boiling point of the ethanol. The ethanol begins to boil. A mixture of ethanol and water vapours rises up the column. Since water has a higher boiling point than ethanol, it condenses back into the flask whereas the ethanol vapours moves up the column into the condenser, gets condensed into liquid ethanol and is collected in the beaker. When all ethanol is distilled over, the temperature reading on the thermometer rises to 100°C i.e., the boiling point of water. The water begins to boil and the vapours rises up the column and enter the condenser where it gets condensed and get collected in another beaker.

Note

The difference in the boiling points of liquids comprising the mixture is the basis for their separation by distillation process, i.e.,

- If the difference in the boiling points of the liquid components in a mixture is more than 25°C, separation is carried out through simple distillation.

- If the difference in the boiling points of the liquid component in a mixture is less than 25°C, separation is carried out through fractional distillation.

Examples

The following mixtures can be separated by the process of fractional distillation :

(i) A mixture of alcohol and water.
(ii) A mixture of sulphur dioxide and chlorine.
(iii) A mixture of ammonia and water.
(iv) A mixture (of liquid air) can be used to separate gases of the air.
(v) The mixture of crude oil petroleum can be separated into useful fractions.

Applications of Fractional Distillation

One of the main application of fractional distillation is to separate the gases of the air. Let us discuss how fractional distillation helps to separate the gases from air in detail.

Separation of Gases

We know that air is a homogeneous mixture and hence can be separated into its components by fractional distillation. But how can we obtain different gases from air?

We have already studied that air is a mixture of gases like carbon dioxide, oxygen, nitrogen, argon, helium, krypton, neon, xenon etc. But the major component of air is nitrogen (78.03%) and then oxygen (20.99%) followed by argon (0.93%). All the remaining gases of air constitute only 0.05% of air. The various gases of air can be separated from one another by fractional distillation of liquid air. The fractional distillation is based on the fact that the liquid air contains all the component gases in the liquid form which have different boiling points and so, when it is warmed, the liquefied gases present in it boil at different temperatures and gets collected separately at different heights in the fractional distillation column. The boiling points of three major components of air are tabulated below :

Boiling Points of the three Major Components of Air.

S. No	Gases	Boiling Point of liquefied gases
1.	Nitrogen	−196°C lowest
2.	Argon	−186°C
3.	Oxygen	−183°C highest

The liquid air can be separated into its constituent gases in the following steps :

Step 1– The air is first filtered to remove dust particles, water vapour and carbon dioxide.

Note

- If water vapour and carbon dioxide are not removed, they would become solid and block the pipes.

Step 2– The air is then compressed to a high pressure and cooled to expand quickly into a chamber through a jet.

Note

- This step helps to cool the air even more.

Step 3– The process of compression, cooling and quick expansion of air is repeated again and again in order to make the air cooler so that it turns into a liquid to obtain liquid air.

Step 4– The liquid air is fed into a fractional distillation column from its bottom and warmed slowly (Fig. 2.85).

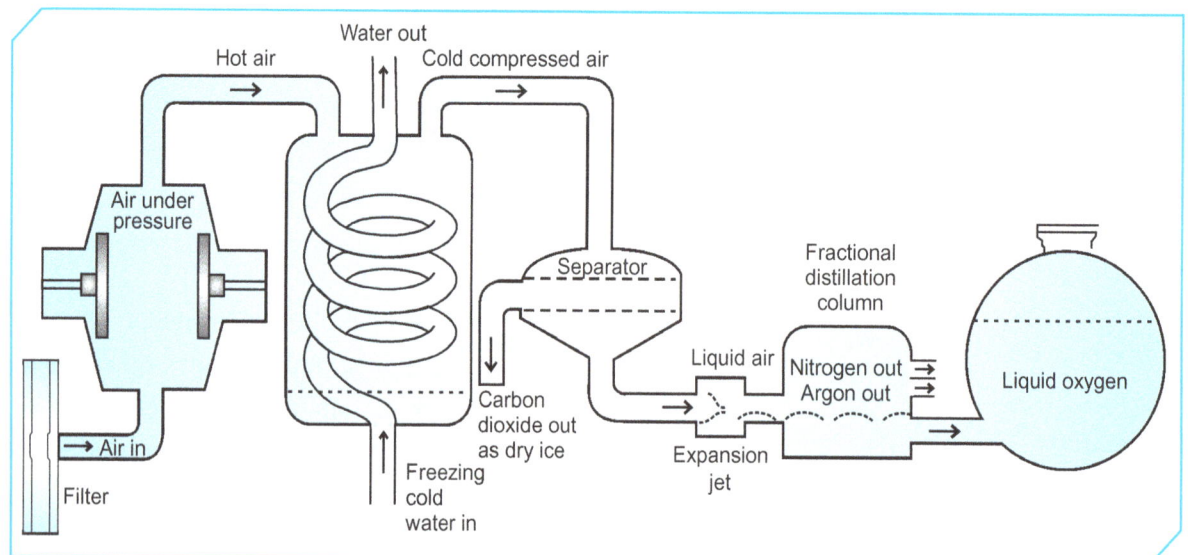

Fig. 2.85 : This figure shows separation of the components of air by fractional distillation.

OBSERVATION

(a) The liquid nitrogen which has the lowest boiling point of -196°C boils off first to form nitrogen gas and is collected from the top part of fractional distillation column.

(b) The liquid argon which has a slightly higher boiling point of -186°C than liquid nitrogen boils off next and is collected as argon gas in the middle part of the fractional distillation column.

(c) The liquid oxygen which has still higher boiling point of -183°C than argon boils off last and get collected as oxygen gas from the bottom part of the fractional distillation column.

The flow diagram given below shows the steps involved in separating the different gases from air (Fig. 2.86) :

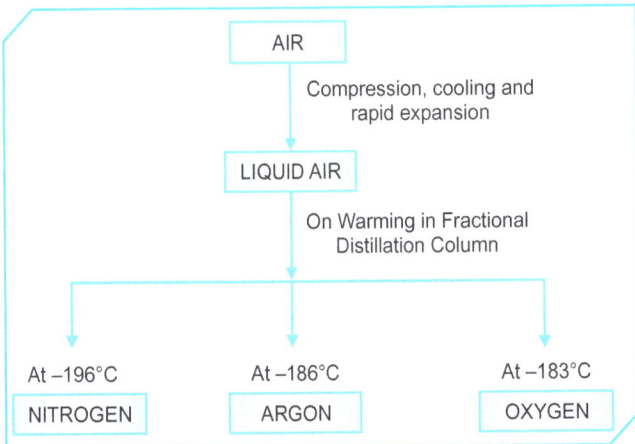

Fig. 2.86 : The flow chart shows the steps involved in the separation of different gases from air.

2.15 SEPARATION OF SOLID – GAS MIXTURES

This method is based on the fact that very fine solid particles in air can be settled by wetting with steam or by passing electricity. Air is thus freed of carbon particles present in smoke, or from local dust particles in coal mines. These methods are often adopted in industrial areas to have a pollution-free environment.

(a) **With Steam :** When steam is introduced into a chamber of smoke, water vapours condense on the carbon particles present in the smoke. The wet carbon particles become heavy and settle at the bottom of the chamber.

(b) **By Electricity :** Electricity is passed through a mixture of fine solid particles, carbon or dust particles in air. The solid particles gather together and on becoming heavy, settle under gravity.

2.16 PHYSICAL AND CHEMICAL CHANGE

Physical Change

A physical change is one in which the shape, size, appearance or state of a substance may alter, but its chemical composition remains the same. No new substance is formed. It is usually a change, which is reversible. By reversing the process, the original substance can be obtained.

For instance, a goldsmith can make a large variety of ornaments using gold pieces. But all of them consist of the same substance, namely gold. A more common example is that of water, which can be converted into solid ice, liquid water, and gaseous water vapour. It can be reconverted to its previous state by various methods. Yet, in all the three forms, the chemical composition of water is not altered. No new substance with new chemical properties is formed. In all these, water consists of two atoms of hydrogen and one atom of oxygen. Let us explain the physical changes with few examples (Fig. 2.87).

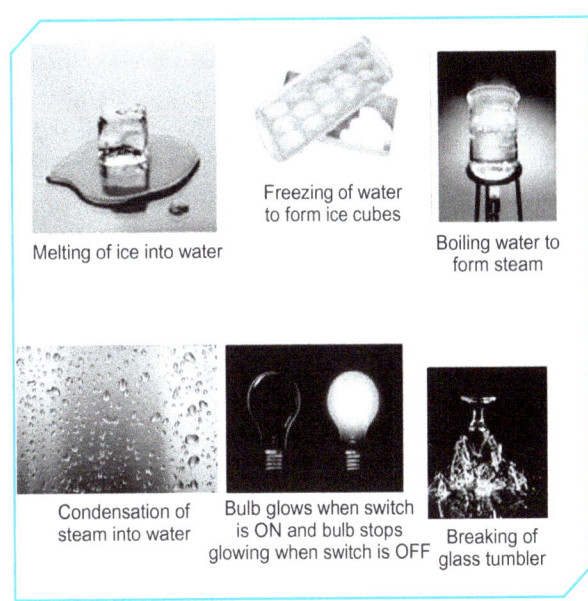

Fig. 2.87 : This figure shows the examples of physical changes

Example 1 : **Heating of Ice :** When ice is kept at room temperature, it starts melting to form water. Though ice and water are physically different, both are made up of water molecules.

Example 2 : **Freezing of Ice :** When water is refrigerated or cooled, it solidifies to form ice.

Example 3 : **Boiling of Water to Steam :** When water is heated strongly, it starts boiling to form steam. Though steam and water look different, both are made up of water molecules.

Example 4 : **Condensation of Steam :** When steam is cooled, it condenses to form water.

Example 5 : **Glowing of an Electric Bulb :** When an electric bulb is switched on, the electric current passes through its filament and it glows to give light. On the other hand, when the current is switched off, the filament returns to its normal condition and the bulb stops glowing. Hence, no new substance is formed during the process.

Example 6 : Breaking of a Glass Tumbler : When a glass tumbler breaks, it forms many small pieces. However, all the pieces are glasses. Thus, during the breaking of a glass tumbler, no new substance is formed.

Chemical Change

A change in which the composition of a substance is altered is called as chemical change. As a result, the original properties get changed and one or more new substances are formed. This means that chemical changes are irreversible. The components of a new substance formed cannot be separated by physical methods. It includes, burning of candle wax, burning of paper, ripening of fruits, growth of a plant, digestion of food, rusting of iron, formation of curd from milk, burning of fuels, formation of iron sulphide etc. Let us discuss the chemical change in detail with a few examples (Fig. 2.88).

Example 1 : Burning of Paper : When a sheet of paper is burnt, new substances like carbon dioxide, water vapour, smoke and ash are produced.

Example 2 : Cooking of Food : When we cook vegetables, a new substance i.e., a dish is formed. The vegetables contain organic substances like proteins and carbohydrates in various proportions. On heating, these organic substances break up into simpler or different compounds which give a different flavour to the cooked food.

Example 3 : Heating of Magnesium Wire : When magnesium wire is heated, it burns to form a new substance, white powder of magnesium oxide.

Since during all the above process, a new chemical substance is formed, all are chemical changes.

Fig. 2.88 : This figure shows the examples of chemical changes.

The necessary conditions required for a chemical change to occur are :

(a) A minimum amount of energy needed to initiate a reaction (activation energy) should be supplied in the form of heat, light or electric current. Since new products are formed in a chemical change, it is necessary to break the old bonds of the reactants to form new bonds. This breakage is done by the activation energy.

(b) For the occurrence of any reaction, the molecules or atoms of the reactants must collide with one another, in order to break old bonds and form new bonds.

Note

- The speed with which the chemical reaction takes place is called the rate of the chemical reaction.
- For example, both oxygen and water or water vapours are essential for rusting.

$$Fe + O_2 + H_2O \rightarrow Fe_2O_3.H_2O \text{ (Rust)}$$
Iron Oxygen water   Iron oxide
        (From air)

Let us try to differentiate physical and chemical change.

Differences between Physical Change and Chemical Change.

S. No	Characteristics	Physical Change	Chemical Change
1.	New substance	New substance is not formed.	New substance is formed.
2.	Nature	Temporary change.	Permanent change.
3.	Heat energy	It absorbs or gives out very little heat energy.	It absorbs or gives out lot of heat energy.
4.	Mass	Mass of the substance does not change.	Mass of the substance changes.
5.	Reversibility	It is easily reversible.	It is irreversible.

IS MATTER AROUND US PURE

Let us now try to solve the following questions.

PAPER – PEN TEST : 13

1. What are miscible and immiscible liquids? Give an example for each.
2. How are miscible liquids separated?
3. Name the process by which immiscible liquids are separated.
4. What is the principle of separating immiscible liquids using separating funnel?
5. Explain the process of separating oil and water using separating funnel.
6. Give any three examples of separation of immiscible liquids using separating funnel.
7. What is meant by fractional distillation?
8. What is the principle of fractional distillation?
9. Explain the fractional column apparatus with a neat sketch.
10. Explain the process of separating a mixture of alcohol and water by the process of fractional distillation with a neat sketch.
11. What is the difference between simple distillation and fractional distillation?
12. Give any three examples of separating miscible liquids using fractional distillation.
13. Give one application of fractional distillation.
14. Define air.
15. Name the major component of air.
16. What is the basis of separation of the different component gases from liquid air?
17. What would happen if water vapour and carbon dioxide are not removed in the process of separating air?
18. What is use of compressing the air to a high pressure?
19. Name the components of air collected in the order of decreasing temperature.
20. Draw a flow diagram to show the steps involved in separating the different gases from air.
21. Explain how solid and gaseous mixtures are separated?
22. Define physical change with an example.
23. Define chemical change with an example.
24. Differentiate between physical change and chemical change.
25. What are the conditions required for a chemical change to take place?
26. Define rate of a chemical reaction.
27. Give the chemical formula of rust.
28. What are the necessary conditions for rusting to take place?
29. Identify the physical change from the following: formation of clouds, mixing of iron filings and sand, formation of curd from milk, rusting of iron, melting of wax.

COMPENDIUM

- Anything which has mass and occupies space is called matter.
- Matter can be classified as pure substances or mixtures.
- A pure substance may either contain constituent particles of only one kind or of different kinds.
- A pure substance has a fixed composition.
- An element is a basic form of matter which cannot be broken down into simpler substances by any physical or chemical means.
- Elements can be broadly classified as- Metals, Non-metals and Metalloids.
- Metals are one category of elements that have lustre, conduct heat and electricity, sonorous, malleable and ductile.
- Non-metals are non-lustrous, non-sonorous and are bad conductors of heat and electricity.
- Metalloids are elements having properties intermediate between those of metals and non-metals.
- A compound is a pure substance composed of two or more elements chemically combined in a fixed proportion.
- A compound can be broken down into simpler substances by chemical or electrochemical methods.

- A mixture contains two or more elements or compounds which are mixed together in any proportion. In a mixture, no new compound is formed.
- A mixture shows the properties of its constituent substances.
- Mixtures are classified into two types namely, Homogeneous mixtures and Heterogeneous mixtures.
- Mixtures whose components mix completely with each other to make a uniform composition are called homogeneous mixtures.
- A heterogeneous mixture has a non-uniform composition.
- The ability of a substance to dissolve in another substance is called solubility.
- Homogeneous mixture of two or more substances is called a solution.
- The component of a solution present in smaller quantity is called a solute.
- The component of a solution present in large excess is called a solvent.
- The solution with high solute concentration is called concentrated solution and that with low concentration is called dilute solution.
- A solution that has dissolved maximum amount of solute at any particular temperature is said to be a saturated solution.
- If the amount of solute contained in a solution is less than the saturation level, it is called an unsaturated solution.
- The concentration of a solution is the amount of solute present in a given amount (mass or volume) of solvent or solution.
- Percentage by mass is one of the methods of expressing concentration of solution.
- There are two kinds of heterogeneous mixtures, colloids and suspensions.
- The colloids are mixtures with particle sizes from 1 nm to 1000 nm.
- The component of colloid present in small amount is called dispersed phase.
- The medium in which the colloidal particles are dispersed or suspend themselves is called dispersion medium.
- In a colloidal system, particles are always suspended and do not settle down. This constant collision of the particles in continuous motion is called Brownian movement.
- Scattering of a beam of light when light is passed through a colloidal solution is called the Tyndall effect.
- The colloids are classified according to the state (solid, liquid or gas) of the dispersed medium or dispersing medium and the dispersed phase.
- The colloid in which dispersed medium is a liquid and dispersed phase is solid, is called as sol.
- The colloid in which both dispersed phase and dispersed medium are in liquid state is called an emulsion.
- The colloid in which dispersed phase is either liquid or a solid and dispersed medium is a gas is called an aerosol.
- A suspension is a heterogeneous mixture in which the solute particles do not dissolve but remain suspended throughout bulk of medium.
- The particles of suspension are visible to naked eye.
- Suspensions are heterogeneous mixtures with particles that have a size greater than 1000 nanometers (nm).
- Magnetic impurities can be separated from non-magnetic impurities by magnetic separation.
- The volatile compounds can be separated from non-volatile compound by sublimation.
- Mixtures of two or more liquid components can be separated by simple or fractional distillation or by using a separating funnel.
- Simple distillation is used for separating liquids having a difference in boiling points of more than or equal to 25 K.
- Fractional distillation is used for separating liquids having a difference in boiling points of less than 25 K.
- Liquids that are immiscible in each other differ in their densities and so can be separated by making use of a separating funnel.
- The process, by which a soluble solid can be obtained from a solution by allowing the solvent to vaporize, is called evaporation.
- Chromatography is used for separation of those solutes which dissolve in same solvent.
- Chromatography is a method of separating and identifying various components in a mixture, which are present in small trace quantities.

- Mixture containing two solid substances out of which one is soluble in a particular solvent and other is insoluble can be separated by dissolving the soluble constituent in a suitable solvent and then separating the insoluble substance through filtration.
- The process of separating the suspended particles of an insoluble substance, from a liquid, by rotating it at high speed is called centrifugation.
- The change in which the shape, size, appearance or state of a substance may alter but its chemical composition remains the same is called a physical change.
- In a physical change no new substance is formed.
- Any change that involves the formation of a new substance and leads to a transformation of chemical identity is called chemical change.
- The chemical changes are usually accompanied with heat exchanges.
- The chemical changes are permanent changes which are usually irreversible.

EXERCISES (SOLVED)

NCERT INTEXT QUESTIONS

1. What is meant by a pure substance?

Ans : It is the substance which consists of only one type of particles having same chemical nature.

2. Differentiate between homogeneous and heterogeneous mixtures with examples.

Ans :

S. No	Homogeneous mixtures	Heterogeneous mixtures
1.	A homogeneous mixture is a mixture having a uniform composition throughout the mixture.	A heterogeneous mixture is a mixture having a non-uniform composition throughout the mixture.
2.	Examples – salt in water, sugar in water, copper sulphate in water, iodine in alcohol, alloy and air.	Examples – sodium chloride and iron filings, salt and sulphur, water and oil, chalk powder in water, wheat flour in water, milk and water.

3. How are sol, solution and suspension different from each other?

Ans :

S. No	Sol	Solution	Suspension
1.	It is a heterogeneous mixture.	It is a homogeneous mixture.	It is a heterogeneous mixture.
2.	The solute particles are so small that they cannot be seen with the naked eye.	The solute particles dissolve.	The solute particles can be seen with naked eye.
3.	The solute particles spread uniformly throughout the mixture.	The solute particles spread uniformly throughout the mixture.	The solute particles remain suspended throughout the bulk of the medium.

4. To make a saturated solution, 36 g of sodium chloride is dissolved in 100 g of water at 293 K. Find its concentration at this temperature.

Ans : Given,

Mass of sodium chloride (solute) = 36 g

Mass of water (solvent) = 100 g

Therefore,

Mass of solution = Mass of solute + Mass of solvent

Mass of solution = 36 + 100 = 136 g

Hence,

The concentration or mass percentage of the solution will be,

$$= \frac{\text{Mass of solute}}{\text{Mass of solution}} \times 100\%$$

$$= \frac{36}{136} \times 100 = 26.47\%$$

Hence, the concentration of sodium chloride is 26.47% by mass at 293K.

5. How will you separate a mixture containing kerosene and petrol (difference in their boiling points is more than 25°C), which are miscible with each other?

Ans : A mixture of miscible liquids having a difference in their boiling points more than 25°C can be separated without decomposition by distillation method. Thus, petrol and kerosene can be separated by distillation.

6. Name the technique to separate :
   (a) Butter from curd
   (b) Salt from sea water
   (c) Camphor from salt

Ans : (a) Centrifugation
   (b) Evaporation
   (c) Sublimation

7. What type of mixtures are separated by the technique of crystallization?

Ans : The process of crystallization is used to separate a mixture of solid containing impurities and a liquid. In this process, a pure solid in the form of crystals are separated from the solution.

8. Classify the following as physical or chemical change.
   (a) Cutting of trees.
   (b) Melting of butter in a pan.
   (c) Rusting of almirah.
   (d) Boiling of water to form steam.
   (e) Passing of electric current through water and the water breaking down into hydrogen and oxygen gases.
   (f) Dissolving common salt in water.
   (g) Making a fruit salad with raw fruits.
   (h) Burning of paper and wood.

Ans : (a) Physical change
   (b) Physical change
   (c) Chemical change
   (d) Physical change
   (e) Chemical change
   (f) Physical change
   (g) Physical change
   (h) Chemical change

9. Try segregating the things around you as pure substances and impure substances or mixtures.

Ans : Pure substances – Water, salt, sugar.

Mixtures – Soil, wood, air, rubber, milk, food, clothes.

NCERT EXERCISES QUESTIONS

1. Which separation techniques will you apply for the separation of the following?
   (a) Sodium chloride from its solution in water.
   (b) Ammonium chloride from a mixture containing sodium chloride and ammonium chloride.
   (c) Small pieces of metal in the engine oil of a car.
   (d) Different pigments from an extract of flower petals.
   (e) Butter from curd.
   (f) Oil from water.
   (g) Tea leaves from tea.
   (h) Iron pins from sand.
   (i) Fine mud particles suspended in water.

Ans : (a) Evaporation.
   (b) Sublimation.
   (c) Centrifugation and filtration.
   (d) Chromatography.
   (e) Centrifugation.
   (f) Using separating funnel.
   (g) Filtration.
   (h) Magnetic separation.
   (i) Centrifugation.

2. Write the steps you would use for making tea. Use the words: solution, solvent, solute, dissolve, soluble, insoluble, filtrate and residue.

Ans : Water is taken as a solvent in a saucer pan. The water (solvent) is allowed to boil. During heating, milk and tea leaves are added to the solvent as solutes to form a solution. The water (solvent) at higher temperature increases the solubility of compounds from the tea leaves which produces the typical tea flavour. The solution is heated for some time to allow more of the tea compounds to dissolve in the solution. Then, the solution is poured through a strainer (filter). The insoluble part of the solution remains on the strainer as residue. Sugar is added to the filtrate which dissolves in it. The resulting solution is the tea.

3. Pragya tested the solubility of four different substances at different temperatures and collected the data as given below: (results are given in the following table, as grams of substance dissolved in 100 grams of water to form a saturated solution).

Substance Dissolved (g)	Temperature in Kelvin (K)				
	283	293	313	333	353
Potassium nitrate	21	32	62	106	167
Sodium chloride	36	36	36	37	37
Potassium chloride	35	35	40	46	54
Ammonium chloride	24	37	41	55	66

(a) What mass of potassium nitrate would be needed to produce a saturated solution of potassium nitrate in 50 grams of water at 313 K?

(b) Pragya makes a saturated solution of potassium chloride in water at 353 K and leaves the solution to cool at room temperature. What would she observe as the solution cools? Explain.

(c) Find the solubility of each salt at 293 K. Which salt has the highest solubility at this temperature?

(d) What is the effect of change of temperature on the solubility of a salt?

Ans : (a) In order to prepare saturated solution, the mass of potassium nitrate required at 313 K is 62 g i.e., 62 g of potassium nitrate is required in 100 g of water at 313 K. Hence, in 50 g of water, the potassium nitrate required will be,

$$\frac{62 \times 50}{100} = 31 g$$

(b) The amount of potassium chloride required to prepare saturated solution at 353 K is 54 g, at 293 K is 35 g. Hence,

54 – 35 = 19 g

Thus, 19 g of potassium chloride will come out as undissolved salt.

(c) The solubility of potassium nitrate, sodium chloride, potassium chloride and ammonium chloride at 293 K is 32, 36, 35 and 37 g respectively. Hence, ammonium chloride has the highest solubility at 293 K.

(d) The solubility of salt increases with increase in temperature and decreases with decrease in temperature.

4. Explain the following giving examples.
   (a) Saturated solution
   (b) Pure substance
   (c) Colloid
   (d) Suspension

Ans : (a) A solution in which no more solute can be dissolved in a definite amount of solvent at a given temperature is called a saturated solution. If more solute is added, it will settle down at the bottom of the container as a precipitate. For example – If 500 g of a solvent dissolves a maximum of 150 g of a particular solute at 40°C, then the solution obtained by dissolving 150 g of that solute in 500 g of that solvent at 300 K is said to be a saturated solution at 300 K.

(b) A pure substance is a substance consisting of only one type of particles having same chemical nature. For example salt, sugar and water are pure substances.

(c) A colloid is a heterogeneous mixture in which the size of the solute particles is so small that they cannot be seen with naked eyes. The particles of the solute get distributed uniformly throughout the mixture. The solute particles do not settle down when the mixture is left undisturbed. Hence, colloid is stable. Colloids cannot be separated by the process of filtration but can be separated by centrifugation process. Colloids show Tyndall effect. For example, smoke, clouds, milk, butter, foam, fog etc.

(d) Suspensions are heterogeneous mixtures in which the solute particles remain suspended throughout the bulk of the medium. The particles can be seen with naked eyes. Suspension shows Tyndall effect. The solute particles settle down when the mixture is left undisturbed. Hence, suspension is unstable. Suspensions can be separated by the process of filtration. For examples, chalk powder and water, wheat flour and water.

5. Classify each of the following as a homogeneous or heterogeneous mixture.

(a) Soda water
(b) Wood
(c) Air
(d) Soil
(e) Vinegar
(f) Filtered tea

Ans : (a) Homogeneous mixture
(b) Heterogeneous mixture
(c) Homogeneous mixture
(d) Heterogeneous mixture
(e) Homogeneous mixture
(f) Heterogeneous mixture

6. How would you confirm that a colourless liquid given to you is pure water?

Ans : Every liquid has characteristic boiling point. Likewise, pure water has boiling point of 373 K or 100°C at 1 atmospheric pressure. If the given colourless liquid boils at even slightly above or below 100°C, at 1 atmospheric pressure, then the given liquid is not pure water.

7. Which of the following materials fall in the category of a "pure substance"?

(a) Ice
(b) Milk
(c) Iron
(d) Hydrochloric acid
(e) Calcium oxide
(f) Mercury
(g) Brick
(h) Wood
(i) Air

Ans : Ice, iron, hydrochloric acid, calcium oxide and mercury are pure substances.

8. Identify the solutions among the following mixtures.

(a) Soil
(b) Sea water
(c) Air
(d) Coal
(e) Soda water

Ans : Sea water, air and soda water are solutions.

9. Which of the following will show Tyndall effect ?

(a) Salt solution
(b) Milk
(c) Copper sulphate solution
(d) Starch solution

Ans : Milk and starch solution will show Tyndall effect.

10. Classify the following into elements, compounds and mixtures.

(a) Sodium
(b) Soil
(c) Sugar solution
(d) Silver
(e) Calcium carbonate
(f) Tin
(g) Silicon
(h) Coal
(i) Air
(j) Soap
(k) Methane
(l) Carbon dioxide
(m) Blood

Ans : **Element :** Sodium, Silver, Tin, Silicon

Mixture : Soil, Sugar Solution, Coal, Air, Soap, Blood

Compound : Calcium Carbonate, Methane, Carbon dioxide

11. Which of the following are chemical changes?

(a) Growth of a plant
(b) Rusting of iron

(c) Mixing of iron filings with sand
(d) Cooking of food
(e) Digestion of food
(f) Freezing of water
(g) Burning of a candle

Ans : Growth of a plant, rusting of iron, cooking of food, digestion of food and burning of a candle are chemical changes.

NCERT EXEMPLAR QUESTIONS

1. Which of the following statements are true for pure substances?
   (i) Pure substances contain only one kind of particles.
   (ii) Pure substances may be compounds or mixtures.
   (iii) Pure substances have the same composition throughout.
   (iv) Pure substances can be exemplified by all elements other than nickel.
   (a) (i) and (ii) (b) (i) and (iii)
   (c) (iii) and (iv) (d) (ii) and (iii)

2. Rusting of an article made up of iron is called :
   (a) Corrosion and it is a physical as well as chemical change
   (b) Dissolution and it is a physical change
   (c) Corrosion and it is a chemical change
   (d) Dissolution and it is a chemical change

3. A mixture of sulphur and carbon disulphide is :
   (a) Heterogeneous and shows Tyndall effect.
   (b) Homogeneous and shows Tyndall effect.
   (c) Heterogeneous and does not show Tyndall effect.
   (d) Homogeneous and does not show Tyndall effect.

4. Tincture of iodine has antiseptic properties. This solution is made by dissolving :
   (a) Iodine in potassium iodide
   (b) Iodine in vaseline
   (c) Iodine in water
   (d) Iodine in alcohol

5. Which of the following are homogeneous in nature?
   (i) ice (ii) wood (iii) soil (iv) air
   (a) (i) and (iii) (b) (ii) and (iv)
   (c) (i) and (iv) (d) (iii) and (iv)

6. Which of the following are physical changes?
   (i) Melting of iron metal
   (ii) Rusting of iron
   (iii) Bending of an iron rod
   (iv) Drawing a wire of iron metal
   (a) (i), (ii) and (iii) (b) (i), (ii) and (iv)
   (c) (i), (iii) and (iv) (d) (ii), (iii) and (iv)

7. Which of the following are chemical changes?
   (i) Decaying of wood
   (ii) Burning of wood
   (iii) Sawing of wood
   (iv) Hammering of a nail into a piece of wood
   (a) (i) and (ii) (b) (ii) and (iii)
   (c) (iii) and (iv) (d) (i) and (iv)

8. Two substances, A and B were made to react to form a third substance, A_2B according to the following reaction
   $$2A + B \rightarrow A_2B$$
   Which of the following statements concerning this reaction are incorrect?
   (i) The product A_2B shows the properties of substances A and B
   (ii) The product will always have a fixed composition
   (iii) The product so formed cannot be classified as a compound
   (iv) The product so formed is an element
   (a) (i), (ii) and (iii), (b) (ii), (iii) and (iv)
   (c) (i), (iii) and (iv) (d) (ii), (iii) and (iv)

9. Two chemical species X and Y combine together to form a product P which contains both X and Y
   $$X + Y \rightarrow P$$
   X and Y cannot be broken down into simpler substances by simple chemical reactions. Which of the following concerning the species X, Y and P are correct?
   (i) P is a compound
   (ii) X and Y are compounds

(iii) X and Y are elements

(iv) P has a fixed composition

(a) (i), (ii) and (iii),   (b) (i), (ii) and (iv)

(c) (ii), (iii) and (iv)   (d) (i), (iii) and (iv)

ANSWERS

1. (b), 2. (c), 3. (d), 4. (d), 5. (c), 6. (c), 7. (a), 8. (c), 9. (d).

10. Suggest separation technique(s) one would need to employ to separate the following mixtures :

    (a) Mercury and water

    (b) Potassium chloride and ammonium chloride

    (c) Common salt, water and sand

    (d) Kerosene oil, water and salt

Ans : (a) Separation by using separating funnel.

(b) Sublimation.

(c) Filtration followed by evaporation or centrifugation followed by evaporation or distillation.

(d) Separation by using separating funnel to separate kerosene oil followed by evaporation or distillation.

11. Which of the tubes in figure given below will be more effective as a condenser in the distillation apparatus?

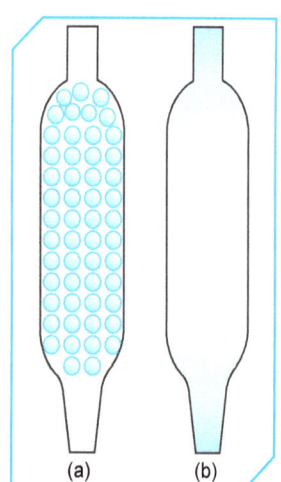

Ans : Tube (a) will be more effective as condenser because the presence of beads in tube would provide a larger surface area for cooling.

12. Salt can be recovered from its solution by evaporation. Suggest some other technique for the same?

Ans : Crystallization, distillation.

13. The 'sea-water' can be classified as a homogeneous as well as heterogeneous mixture. Comment.

Ans : Since sea water contains mixture of salts and water, it is considered as homogeneous mixture. But it also contains suspended impurities like mud, decayed plant or animal material etc. Hence, it is also classified as heterogeneous mixture. Also samples of sea water from different geographical areas might show slightly different constitution or properties in terms of salts constitution and impurity constitution. Hence it is also classified as heterogeneous mixture.

14. While diluting a solution of salt in water, a student by mistake added acetone (boiling point 56°C). What technique can be employed to get back the acetone? Justify your choice.

Ans : Since, the boiling point of acetone is 56°C and boiling point of water is 100°C, and for distillation the minimum difference in temperature should be 25°C. Thus, the process of distillation can be employed to get back the acetone. Acetone, being more volatile than water will separate out first.

15. What would you observe when?

    (a) A saturated solution of potassium chloride prepared at 60°C is allowed to cool to room temperature.

    (b) An aqueous sugar solution is heated to dryness.

    (c) A mixture of iron filings and sulphur powder is heated strongly.

Ans : (a) Solid potassium chloride will separate out.

(b) Initially, the water will evaporate and then sugar will get charred.

(c) Iron sulphide will be formed.

16. Explain why particles of a colloidal solution do not settle down when left undisturbed, while in the case of a suspension they do.

Ans : Particle size in a suspension is larger than those in a colloidal solution. Hence, the molecular interaction in a suspension is not strong enough to keep the particles suspended and so they settle down. But the particles of a colloidal solution do not settle down when left undisturbed.

17. Smoke and fog both are aerosols. In what way are they different?

Ans : Both fog and smoke have gas as the dispersion medium. The only difference is that the dispersed phase in fog is liquid (water droplets) and in smoke it is solid (carbon and ash particles).

18. Classify the following as physical or chemical properties.

    (a) The composition of a sample of steel is: 98% iron, 1.5% carbon and 0.5% other elements.

    (b) Zinc dissolves in hydrochloric acid with the evolution of hydrogen gas.

    (c) Metallic sodium is soft enough to be cut with a knife.

    (d) Most metal oxides form alkalis on interacting with water.

Ans : Physical properties – (a) and (c)

Chemical properties – (b) and (d)

19. The teacher instructed three students 'A', 'B' and 'C' respectively to prepare 50% (mass by volume) solution of sodium hydroxide (NaOH). 'A' dissolved 50g of NaOH in 100 mL of water, 'B' dissolved 50g of NaOH in 100g of water while 'C' dissolved 50g of NaOH in water to make 100 mL of solution. Which one of them has made the desired solution and why?

Ans : 'C' has made the desired solution. This is because :

$$\text{Mass by volume\%} = \frac{\text{Mass of solute}}{\text{Volume of solution}} \times 100\%$$

$$= \frac{50}{100} \times 100$$

$$= 50\% \text{ mass by volume}$$

20. Name the process associated with the following:

    (a) Dry ice is kept at room temperature and at one atmospheric pressure.

    (b) A drop of ink placed on the surface of water contained in a glass spreads throughout the water.

    (c) A potassium permanganate crystal is in a beaker and water is poured into the beaker with stirring.

    (d) An acetone bottle is left open and the bottle becomes empty.

    (e) Milk is churned to separate cream from it.

    (f) Settling of sand when a mixture of sand and water is left undisturbed for some time.

    (g) Fine beam of light entering through a small hole in a dark room, illuminates the particles in its paths.

Ans : (a) Sublimation.

(b) Diffusion.

(c) Dissolution or diffusion.

(d) Evaporation, diffusion.

(e) Centrifugation.

(f) Sedimentation.

(g) Scattering of light (Tyndall effect).

21. You are given two samples of water labelled as 'A' and 'B'. Sample 'A' boils at 100°C and sample 'B' boils at 102°C. Which sample of water will not freeze at 0°C? Comment.

Ans : Sample 'B' will not freeze at 0°C because it is not pure water. At 1 atm, the boiling point of pure water is 100°C and the freezing point of pure water is 0°C.

22. What are the favourable qualities given to gold when it is alloyed with copper or silver for the purpose of making ornaments?

Ans : Pure gold is very soft as compared to gold alloyed with silver or copper. Thus, for providing strength to gold, it is alloyed.

23. An element is sonorous and highly ductile. Under which category would you classify this element? What other characteristics do you expect the element to possess?

Ans : The element is a metal. Other characteristics expected to be possessed by the element are– lustre, malleability, heat and electrical conductivity.

24. Give an example each for the mixture having the following characteristics. Suggest a suitable method to separate the components of these mixtures.

    (a) A volatile and a non-volatile component.

    (b) Two volatile components with appreciable difference in boiling points.

    (c) Two immiscible liquids.

    (d) One of the component changes directly from solid to gaseous state.

    (e) Two or more coloured constituents soluble in some solvent.

Ans : (a) Example : Salt from sea water

Evaporation or distillation

(b) Example : Mixture of acetone (boiling point 56.5°C) and water (boiling point 100°C)

Distillation

(c) Example : Separating oil and water
Separation by using separating funnel

(d) Example : Mixture of Iodine and sand
Sublimation

(e) Example : Coloured dyes from ink
Chromatography

25. Fill in the blanks :

(a) A colloid is a ---------------------- mixture and its components can be separated by the technique known as ------------.

(b) Ice, water and water vapour look different and display different ----------------------- properties but they are ----------------------- the same.

(c) A mixture of chloroform and water taken in a separating funnel is mixed and left undisturbed for some time. The upper layer in the separating funnel will be of ---------- and the lower layer will be that of -------------

(d) A mixture of two or more miscible liquids, for which the difference in the boiling points is less than 25 K can be separated by the process called ------------------.

(e) When light is passed through water containing a few drops of milk, it shows a bluish tinge. This is due to the -------------of light by milk and the phenomenon is called ------------------. This indicates that milk is a ------------- solution.

Ans : (a) Heterogeneous, centrifugation

(b) Physical, chemically

(c) Water, chloroform (hint- density of water is less than that of chloroform)

(d) Fractional distillation

(e) Scattering, Tyndall effect, colloidal

26. Sucrose (sugar) crystals obtained from sugarcane and beetroot are mixed together. Will it be a pure substance or a mixture? Give reasons for the same.

Ans : It is a pure substance because chemical composition of sugar crystals is same irrespective of its source.

27. Give some examples of Tyndall effect observed in your surroundings?

Ans : Tyndall effect can be seen when light passes through a heterogeneous mixture. Example, when sunlight passes through the canopy of trees in a dense forest.

28. Can we separate alcohol dissolved in water by using a separating funnel? If yes, then describe the procedure. If not, explain.

Ans : Water and alcohol are miscible therefore; they cannot be separated using a separating funnel.

29. On heating, calcium carbonate gets converted into calcium oxide and carbon dioxide.

(a) Is this a physical or a chemical change?

(b) Can you prepare one acidic and one basic solution by using the products formed in the above process? If so, write the chemical equation involved.

Ans : (a) Chemical change

(b) Acidic and basic solutions can be prepared by dissolving the products of the above process in water.

$CaO + H_2O \rightarrow Ca(OH)_2$ (basic solution)

$CO_2 + H_2O \rightarrow H_2CO_3$ (acidic solution)

30. Non-metals are usually poor conductors of heat and electricity. They are non-lustrous, non-sonorous and non-malleable and are coloured.

(a) Name a lustrous non-metal.

(b) Name a non-metal which exists as a liquid at room temperature.

(c) Name the allotropic form of a non-metal which is a good conductor of electricity.

(d) Name a non-metal which is known to form the largest number of compounds.

(e) Name a non-metal other than carbon which shows allotropy.

(f) Name a non-metal which is required for combustion.

Ans : (a) Iodine

(b) Bromine

(c) Graphite

(d) Carbon

(e) Sulphur, phosphorus

(f) Oxygen

31. Classify the substances given in the figure below into elements and compounds

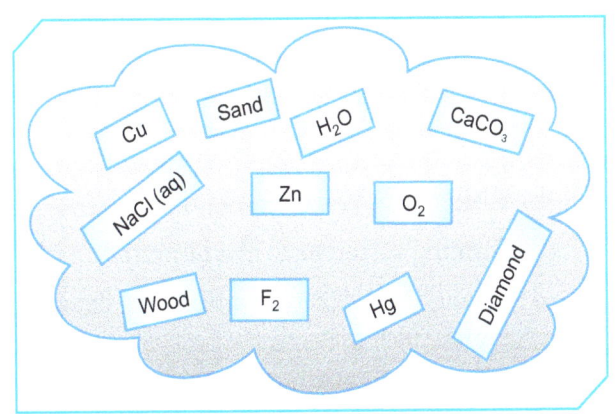

Ans : Elements – Cu, Zn, F_2, O_2, Diamond (carbon), Hg

Compounds : $CaCO_3$, H_2O

32. Which of the following are not compounds?

(a) Chlorine gas

(b) Potassium chloride

(c) Iron

(d) Iron sulphide

(e) Aluminium

(f) Iodine

(g) Carbon

(h) Carbon monoxide

(i) Sulphur powder

Ans : Chlorine gas, iron, aluminium, iodine, carbon, sulphur powder are not compounds.

33. Fractional distillation is suitable for separation of miscible liquids with a boiling point difference of about 25 K or less. What part of fractional distillation apparatus makes it efficient and possess an advantage over a simple distillation process. Explain with the help of a diagram.

Ans : The fractionating column packed with glass beads provides a surface for the vapours to collide and lose energy so that they can be quickly condensed and distilled. Also, length of the column would increase the efficiency. Hence, fractionating column of fractional distillation apparatus makes it more efficient as compared to the simple distillation process.

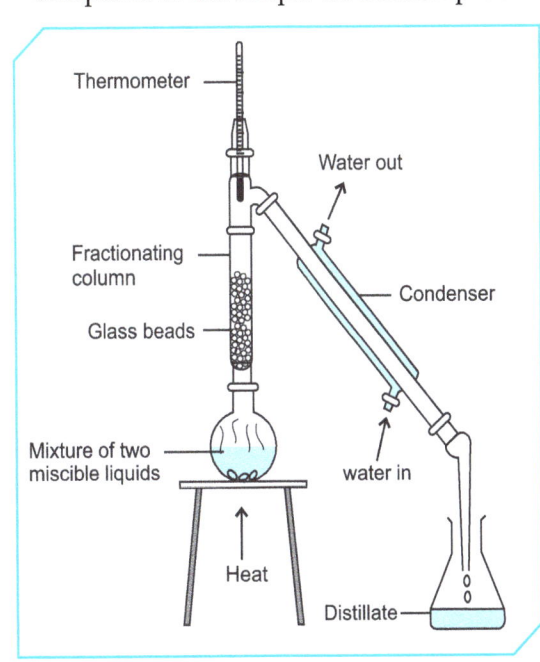

34. (a) Under which category of mixtures will you classify alloys and why?

(b) Comment: "A solution is always a liquid".

(c) Can a solution be heterogeneous?

Ans : (a) Homogenous mixture, because they have a uniform composition throughout.

(b) No, solid solutions and gaseous solutions are also possible. Examples - brass and air.

(c) No, solution is a homogenous mixture of two or more substances.

35. A child wanted to separate the mixture of dyes constituting a sample of ink. He marked a line by the ink on the filter paper and placed the filter paper in a glass containing water as shown in the given figure. The filter paper was removed when the water moved near the top of the filter paper.

(i) What would you expect to see, if the ink contains three different coloured components?

(ii) Name the technique used by the child.

(iii) Suggest one more application of this technique.

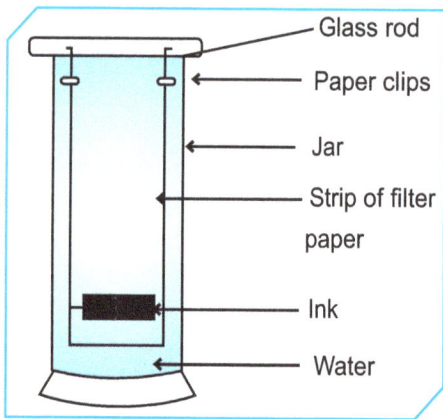

Ans : (i) Three different coloured bands will be observed.

(ii) Chromatography.

(iii) To separate the pigments present in Chlorophyll.

36. A group of students took an old shoe box and covered it with a black paper from all sides. They fixed a source of light (a torch) at one end of the box by making a hole in it and made another hole on the other side to view the light. They placed a milk sample contained in a beaker or tumbler in the box as shown in the figure given below. They were amazed to see that milk taken in the tumbler was illuminated. They tried the same activity by taking a salt solution but found that light simply passed through it?

(a) Explain why the milk sample was illuminated. Name the phenomenon involved.

(b) Same results were not observed with a salt solution. Explain.

(c) Can you suggest two more solutions which would show the same effect as shown by the milk solution?

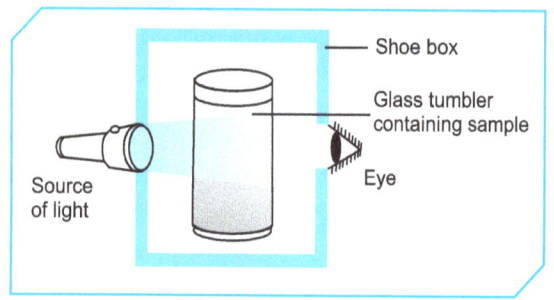

Ans : (a) Milk is a colloid and would show Tyndall effect.

(b) Salt solution is a true solution and would not scatter light.

(c) Detergent solution, sulphur solution.

37. Classify each of the following as a physical or a chemical change. Give reasons.

(a) Drying of a shirt in the sun.

(b) Rising of hot air over a radiator.

(c) Burning of kerosene in a lantern.

(d) Change in the colour of black tea on adding lemon juice to it.

(e) Churning of milk cream to get butter.

Ans : Physical changes — (a), (b), (e)

Chemical changes — (c), (d)

38. During an experiment the students were asked to prepare a 10% (Mass/Mass) solution of sugar in water. Ramesh dissolved 10g of sugar in 100g of water while Sarika prepared it by dissolving 10g of sugar in water to make 100g of the solution.

(a) Are the two solutions of the same concentration?

(b) Compare the mass percentage of the two solutions.

Ans : (a) No.

(b) We know,

$$\text{Mass}(\%) = \frac{\text{Mass of solute}}{\text{Mass of solute + Mass of solvent}} \times 100\%$$

Solution made by Ramesh

Mass of solute = 10 gram

Mass of solution = 100 gram + 10 gram = 110 gram

Hence, $\text{Mass \%} = \left(\frac{10}{10+100}\right) \times 100\%$

$= \frac{10}{110} \times 100 = 9.09\%$

Solution made by Sarika

Mass of solute = 10 gram

Mass of solution = 100 gram

Hence,

$\text{Mass \%} = \frac{10}{100} \times 100 = 10\%$

39. You are provided with a mixture containing sand, iron filings, ammonium chloride and sodium chloride. Describe the procedures you would use to separate these constituents from the mixture?

Ans : Step 1- Separate iron filings with the help of a magnet.

Step 2- Sublimation of the remaining mixture separates ammonium chloride.

Step 3- Add water to the remaining mixture, stir and filter.

Step 4- The filtrate can be evaporated to get back sodium chloride. The residue in filter paper is sand.

40. Arun has prepared 0.01% (by mass) solution of sodium chloride in water. Which of the following correctly represents the composition of the solutions?

(a) 1.00 g of NaCl + 100g of water

(b) 0.11g of NaCl + 100g of water

(c) 0.01 g of NaCl + 99.99g of water

(d) 0.10 g of NaCl + 99.90g of water

Ans : (c)

Reason :

$$\text{Mass \%} = \frac{\text{Mass of solute}}{\text{Mass of solute + Mass of solvent}} \times 100\%$$

$$= \frac{0.01}{0.01 + 99.99} \times 100 = \frac{0.01}{100} \times 100 = 0.01$$

41. Calculate the mass of sodium sulphate required to prepare its 20% (mass percent) solution in 100g of water?

Ans : Let,

The mass of sodium sulphate required be = xg

The mass of solution would be = $(x + 100)$g

xg of solute in $(x + 100)$ g of solution,

$$20\% = \frac{x}{x + 100} \times 100$$

$$20x + 2000 = 100x$$

$$80x = 2000$$

$$x = \frac{2000}{80} = 25g$$

Hence, to prepare 20% solution in 100 gram of water 25 gram of sodium sulphate is needed.

HIGHER ORDER THINKING SKILL QUESTIONS (HOTS)

1. Ravi added solid A to water, it dissolved with the evolution of a lot of heat and releasing a gas which burnt with a pop sound. The products B and C. were formed. The properties of B and C was entirely different from A as well as water. The products B and C can also be converted into solid A and water. He was totally confused about the result and asked his teacher for the questions. The teacher explained to him everything in detail.

(a) What type of change took place when solid A was dissolved in water? Give reason for your answer.

(b) Name a metal which could behave like solid A.

(c) Identify the products B and C.

Ans : (a) Chemical change. This is because the properties of the products B and C are entirely different from those of solid A.

(b) Sodium.

(c) The product B is sodium hydroxide and the product C is hydrogen.

2. Sam was given two liquids, one a solution and the other a compound. He was asked to distinguish the solution from a compound. He asked his friend Krishna for help. Krishna suggested him an activity. Sam answered to teacher and was applauded by his school mates.

(a) What is a solution?

(b) What idea would have been suggested by Krishna to differentiate the solution from a compound?

Ans : (a) Solution is a mixture.

(b) In order to differentiate solution and a compound, we should evaporate them separately. The liquid which evaporates completely leaving no residue is a pure compound and the liquid which leaves behind a residue on evaporation is a solution.

3. Observe the diagram and answer the following questions.

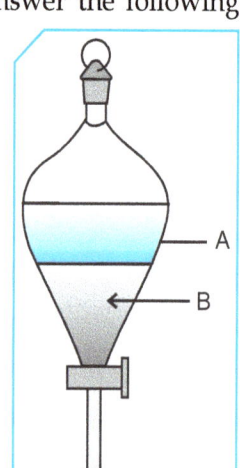

(a) Identify the process.

(b) Name the component A and B as solid, liquid, gas or mixture.

(c) Give an example.

Ans : (a) Separation of mixture of two immiscible liquids by separating funnel.

(b) A – Liquid; B – Liquid.

(c) Kerosene, oil and water.

4. Observe the diagram and answer the following questions.

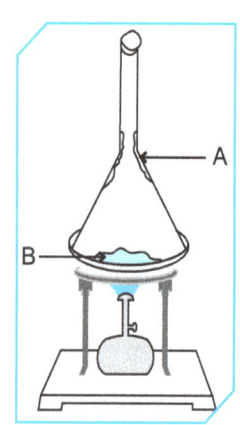

(a) Identify the process.

(b) Name the component A and B as solid, liquid, gas or mixture.

(c) Give an example.

Ans : (a) Sublimation.

(b) A – Solid; B – Mixture of two solids.

(c) Ammonium chloride and salt.

5. Observe the diagram and answer the following questions.

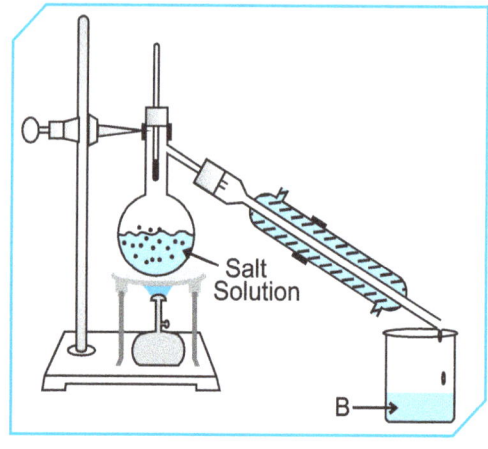

(a) Identify the process.

(b) Name the component A and B as solid, liquid, gas or mixture.

(c) Give an example.

Ans : (a) Separation of two miscible liquids by distillation.

(b) A – Mixture of two miscible liquids; B – Liquid.

(c) Acetone and water.

6. Observe the diagram and answer the following questions :

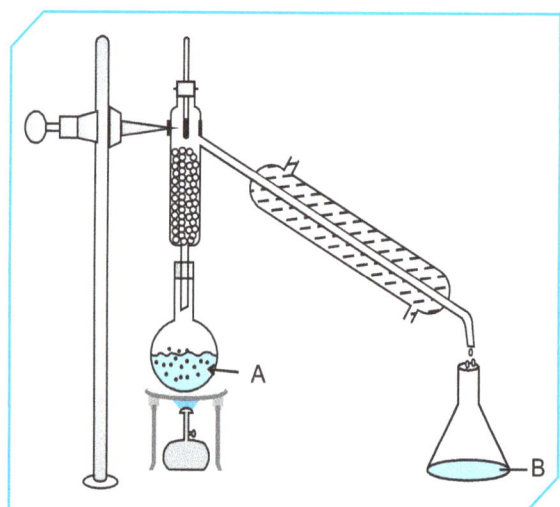

(a) Identify the process.

(b) Name the component A and B as solid, liquid, gas or mixture.

(c) Give an example.

Ans : (a) Separating two or more miscible liquids having boiling points less than 25 K by fractional distillation.

(b) A – Mixture of two miscible liquids; B – Liquid.

(c) Alcohol and water.

7. The diagram below shows the separation of different gases from air.

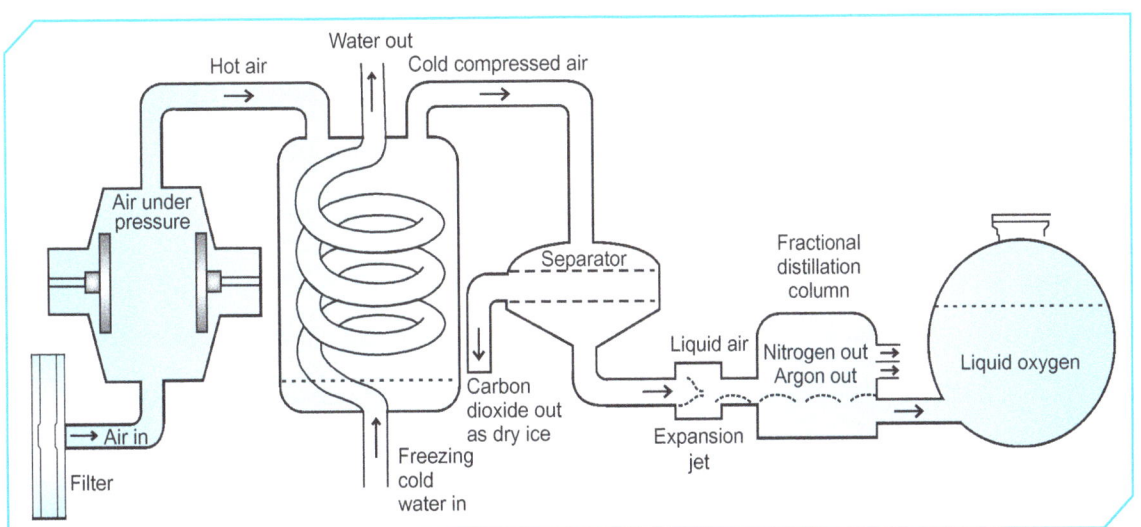

(a) Identify the process.

(b) Which gas forms the liquid first as the air is cooled?

(c) Name the inert gas present which is the main constituent by volume.

Ans : (a) Fractional distillation.

(b) Nitrogen.

(c) Argon.

MULTIPLE CHOICE QUESTIONS (MCQs)

1. Which one of the following may be termed as a pure substance?
   (a) Sodium chloride (b) Soft drink
   (c) Aerosol (d) Soil

2. Which of the following is a compound?
   (a) Air (b) Solution
   (c) Marble (d) Stainless steel

3. A substance in which all atoms are alike is called an :
   (a) Compound (b) Mixture
   (c) Element (d) None of these

4. Select a colloidal solution out of the following:
   (a) Gold ornaments (b) Sand grains
   (c) Lime water (d) Paint

5. Identify solution among the following mixtures:
   (a) Gun powder (b) Aerated water
   (c) Soil (d) Blood

6. The size of particles in a solution is :
   (a) Smaller than 10^{-7} cm
   (b) Larger than 10^{-5} cm
   (c) Between 10^{-5} and 10^{-8} cm
   (d) Smaller than 10^{-5} cm.

7. Common salt is obtained from sea water by :
   (a) Evaporation (b) Sublimation
   (c) Filtration (d) Fractional distillation

8. Solution of soap in water is a :
   (a) True solution (b) Colloidal solution
   (c) Suspension (d) None of the above

9. Gases are separated from each other by :
   (a) Fractional evaporation
   (b) Fractional distillation
   (c) Fractional crystallization
   (d) Fractional sublimation

10. Select the non-metal from the following :
    (a) Diamond (b) Gold
    (c) Silver (d) Platinum

11. Shaving cream is colloidal solution of :
    (a) Gas in liquid (b) Liquid in liquid
    (c) Solid in liquid (d) Gas in solid

12. A mixture of ammonium chloride and sand can be separated by :
    (a) Decantation (b) Sublimation
    (c) Evaporation (d) Centrifugation

13. Impure salts can be purified by the process :
    (a) Fractional evaporation
    (b) Distillation
    (c) Fractional purification
    (d) Crystallization

14. Components retain their properties in a :
    (a) Compound (b) Mixture
    (c) Element (d) None of these

15. Emulsion is a colloidal solution of liquid in :
    (a) Solid (b) Liquid
    (c) Gas (d) Air

16. Particles of which are visible by naked eyes :
    (a) Mixture (b) Colloidal solution
    (c) Suspension (d) None of these

17. Which one of the following is a physical change?
    (a) Burning of magnesium
    (b) Exposure of iron to moisture
    (c) Dissolution of sugar in water
    (d) Formation of a compound

18. Which is a homogeneous mixture?
    (a) It has a fixed composition
    (b) It has uniform composition
    (c) It has non-uniform composition
    (d) It cannot be broken down to simpler substances

19. Most elements are :
    (a) Solids (b) Liquids
    (c) Gases (d) Mixtures

20. Which one of the following does not have fixed melting or boiling point?
    (a) Oxygen (b) Gold
    (c) Ethanol (d) Air

21. Which one of the following is or are homogeneous in nature?
    (a) Ice and wood (b) Wood and soil
    (c) Air and ice (d) Ice and soil

22. Which one of the following is or are compounds?
    (a) CO (b) NO
    (c) CO and NO (d) None of these

23. Which one of the following is solid foam?
    (a) Ruby (b) Shaving cream
    (c) Bread (d) Butter

24. The liquid which leaves behind a residue on heating is ....
    (a) Alcohol (b) Bromine
    (c) Mercury (d) Brine

25. Which one of the following is not a chemical change?
    (a) Corrosion of gate
    (b) Sublimation of naphthalene
    (c) Ripening of banana
    (d) Formation of curd

26. Which one of the following is suspension?
    (a) Vinegar (b) Salt solution
    (c) Milk (d) Milk of magnesia

27. Which one of the following is not an emulsion?
    (a) Shaving cream (b) Face cream
    (c) Butter (d) Milk

28. Which one of the following will exhibit Tyndall effect?
    (a) Potassium permanganate + Water
    (b) Chalk powder + Water
    (c) Potash alum + Water
    (d) Sugar + Water

29. Which is an example of the solution of solid in solid?
    (a) Beryllium (b) Bread
    (c) Brass (d) Boron

30. Which one of the following scrap metal cannot be separated by magnetic separation?
    (a) Chromium (b) Steel
    (c) Cobalt (d) Nickel

ANSWERS

1. (a), 2. (c), 3. (c), 4. (d), 5. (b), 6. (a), 7. (a) 8. (b), 9. (b), 10. (a), 11. (a), 12. (b), 13. (d), 14. (b) 15. (b), 16. (c), 17. (c), 18. (b), 19. (a), 20. (d), 21. (c) 22. (c), 23. (c), 24. (d), 25. (b), 26. (d), 27. (a), 28. (b), 29. (c), 30. (a).

VERY SHORT ANSWER TYPE QUESTIONS

1. Name a metal which is soft and a non-metal which is hard.
2. Name an element, a compound and a mixture.
3. Name three important metalloids.
4. Name a solid, a liquid and a gaseous non-metal.
5. Define sol.
6. Define aerosol.
7. Define foam.
8. Define a physical change.
9. Define a chemical change.

10. How are two solid substances separated from a mixture containing two solid substances?
11. Define sublimate.
12. Define centrifugation.
13. Define distillation.
14. State any two applications of fractional distillation.
15. How will you separate the components of the mixture containing sand, water and mustard oil?
16. Name the process used to recover salt from an aqueous salt solution.
17. Name the technique used to squeeze out water from wet clothes while drying in a washing machine.
18. What is the significance of fractionating column in fractional distillation?
19. How will you detect the traces of poison present in the stomach wash of a person?
20. How are the impurities present in iron removed in industries?

SHORT ANSWER TYPE –I QUESTIONS

1. Differentiate between a solution and a mixture.
2. Define pure substances. Give two examples.
3. Comment: "Air is a mixture and water is a compound".
4. Why hydrogen and oxygen are considered elements whereas water is a compound?
5. Give two points of evidence to show that sodium chloride is a compound.
6. How will you justify that sugar solution is a mixture ?
7. Differentiate between homogeneous and heterogeneous mixtures.
8. Comment: "Copper is a metal while sulphur is a non-metal".
9. Define the following terms :
    (a) Ductility
    (b) Malleability
    (c) Brittleness
10. What is meant by an element and a compound?
11. Give any four examples of mixtures.
12. Define solutions. Give any two examples.
13. Give any two examples of homogeneous and heterogeneous mixtures.
14. What are the elements present in the following compounds?
    (a) Potassium nitrate
    (b) Washing soda
    (c) Baking soda
15. Comment: "Brass is considered as a mixture".

SHORT ANSWER TYPE-II QUESTIONS

1. Compare the properties of metals and non-metals.
2. Differentiate between a suspension and a colloid.
3. Classify different types of solutions with an example for each.
4. Differentiate between a true solution and a colloidal solution.
5. 9.72g of sodium chloride dissolves in 30g of water at 70°C. Calculate the solubility of sodium chloride at that temperature.
6. What happens when a beam of light is passed through a colloidal solution?
7. Explain Tyndall effect.
8. How will you separate ammonium chloride, sand and iron filings?
9. Explain a method to separate common salt from a mixture of chalk powder and common salt.
10. How will you separate kerosene oil and water? Explain with neat sketch.
11. How is cream separated from milk?
12. (a) Define chromatography.
    (b) Define chromatogram.
    (c) State one application of chromatography.
13. How is sugar recovered from sugar solution? Explain.
14. Explain the method of separating iron filings, naphthalene and chalk powder.
15. How is impure copper sulphate purified by the process of crystallization.

LONG ANSWER TYPE QUESTIONS

1. (a) Differentiate between a saturated and a unsaturated solution.
    (b) How will you test whether a given solution is saturated or not?
2. How will you prepare a saturated solution of sodium chloride in water at 25°C? What will happen if this solution is cooled to 10°C?

3. Explain the process of separation of gases from air with a flow diagram.

4. Explain the method of separating ammonium chloride from a mixture of ammonium chloride and common salt with neat sketch.

5. Draw a neat and labelled diagram of the apparatus used to obtain pure water from salt-water mixture.

6. Explain with a neat and labelled sketch how water is purified on a large scale and supplied to the cities.

7. With a help of neat diagram, explain the process of separating a mixture of ethanol and water.

8. Differentiate between colloid, suspension and solution.

EXERCISES (UNSOLVED)

VIVA VOCE QUESTIONS

1. When a saturated solution is heated, does it change into unsaturated solution?
2. How will you separate a mixture of milk and cooking oil?
3. Give an example of solid in liquid solution.
4. How will you separate iron nails from saw dust?
5. What is the size of the particles in suspension?
6. What is the unit of mass percent?
7. What happens if a colloidal solution of sulphur is centrifuged for sometime?
8. Give one property in which a solution of sugar in water resembles a mixture of sugar and sand.
9. Can a mixture of alcohol and water be separated by separating funnel?
10. What happens when a saturated solution of sodium chloride prepared at 60°C is allowed to cool at room temperature?

TRUE OR FALSE

1. The identities of the substances change in a physical change.
2. The chemical changes can be reversed easily.
3. Iodine and sand can be separated by sublimation.
4. When the boiling point between the components in the liquid mixture is less than 25°C, then fractional distillation is used.
5. A liquid mixture of carbon tetrachloride and water can be separated by separating funnel.
6. A separating funnel helps in separating only two immiscible liquids.
7. Sodium chloride undergoes sublimation.
8. A white precipitate of silver chloride formed by mixing solutions of silver nitrate and sodium chloride can be separated by decantation.
9. The process of neutralization of charge on the colloidal particles by adding oppositely charged species is called coagulation.
10. The solution shows Tyndall effect.

FILL IN THE BLANKS

1. Elements combine in a fixed proportion to form ------------------.
2. Air is a ------------------ of several gases.
3. ---------------------- is separated from waste by magnetic separation.
4. Pure liquid from a solution is obtained by ------------------------.
5. -------------------- is the only metal which is in liquid state at room temperature.
6. Tyndall effect is produced by ---------------------.
7. Separating funnel is used to separate two or more ---------------- liquids.
8. New substances are formed in a ---------------- change.
9. A ------------ shows the properties of constituent substances.
10. The properties of a ------------------- are different from the constituent elements.

MATCH THE FOLLOWING

1. Match column 1 and column 2.

S. No	Column 1	Column 2	Correct Match
1.	Iron	Heterogeneous mixture	
2.	Steel	Compound	
3.	Sodium chloride	Element	
4.	Iodized table salt	Homogeneous mixture	

2. Match the column 1 and column 2.

S. No	Column 1	Column 2	Correct Match
1.	Solid in liquid	Clouds	
2.	Liquid in gas	Common salt in water	
3.	Gas in solid	German silver	
4.	Solid in solid	Nitrogen and hydrogen on the surface of nickel metal.	

3. Match the column 1 and column 2

S. No	Column 1	Column 2	Correct Match
1.	Oil from water	Winnowing	
2.	Husk from wheat	Filtration	
3.	Iron scrap from waste	Separating funnel	
4.	Tea leaves from water	Magnetic separation	

4. Match the column 1 and column 2 :

S. No	Column 1	Column 2	Correct Match
1.	Water from salt water	Evaporation	
2.	Common salt from sea water	Fractional distillation	
3.	Impurities from pond water	Distillation	
4.	Gases from air	Decantation	

DIAGRAM BASED QUESTIONS

1. Complete 'X', 'Y' and 'Z'.

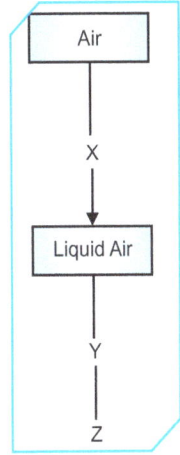

2. Observe the diagram and answer the questions given below :

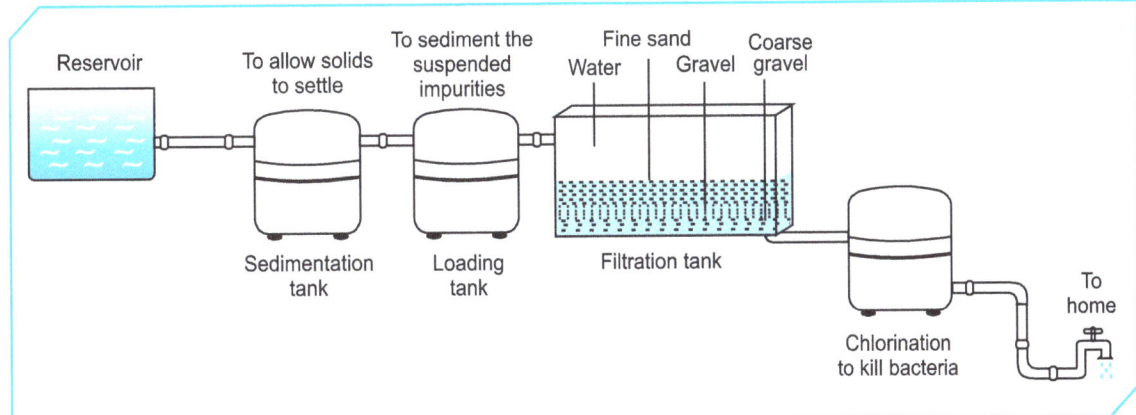

   (a) What is the role of sedimentation tank?
   (b) What is the function of loading tank?
   (c) What is the use of chlorination?

3. Observe the figure and answer the questions given below :
   (a) Identify X and Y.
   (b) Name A, B, C and D.
   (c) Define 1 with respect to A → D.
   (d) Give example in 2 with respect to A → D.

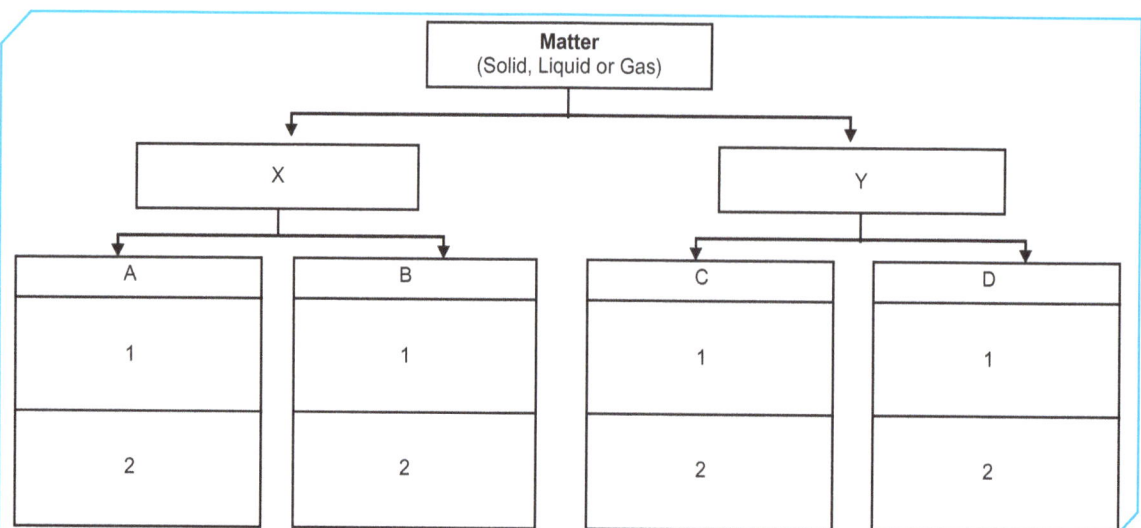

SYMPOSIUM

Divide the class into 4 or more groups depending on the size of the class.

Topic 1 : Methods of separation of mixtures.

Key words :
 (a) Introduction.
 (b) Classification of mixtures.
 (c) Examples of mixtures.
 (d) Methods involved in separating mixtures.
 (e) Explaining each method with diagram.

Topic 2 : Physical change and chemical change.

Key words :
(a) Introduction.
(b) Physical change with examples.
(c) Chemical change with examples.

GROUP DISCUSSION

Topic 1 : Types of mixtures

Key words :
(a) Introduction.
(b) Different types of mixtures.
(c) Illustrating with examples.

Topic 2 : Classification of mixtures

Key words :
(a) Introduction.
(b) Classification of different types of mixtures.
(c) Illustrating each type with example.

ANSWERS

VIVA VOCE QUESTIONS

1. Yes.
2. Separating funnel.
3. Sugar in water or common salt in water.
4. Magnetic separation.
5. 10^{-5} cm.
6. No units.
7. The yellow precipitate of sulphur will settle down at the bottom while the colourless solution is collected above the precipitate.
8. Both taste sweet due to the presence of sugar in both.
9. No.
10. A small amount of salt is collected as a residue.

TRUE OR FALSE

1. False
2. False
3. True
4. False
5. True
6. True
7. False
8. False
9. True
10. False

FILL IN THE BLANKS

1. Compounds
2. Mixture
3. Iron
4. Distillation
5. Mercury
6. Colloids
7. Immiscible
8. Chemical
9. Mixture
10. Compound

MATCH THE FOLLOWING

1.

S. No	Column 1	Column 2	Correct Match
1.	Iron	Heterogeneous mixture	4
2.	Steel	Compound	3
3.	Sodium chloride	Element	1
4.	Iodized table salt	Homogeneous mixture	2

2.

S. No	Column 1	Column 2	Correct Match
1.	Solid in liquid	Clouds	2
2.	Liquid in gas	Common salt in water	1
3.	Gas in solid	German silver	4
4.	Solid in solid	Nitrogen and hydrogen on the surface of nickel metal.	3

3.

S. No	Column 1	Column 2	Correct Match
1.	Oil from water	Winnowing	2
2.	Husk from wheat	Filtration	4
3.	Iron scrap from waste	Separating funnel	1
4.	Tea leaves from water	Magnetic separation	3

4.

S. No	Column 1	Column 2	Correct Match
1.	Water from salt water	Evaporation	2
2.	Common salt from sea water	Fractional distillation	4
3.	Impurities from pond water	Distillation	1
4.	Gases from air	Decantation	3

DIAGRAM BASED QUESTIONS

1. Air → Compress and cool by increasing pressure and decreasing temperature → Liquid Air → Allow to warm up slowly in fractional distillation column → Gases get separated at different heights

2. (a) To allow solids to settle.
   (b) To sediment the suspended impurities.
   (c) To kill the bacteria.

3.

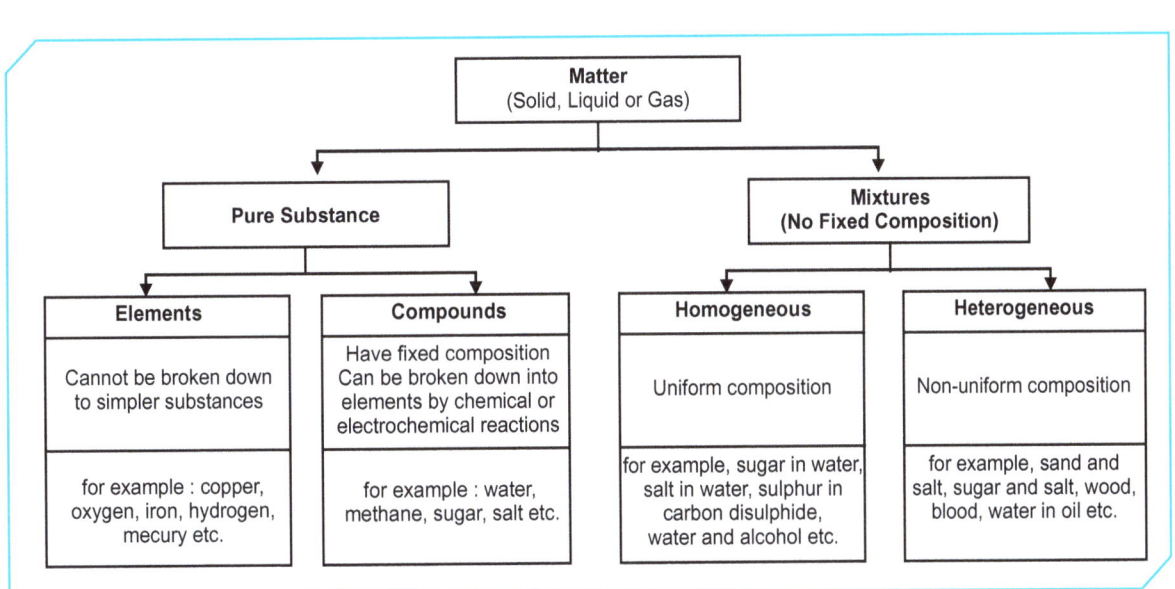

MOCK TEST-1

Time : 2 Hours   Max. Marks : 50

General Instructions :

- All questions are compulsory.
- There is no overall choice.
- Questions 1 to 5 are one mark questions. These are to be answered in one word or in one sentence.
- Questions 6 to 10 are two marks questions. These are to be answered in about 30 words each.
- Questions 11 to 15 are three marks questions. These are to be answered in about 50 words each.
- Questions 16 to 19 are five marks questions. These are to be answered in about 70 words each.

1. Which method is better for recovering sugar from sugar solution? Evaporation or Crystallization.
2. Define chromatogram.
3. Name the apparatus used to separate oil from water.
4. Name the solvent you would use to separate a mixture of sulphur and carbon.
5. What is the name of the clear liquid formed when a solid dissolves in a liquid?
6. What is the concentration of a solution which contains 16g of urea in 120g of solution?
7. Differentiate between a solution and a mixture.
8. How will you confirm that a colourless liquid given is pure water?
9. How will you distinguish the solutions and a compound?
10. What will happen if a saturated solution is heated or cooled?
11. Sam was given two liquids, one a solution and the other a compound. He was been asked to distinguish the solution from a compound. He asked his friend Krishna for help. Krishna suggested him with an activity. Sam answered correctly to the method that could be used for the seperation and the teacher was satisfied. This was also applauded by his school mates.

    (a) What values of Krishna has been displayed?
    (b) What is a solution?
    (c) What idea would have been suggested by Krishna to differentiate the solution from a compound?

12. The diagram below shows the separation of different gases from air.

    (a) Identify the process.
    (b) Which gas turns to liquid first as the air is cooled?
    (c) Name the inert gas present which is the main constituent by volume.

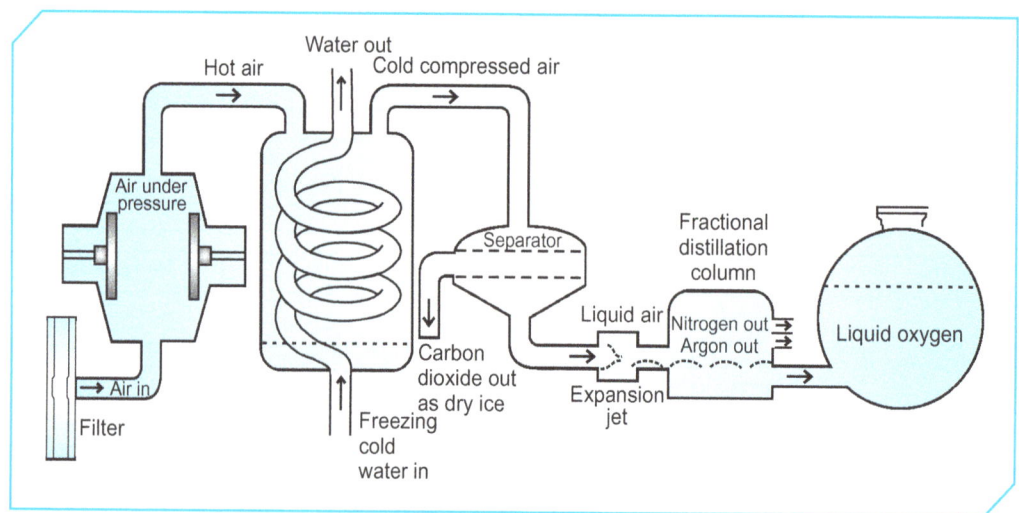

13. Explain Tyndall effect.
14. Compare the properties of metals and non-metals.
15. 9.72g of sodium chloride dissolves in 30g of water at 70°C. Calculate the solubility of sodium chloride at that temperature.
16. (a) Differentiate between a saturated and an unsaturated solution.
    (b) How will you test whether a given solution is saturated or not?
17. Draw a neat and labelled diagram of the apparatus used to obtain pure water from salt-water mixture.
18. Explain the process of separation of gases from air with a flow diagram.
19. Explain with a neat and labelled sketch how water is purified on a large scale and supplied to the cities.

MOCK TEST–2

Time : 2 Hours   Max. Marks : 50

General Instructions :

- All questions are compulsory.
- There is no overall choice.
- Questions 1 to 5 are one mark questions. These are to be answered in one word or in one sentence.
- Questions 6 to 10 are two marks questions. These are to be answered in about 30 words each.
- Questions 11 to 15 are three marks questions. These are to be answered in about 50 words each.
- Questions 16 to 19 are five marks questions. These are to be answered in about 70 words each.

1. What does the term '5% sugar solution' refers to?
2. What happens to a saturated sugar solution when the temperature is increased?
3. Which will scatter light : Sugar solution or Soap solution?
4. Name a metal and a non-metal which exists as liquid at room temperature.
5. State one application of centrifugation.
6. What is the use of fractionating column in fractional distillation?
7. How will you separate a mixture of salt and sugar?
8. How will you separate a mixture of sand, kerosene and water?
9. Give a schematic representation of separation of gases from air.
10. Mention any two applications of fractional distillation.
11. Observe the diagram and answer the following questions.
    (a) Identify the process.
    (b) Name the component A and B as solid, liquid, gas or mixture.
    (c) Give an example.

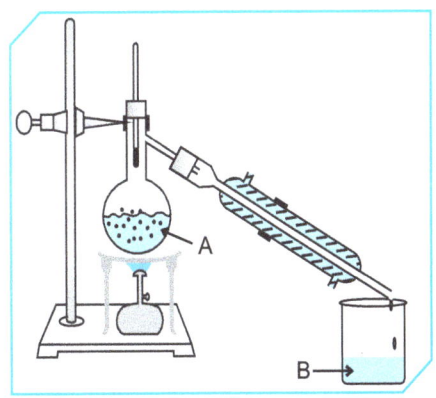

12. Ravi added solid A to water, it dissolved with the evolution of a lot of heat making little explosions to form the products B and C. The properties of B and C was entirely different from A as well as water. The products B and C can also be converted into solid A and water. He was totally confused about the result and asked his teacher for the questions. The teacher explained to him everything in detail.
    (a) What type of change took place when solid A was dissolved in water? Give reason for your answer.
    (b) Name a metal which could behave like solid A. Identify the products B and C.

(c) What are the values of teacher displayed?

(d) How will you separate ammonium chloride, sand and iron filings?

13. Explain a method to separate common salt from a mixture of chalk powder and common salt.

14. How will you separate kerosene oil and water? Explain with neat sketch.

15. How is cream separated from milk?

16. How will you prepare a saturated solution of sodium chloride in water at 25°C? What will happen if this solution is cooled to 10°C?

17. Explain the method of separating ammonium chloride from a mixture of ammonium chloride and common salt with neat sketch.

18. With a help of neat diagram, explain the process of separating a mixture of ethanol and water.

19. Differentiate colloid, suspension and a solution.

3 ATOMS AND MOLECULES

CONTENTS

3.0 Introduction
3.1 Laws of Chemical Combination
3.2 Law of Conservation of Mass
3.3 Law of Constant or Definite Proportions
3.4 Atomic Theory of Matter
3.5 Dalton's Atomic Theory
3.6 Atoms
3.7 Atomic Symbols or Symbols of Elements
3.8 Atomic Mass of an Element
3.9 Existence of Atoms
3.10 Molecules
3.11 Chemical Formulae
3.12 Ions and Ionic Compounds
3.13 Writing Chemical Formulae
3.14 Gram Atomic Mass and Gram Molecular Mass
3.15 Percentage Composition
3.16 Mole Concept

3.0 INTRODUCTION

Chemistry is the branch of science which deals with the structure, composition, properties and interaction of matter. Since, matter constitutes of atoms and molecules, chemistry is also called the science of atoms and molecules. Ancient Indian and Greek philosophers have always wondered about the unknown and unseen form of matter. An Indian philosopher **Maharishi Kanad,** postulated that if matter (called as *Padarth* in Hindi) is continuously divided and it forms smaller and smaller particles. But, in the end there occurs a stage of smallest particles beyond which further division will not be possible. He named these particles *Parmanu*. Later, Greek philosophers, **Democritus** and **Leucippus** called these indivisible particles as *atomos* (meaning indivisible). Another Indian philosopher, **Pakudha Katyayama,** said that these particles of matter normally exist in a combined form (now called as molecules) which gives us various forms of matter. However, all this work was based on philosophical considerations and not much experiment could be done to validate these ideas.

Later, scientists recognized the differences between elements and compounds and started to find out how and why elements combine and what happens when they combine.

3.1 LAWS OF CHEMICAL COMBINATION

The combination of elements to form compounds is governed by the following four basic laws called the laws of chemical combinations namely,

(a) Law of Conservation of Mass
(b) Law of Constant or Definite Proportions
(c) Law of Multiple Proportions
(d) Law of Reciprocal Proportions

Antoine L. Lavoisier laid the foundation of two important laws of chemical combination which deals with mass. Thus, whenever substances react they do so according to these laws. These laws form the basis of Dalton's atomic theory of matter.

3.2 LAW OF CONSERVATION OF MASS

It has been observed that when a chemical reaction takes place in a closed container, there was no change in the mass of the reactants. This resulted in the formulation of law of conservation of mass. The law of conservation of mass was proposed by **Antoine L. Lavoisier** in 1774 (Fig. 3.1).

Fig. 3.1 : Antoine L. Lavoisier, the chemist who formulated the law of conservation of mass.

He made careful quantitative measurements in chemical reactions and established that mass is neither created nor destroyed in a chemical change. According to law of conservation of mass,

"Mass is neither created nor destroyed during a chemical reaction, but it only changes from one form to another form"

In a chemical reaction, the substances which combine together are known as *'reactants'* whereas the new substances formed are known as *'products'*. During a chemical reaction, the reactants are converted into products. But the total mass of the reactants and products remains the same. This law is also called as the *law of indestructibility of matter.*

Let us illustrate the law of conservation of mass with few examples.

Illustration 1 : In the reaction, when mercuric oxide is heated it, produces mercury and oxygen gas (Fig. 3.2).

$$2HgO \xrightarrow{\Delta} 2Hg + O_2$$
Mercuric oxide → Mercury + Oxygen

The sum of masses of mercury and oxygen was found to be equal to the mass of mercuric oxide. Let us work out the mass of mercury and oxygen. The atomic weight of mercury is 80 u while that of oxygen is 16u. Hence, the mass of mercuric oxide, mercury and oxygen is as follows :

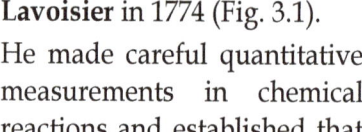

Mercuric oxide		Mercury+Oxygen
Reactants		Products
2× (80 + 16)	→	(2 × 80) + (16 × 2)
2 × 96	→	160 + 32
192 u	→	192 u

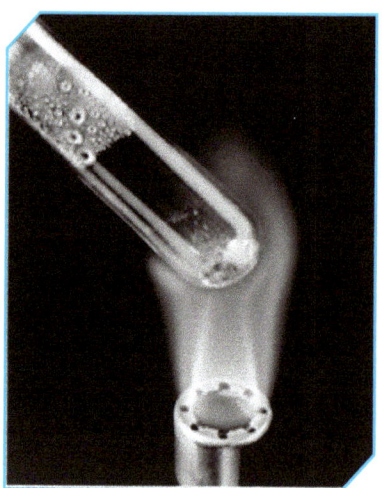

Fig. 3.2 : This figure shows the decomposition of mercuric oxide on heating.

Illustration 2 : When calcium carbonate is heated, it produces carbon dioxide and calcium oxide.

$$CaCO_3 \xrightarrow{\Delta} CaO + CO_2$$
Calcium carbonate → Calcium oxide + Carbon dioxide

The sum of masses of calcium oxide and carbon dioxide was found to be equal to the mass of calcium carbonate. Let us work out the mass of calcium oxide and carbon dioxide. The atomic weight of calcium is 40u, carbon is 12u and oxygen is 16u. Hence, the mass of calcium carbonate, calcium oxide and carbon dioxide is as follows :

Calcium carbonate		Calcium oxide + Carbon dioxide
40 + 12 + (16 × 3)	→	(40 + 16) + 12 + (16 × 2)
40 + 12 + 48	→	56 + 12 + 32
100 u	→	100 u

Both the examples illustrated above support the law of conservation of mass because in both the examples, the total mass of reactants and products remain conserved. Thus, we can verify the law of conservation in the chemical laboratory by taking known masses of two chemicals called reactants, allowing them to react by mixing them and then finding the masses of the products formed. There should be no change in the mass. Let us now verify the law of conservation of mass experimentally.

Experimental Verification of Law of Conservation of Mass

Procedure

Step 1- Take a clean conical flask fitted with a rubber cork, a small test tube having a long thread tied to its neck.

Step 2- Weigh all these together on a balance and note down the initial mass of the apparatus.

Step 3- Now take 20.8g of sodium chloride solution in the conical flask.

Step 4- Then, add 14.2 g of silver nitrate solution in the small test tube and lower it carefully into the conical flask by holding the free end of thread tied to its neck.

Step 5- Fix the rubber cork in the mouth of the conical flask to hold the thread tightly.

Step 6- Make sure that the mouth of the small test tube remains above the sodium chloride solution level, so that the reactants do not get mixed (Fig 3.3 a).

Step 7- Note down the mass of apparatus along with the reactants by weighing it on a balance.

Step 8- If we subtract the initial mass of apparatus from this mass, we will obtain the mass of the reactants. Assume the mass of the reactants as 'x'.

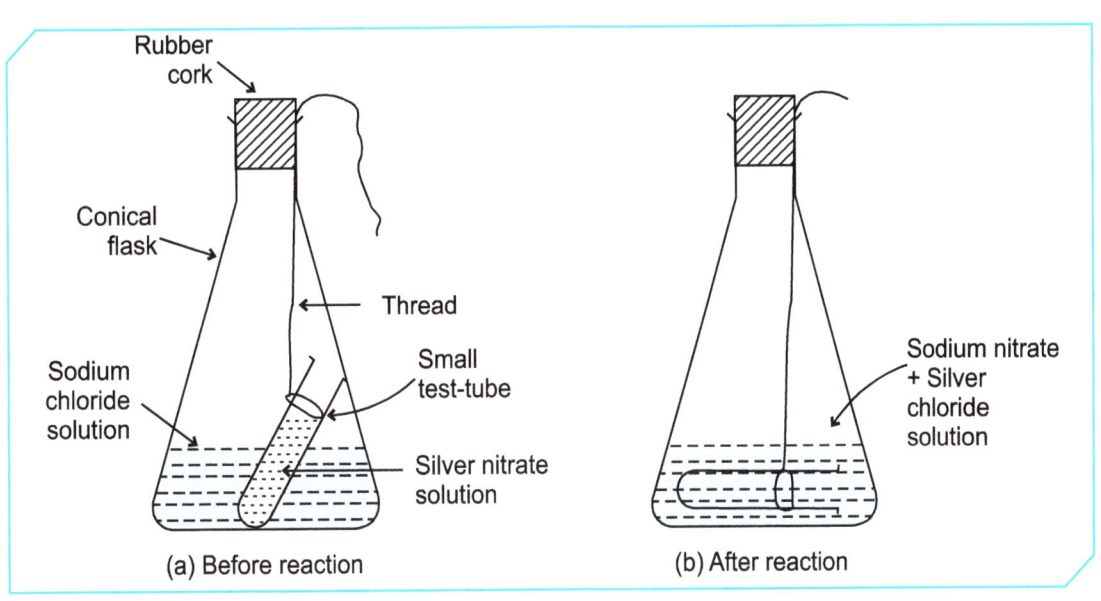

Fig. 3.3 : Experimental verification of the law of conservation of mass.

Step 9- Remove the rubber cork from the mouth of the conical flask so that the thread becomes loose.

Step 10- The silver nitrate solution gets mixed with sodium chloride solution.

Step 11- This results in the formation of white precipitate of silver chloride and sodium nitrate solution (Fig. 3.3 (b) and (Fig. 3.4).

Step 12- Note down the mass of apparatus along with the products formed. Assume the mass of the products as 'y'.

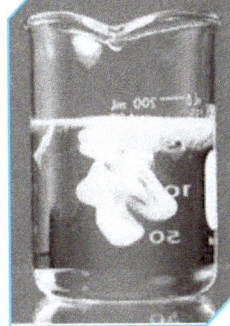

Fig. 3.4 : This figure shows the formation of white precipitate of silver chloride on mixing the solution of sodium chloride with silver nitrate.

Calculation

The chemical reaction of the experiment is :

Sodium chloride + Silver nitrate ⟶ Silver chloride + Sodium nitrate

Mass of sodium chloride taken = 20.8g
Mass of silver nitrate taken = 14.2g
Mass of silver chloride formed = 23.3g
Mass of sodium nitrate formed = 11.7g

Thus,
Total mass of reactants = Sodium chloride + Silver nitrate
= 20.8g + 14.2g
= 35.0g

Total mass of products = Silver chloride + Sodium nitrate
= 23.3g + 11.7g
= 35.0g

Observation

The total mass of products (y) formed is equal to the total mass of reactants (x), confirming the law of conservation of mass.

Result

This experiment verifies the law of conservation of mass. Let us perform an activity to prove the law of conservation of mass.

Activity 3.1– To understand the law of conservation of mass.

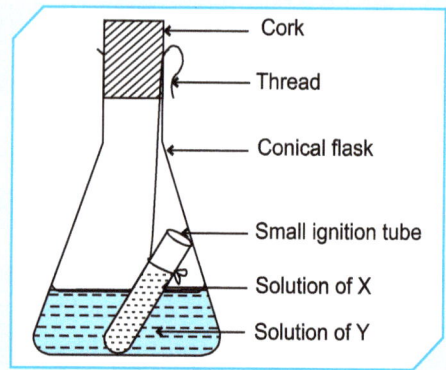

Fig. 3.5 : Ignition tube containing solution of X, dipped in a conical flask containing solution of Y

PROCEDURE

Step 1– Take one of the following sets, X and Y of chemicals

	X	Y
(a)	Copper sulphate	Sodium carbonate
(b)	Barium chloride	Sodium sulphate
(c)	Lead nitrate	Sodium chloride

Step 2– Prepare separately a 5% solution of any one pair of substances listed under X and Y in water.

Step 3– Take a little amount of solution of Y in a conical flask and some solution of X in an ignition tube.

Step 4– Hang the ignition tube in the flask carefully; see that the solutions do not get mixed.

Step 5– Put a cork on the flask.

Step 6– Weigh the flask with its contents carefully.

Step 7– Now tilt and swirl the flask, so that the solutions X and Y get mixed.

Step 8– Weigh again.

Step 9– What happens in the reaction flask?

Step 10– Do you think that a chemical reaction has taken place?

Step 11– Why should we put a cork on the mouth of the flask?

Step 12– Does the mass of the flask and its contents change?

OBSERVATION

On tilting the flask the X and Y solution gets mixed. Yes the chemical reaction has taken place. A cork was put on the mouth of the conical flask to ensure there is no loss in the mass by releasing gas. No, there is no change in the mass of the contents.

CONCLUSION

Law of conservation of mass states that "mass can neither be created nor destroyed in a chemical reaction".

Let us now solve some problems based on the law of conservation of mass.

Solved Sample Problems

Sample Problem 1 : 10.0g of calcium carbonate decomposes completely to form 5.6g of calcium oxide. Calculate the mass of carbon dioxide formed.

Solution : Given,

$$\text{Calcium carbonate} \rightarrow \text{Calcium oxide} + \text{Carbon dioxide}$$
$$10.0g \qquad\qquad 5.6g \qquad\qquad x\,g$$

Mass of calcium carbonate taken = 10.0g

Mass of calcium oxide formed = 5.6g

Mass of carbon dioxide formed, x = Mass of calcium carbonate – Mass of calcium oxide

Substituting the values, we get

Mass of carbon dioxide, x = 10.0 – 5.6 = 4.4g

Hence, 10.0g of calcium carbonate produces 5.6g of calcium oxide and 4.4g of carbon dioxide.

Sample Problem 2 : Sodium carbonate reacts with ethanoic acid to form sodium ethanoate, carbon dioxide and water. In an experiment, 5.3g of sodium carbonate reacts with 6g of ethanoic acid to form 8.2g of sodium ethanoate, 2.2g of carbon dioxide and 0.9g of water. Show that this data confirms the law of conservation of mass.

Solution : Given,

$$\text{Sodium carbonate} + \text{Ethanoic acid} \rightarrow \text{Sodium ethanoate} + \text{Carbon dioxide} + \text{Water}$$
$$5.3g \qquad\qquad 6g \qquad\qquad 8.2g \qquad\qquad 2.2g \qquad\qquad 0.9g$$

Mass of sodium carbonate taken = 5.3g

Mass of ethanoic acid taken = 6g

Mass of sodium ethanoate formed = 8.2 g

Mass of carbon dioxide formed = 2.2g

Mass of water formed = 0.9g

Now, the mass of reactants (Sodium carbonate + Ethanoic acid) = 5.3 + 6 = 11.3g

The mass of products formed (Sodium ethanoate + Carbon dioxide + Water) = 8.2 + 2.2 + 0.9 = 11.3g

Hence, the total mass of reactants is equal to the total mass of products. Hence, the law of conservation of mass is proved.

Try Yourself

1. 9.4g of magnesium carbonate on heating gave 4.4g of carbon dioxide and 5.0g of magnesium oxide. Show that these observations are in agreement with law of conservation of mass.
2. 30.0g of potassium chlorate decomposes to produce 14.9g of potassium chloride and 9.6g of oxygen. What mass of potassium chlorate remains undecomposed?　　　　[5.5g]
3. 10.0g of calcium carbonate on heating gave 4.4g of calcium oxide and 5.6g of carbon dioxide. Show that these observations are in agreement with law of conservation of mass.
4. When 20.8g of barium chloride is added with 14.2g of sodium sulphate, 23.3g of barium sulphate and 11.7g of sodium chloride are formed. Show that these observations are in agreement with the law of conservation of mass.
5. If 6.3g of sodium bicarbonate are added to 15.0g of acetic acid solution, the residue is found to weigh 18.0g. What is the mass of carbon dioxide released in the reaction?　　　　[3.3g]

PAPER-PEN TEST: 1

1. What are the different laws of chemical combination?
2. Who laid the foundation of two important laws of chemical combination which deals with mass?
3. What is the basis of the law of chemical combinations?
4. Which resulted in the formulation of law of conservation of mass?
5. The law of conservation of mass was proposed by ------------------- in --------------.
6. Define law of conservation of mass.
7. Which law is also called as the law of indestructibility of matter?
8. What are reactants and products?
9. Illustrate the law of conservation of mass with an example.
10. How will you verify the law of conservation of mass experimentally?
11. Perform an activity to prove the law of conservation of mass.

3.3 LAW OF CONSTANT OR DEFINITE PROPORTIONS

The law of constant proportions was proposed by French chemist, **Joseph Proust** in 1799 (Fig. 3.6). Proust proved experimentally that compound obtained from different sources will always contain same elements combined together in fixed proportions. According to the law of constant proportions,

Fig. 3.6 : Joseph Proust, a French chemist who formulated the law of constant proportions.

"When different elements combine to give a pure compound, the ratio between the masses of these elements will always remain the same"

This means that whatever the source may be, a pure chemical compound is always made up of same elements in the same mass percentage. For instance, water can be obtained from different sources such as river, ocean, well, canal, tube well, rain or by the chemical combination of hydrogen and oxygen. But, if different samples of water are analyzed we can find that it will always have two elements, hydrogen and oxygen combined together and the ratio between their mass is 1 : 8. Let us illustrate the law of constant proportion with few more examples.

Illustration 1 : The compound carbon dioxide can be formed in the number of ways as follows :

(a) By heating lime stone (calcium carbonate).

(b) By the reaction of sodium carbonate with dilute hydrochloric acid (Fig. 3.7).

(c) By burning carbon or coke in air or oxygen.

The formation of carbon dioxide by any one of the above methods will have the mass of carbon (C) and oxygen (O) in the same constant ratio of 12: 32 or 3 : 8.

145

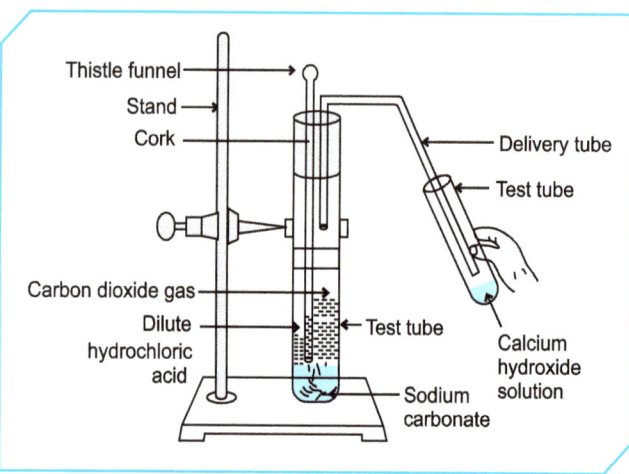

Fig. 3.7 : This figure shows the formation of carbon dioxide gas by the reaction of sodium carbonate and hydrochloric acid.

Illustration 2 : The compound ammonia always contains the same two elements, nitrogen and hydrogen combined together in the same ratio of 14 : 3 by mass.

Let us now solve the problems based on the law of constant proportions.

Solved Sample Problems

Sample Problem 1 : When 1.375g of cupric oxide was reduced on heating in a current of hydrogen, the weight of copper that remained was 1.098g. In another experiment 1.179g of copper was dissolved in nitric acid and resulting copper nitrate was converted into cupric oxide by ignition. The weight of cupric oxide formed was 1.476g. Show that these results illustrate the law of constant proportion.

Solution : In the first experiment

Given, Mass of cupric oxide = 1.375g

Mass of copper left = 1.098g

Mass of oxygen present = Mass of cupric oxide − Mass of copper

= 1.375 − 1.098 = 0.277g

$$\% \text{ of oxygen in a compound} = \frac{\text{Mass of oxygen in compound}}{\text{Mass of compound}} \times 100$$

$$\% \text{ of oxygen in CuO} = \frac{0.277}{1.375} \times 100$$

$$= 20.14\%$$

In the second experiment

Given,
Mass of copper taken = 1.179g
Mass of cupric oxide formed = 1.476g
Mass of oxygen present = Mass of cupric oxide − Mass of copper
= 1.476 − 1.179
= 0.297g

$$\% \text{ of oxygen in a compound} = \frac{\text{Mass of oxygen in compound}}{\text{Mass of compound}} \times 100$$

Since, the percentage of oxygen is approximately the same in both the above cases, so the law of constant composition is illustrated.

$$\% \text{ of oxygen in CuO} = \frac{0.297}{1.476} \times 100$$

$$= 20.12\%$$

Sample Problem 2 : 0.24g of sample of compound contains 0.096g of boron and 0.144g of oxygen. Calculate the percentage composition of the sample.

Solution : Given, Mass of the sample compound = 0.24g
Mass of boron in the compound = 0.096g
Mass of oxygen in the compound = 0.144g

$$\% \text{ of boron in the sample compound} = \frac{\text{Mass of boron in the sample compound}}{\text{Mass of sample compound}} \times 100$$

% of boron in the sample = $\dfrac{0.096}{0.24} \times 100$

= 40%

% of oxygen in the sample compound = $\dfrac{\text{Mass of oxygen in sample compound}}{\text{Mass of sample compound}} \times 100$

% of oxygen in sample = $\dfrac{0.144}{0.24} \times 100 = 60\%$

Thus, the percentage composition of the sample compound is Boron- 40% and Oxygen-60%.

Try Yourself

1. In the first experiment, a sample of ascorbic acid produced in the laboratory contains 15.0g of carbon and 20.0g of oxygen. In the second experiment, ascorbic acid is isolated from lemon containing 42.9% carbon. Show that the data is in accordance with the law of constant proportion.
2. In first experiment, 1.288g of copper oxide was obtained from 1.03g of copper. In second experiment, 3.672g of copper oxide gave 2.938g of copper. Show that the data is in accordance with the law of constant proportion.
3. Hydrogen and oxygen combine in the ratio of 1:8 by mass to form water. What mass of oxygen gas would be required to react completely with 3g of hydrogen gas?
4. When 3g of carbon is burnt in 8g of oxygen, 11g of carbon dioxide is produced. What mass of carbon dioxide will be formed when 3g of carbon is burnt in 50g of oxygen? Show that the data is in accordance with the law of constant proportion.

PAPER-PEN TEST : 2

1. The law of constant proportions was proposed by ------------------ in ---------------.
2. Define law of constant proportion.
3. What are the different ways by which carbon dioxide is formed?
4. What is the ratio of nitrogen and hydrogen in ammonia?
5. What is the ratio of carbon and oxygen in carbon dioxide?

3.4 ATOMIC THEORY OF MATTER

About 300 BC, **Aristotle** argued that both matter and motion are continuous. According to him, matter could be divided infinite number of times and even the smallest particle could be further divided into fundamental particles. Later around 400 BC, the early Indians and Greek philosophers suggested that matter is composed of tiny discrete particles. However, the idea of atom was only speculative and was not verified experimentally. Then, John Dalton, a British school teacher known as father of modern atomic theory put forward that the atom as the ultimate particle of matter is incapable of being created or destroyed.

3.5 DALTON'S ATOMIC THEORY

British chemist **John Dalton** provided the basic theory about the nature of matter in 1808. He used the name 'atoms' as given by the Greeks and said that the smallest particles of matter are atoms. His theory was based on the laws of chemical combination. According to Dalton's atomic theory,

"All matter, whether an element, a compound or a mixture is composed of small particles called atoms"

Based on his studies and observations, he came out with the statement that the smallest part of matter which cannot be divided any further is an atom. He then postulated his atomic theory which became one of the foundations of modern chemistry (Fig. 3.8).

Fig. 3.8 : John Dalton, the chemist who proposed the atomic theory of matter, popularly known as the Dalton's atomic theory.

Postulates of Dalton's Atomic Theory

The postulates of Dalton's Atomic Theory of matter are stated as follows :

(a) All matter is made of extremely small particles called 'atoms'.
(b) Atoms are indivisible particles, which mean they cannot be further divided into smaller particles.

(c) Atoms can neither be created nor be destroyed in a chemical reaction.

(d) All the atoms of a given element are identical in mass, size and chemical properties.

(e) Atoms of different elements have different size, mass and chemical properties.

(f) Atoms combine in the ratio of small whole numbers to form compounds.

(g) Atoms of same elements or different elements combine to form molecules.

(h) The relative number and kinds of atoms are constant in a given compound.

Dalton's Atomic Theory based on the Laws of Chemical Combination

Dalton was the first person who attempted to describe the behavior of matter in terms of atoms. His theory was accepted because it could explain the laws of chemical combination in terms of atoms. His theory provided a simple explanation for the laws of chemical combination. Let us discuss the law of conservation of mass in terms of atoms. According to Dalton's atomic theory,

"Atoms can neither be created nor be destroyed"

In a chemical reaction, the number of various types of atoms in the products is the same as the number of all those atoms in the reactants. In other words, in a chemical reaction, atoms only rearrange themselves to form products. Thus, the total mass of the product remains equal to the total mass of the reactants during a chemical reaction. For example, when calcium carbonate ($CaCO_3$) undergoes decomposition, it gives calcium oxide (CaO) and carbon dioxide (CO_2). In this equation, the reactant calcium carbonate is made up of 1 calcium atom, 1 carbon atom and 3 oxygen atoms. On the other hand, the products contain 1 calcium atom in calcium oxide, 1 carbon atom in carbon dioxide and 3 oxygen atoms i.e., one from calcium oxide and two from carbon dioxide. This shows that there is no change in the mass during the decomposition of calcium carbonate to form calcium oxide and carbon dioxide. Hence, the mass remains conserved (Fig. 3.9 and 3.10).

$$CaCO_3 \xrightarrow{\Delta} CaO + CO_2$$
Calcium carbonate   Calcium oxide   Carbon dioxide

Fig. 3.9 : This figure shows Calcium carbonate. Its chemical formula is $CaCO_3$.

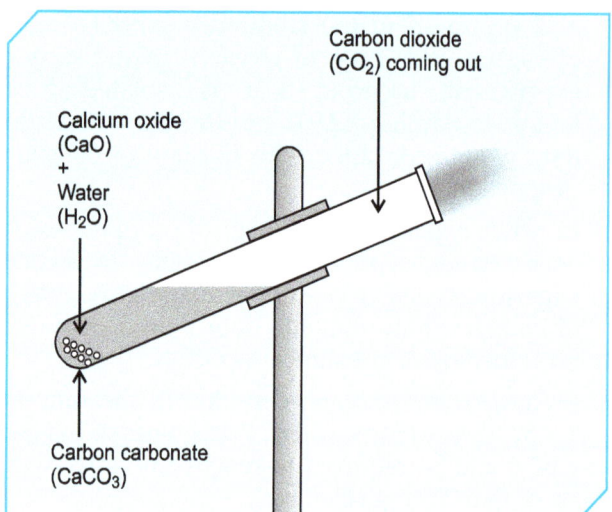

Fig. 3.10 : This figure shows the decomposition of Calcium carbonate.

Let us now discuss the law of constant proportions in terms of atoms. According to Dalton's atomic theory,

"Every element consists of small particles called atoms, each having a fixed mass"

This shows that the atoms of different elements combine in a fixed ratio to form compounds and the mass of each element in that compound is fixed. Hence, whatever be the source of the compound, a compound will always have the fixed ratio of atoms of different types combined together in the same proportion by mass. For example, 2 hydrogen atoms and 1 oxygen atom combines to form a molecule of water. Since a water molecule always contains 2 atoms of hydrogen and 1 oxygen atom, thus, the masses of hydrogen and oxygen elements in water will also be in constant proportion.

Limitations of Dalton's Atomic Theory

Though Dalton's atomic theory could explain the laws of chemical combination, it failed in the following features :

(a) According to Dalton's atomic theory, atoms were thought to be indivisible. However, under certain circumstances atoms can be further divided into smaller particles such as electrons, protons and neutrons.

(b) His theory proposed that all the atoms of an element will have exactly the same mass. However, it was later known that the atoms of the same element can have different masses (isotopes).

(c) It failed to explain different properties of the elements.

(d) His theory suggested that the atoms of different elements have different masses. However, it was known that even atoms of different elements can have the same mass.

(e) It also failed to explain why and how atoms of different elements combine to form compounds or molecules.

(f) It failed to explain the nature of bonding forces that keeps the atoms together in a molecule.

PAPER-PEN TEST : 3

1. Define Dalton's atomic theory.
2. Who provided the basic theory about the nature of matter?
3. The smallest particles of matter are --------------.
4. Explain the postulates of Dalton's atomic theory.
5. Justify: "The total mass of the products remains equal to the total mass of the reactants during a chemical reaction."
6. What happens when calcium carbonate undergoes decomposition?
7. Define the law of constant proportions.
8. What are the drawbacks of Dalton's atomic theory?
9. Why Dalton's atomic theory was accepted?
10. Complete the equation : $CaCO_3 \xrightarrow{\Delta}$

3.6 ATOMS

All forms of matter such as elements, compounds or mixture are made up of atoms. Thus, we can say that atoms are the building blocks of all matter around us. Atoms are so small that we cannot see them even with a microscope. Now, it has been proved that atoms are further made up of three basic particles called *protons, electrons* and *neutrons*. There are as many kinds of atoms as there are elements. Since an atom has no overall charge, the number of electrons outside the nucleus is equal to the number of protons inside the nucleus. The atoms of most of the elements are very reactive and hence, do not exist in free state (Fig. 3.11). But a few exist in combination with the atoms of same element or different element. However, the atoms of noble gases like helium, neon, argon, krypton etc., are capable of independent existence. Thus, we can define atom as,

"The smallest particle of an element that can take part in a chemical reaction."

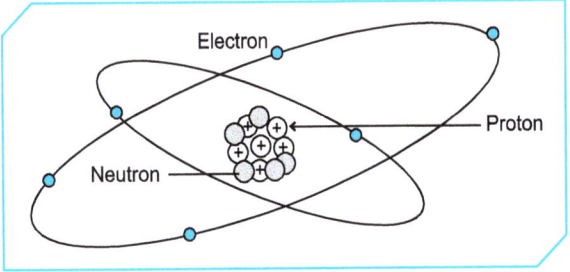

Fig. 3.11 : This figure shows the smallest unit of matter, i.e, atom.

How Big are Atoms?

Atoms are so small that we cannot see them even under a powerful microscope. The modern and advanced technique i.e., *Scanning Tunneling Electron Microscope* (STEM) has been used to study the magnified images of the surfaces of some elements. The images obtained by this technique shows atoms as blurred spheres on the surface of the element (Fig. 3.12). The idea of size of an atom is obtained from the radius of the atom. The radius of an atom or the atomic radius is measured in nanometers (nm).

$$1 \text{ nm} = \frac{1}{10^9} \text{ (metre)}$$

Or, $1 \text{ nm} = 10^{-9}$ m

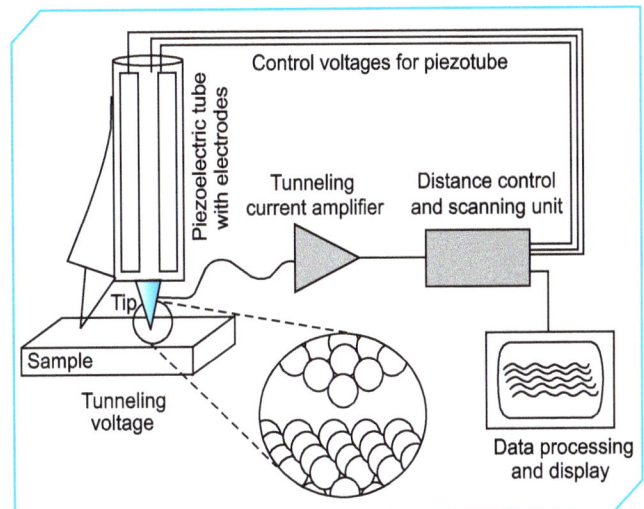

Fig. 3.12 : The figure shows schematic view of a Scanning Tunneling Electron Microscope.

Hydrogen atom is the smallest of all atoms. Its atomic radius is of the order 0.037nm (in metres, the radius will be 0.037 x 10^{-9}m). The atomic radius (Fig. 3.13) may be defined as,

"The distance between the nucleus of an atom and its valence or outer shell"

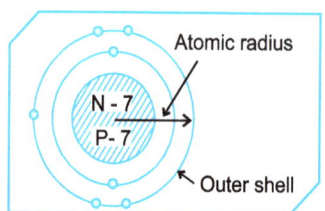

Fig. 3.13 : This figure shows the pictorial representation of atomic radius of an element.

The relative atomic radii of few elements are given in the table below :

Relative Atomic Radii of Some Important Elements

S. No	Elements	Symbol of the elements	Atomic radius or radius of atom	Diagrammatic sketch
1.	Hydrogen	H	0.037 nm	1 H
2.	Oxygen	O	0.073 nm	8 O
3.	Nitrogen	N	0.074 nm	7 N
4.	Carbon	C	0.077 nm	6 C
5.	Chlorine	Cl	0.099 nm	17 Cl
6.	Sulphur	S	0.104 nm	16 S
7.	Iron	Fe	0.126 nm	26 Fe
8.	Copper	Cu	0.128 nm	29 Cu
9.	Gold	Au	0.144 nm	79 Au
10.	Magnesium	Mg	0.160 nm	12 Mg
11.	Sodium	Na	0.191 nm	11 Na
12.	Calcium	Ca	0.197 nm	20 Ca

The relative sizes of some common substances are tabulated below :

Relative Radii of Some Common Substance

S. No.	Common Substances	Relative Sizes
1.	Atom of hydrogen	10^{-10} m
2.	Molecule of water	10^{-9} m
3.	Molecule of Haemoglobin	10^{-8} m
4.	Grain of sand	10^{-4} m
5.	Ant	10^{-2} m
6.	Watermelon	10^{-1} m

Though the atoms are so insignificant in size, they are important because our entire world is made up of atoms. We may not be able to see them, but they are constantly affecting whatever we do.

PAPER-PEN TEST : 4

1. ---------------- are the building blocks of all matter.
2. What are the three basic particles in atoms?
3. Why atoms do not exist in free state?
4. Name a few atoms which exist in free state.
5. Define atom.
6. Name the technique used to study the magnified images of the surfaces of some elements.
7. How do we obtain size of an atom?
8. The radius of an atom or the atomic radius is measured in -------------------.
9. 1 nm = ------------ m.
10. Define atomic radius.
11. Which is the smallest atom?
12. What is the atomic radius of hydrogen atom?

3.7 ATOMIC SYMBOLS OR SYMBOLS OF ELEMENTS

Symbols, short names and abbreviations are common these days as these are used for the sake of simplicity. In chemistry, the shortened names of the elements are known as *symbols*. A symbol may be defined as, *"A short hand representation of the name of an element."*

Ancient Symbols of Atoms of Different Elements

Alchemists, who were also called fire philosophers, were the ancient chemists. They used few signs and symbols based on mythological origin to represent some of the elements. A few symbols for some elements are shown in (Fig. 3.14) below :

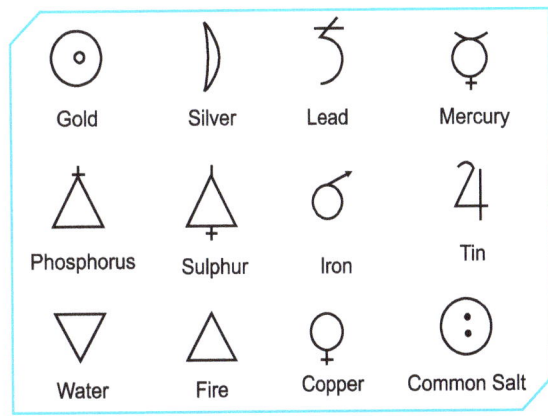

Fig. 3.14 : Symbols of some elements as proposed by ancient chemists.

Later, Dalton was the first scientist to identify the symbols for elements and compounds. When he used a symbol for an element, he also meant a definite quantity of that element, i.e., one atom of that element. In order to differentiate element and compounds, he used certain signs inside the circles. A few symbols for some elements and compounds are shown (Fig. 3.15) below :

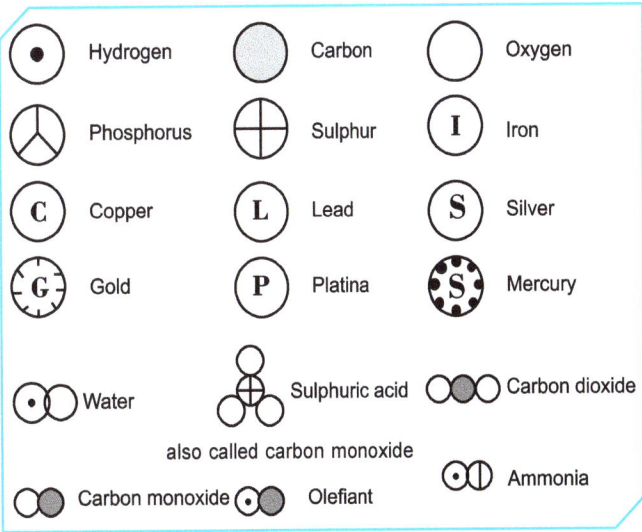

Fig. 3.15 : Symbols of some elements and compounds as proposed by Dalton.

However, the symbols of elements as proposed by **Dalton** were difficult to draw and memorize. Therefore, an alternative method of representing elements was proposed by **J.J. Berzelius** who formulated the modern day symbols of representing elements.

Modern Day Symbols of Atoms of Different Elements

J.J. Berzelius introduced the modern chemical symbols of different elements (Fig. 3.16). He suggested that the symbols of elements can be made from one or two letters of the English or Latin name of the element. The names of elements were derived from the name of the place where they were found for the first time. For example, the name copper was taken from Cyprus. Some names were taken from specific colours. For example, 'gold' was taken from the English word meaning 'yellow'.

Fig. 3.16 : J.J. Berzelius: the scientist who first introduced the modern symbols of the different elements.

Now-a-days, IUPAC (International Union of Pure and Applied Chemistry) approves names of elements. According to IUPAC, the symbols are the first one or two letters of the element's name in English. The first letter of a symbol is always written as a capital letter (uppercase) and the second letter as a small letter (lowercase). For instance, Aluminium is written as Al and not AL, Cobalt is written as Co and not CO etc.

The symbols of some elements are formed from the first letter of the name and a letter, appearing later in the name. For instance, Chlorine is written as Cl, Zinc is written as Zn etc. Some symbols have been taken from the names of elements in Latin, German or Greek. For instance, Iron is Fe from its Latin name 'ferrum', sodium is Na from 'natrium,' potassium is K from 'kalium'. Therefore, each element has a name and a unique chemical symbol.

In some elements, the first letter of their English names is taken as their symbols. For instance, in case of hydrogen, oxygen and iodine, the first letter of their English name represents their symbols, i.e., H, O and I. However, there are a number of elements whose names begin with the same letter. For instance, Barium, Boron, Bismuth, Beryllium etc., starts with the letter 'B'. In order to differentiate these elements, one of the element is given a one letter symbol, whereas the first and second letter of the element's name is taken as a symbol of all other elements as Boron (B), Barium (Ba), Bismuth (Bi) and Beryllium (Be). The symbols of some of the important elements derived from their English names are tabulated below:

Chemical Symbols of Some of the Elements Derived from their English Names

English name of the elements	Symbol	English name of the elements	Symbol	English name of the elements	Symbol
Aluminium	Al	Beryllium	Be	Nitrogen	N
Argon	Ar	Fluorine	F	Oxygen	O
Boron	B	Krypton	Kr	Nickel	Ni
Bromine	Br	Hydrogen	H	Silicon	Si
Barium	Ba	Helium	He	Manganese	Mn
Calcium	Ca	Iron	Fe	Iodine	I
Carbon	C	Lithium	Li	Sulphur	S
Chlorine	Cl	Magnesium	Mg	Uranium	U
Cobalt	Co	Neon	Ne	Zinc	Zn

Some elements have both English as well as Latin or German names. Therefore, in order to avoid confusion, symbols of some of the important elements are derived from their Latin or German names. A few elements derived from Latin or German are tabulated below :

Chemical Symbols of Some of the Elements Derived from their Latin or German Names

S. No	English name of the elements	Latin / German name	Symbol
1.	Silver	Argentum	Ag
2.	Tungsten	Wolfram	W
3.	Potassium	Kalium	K
4.	Gold	Aurum	Au

5.	Sodium	Natrium	Na
6.	Lead	Plumbum	Pb
7.	Mercury	Hydrargyrum	Hg
8.	Antimony	Stibium	Sb
9.	Copper	Cuprum	Cu
10.	Iron	Ferrum	Fe
11.	Tin	Stannum	Sn

Note

- For certain elements, the first two letters of the name of the element are taken. However, it should be noted that in a 'two letter' symbol, the first letter is the first letter of the element whereas another letter may or may not always be the second letter of the element.

Let us discuss a few elements having their first two letters as their symbols.

Chemical Symbols of Some of the Elements Having First two Letters as their Symbols.

S.No.	English Name of the Elements	Symbol
1.	Calcium	Ca
2.	Aluminium	Al
3.	Neon	Ne
4.	Germanium	Ge
5.	Silicon	Si
6.	Argon	Ar
7.	Nickel	Ni
8.	Helium	He
9.	Cobalt	Co
10.	Barium	Ba
11.	Bromine	Br

Let us now discuss the significance of the symbol of an element.

Significance of the Symbol of an Element

The symbol of an element represents the name of the element, one atom of the element, one mole of the element and a definite mass of the element equal to atomic mass expressed in grams. For example, the element nitrogen (N) represents :

(a) The name of the element as Nitrogen.

(b) One atom of the Nitrogen element.

(c) One mole of nitrogen atoms which is equal to 6.022×10^{23} atoms.

(d) A definite mass of the element which is equal to the atomic mass expressed in grams. In other words, 14g of nitrogen is equal to the atomic mass of nitrogen.

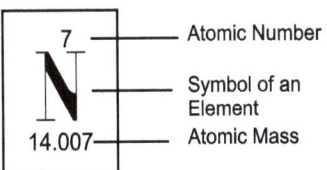

PAPER-PEN TEST : 5

1. What are symbols?
2. Alchemists were also called ----------------------.
3. The signs and symbols used by the ancient chemist were based on ---------------.
4. Who was the first scientist to identify the symbols for elements and compounds?
5. What did Dalton do to differentiate between elements and compounds?
6. Who proposed an alternative method of representing elements?
7. Who formulated the modern day symbols of representing elements?
8. Name an element which was derived from the name of the place where they were found for the first time.
9. Expand IUPAC.
10. Give the chemical symbols of five elements derived from their English names.
11. Give the chemical symbols of five elements derived from Latin or German names.

12. Name five elements having first two letters as their symbols.
13. Mention the significance of symbol of an element.

3.8 ATOMIC MASS OF AN ELEMENT

According to Dalton's atomic theory, each element has a characteristic atomic mass. His theory explained the law of constant proportion so well that scientists were prompted to measure the atomic mass of an atom. Since determining the mass of an individual atom was a difficult task, relative atomic masses were determined using the laws of chemical combinations and the compounds formed. For instance, the compound carbon monoxide (CO) formed by carbon and oxygen was observed experimentally. It was found that 3 g of carbon combines with 4 g of oxygen to form carbon monoxide (CO). Thus, we can define atomic mass as,

"The mass of an atom of an element."

The atomic mass can be expressed in milligrams (mg), kilograms (kg), grams (g) etc. The actual mass of the atoms of the elements are very, very small. It is extremely inconvenient to write and measure such small masses while carrying out calculations. Therefore, it was necessary to define atomic masses in simple way. In 1961, IUPAC has accepted the atomic mass unit (earlier abbreviated as 'amu' but now, it is written as 'u' or unified mass) scale to be used for expressing atomic masses of elements. In order to understand the definition of atomic mass on amu scale, we should know the meaning of carbon – 12 atom (C-12). Carbon – 12 is the atom of carbon which has 6 protons and 6 neutrons in its nucleus, so that its mass number is 12. If we define the atomic mass unit as equal to the mass of one carbon atom, then we would assign carbon an atomic mass of 1.0 u and oxygen an atomic mass of 1.33 u. However, it is more convenient to have these numbers as whole numbers. Initially scientists took 1/16 of the mass of an atom of naturally occurring oxygen as the unit due to two reasons :

(a) Oxygen reacted with a large number of elements and formed compounds.

(b) This atomic mass unit gave masses of most of the elements as whole numbers.

However, for a universally accepted atomic mass unit, the most stable carbon-12 isotope was chosen as the standard reference for measuring atomic masses. Thus, one atomic mass unit is defined as :

"The quantity of mass equal to exactly one twelfth (1/12th) of the mass of an atom of carbon-12"

The atomic masses of all other elements have been found by comparing their mass with respect to an atom of carbon-12. Thus, atomic mass of an element is defined as,

"The relative mass of its atom as compared with the mass of a carbon-12 taken as 12 units"

The relative atomic mass of an element can be expressed as,

$$\text{Atomic mass of an element} = \frac{\text{Mass of one atom of the element}}{1/12 \times \text{Mass of one atom of C-12}}$$

Applying the above expression, relative atomic masses of some of the common elements are tabulated below :

Relative Atomic Masses of Some Common Elements
(Standard $^{12}_{6}C = 12.000$)

Element	Symbol	Atomic Mass (u)	Element	Symbol	Atomic Mass (u)
Hydrogen	H	1 u	Aluminium	Al	27 u
Carbon	C	12 u	Phosphorus	P	31 u
Nitrogen	N	14 u	Potassium	K	39 u
Oxygen	O	16 u	Iron	Fe	56 u
Sodium	Na	23 u	Copper	Cu	63.5 u
Magnesium	Mg	24 u	Chlorine	Cl	35.5 u
Sulphur	S	32 u	Calcium	Ca	40 u

Since the experimentally measured mass of an atom of carbon-12 is 1.9926×10^{-23} gram, we can get the absolute mass of the atomic mass unit by dividing this mass by 12, which is equal to 1.6605×10^{-24} gram. Thus, by using this value of atomic mass unit, we can find the actual mass or absolute mass of the atoms of any element.

3.9 EXISTENCE OF ATOMS

Most of the atoms are chemically reactive and hence do not exist in the Free State (as independent atoms). A few elements such as noble gases are chemically unreactive and exist in the Free State (as independent atoms). Generally, atoms exist in the form of molecules and ions. These molecules or ions aggregate in large numbers to form the matter that can be seen, felt or touched. When atoms form molecules or ions, they become stable. Thus,

"The compounds containing molecules are called molecular compounds."

"The compounds containing ions are called ionic compounds."

We cannot see the individual molecules or ions with our eyes. However, we can see the substances which are a collection of molecules or ions held together through interparticle forces. For instance, we cannot see the individual sodium ions and chloride ions with our eyes, but we can see the sodium chloride compound or molecule because it is aggregate of millions of sodium and chloride ions. Similarly, we cannot see the individual iodine molecules with our eyes, but we can see violet coloured iodine crystal(Fig. 3.17a and b).

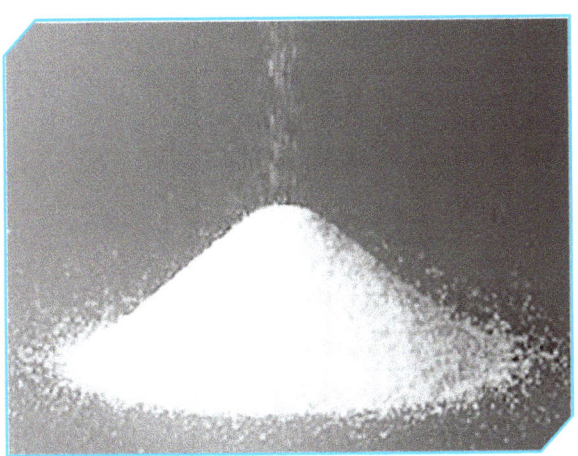

Fig. 3.17 : (a) Sodium chloride (NaCl) compound.

(b) Iodine crystals.

PAPER-PEN TEST : 6

1. Define atomic mass.
2. How are the atomic masses measured?
3. Why it was necessary to measure the atomic mass?
4. What is C-12?
5. Define one amu.
6. Define relative atomic mass.
7. How will you find the actual mass or absolute mass of the atoms of any element?
8. Atoms exist in the form of ------------------ and ------------.
9. Why we cannot see the individual sodium ions and chloride ions with our eyes, but we can see the sodium chloride compound?
10. Give the atomic mass of : (a) Magnesium (b) Calcium (c) Potassium

3.10 MOLECULES

A molecule is a group of two or more atoms that are chemically bonded together by attractive forces. They are electrically neutral and can exist in Free State. A molecule, thus can be defined as,

"The smallest particle of an element or a compound that is capable of an independent existence and shows all the properties of that substance"

Atoms of the same element or of different elements can join together to form molecules. In other words, molecules can be formed either by combining atoms of the same element or of different elements. Let us discuss the two types of molecules :

Molecules of Elements

The molecules of an element contains the same type of atoms i.e., two or more similar atoms chemically combined together. Molecules of many metals, such as argon (Ar), helium (He), neon (Ne), krypton (Kr), sodium (Na), aluminium (Al), iron (Fe) etc., are made up of only one atom of that element. But this is not the case with most of the non-metals. For instance, a molecule of oxygen consists of two atoms of oxygen as O_2, a molecule of chlorine consists of two atoms of chlorine as Cl_2, a molecule of nitrogen gas consists of two atoms of nitrogen as N_2 and a molecule of iodine gas consists of two atoms of iodine as I_2.

Ozone gas has three oxygen atoms combined together; therefore it exists as O_3 molecule. Similarly, phosphorus element has four phosphorus atoms combined together and so it exists as P_4 molecule, the sulphur element has eight sulphur atoms combined together and so it exists as S_8 molecule. We will now discuss the atomicity of elements (Fig. 3.18).

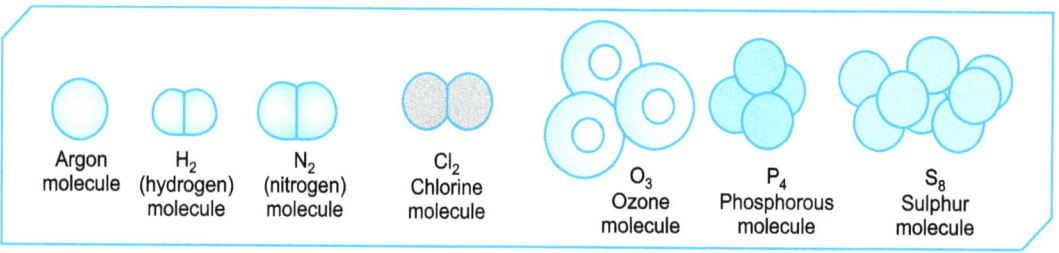

Fig. 3.18 : This figure shows some of the examples of molecules of elements.

Atomicity

Metals and some other elements, such as carbon, do not have a simple structure but consist of a very large and indefinite number of atoms bonded together. We can define atomicity as,

"The number of atoms present in one molecule of an element."

(a) Noble gases such as helium (He), argon (Ar), neon (Ne) etc., have one atom each in their molecules and so, the atomicity of helium, argon and neon is 1. Such molecules are called as monoatomic.

(b) The metal elements such as iron (Fe), zinc (Zn), sodium (Na), nickel (Ni), cobalt (Co), aluminium (Al), magnesium (Mg), copper (Cu), etc., have one atom each in their molecules and therefore, their atomicity is also taken as 1. Thus, metals are called as monoatomic.

(c) The molecules of hydrogen (H_2), chlorine (Cl_2), oxygen (O_2), bromine (Br_2), etc, have two atoms in their molecules and so, the atomicity of hydrogen, chlorine, oxygen and bromine is 2. Such molecules are called as diatomic.

(d) Ozone (O_3) has three atoms of oxygen in its molecule and so, the atomicity of ozone is 3. Such molecules are called as triatomic.

(e) Phosphorus (P_4) has four atoms of phosphorus in its molecule and so, the atomicity of phosphorus is 4. Such molecules are called as tetraatomic.

(f) Sulphur (S_8) has eight atoms of sulphur in its molecule and so, the atomicity of sulphur is 8. Such molecules are called as polyatomic.

The atomicity of some of the important elements is tabulated below :

Atomicity of Some of the Important Elements

Name of the element	Atomicity	Number of atoms	Diagrammatic sketch
Argon	Monoatomic	1	Ar
Helium	Mono atomic	1	He
Sodium	Monoatomic	1	Na
Magnesium	Monoatomic	1	Mg
Aluminium	Monoatomic	1	Al

Oxygen	Diatomic	2	O—O
Hydrogen	Diatomic	2	H—H
Nitrogen	Diatomic	2	N—N
Chlorine	Diatomic	2	Cl—Cl
Ozone	Triatomic	3	O—O—O
Phosphorus	Tetraatomic	4	(tetrahedral structure)
Sulphur	Polyatomic	8	(ring and crown structures, Top view / Side view)

Molecules of Compounds

Atoms of different elements join together in definite proportions to form molecules of compounds. In other words, the molecule of a compound contains two or more of different types of atoms chemically combined together. In order to understand it more clearly, we can take the following examples :

(a) A molecule of water (H_2O) is formed from two different atoms, hydrogen atom (H) and oxygen atom (O).

(b) A molecule of ammonia (NH_3) is formed from two different types of atoms, hydrogen atom (H) and nitrogen atom (N).

(c) A molecule of carbon dioxide (CO_2) is formed from two different atoms, carbon atom (C) and oxygen atom (O).

(d) A molecule of methane (CH_4) is formed from two different atoms, carbon atom (C) and hydrogen atom (H).

(e) A molecule of sulphur dioxide (SO_2) is formed from two different atoms, sulphur atom (S) and oxygen atom (O).

(f) A molecule of hydrogen chloride (HCl) is formed from two different atoms, hydrogen atom (H) and chlorine atom (Cl).

We can summarize the above discussion in a tabular column as follows :

Structure of Some Important Molecules of Compounds

Compound	Combining elements	Structure of compound
Water (H_2O)	Hydrogen, Oxygen	H – O – H
Ammonia (NH_3)	Nitrogen, Hydrogen	H – N – H | H
Carbon dioxide (CO_2)	Carbon, Oxygen	O = C = O
Methane (CH_4)	Carbon, Hydrogen	H | H – C – H | H
Sulphur dioxide (SO_2)	Sulphur, Oxygen	O = S = O
Hydrogen chloride (HCl)	Hydrogen, Chlorine	H – Cl

3.11 CHEMICAL FORMULAE

The chemical formula of a compound is a symbolic representation of its composition. We can define chemical formulae as,

"The composition of a molecule of the substance in terms of symbols of the elements present in the molecule is known as chemical formulae"

The chemical formula denotes the number of atoms present in one molecule of the compound. The chemical formulae also indicates the fixed proportion by mass of the combining atoms. Generally, the chemical formulae is classified into two types namely,

(a) Empirical formulae
(b) Molecular formulae

(a) Empirical Formulae

The empirical formula of a compound is calculated from the percentage of various elements present in the compound. Thus, we can define empirical formula as,

"The simplest ratio of atoms of different elements present in a molecule of the compound"

The percentage of the elements in the compound can be determined from the given data and the empirical formulae can be determined as follows :

Step 1– Divide the percentage given for each element by its atomic mass to get the relative number of moles of various elements present in the compound.

Step 2– Divide the quotients obtained in step 1 by the smallest of them to get a simple ratio of moles of various elements.

Step 3– Multiply the figures obtained by a suitable integer to get a whole number ratio.

Step 4– Write down the symbols of the elements side by side and give the numbers obtained from the above step as the subscripts to the lower right hand side of each symbol. This gives us the empirical formula.

Let us now try to solve few problems based on empirical formula.

Solved Sample Problems

Sample Problem 1 : A compound contains 75% carbon and 25% hydrogen. Find its empirical formula. Atomic weight of C = 12u, H = 1u

Solution : Given : Atomic mass of carbon = 12u
Atomic mass of hydrogen = 1u

Elements	Percentage Composition	Relative no. of moles	Simple ratio of moles	Simplest whole number ratio
C	75	$\frac{75}{12} = 6.25$	$\frac{6.25}{6.25} = 1$	1
H	25	$\frac{25}{1} = 25$	$\frac{25}{6.25} = 4$	4

Hence, the empirical formula of the compound is CH_4.

Sample Problem 2 : A compound contains 25% carbon and 75% oxygen. Find its empirical formula. Atomic weight of C = 12u, O = 16u

Solution : Given : Atomic mass of carbon = 12u
Atomic mass of oxygen = 16u

Elements	Percentage Composition	Relative no. of moles	Simple ratio of moles	Simplest whole number ratio
C	25	$\frac{25}{12} = 2.08$	$\frac{2.08}{2.08} = 1$	1
O	75	$\frac{75}{16} = 4.69$	$\frac{4.69}{2.08} = 2.25$	2

Hence, the empirical formula of the compound is CO_2.

Try Yourself

1. A compound has 54.54% carbon, 9.09% hydrogen and 36.36% oxygen. Find its empirical formula.
   [C_2H_4O]

2. A compound contains 80% carbon and 20% hydrogen. Find its empirical formula.
   [CH_3]

3. A substance contains 43.4% sodium, 11.3% carbon and 43.3% oxygen. Calculate its empirical formula.
   [Na_2CO_3]

4. A compound contains 14.31% sodium, 9.97% sulphur, 6.22% hydrogen and 69.5% oxygen. Calculate its empirical formula.

[$Na_2SH_{20}O_{14}$]

5. A compound contains 40.65% carbon, 8.55% hydrogen and 23.7% nitrogen. Find its empirical formula.

[C_2H_5N]

PAPER-PEN TEST : 7

1. Define a molecule.
2. Atoms of the same element or of different elements can join together to form ------------.
3. How are molecules formed?
4. What do the molecules of an element contain?
5. Name three monoatomic molecules.
6. Name three diatomic molecules.
7. What are triatomic molecules? Give an example.
8. What are tetratomic molecules? Give an example.
9. What are polyatomic molecules? Give an example.
10. What are the combining elements in :
    (a) Hydrogen chloride
    (b) Sulphur dioxide
    (c) Methane
    (d) Carbon dioxide
    (e) Ammonia
11. Define chemical formulae.
12. What are the two types of chemical formulae?
13. What do the chemical formulae denote?
14. Define empirical formulae.
15. How will you determine the empirical formulae?

(b) Molecular Formulae

In the molecular formulae, the symbol represents the element while the figure written in the subscript of the symbol of an element represents the number of atoms present in one molecule. We can define molecular formulae as,

"A symbolic representation of a molecule of a substance representing the actual number of various atoms present in it is called molecular formula"

For example, the molecular formula of carbon dioxide is CO_2. This formulae shows that one molecule of carbon dioxide contains one atom of carbon and two atoms of oxygen. Similarly, the molecular formula of hydrogen is H_2. This formulae shows that one molecule of hydrogen contains 2 atoms of hydrogen. The chemical formula can be of an element or of a compound. Let us discuss this in detail below.

Formulae of Elements

The chemical formula of an element is the composition of its molecule, in which the symbol refers to the element and the mathematical figure in subscript tells us how many atoms are present in a molecule. For example, one molecule of chlorine element contains two atoms of chlorine. Therefore, the formula of the chlorine is Cl_2. Similarly, one molecule of oxygen element contains two atoms of oxygen. Therefore, the formula of oxygen is O_2. On the other hand, the inert gases like neon, helium and argon have only one atom per molecule, so their formula is Ne, He and Ar respectively. Let us see the molecular formulae of some common elements as shown in a table below :

Molecular formulae of Some Common Elements

S. No	Elements	Formula	No. of atoms
1.	Hydrogen	H_2	2
2.	Nitrogen	N_2	2
3.	Oxygen	O_2	2
4.	Chlorine	Cl_2	2
5.	Bromine	Br_2	2
6.	Iodine	I_2	2
7.	Phosphorus	P_4	4
8.	Sulphur	S_8	8
9.	Argon	Ar	1
10.	Helium	He	1

Formulae of Compounds

The chemical formula of a compound has chemical symbols representing the elements present, and the mathematical figure in the subscript represents the number of atoms of each element present in one molecule of compound. For example, aluminium oxide is a compound having the formula Al_2O_3. This formula shows that the compound is made up of aluminium atoms and oxygen atoms in the ratio of 2 : 3 respectively. In other words, the compound aluminium oxide contains 2 atoms of aluminium and 3 atoms of oxygen. Similarly, in case of sodium chloride compound, the formula of compound is NaCl. The formula NaCl, does not show any subscripts and hence it is taken as 1. Thus, the formula shows that the compound is made up of sodium atoms and chlorine atoms in the ratio of 1 : 1 respectively. The mathematical figure given in front of the formula of a compound represents the number of molecules. For example, $6CO_2$ means 6 molecules of carbon dioxide. The formulae of some common molecular compounds and the elements present in them are tabulated below :

Formulae of Some Common Molecular Compounds

Name of the compound	Formula	Elements present	Ratio	Structure of the compound
Water	H_2O	Hydrogen and Oxygen	2:1	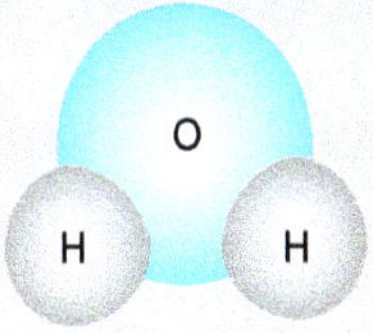
Carbon dioxide	CO_2	Carbon and Oxygen	1:2	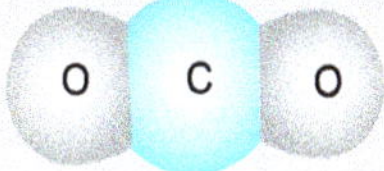
Sulphur dioxide	SO_2	Sulphur and Oxygen	1:2	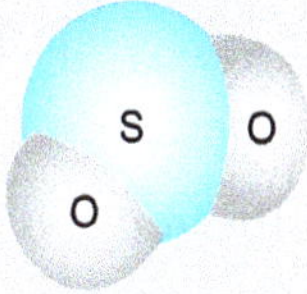
Ammonia	NH_3	Nitrogen and Hydrogen	1:3	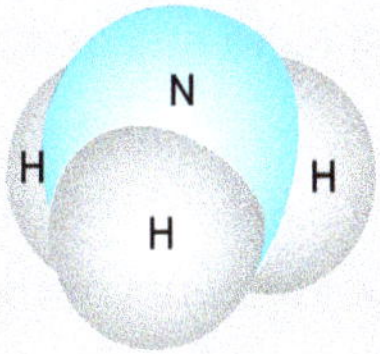
Methane	CH_4	Carbon and Hydrogen	1:4	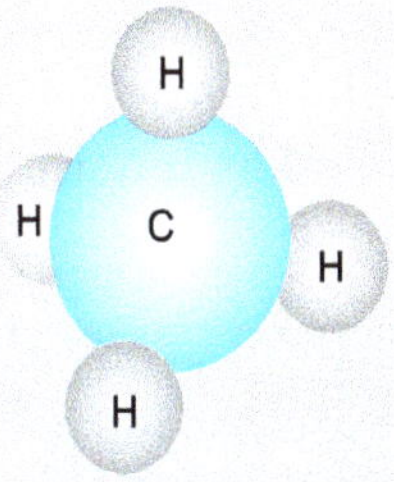
Ethanol	C_2H_5OH	Carbon, Hydrogen and Oxygen	2:6:1	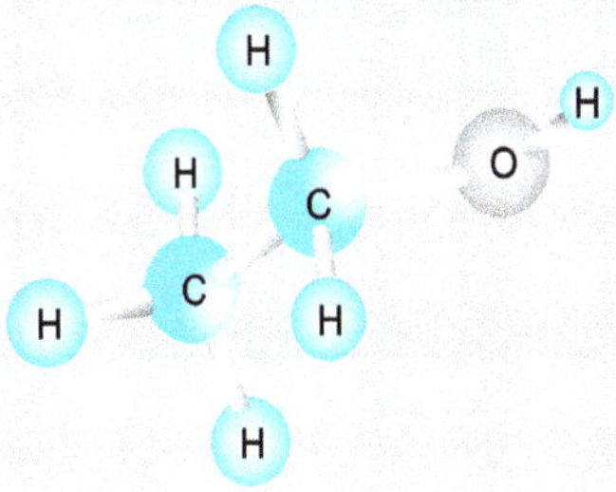
Hydrogen chloride	HCl	Hydrogen and Chlorine	1:1	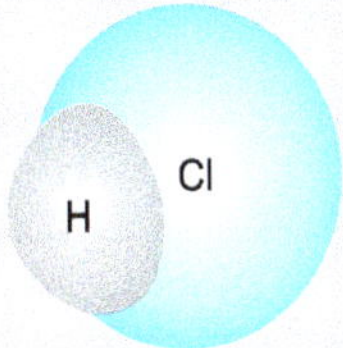

Hydrogen sulphide	H_2S	Hydrogen and Sulphur	2 : 1	
Carbon disulphide	CS_2	Carbon and Sulphur	1 : 2	

We can also calculate the ratio of molecules in a given compound as shown in the activity below.

Activity 3.2– To calculate the ratio of number of atoms of elements present in the molecules of compound.

PROCEDURE

Step 1– If hydrogen and oxygen combines in the ratio of 1 : 8, find the ratio by number of the atoms of elements in the molecules of compound.

Step 2– If nitrogen and oxygen combines in the ratio of 28 : 3, find the ratio by number of the atoms of elements in the molecules of compound.

Step 3– If carbon and oxygen combines in the ratio of 3 : 8, find the ratio by number of the atoms of elements in the molecules of compound.

CALCULATION

The ratio by number of atoms for a water molecule can be found as follows :

(a)

Element	Ratio by mass	Atomic mass (u)	Mass ratio/ Atomic mass	Simplest whole number ratio
H	1	1	1/1 = 1	2
O	8	16	8/16 = 1/2	1

(b)

Element	Ratio by mass	Atomic mass (u)	Mass ratio/ Atomic mass	Simplest whole number ratio
N	28	14	14/28 = 2/1	2
O	3	16	3/16 = 1/5.3	5

(c)

Element	Ratio by mass	Atomic mass (u)	Mass ratio/ Atomic mass	Simplest whole number ratio
C	3	12	3/12 = 1/4	1
O	8	16	8/16 = 1/2	2

CONCLUSION

(a) The ratio by number of atoms for H : O = 2 : 1
= H_2O

(b) The ratio by number of atoms for N : O = 2 : 5
= N_2O_5

(c) The ratio by number of atoms for C : O = 1 : 2
= CO_2

Significance of Molecular Formulae

The molecular formulae has the following significances :

(a) It indicates the number of atoms of each element present in one molecule of the compound.

(b) It indicates the number of different elements present in the compound.

(c) It helps to calculate the relative molecular mass of the compound.

Relationship between Molecular Formulae and Empirical Formulae

The molecular formulae and the empirical formulae are related as,

n × Empirical formula = Molecular formula

Where 'n' is a positive integer.

Thus,

$$n = \frac{\text{Molecular mass of the compound}}{\text{Empirical formula mass}}$$

Molecular Mass

The molecular mass is the mass of one molecule, i.e., the number of times a molecule is heavier than 1/12th of the weight of a C-12 atom. We can thus define molecular mass as,

"The molecular mass of a substance is the relative mass of its molecule compared with the mass of a carbon-12 atom taken as 12 units"

$$\text{Molecular mass} = \frac{\text{Weight of one molecule of a substance}}{1/12\text{th of the weight of one carbon} - 12 \text{ atom}}$$

Since, the molecular mass is a ratio, it has no units. Generally it is expressed in atomic mass unit (amu).

Calculation of Molecular Mass

In order to obtain the molecular mass, we need to know the molecular formula of a substance. This is because molecular mass is equal to the sum of the atomic masses of all the atoms present in one molecule of the substance. Let us illustrate the calculation of molecular mass with an example.

Let us calculate the molecular mass of water. The molecular mass of water will be equal to the sum of the masses of two hydrogen atoms, and one oxygen atom as we know that one molecule of water contains two atoms of hydrogen and one atom of oxygen. By knowing the atomic mass of hydrogen as 1u and oxygen as 16 u, we can calculate the molecular mass as follows :

Mass of hydrogen (H) atom = 1u

Mass of oxygen (O) atom = 16 u

Molecular mass of water (H_2O) = Mass of two hydrogen atoms + Mass of one oxygen atom

= 1 x 2 + 16 = 18 u

Thus, the molecular mass of water (H_2O) is 18 u.

Solved Sample Problems

Sample Problem 1 : Calculate the relative molecular mass of sulphuric acid (H_2SO_4). Atomic Masses : H = 1 u, O = 16 u and S = 32 u.

Solution : Given : Atomic mass of hydrogen (H) atom = 1u,

Atomic mass of oxygen (O) atom = 16 u

Atomic mass of sulphur (S) atom = 32 u

So the molecular mass of water, which contains two atoms of hydrogen, atom of sulphur and four atoms of oxygen is :

Molecular mass of H_2SO_4 = Mass of 2H atom + Mass of 5 atom + mass of 40 atom

= (2 × 1) + (32 × 1) + (16 × 4)

= 2 + 32 + 64 = 98 u

Hence, the molecular mass of sulphuric acid is 98 u.

Sample Problem 2 : Calculate the molecular mass of nitric acid (HNO_3). Atomic Masses : N = 14u, H = 1u, O = 16 u

Solution : Given : Atomic mass of hydrogen (H) atom = 1u,

Atomic mass of oxygen (O) atom = 16 u,

Atomic mass of nitrogen (N) atom = 14u

Now,

Molecular mass of HNO_3 = Atomic mass of H + Atomic mass of N + 3 × Atomic mass of O

= 1 + 14 + 3 x 16

= 63 u

Hence, the molecular mass of nitric acid (HNO_3) is 63u.

Sample Problem 3 : Calculate the molecular mass of chloroform ($CHCl_3$). Atomic Masses : H = 1u, C = 12 u, Cl = 35.5 u

Solution : Given : Atomic mass of hydrogen (H) atom = 1u, Atomic mass of carbon (C) atom = 12u, Atomic mass of Chlorine (Cl) atom = 35.5u

Now,

Molecular mass of $CHCl_3$ = Atomic mass of C + Atomic mass of H + 3 x Atomic mass of Cl

= 12 + 1 + 3 x 35.5

= 13 + 106.5 = 119.5u

Hence, the molecular mass of Chloroform ($CHCl_3$) is 119.5 u.

Try Yourself

1. Calculate the molecular mass of sulphuric acid (H_2SO_4). Given Atomic masses : H = 1 u, S = 32u, O = 16u

2. Calculate the molecular mass of calcium carbonate ($CaCO_3$). Atomic masses : Ca = 20u, C = 12u, O = 16u

3. Calculate the molecular mass of potassium nitrate (KNO_3). Atomic masses: K = 38u, N = 14u, O = 16u

4. Calculate the molecular masses of :
   (a) H_2 (b) O_2 (c) Cl_2 (d) CO_2 (e) NH_3
   Atomic Masses : N = 14u, H = 1u, O = 16u, Cl = 35.5 u

5. Calculate the molecular masses of :
   (a) CH_4 (b) C_2H_6 (c) C_2H_4 (d) CH_3OH
   Atomic Masses : C = 12u, O = 16u, H = 1u

Significance of the Formula of a Substance

The formula of a substance has the following significances :

(a) The formula indicates the name of the substance.
(b) The formula gives the names of all the elements present in the molecule.
(c) The formula represents one molecule of the substance.
(d) The formula gives the number of atoms of each element present in one molecule.
(e) The formula represents a definite mass of the substance.
(f) The formula represents one mole of the substance.

PAPER-PEN TEST : 8

1. Define molecular formula.
2. In a molecular formula, what does the figure written in the subscript of the symbol of an element represent?
3. Give the formula of : (a) Sulphur, (b) Phosphorus (c) Bromine.
4. What does the mathematical figure given in front of the formula of a compound represent?
5. Give the formula, elements and their ratio in (a) Sulphur dioxide (b) Hydrogen sulphide (c) Carbon disulphide.
6. If nitrogen and oxygen combines in the ratio of 14:3, find the ratio by number of the atoms of elements in the molecules of compounds.
7. Mention the significances of molecular formulae.
8. Give the relationship between molecular formulae and empirical formulae.
9. Define molecular mass.
10. How is molecular mass expressed?
11. How will you calculate the molecular mass?
12. Give the significance of the formula of a substance.

3.12 IONS AND IONIC COMPOUNDS

Ions

They are also known as radicals. When an atom loses or gains electrons, it gets a charge (either positive or negative). The charged species are known as ions. Compounds composed of metals and non-metals contain charged species. Ions may consist of a single charged atom or a group of atoms that have a net charge on them. A group of atoms carrying a charge is known as a polyatomic ion. We can define ion as,

"The electrically charged atoms are called ions"

In other words, an atom that acquires either positive or negative electrical charge is called an ion. It includes chloride ions (Cl^-), magnesium ions (Mg^{2+}) and oxide ions (O^{2-}) etc. These ions are formed by the loss or gain of electrons by an atom and contain an unequal number of electrons and protons. There are two types of ions, namely

(a) *Cations*
(b) *Anions*

An ion is a charged particle which may be negatively or positively charged. A negatively charged ion is called an *'anion'* and the positively charged ion, is called a *'cation'*. Before we proceed, we need to know why atoms lose or gain electrons.

Why do Atoms Lose or Gain Electrons ?

The inert gas elements like helium (He), argon (Ar), neon (Ne) etc., are chemically inactive or inert. This means these elements do not react with other elements. Hence, we can say that these elements are stable. This stability is because of the fact that the last shell in all these elements has eight electrons.

Thus, when an atom has eight electrons in the last shell, they are said to be highly stable. All atoms lose or gain electrons to get eight electrons in the last shell to attain stability. Let us now study about cations first.

(a) Cations

Positively charged ions are called cations (Fig. 3.19). It is formed by the loss of one or more electrons by an atom. It includes sodium ions (Na^+), magnesium ions (Mg^{2+}), calcium ions (Ca^{2+}) etc. We will now discuss the formation of cation with few examples.

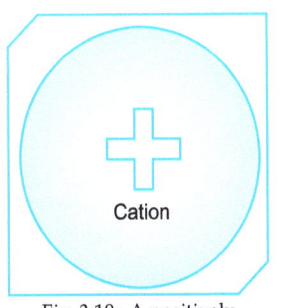

Fig. 3.19 : A positively charged ion or Cation

Example 1 : Sodium Atom

Symbol – Na

Atomic Number – 11

Electronic Configuration – 2, 8, 1

When sodium (Na) atom loses one electron, it becomes positively charged sodium ion or cation (Na^+). The cation thus formed contains one less electron than a normal sodium atom. Thus, a normal atom is said to contain an equal number of protons and electrons whereas a cation contains less electrons than protons.

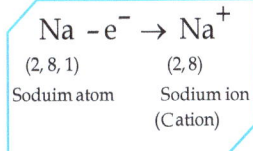

Let us write the number of protons and electrons in a sodium atom as well as in sodium ion.

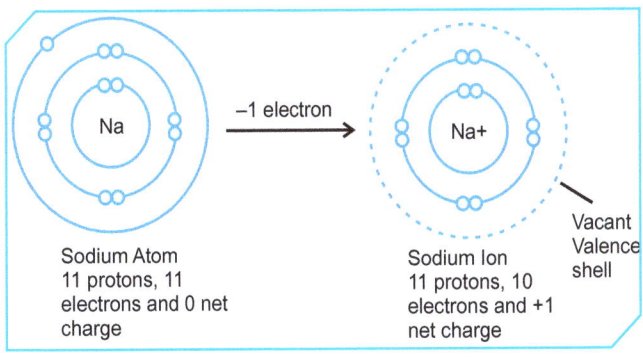

Fig. 3.20 : This figure shows the number of protons, electrons and net charge on sodium atom and sodium ion.

Since, the number of protons and electrons in a sodium (Na) atom is equal, we can say that it is electrically neutral having no overall charge. On the other hand, in the sodium (Na^+) ion, there are 11 protons and 10 electrons. This means there is 1 proton more than electrons and hence a sodium ion has one unit positive charge and is written as Na^+ (Fig. 3.20).

Example 2 : Magnesium Atom

Symbol – Mg

Atomic Number – 12

Electronic Configuration – 2, 8, 2

When magnesium (Mg) atom loses two electrons, it becomes a magnesium (Mg^{2+}) ion or cation. The cation thus formed contain two electrons less than a normal atom. Thus, a normal atom is said to contain an equal number of protons and electrons whereas a cation contain less electrons than proton.

Let us write the number of protons and electrons in a magnesium atom as well as magnesium ion.

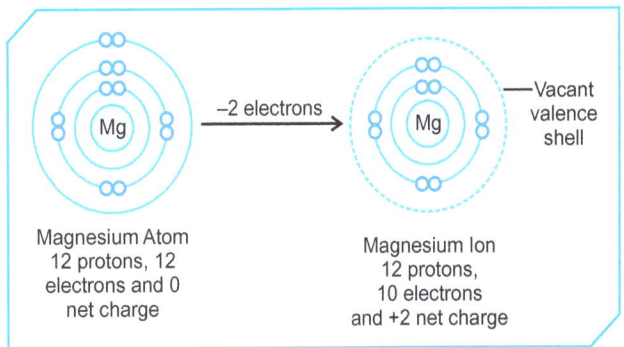

Fig. 3.21 : This figure shows the number of protons, electrons and net charge on magnesium atom and magnesium ion.

Since, the number of protons and electrons in a magnesium (Mg) atom is equal, we can say that they are electrically neutral having no overall charge. On the other hand, in the magnesium (Mg^{2+}) ions, there are 12 protons and 10 electrons. This means there are 2 protons more than electrons, and hence a magnesium ion has two unit positive charge and is written as Mg^{2+} (Fig. 3.21).

Similarly, you can work for other metals such as calcium (Ca), potassium (K) etc., All metal atoms lose electrons to form cations which are accepted by a non-metal atom in a chemical reaction. Do you know that even non-metal elements such as hydrogen and ammonia also form cations? They form hydrogen (H^+) ion and ammonium NH_4^+ ion respectively, by the loss of an electron.

Thus, we can conclude that,

(i) If an atom loses one electron, then the cation formed has one unit positive charge. Example, sodium ion (Na⁺), potassium ion (K⁺).

(ii) If an atom loses two electrons, then the cation formed has two units positive charge. Example, magnesium ion (Mg^{2+}), calcium ion (Ca^{2+}), zinc ion (Zn^{2+}).

(iii) If an atom loses three electrons, then the cation formed has three units positive charge. Example, aluminium ion (Al^{3+}), iron (III) or ferric ion (Fe^{3+}).

Note
- It is not possible to remove more than three electrons from an atom. This is because a very high energy is required to remove these electrons.

Let us now discuss about anions.

(b) Anions

Negatively charged ions are called anions (Fig. 3.22). It is formed by the gaining of one or more electrons by an atom. It includes chloride ion (Cl⁻), oxide ion (O^{2-}), nitride ion (N^{3-}) etc. We will now discuss the formation of anion with few examples.

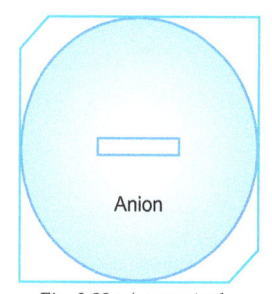

Fig. 3.22 : A negatively charged ion or anion

Example 1 : Chlorine Atom

Symbol – Cl

Atomic Number – 17

Electronic configuration – 2, 8, 7

When chlorine (Cl) atom gains an electron, it becomes a chloride (Cl⁻) ion or anion. The anion thus formed contains one electron more than a normal atom. Thus, a normal chloride atom is said to contain an equal number of protons and electrons whereas an anion contains more electrons than protons.

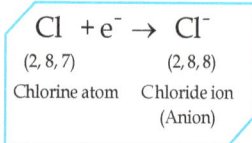

Cl + e⁻ → Cl⁻
(2, 8, 7)   (2, 8, 8)
Chlorine atom Chloride ion
(Anion)

Let us write the number of protons and electrons in a chlorine atom as well as in chloride ion.

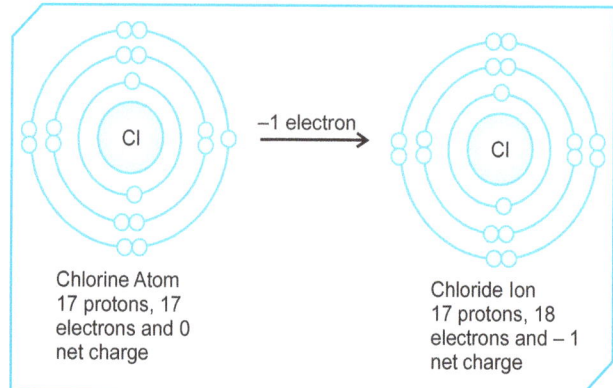

Chlorine Atom
17 protons, 17 electrons and 0 net charge

Chloride Ion
17 protons, 18 electrons and – 1 net charge

Fig. 3.23 : This figure shows the number of protons, electrons and net charge on chlorine atom and chloride ion.

Since, the number of protons and electrons in a chlorine (Cl) atom is equal, we can say that they are electrically neutral having no overall charge. On the other hand, in the chloride (Cl⁻) ion, there are 17 protons and 18 electrons. This means there is 1 electron more than protons and hence, a chloride ion has one unit negative charge and is written as Cl⁻ (Fig. 3.23).

Example 2 : Oxygen Atom

Symbol – O

Atomic Number – 8

Electronic Configuration – 2, 6

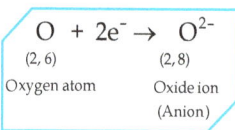

O + 2e⁻ → O^{2-}
(2, 6)   (2, 8)
Oxygen atom   Oxide ion
              (Anion)

When oxygen (O) atom gains two electrons, it becomes an oxide (O^{2-}) ion. The anion thus formed contain two electrons more than a normal atom. Thus, a normal atom is said to contain an equal number of protons and electrons whereas an anion contains more electrons than protons.

Let us write the number of protons and electrons in an oxygen atom as well as oxide ion.

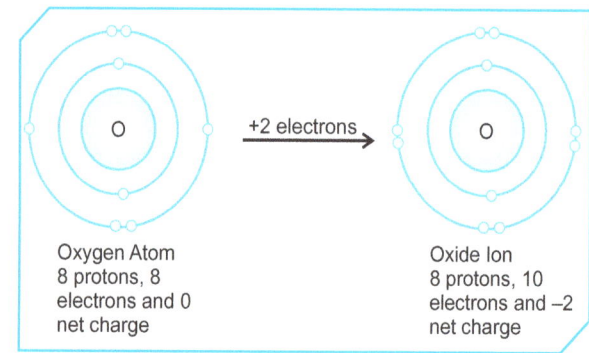

Oxygen Atom
8 protons, 8 electrons and 0 net charge

Oxide Ion
8 protons, 10 electrons and –2 net charge

Fig. 3.24 : This figure shows the number of protons, electrons and net charge on oxygen atom and oxide ion.

Since, the number of protons and electrons in an oxygen (O) atom is equal, we say that they are electrically neutral having no overall charge. On the other hand, in the oxide (O^{2-}) ion, there are 8 protons and 10 electrons. This means, there are two electrons more than protons and hence an oxide ion has two units negative charge and is written as O^{2-} (Fig. 3.24).

All the non-metal ions are anions except hydrogen and ammonium ion. They accept electrons given by the metals during chemical reaction and become negatively charged. Thus, we can conclude that,

(i) If an atom gains one electron, then the anion formed has one unit negative charge. Example, chloride ion (Cl^-), bromide ion (Br^-) etc.

(ii) If an atom gains two electrons, then the anion formed has two units negative charges. Example, oxide ion(O^{2-}), sulphide ion (S^{2-}) etc.

(iii) If an atom gains three electrons, then the anion formed has three units of negative charge. Example, nitride ion(N^{3-}), phosphate ion (PO_4^{3-}) etc.

PAPER-PEN TEST : 9

1. Define ions.
2. Ions are also called as ------------------.
3. What is polyatomic ion?
4. What are the two types of ions?
5. Why elements are stable?
6. What are cations?
7. How are cations formed?
8. Explain the formation of sodium ion from sodium atom.
9. Illustrate the formation of magnesium ion from magnesium atom.
10. What are anions?
11. How are anions formed?
12. Explain the formation of chloride ion from chlorine atom.
13. Illustrate the formation of oxide ion from oxygen atom.
14. Name the anion having three units of negative charge.
15. Name the cation having two units of positive charge.

Simple Ions

Those ions which are formed from single atoms are called simple ions. Hence, they are also known as monatomic ions. Some of the common simple ions and their symbols are given below :

(a) Sodium ion (Na^+) is a simple ion. This is because it is formed from a single sodium atom.

(b) Magnesium ion (Mg^{2+}) is a simple ion. This is because it is formed from a single magnesium atom.

(c) Chloride ion (Cl^-) is a simple ion. This is because it is formed from a single chlorine atom.

(d) Oxide ion (O^{2-}) is a simple ion. This is because it is formed from a single oxygen atom.

(e) Aluminium ion (Al^{3+}) is a simple ion. This is because it is formed from a single aluminium atom.

Compound Ions

Those ions which are formed from groups of joined atoms are called compound ions. Hence, they are also called as polyatomic ions. Some of the common compound ions and their symbols are given below:

(a) Ammonium ion is a compound ion (NH_4^+). This is because, it is formed from nitrogen and hydrogen atom.

(b) Carbonate ion is a compound ion (CO_3^{2-}). This is because, it is formed from carbon and oxygen atom.

(c) Sulphate ion is a compound ion (SO_4^{2-}). This is because, it is formed from sulphur and oxygen atom.

(d) Nitrate ion is a compound ion (NO_3^{2-}). This is because; it is formed from nitrogen and oxygen atom.

Let us tabulate some of the common simple ions and compound ions (polyatomic ions) and their symbols in a table given below :

Some Common Simple Ions and Compound Ions

Name of the Ion	Symbol	Name of the ion	Symbol
Potassium ion	K^+	Bromide ion	Br^-
Sodium ion	Na^+	Hydroxide ion	OH^-
Magnesium ion	Mg^{2+}	Chloride ion	Cl^-
Calcium ion	Ca^{2+}	Oxide ion	O^{2-}

Copper (II) ion	Cu^{2+}	Sulphide ion	S^{2-}
Zinc ion	Zn^{2+}	Carbonate ion	CO_3^{2-}
Iron (II) ion	Fe^{2+}	Nitrate ion	NO_3^-
Aluminium ion	Al^{3+}	Sulphate ion	SO_4^{2-}
Ammonium	NH_4^+	Phosphate ion	PO_4^{3-}

Ionic Compounds

Generally metals do not react with other metals, but non-metals react with other non-metals to form covalent compounds. When a metal reacts with a non-metal, an ionic compound is formed. In an ionic compound, when atoms of the elements combine, a force of attraction is developed between the two oppositely charged ions which hold them together. This force which holds the ions together in an ionic compound is called an *ionic or electrovalent bond*. In an ionic compound, the number of positively charged ions and the number of negatively charged ions are equal and hence, the overall charge on an ionic compound is zero. For instance, sodium chloride(NaCl) is an ionic compound. This is because, it has equal number of positively charged sodium (Na^+) ions and negatively charged chloride (Cl^-) ions. Let us tabulate some of the common ionic compounds, their formula and ions present in them as follows :

Some Common Ionic Compounds

Name	Chemical formula	Ions present
Sodium chloride	NaCl	Na^+ and Cl^-
Potassium chloride	KCl	K^+ and Cl^-
Ammonium chloride	NH_4Cl	NH_4^+ and Cl^-
Magnesium chloride	$MgCl_2$	Mg^{2+} and Cl^-
Aluminium oxide	Al_2O_3	Al^{3+} and O^{2-}
Calcium oxide	CaO	Ca^{2+} and O^{2-}
Calcium nitrate	$Ca(NO_3)_2$	Ca^{2+} and NO_3^-
Copper (II) Sulphate	$CuSO_4$	Cu^{2+} and SO_4^{2-}
Calcium chloride	$CaCl_2$	Ca^{2+} and Cl^-
Sodium hydroxide	NaOH	Na^+ and OH^-
Potassium hydroxide	KOH	K^+ and OH^-
Calcium chloride	$CaCl_2$	Ca^{2+} and Cl^-

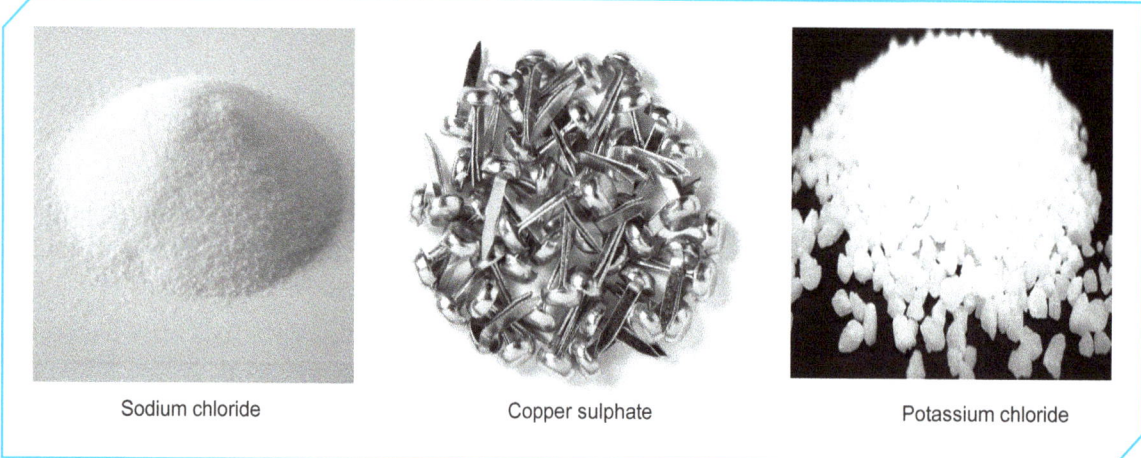

Sodium chloride   Copper sulphate   Potassium chloride

Fig. 3.25 : This figure shows some of the common ionic compounds.

From the above discussion, we can conclude that when a compound is made up of a metal and a non-metal, we can say that it is an ionic compound (Fig. 3.25). Some ionic compounds along with their constituent elements and ratio by mass have been tabulated on next page :

Constituent Elements of Some Common Ionic Compounds along with Ratio by Mass

Ionic Compound	Constituting Elements	Ratio by Mass
Magnesium sulphide	Magnesium, Sulphur	3 : 4
Sodium chloride	Sodium, Chlorine	23 : 35.5
Calcium oxide	Calcium, Oxygen	5 : 2

Let us now try to solve problems based on the ionic compounds.

Solved Sample Problems

Sample Problem 1 : Write down the name of the compound represented by the formula K_2SO_4 along with its constituent ions.

Solution : The letter 'K' belongs to potassium while 'SO$_4$' belongs to sulphate. Therefore, the name of the compound is potassium sulphate. The ions present in potassium sulphate are K^+ and SO_4^{2-}.

Sample Problem 2 : Write down the name of the compound represented by the formula $Al_2(SO_4)_3$ along with its constituent ions.

Solution : The letter 'Al' belongs to aluminium while 'SO$_4$' belongs to sulphate. Therefore, the name of the compound is aluminium sulphate. The ions present in aluminium sulphate are Al^{3+} and SO_4^{2-}.

Try Yourself

Write down the names of compounds represented by the formulae and their constituent ions :

1. $CaCO_3$
2. $CaCl_2$
3. $CaSO_4$
4. $MgSO_4$
5. KNO_3

Formula Mass of Ionic Compounds

We have studied that ionic compounds contain ions as their constituent particles and there are no molecules in them. So, in order to calculate the mass of an ionic compound we use the term 'formula mass' instead of 'molecular mass'. Thus, we can define formula mass of an ionic compound as,

"The sum of the atomic masses of all the atoms (or ions) present in a molecule of an ionic compound"

In order to calculate the formula mass of an ionic compound, we should know the formula of the ionic compound as well as the atomic masses of all the atoms (or ions) present in the formula.

Note

- The formula mass is calculated in a way similar to the calculation of molecular mass.
- Atomic mass of an atom and its ion is same.

Solved Sample Problems

Sample Problem 1 : Calculate the formula mass of potassium carbonate (K_2CO_3). Given : Atomic masses of K = 39u, C = 12 u, O = 16u

Solution : We know that:

Formula mass of K_2CO_3 = Mass of 2 K atom + Mass of C atom + Mass of 3 O atoms

Substituting the atomic masses in the formula above, we get

Formula mass of K_2CO_3 = 2 × 39 + 12 + 3 × 16
= 78 + 12 + 48
= 138 u

Hence, the formula mass of potassium carbonate is 138 u

Sample Problem 2 : Calculate the formula mass of calcium chloride ($CaCl_2$). Given : Atomic masses of Ca = 40u, Cl = 35.5 u

Solution : We know that :

Formula mass of $CaCl_2$ = Mass of Ca atom + Mass of 2 Cl atoms

Substituting the atomic masses in the formula above, we get

Formula mass of $CaCl_2$ = 40 + 2 × 35.5
= 40 + 71
= 111 u

Hence, the formula mass of calcium chloride is 111 u.

Try Yourself

1. Calculate the formula mass of sodium carbonate (Na_2CO_3). (Given: Atomic masses of Na = 23u, C = 12 u, O = 16u)
2. Calculate the formula mass of potassium sulphate (K_2SO_4). (Given : Atomic masses of K = 39u, S = 32 u, O = 16u)
3. Calculate the formula mass of potassium nitrate (KNO_3). (Given : Atomic masses of K = 39u, N = 14 u, O = 16u)
4. Calculate the formula mass of sodium nitrate ($NaNO_3$). (Given : Atomic masses of Na = 23u, N = 14 u, O = 16u)
5. Calculate the formula mass of ammonium carbonate (NH_4CO_3). (Given : Atomic masses of N = 14u, H = 1 u, C = 12 u, O = 16u)
6. Calculate the formula masses of zinc oxide (ZnO), sodium oxide (Na_2O), potassium carbonate (K_2CO_3) if the atomic masses of Zn = 65 u, Na = 23 u, K = 39 u, C = 12 u, and O = 16u.

PAPER-PEN TEST : 10

1. Define simple ions.
2. Simple ions are also called ------------------.
3. What are compound ions?
4. Give the formula of (a) Phosphate ion (b) Aluminium ion (c) Hydroxide ion
5. Sodium chloride is an ionic compound. Justify.
6. How is an ionic compound formed?
7. Give the chemical formulae of (a) Potassium hydroxide (b) Aluminium oxide.
8. Name the ions present in (a) Calcium chloride (b) Potassium nitrate.
9. Write down the name of the compound represented by the formula $Ca(NO_3)_2$ along with its constituent ions.
10. Differentiate between simple and compound ions.
11. Define formula mass of ionic compounds.
12. How will you calculate the formula mass of an ionic compound?

3.13 WRITING CHEMICAL FORMULAE

The chemical formula of a compound is a type of shorthand representation that describes the composition of elements in terms of their symbols in a compound. In other words, it represents the symbols of different elements in the compound and the ratio of the elements to one another. In a chemical formula, if a substance contains more than one atom of a particular element, this quantity is indicated by writing the mathematical figure 2, 3, 4, 5 etc. as subscript after the chemical symbol. Thus, we can define chemical formula as,

"It is a shorthand representation of the composition of a molecule of the compound in terms of the symbols of the elements present in it"

For example, the chemical formula for water is H_2O, which indicates that 2 atoms of hydrogen combine with 1 atom of oxygen. Similarly, the chemical formula for sodium chloride is NaCl indicating that 1 atom of sodium combines with 1 atom of chlorine in a one to one ratio. In the formula of the compound magnesium bromide, $MgBr_2$, the subscript 2 indicates two bromine atoms.

When two different non-metals combine to form a molecular compound, then the name of the less electronegative element is written first as such, whereas the name of more electronegative non-metal is written second with the ending of the name changed to 'ide'. For example- HCl is named as hydrogen chloride (H is written first as it is a less electronegative element whereas Cl is written second with its ending changed to chloride as it is more electronegative element).

Prefixes are used to indicate the number of atoms in a molecular compound when there is more than one atom of an element in the formula. The prefix used to indicate the number of atoms of an element in a molecular formula is as follows :

Prefix to Indicate the Number of Atoms in a Molecular Compound

Number of atoms	Prefix
1	mono
2	di
3	tri
4	tetra
5	penta
6	hexa
7	hepta
8	octa

ATOMS AND MOLECULES

For example, CO is named by adding prefix 'mono' to oxygen atom as carbon monoxide; CO_2 is named by adding prefix 'di' to oxygen atom as carbon dioxide. Similarly, SO_3, PCl_4 and PCl_5 are named as sulphur trioxide, phosphorus tetrachloride and phosphorus pentachloride respectively.

Before we discuss the rules for writing the chemical formulae of binary compounds (i.e., molecular and ionic compounds), it is important to remember the valencies of different elements and ions. Let us discuss this in detail first.

Valency

The combining power or capacity of an element is known as its valency. It can be used to find out how the atoms of an element will combine with the atom(s) of another element to form a chemical compound. Some elements exhibit more than one valency. Such elements are said to possess variable valency. For example, copper and iron metal show valencies of (1 and 2) and (2 and 3) respectively. Similarly, non-metals such as nitrogen and phosphorous show valencies of 3 and 5 each. Whereas, sulphur shows valencies of 2, 4 and 6. The elements exhibiting the valency 1, 2, 3, 4, 5, 6, 7 are called monovalent, divalent, trivalent, tetravalent, pentavalent, hexavalent and heptavalent respectively. Valencies of some common metals and non-metals which will help in writing the chemical formula of the compounds, are given below in the table.

Valencies of Some Common Metal and Non-Metal Elements

Element	Symbol	Valency
Hydrogen	H	1
Fluorine	F	1
Chlorine	Cl	1
Bromine	Br	1
Iodine	I	1
Sodium	Na	1
Potassium	K	1
Oxygen	O	2
Nitrogen	N	3
Phosphorous	P	3
Boron	B	3
Sulphur	S	2, 4, 6
Carbon	C	4
Chromium	Cr	2, 3, 6
Copper	Cu	1, 2
Gold	Au	1, 3
Iron	Fe	2, 3
Lead	Pb	2, 4
Manganese	Mn	2, 3, 4, 6, 7
Mercury	Hg	1, 2
Nitrogen	N	1, 2, 3, 5
Phosphorus	P	3, 5
Aluminium	Al	3
Tin	Sn	2, 4
Calcium	Ca	2

According to old system of naming, if an element exhibits variable valency, then the name of the atom with lower valency is denoted by the suffix-ous and the one with higher valency is denoted by the *suffix-ic*. For example, copper having valency 1 is named as cuprous whereas the copper element with valency 2 is named as cupric. However, according to the new IUPAC system, the copper having the valency 1 is named as copper (I) while the copper having the valency 2 is named as copper (II).

Note
- Cation is positively charged, so it has positive valency.
- Anion is negatively charged, so it has negative valency.

As we know that, ionic compounds are formed by the combination of positive ion and negative ion. Therefore, the valency of the positive ion and the negative ion is needed in order to write the formulae of an ionic compound. The valency of an ion is equal to its charge. For example, if a positive ion has 1 unit charge, then its valency is +1 and it is called a monovalent ion. Similarly, if a negative ion has 1 unit charge, then its valency is -1 and it is also called a monovalent ion.

Based on the number or amount of charge on the ion or radicals, they are further classified as monovalent, divalent, trivalent, tetravalent ions. Let us now tabulate a few positive radicals i.e., cations showing monovalent, divalent, trivalent and tetravalent valencies.

Valencies of Some Common Cations (Positive Ions)

Type of ion	Name of positive ion	Formula of positive ion	Valency
Monovalent	Hydrogen ion	H^+	+1
Monovalent	Sodium ion	Na^+	+1

Monovalent	Copper (I) ion (Cuprous ion)	Cu^+	+1
Monovalent	Mercury (I) ion (Mercurous ion)	Hg^+	+1
Monovalent	Ammonium ion	NH_4^+	+1
Monovalent	Silver (I) ion (Argentous ion)	Ag^+	+1
Monovalent	Potassium ion	K^+	+1
Bivalent	Copper (II) ion (Cupric ion)	Cu^{2+}	+2
Bivalent	Iron (II) ion (Ferrous ion)	Fe^{2+}	+2
Bivalent	Mercury (II) ion (Mercuric ion)	Hg^{2+}	+2
Bivalent	Tin (II) ion (Stannous ion)	Sn^{2+}	+2
Bivalent	Lead (II) ion (Plumbous ion)	Pb^{2+}	+2
Bivalent	Silver (II) ion (Argentic ion)	Ag^{2+}	+2
Bivalent	Magnesium ion	Mg^{2+}	+2
Bivalent	Calcium ion	Ca^{2+}	+2
Trivalent	Iron (III) ion (Ferric ion)	Fe^{3+}	+3
Trivalent	Aluminium ion	Al^{3+}	+3
Tetravalent	Lead (IV) ion (Plumbic ion)	Pb^{4+}	+4
Tetravalent	Tin (IV) ion (Stannic ion)	Sn^{4+}	+4

Let us now tabulate a few negative radicals i.e., anions showing monovalent, divalent and trivalent valencies.

Valencies of Some Common Anions (Negative Ions)

Type of ion	Name of negative ion	Formula of negative ion	Valency
Monovalent	Hydroxide/hydroxyl ion	OH^-	-1
Monovalent	Fluoride ion	F^-	-1
Monovalent	Chloride ion	Cl^-	-1
Monovalent	Bromide ion	Br^-	-1
Monovalent	Iodide ion	I^-	-1
Monovalent	Hydride ion	H^-	-1
Monovalent	Nitrate ion	NO_3^-	-1
Monovalent	Nitrite ion	NO_2^-	-1
Monovalent	Hypochlorite ion	ClO^-	-1
Monovalent	Chlorate ion	ClO_3^-	-1
Monovalent	Chlorite ion	ClO_2^-	-1
Monovalent	Perchlorate ion	ClO_4^-	-1
Monovalent	Acetate ion	CH_3COO^-	-1
Monovalent	Formate ion	$HCOO^-$	-1
Monovalent	Bisulphate/Hydrogen sulphate ion	HSO_4^-	-1
Monovalent	Bisulphite ion	HSO_3^-	-1
Monovalent	Bisulphide ion	HS^-	-1

Monovalent	Bicarbonate or Hydrogen carbonate ion	HCO_3^-	–1
Bivalent	Oxide ion	O^{2-}	–2
Bivalent	Peroxide ion	O_2^{2-}	–2
Bivalent	Carbonate ion	CO_3^{2-}	–2
Bivalent	Sulphate ion	SO_4^{2-}	–2
Bivalent	Sulphite ion	SO_3^{2-}	–2
Bivalent	Sulphide ion	S^{2-}	–2
Trivalent	Phosphate ion	SO_3^{2-}	–3
Trivalent	Phosphide ion	P^{3-}	–3
Trivalent	Nitride ion	N^{3-}	–3

Rules for Writing the Chemical Formulae of Binary Compounds

The chemical formula of different compounds can be written easily if we know the symbols and combining capacity of the elements. The simplest compounds, which are made up of two different elements are called *binary compounds*. For them, the valencies of ions are used to write formulae for compounds. While writing the chemical formulae for compounds, the constituent elements and their valencies must crossover. The rules for writing chemical formulae are as follows :

(a) Write down the symbols of the elements which form the compound.
(b) Below the symbol of each element, write down its valency.
(c) Finally, cross-over the valencies of the combining atoms and this gives the chemical formula of a molecular compound.

Let us illustrate the method to deduce the chemical formulae with a few examples.

Solved Sample Problems

Sample Problem 1 : Deduce the chemical formula of hydrogen chloride

Solution :

Step 1- Write down the symbols of the elements.
Symbol   H   Cl
Step 2- Write down the valency below the symbol.
Symbol   H   Cl
Valency   1   1

Step 3- Cross - over the valencies

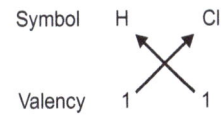

Thus, the formula of hydrogen chloride is HCl

Sample Problem 2 : Deduce the chemical formula of hydrogen sulphide

Solution :

Step 1- Write the symbols of the elements.
Symbol   H   S
Step 2- Write down the valency below the symbol.
Symbol   H   S
Valency   1   2
Step 3- Cross - over the valencies

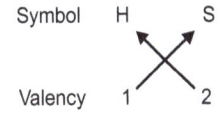

Thus, the formula of hydrogen sulphide is H_2S

Sample Problem 3 : The valency of carbon is 4 and that of chlorine is 1. What will be the chemical formula of carbon tetrachloride?

Solution :

Step 1- Write down the symbols of the elements.
Symbol   C   Cl
Step 2- Write down the valency below the symbol.
Symbol   C   Cl
Valency   4   1

Step 3– Cross - over the valencies

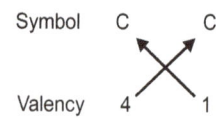

Thus, the formula of carbon tetrachloride is CCl_4

Sample Problem 4 : The valency of magnesium is 2 and that of chlorine is 1. What will be the formula of magnesium chloride?

Solution :
Step 1– Write down the symbols of the elements.
Symbol   Mg   Cl
Step 2– Write down the valency below the symbol.
Symbol   Mg   Cl
Valency   2   1
Step 3– Cross - over the valencies

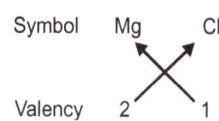

Thus, the formula of magnesium chloride is $MgCl_2$

Sample Problem 5 : What will be the formula of calcium carbonate ?

Solution :
Step 1– Write the symbols present in the formulae
Symbol   Ca CO_3
Step 2– Write down the valency below the symbol.
Symbol   Ca CO_3
Valency   2   2
Step 3– Cross-over the valencies

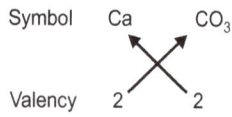

Thus, the formula of calcium carbonate is $CaCO_3$

Try Yourself

1. Write down the chemical formulae of the following molecular compounds :
   (a) Sodium oxide
   (b) Aluminium chloride
   (c) Sodium sulphide
   (d) Magnesium hydroxide
   (e) Aluminium oxide
   (f) Calcium oxide
   (g) Sodium nitrate
   (h) Calcium hydroxide
   (i) Sodium carbonate
   (j) Ammonium sulphate

2. Write down the names of compounds represented by the following molecular formulae:
   (a) $Al_2(SO_4)_3$
   (b) $CaCl_2$
   (c) K_2SO_4
   (d) KNO_3
   (e) $CaNO_3$.

PAPER-PEN TEST : 11

1. Define chemical formula.
2. What does the chemical formula for water indicate ?
3. What is the significance of prefixes in a chemical formula ?
4. Define valency.
5. Name two elements possessing two valencies.
6. What are the rules for writing the chemical formulae of the ionic compounds ?
7. Give the valency of (a) Nitrogen (b) Carbon (c) Iodine
8. The valency of an ion is equal to its -------------.
9. How can we classify ions ?
10. Name three monovalent cations with their formula and valencies.
11. Name three divalent cations with their formulae and valencies.
12. Name a trivalent cation with its formulae and valency.
13. Name two tetravalent cations with their formulae and valencies.
14 Name three monovalent anions with their formulae and valencies.
15. Name three bivalent anions with their formulae and valencies.
16. Name three trivalent anions with their formulae and valencies.

Before we proceed to mole concept, we need to understand the terms 'molar mass', 'gram atomic mass' and 'gram molecular mass'. Let us first discuss gram atomic mass.

3.14 GRAM ATOMIC MASS AND GRAM MOLECULAR MASS

Gram Atomic Mass (GAM)

The relative atomic mass expressed in grams is called gram atomic mass. We can also define it as,

"The amount of a substance whose mass in grams is numerically equal to its atomic mass"

Let us now illustrate the gram atomic mass of a substance with an example.

The atomic mass of carbon, C = 12 u

Therefore, Gram Atomic mass of carbon, C = 12 g

Similarly, Atomic mass of nitrogen, N = 14 u

Therefore, Gram Atomic mass of nitrogen, N = 14 g

Thus, the gram atomic mass of a substance represents the mass of one mole of atoms i.e., 6.022×10^{23} atoms of that substance. This means that the number of atoms present in one gram atomic mass of any substance is 6.022×10^{23} atoms. Let us now discuss the term 'gram molecular mass.

Gram Molecular Mass (GMM)

When the molecular mass is expressed in grams, it is called gram molecular mass or gram molecule or mole molecule. We can also define it as,

"The amount of a substance whose mass in grams is numerically equal to its molecular mass"

Let us now illustrate the gram molecular mass of a substance with an example.

The molecular mass of chlorine,

Cl_2 = 35.5 + 35.5 = 71 u

So, gram molecular mass of chlorine,

Cl_2 = 71 g

Similarly,

The molecular mass of nitrogen, N_2 = 14 + 14 = 28 u

So, gram molecular mass of nitrogen, N_2 = 28 g

Thus, the gram molecular mass of a substance represents the mass of one mole of molecules i.e., 6.022×10^{23} molecules. This means the number of molecules present in one gram molecular mass of any substance is 6.022×10^{23} molecules. Let us discuss the term 'molar mass'.

The molar mass of a substance can be defined as,

"The mass of one mole of that substance".

The unit of molar mass is grams per mole which is abbreviated as g/mol or grams/mol. The molar mass can be of an element or of a molecular compound. The molar mass of an element is numerically equal to the atomic mass expressed in the unit g/mol. Thus, we can conclude that the molar mass of an element is the mass of one mole of its atoms. The molar mass of an element has 6.022×10^{23} atoms of the element in it. Let us illustrate molar mass of an element with an example.

The atomic mass of nitrogen, N = 14 u

Therefore,

The molar mass of nitrogen element, N = 14g/mol

Similarly, the atomic mass of oxygen, O = 16 u

Therefore, the molar mass of oxygen element, O = 16g/mol

Similarly, the molar mass of a molecular substance is numerically equal to its molecular mass expressed in g/mol. Thus, we can conclude that the molar mass of a molecular substance is the mass of one mole of its molecules. The molar mass of a substance has 6.022×10^{23} molecules of the substance in it. Let us illustrate molar mass of a molecular substance with an example.

The molecular mass of chlorine, Cl_2 = 71 u

So, the molar mass of chlorine, Cl_2 = 71 g/mol

Similarly, the molecular mass of oxygen, O_2 = 32 u

So, the molar mass of oxygen, O_2 = 32 g/mol

The term 'molar mass' of an element can be used to replace the term 'gram atomic mass'. Thus, from above discussion, we can conclude that if an element exists as molecules, then it can have gram atomic mass as well as gram molecular mass. But if an element does not exists as molecules, then it can have only gram atomic mass. All the compounds can have only gram molecular mass.

Note
- 'Gram atomic mass of an element' is the same as 'Molar mass of an element'.
- 'Gram molecular mass of a substance' is the same as 'Molar mass of a substance'.

We will now solve some problems based on the calculation of molar mass.

Solved Sample Problems

Sample Problem 1 : Calculate the molar mass of ethyne, C_2H_2. Given atomic masses of C = 12 u, H = 1 u

Solution : Given, Atomic mass of C atom = 12 u, Atomic mass of H atom = 1u

Molar mass of ethyne, $\quad C_2H_2$ = 2 × Mass of carbon + 2 × Mass of hydrogen

Substituting the atomic masses, we get

Molar mass of ethyne, C_2H_2 = 2 x 12 + 2 x 1 = 24 + 2 = 26 g/mol

Sample Problem 2 : Calculate the molar mass of phosphorus molecule, P_4. Given atomic masses of P = 31 u

Solution : Given, Atomic mass of P atom = 31 u

Molar mass of phosphorus molecule,

P_4 = 4 x Mass of phosphorus

Substituting the atomic masses, we get

Molar mass of phosphorus molecule, P_4 = 4 × 31 = 124 g/mol

Try Yourself

1. Calculate the molar mass of nitric acid, HNO_3.
2. Calculate the molar mass of sulphur molecule, S_8.
3. Calculate the molar mass of hydrochloric acid, HCl.
3. Calculate the molar mass of sulphuric acid, H_2SO_4.
4. Calculate the molar mass of acetic acid, CH_3COOH. Given the atomic masses of C = 12 u, H = 1u, S = 32 u, Cl = 35.5u, N = 14u, O = 16 u

3.15 PERCENTAGE COMPOSITION

Another important aspect of formulae is the elemental analysis of a substance. The elemental analysis helps to determine the mass of each element present in 100g of a known compound. It also helps to identify the formula of the unknown compound.

"The proportion by mass of each element present in a compound is called its percentage composition"

Thus, we can write it as,

% of an element by mass present in a compound = $\dfrac{\text{Mass of element in one mole of the compound}}{\text{Gram molecular mass of the compound}} \times 100$

Let us now try to solve a few problems based on the percentage composition.

Solved Sample Problems

Sample Problem 1 : Calculate the percentage composition of carbon and hydrogen in propane (C_3H_8). Given : Atomic weight of carbon, C = 12u and hydrogen, H= 1u

Solution : Given, Atomic weight of C = 12 u , Atomic weight of H = 1 u

Mass of propane, C_3H_8 = 3 x 12 + 8 x 1 = 36 + 8 = 44 g

The molar mass of carbon = 3 x Atomic weight of carbon = 3 x 12 = 36u

The molar mass of hydrogen = 8 x Atomic weight of hydrogen = 8 x 1 = 8 u

Now, we can calculate the percentage composition of each element from the mass of each element in 1 mol of propane divided by molar mass of propane.

$$\text{Percentage of carbon} = \dfrac{\text{Mass of C in 1 mol of propane}}{\text{Mass of propane}} \times 100$$

$$\text{\% of carbon} = \dfrac{3 \times 12 \text{ g}}{44 \text{g}} \times 100$$

$$= 81.82\%$$

$$\text{Percentage of hydrogen} = \dfrac{\text{Mass of H in 1 mol of propane}}{\text{Mass of propane}} \times 100$$

$$\text{\% of hydrogen} = \dfrac{8 \times 1 \text{ g}}{44 \text{g}} \times 100$$

$$= 18.28\%$$

Sample Problem 2 : Calculate the percentage composition of sulphur and oxygen in sulphur dioxide (SO_2). Given: Atomic weight of sulphur, S = 32u and oxygen, O = 16u

Solution : Given : Atomic weight of sulphur, S = 32u and oxygen, O = 16u
Mass of sulphur dioxide, SO_2 = 32 + 2 × 16 = 32 + 32 = 64g
The molar mass of sulphur = 1 × Atomic weight of sulphur = 1 × 32 = 32 u
The molar mass of oxygen = 2 × Atomic weight of oxygen = 2 × 16 = 32 u

$$\text{Percentage of sulphur} = \frac{\text{Mass of S in 1 mol of sulphur dioxide}}{\text{Mass of sulphur dioxide}} \times 100$$

$$= \frac{32}{64} \times 100 = 50\%$$

$$\text{Percentage of oxygen} = \frac{\text{Mass of O in 1 mol of sulphur dioxide}}{\text{Mass of sulphur dioxide}} \times 100$$

$$= \frac{32}{64} \times 100 = 50\%$$

Try Yourself

1. Calculate the percentage composition of oxygen, nitrogen and calcium in calcium nitrate ($Ca(NO_3)_2$). Given : Atomic weight of O = 16u, Ca = 40u, N = 14u

2. Calculate the percentage composition of oxygen and hydrogen in water (H_2O). Given : Atomic weight of H = 1u, O = 16u

3. Calculate the percentage composition of oxygen, hydrogen and sulphur in sulphuric acid (H_2SO_4). Given : Atomic weight of H = 1u, O = 16u, S = 32u

4. Calculate the percentage composition of oxygen and iron in Fe_2O_3. Given : Atomic weight of O = 16u, Fe = 55.8u

PAPER-PEN TEST : 12

1. Define gram atomic mass.
2. What does the gram atomic mass represent?
3. Define gram molecular mass.
4. Illustrate the gram molecular mass.
5. Define molar mass. Give its unit.
6. Illustrate molar mass of an element with an example.
7. Define percentage composition.
8. What is the significance of percentage composition?
9. How will you calculate the percentage of an element by mass present in a compound?

3.16 MOLE CONCEPT

The word "mole" was introduced in 1896 by German physical chemist **Wilhelm Ostwald** (Fig. 3.26) who derived the term from the Latin word *'mole'* meaning a *'heap'* or *'pile'*. The unit mole was accepted in 1967 to provide a simple way of reporting a large number of heap of atoms and molecules in a sample. Moles give the relationship between the mass of the substance and the number of individual chemical units present in it. It is usually represented in SI units as 'mol'. Scientists count atoms and molecules by weighing them. It is clear through experiments that if we weigh an element equal to its atomic mass in grams, then it contains 6.022×10^{23} atoms of the element. Similarly, if we weigh a compound or a substance equal to its molecular mass in grams, then it contains 6.022×10^{23} molecules of the compound.

Fig. 3.26 : Wilhelm Ostwald – a German chemist who first introduced the term 'mole'

In the above cases, the gram atomic mass as well as 6.022×10^{23} atoms of the element or gram molecular mass as well as 6.022×10^{23} molecules of the compound represents 1 mole of the compound. Let us illustrate the mole concept with an example.

Consider the following reaction of hydrogen and oxygen to form water.

$$2H_2 + O_2 \rightarrow 2H_2O$$

The above reaction indicates that :

(a) Two molecules of hydrogen combine with 1 molecule of oxygen to form two molecules of water.

(b) 4u of hydrogen molecules combine with 32 u of oxygen molecules to form 36u of water molecules.

It is clear from the above equation that the quantity of a substance can be characterized by its mass or the number of molecules. But, a chemical equation indicates directly the number of atoms or molecules taking part in the reaction. Thus, it is more convenient to refer to the quantity of a substance in terms of the number of its molecules or atoms, rather than their masses. So, a new unit "mole" was introduced. Thus, we can define mole as,

"One mole of any species (atoms, molecules, ions or particles) is the quantity in number having a mass equal to its atomic or molecular mass in grams"

In other words, we can say that, *"A group of 6.022×10^{23} atoms, molecules or ions of a substance is called a mole of that substance"*

One mole of atoms = 6.022×10^{23} atoms

One mole of molecules = 6.022×10^{23} molecules

Let us illustrate this with an example. Consider oxygen atom (O) and oxygen molecule (O_2). Here, we can have a mole of oxygen atoms or a mole of oxygen molecules,

Therefore,

1 mole of oxygen atoms, (O) = 6.022×10^{23} oxygen atoms

1 mole of oxygen molecules, (O_2) = 6.022×10^{23} oxygen molecules

Thus, we can conclude that a mole represents a definite number of particles such as atoms, molecules or ions of a substance. The number of particles present in one mole of any substance is fixed, with a value of 6.022×10^{23}. This experimentally obtained number is called the *Avogadro Constant* or *Avogadro number* (represented by N_0), named in honour of the Italian scientist, **Amedeo Avogadro** (Fig. 3.27).

Fig. 3.27: Amedeo Avogadro, an Italian scientist in whose honour Avogadro number was named which is equal to 6.022×10^{23} particles (atoms, ions or molecules)

1 mole (of anything) = 6.022×10^{23} in number,

1 dozen = 12 nos.

1 gross = 144 nos.

Another advantage of a mole is that mass of 1 mole of a particular substance is fixed. The mass of 1 mole of a substance is equal to its relative atomic or molecular mass in grams. The atomic mass of an element gives us the mass of one atom of that element in atomic mass units (u). Chemists relate the mass in grams to numbers while carrying out reactions using the number of atoms and molecules.

1 mole = 6.022×10^{23} number of atoms = Relative mass in grams.

Thus, a mole is the chemist's counting unit on knowing the mass of one mole of a substance, we can calculate the mass of any number of moles of that substance using the formula,

Number of moles = $\dfrac{\text{Given mass}}{\text{Molar mass}}$

Number of moles = $\dfrac{\text{Given number of particles}}{\text{Avogadro number}}$

For instance,

6.022×10^{23} atoms of nitrogen (N) weighs 14 g.

6.022×10^{23} molecules of nitrogen (N_2) weighs 28 g.

Here, the molar mass of nitrogen atom is 14 g/mol, while the molar mass of nitrogen molecule is 28 g/mol.

The masses of moles of some of the substances are tabulated below :

Masses of Moles of Some Common Substances

Substance taken	Symbol of the substance	Mass of 1 mole (Molar mass)	1 Mole contains
1 mole of sodium atoms	Na	23g	6.022×10^{23} sodium atoms
1 mole of water molecules	H_2O	18g (2 + 16)	6.022×10^{23} water molecules
1 mole of hydrogen molecules	H_2	2g	6.022×10^{23} hydrogen molecules
1 mole of hydrogen atoms	H	1g	6.022×10^{23} hydrogen atoms
1 mole of carbon atoms	C	12g	6.022×10^{23} carbon atoms

Hence, we can conclude that :

1 mole of atoms of an element = Gram atomic mass of the element (in grams)

1 mole of molecules of a substance = Gram molecular mass of the substance (in grams)

Relationship between Mole, Mass and Avogadro Number

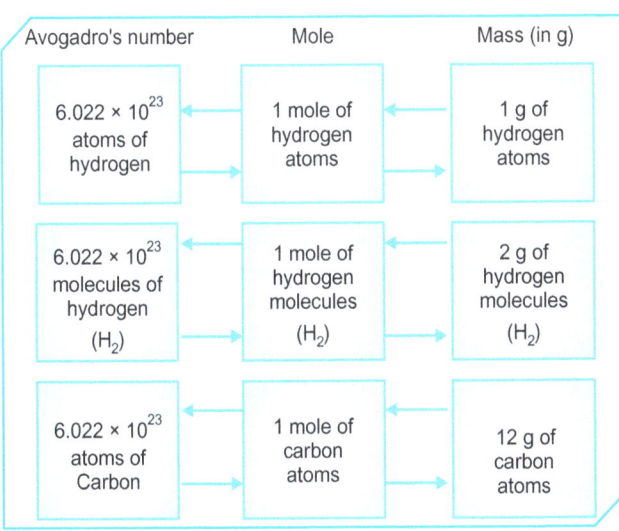

Let us summarize the mole concept.

Relationship of Mole, Mass and Molar mass

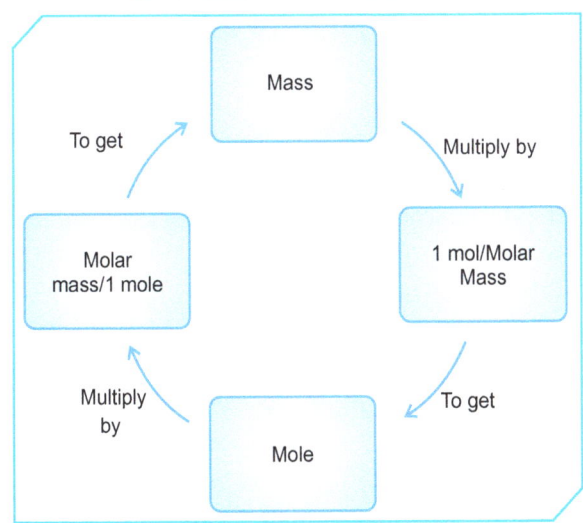

Relation of Mole and Volume

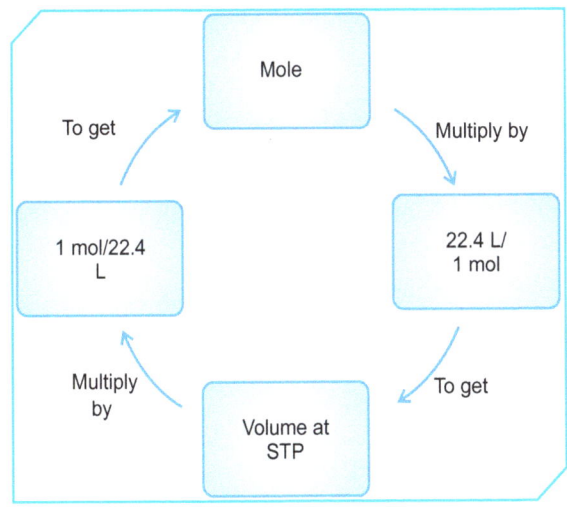

Relation of Mole and Number of Particles

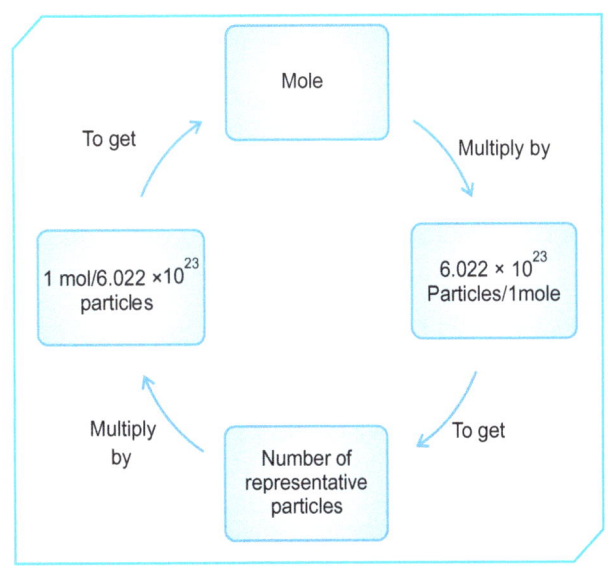

Let us solve few problems based on moles.

Solved Sample Problems

Sample Problem 1 : Calculate the number of moles for the following :

(a) 52 g of helium (He) (finding mole from mass)

(b) 12.044×10^{23} number of helium (He) atoms (finding mole from number of particles).

Solution :

(a) Given : Atomic mass of He = 4 u

Molar mass of He = 4g

Given mass of He = 52 g

The number of moles = $\dfrac{\text{Given mass}}{\text{Molar mass}}$

= 52/4 = 13

(b) Given : 1 mole = 6.022×10^{23}

No. of particles = 12.044×10^{23}

Avogadro number = 6.022×10^{23}

The number of moles = $\dfrac{\text{Given number of particles}}{\text{Avogadro number}}$

= $\dfrac{12.044 \times 10^{23}}{6.022 \times 10^{23}}$

= 2

Sample Problem 2 : Calculate the mass of the following :

(a) 0.5 mole of N_2 gas (mass from mole of molecule)

(b) 0.5 mole of N atoms (mass from mole of atom)

(c) 3.011×10^{23} number of N atoms (mass from number)

(d) 6.022×10^{23} number of N_2 molecules (mass from number)

Solution :

(a) Mass = molar mass × number of moles

$m = M \times n$

$= 28 \times 0.5$

$= 14 g$

(b) Mass = molar mass × number of moles

$m = M \times n$

$= 14 \times 0.5$

$= 7 g$

(c) The number of moles,

$n = \dfrac{\text{Given number of particles (N)}}{\text{Avogadro number (N}_0)}$

$= \dfrac{3.011 \times 10^{23}}{6.022 \times 10^{23}}$

$m = M \times n$

$= \dfrac{14 \times 3.011 \times 10^{23}}{6.022 \times 10^{23}}$

$= 14 \times 0.5$

$= 7 g$

(d) The number of moles,

$n = \dfrac{\text{Given number of particles (N)}}{\text{Avogadro number (N}_0)}$

$m = M \times n$

$= \dfrac{28 \times 6.022 \times 10^{23}}{6.022 \times 10^{23}}$

$= 28 \times 1$

$= 28 g$

Sample Problem 3 : Calculate the number of particles in each of the following :

(a) 46 g of Na atoms (number from mass)

(b) 8 g of O_2 molecules (number of molecules from mass)

(c) 0.1 mole of carbon atoms (number from given moles)

Solution :

(a) Given : mass, m = 46g, molar mass, M = 23g, Avogadro number $N_0 = 6.022 \times 10^{23}$

The no. of atoms

$= \dfrac{\text{Given mass}}{\text{Molar mass}} \times \text{Avogadro number}$

$= \dfrac{46}{23} \times 6.022 \times 10^{23}$

$= 12.044 \times 10^{23}$

(b) Given mass, m = 8 g, molar mass, M = 32 g, Avogadro number, $N_0 = 6.022 \times 10^{23}$

The no. of atoms $= \dfrac{\text{Given mass}}{\text{Molar mass}} \times \text{Avogadro number}$

$= \dfrac{8}{32} \times 6.022 \times 10^{23}$

$= 1.5055$ or 1.51×10^{23}

(c) No. of moles of particles, n = 0.1, Avogadro number,

$N_0 = 6.022 \times 10^{23}$

The number of particles (atoms) = number of moles of particles × Avogadro number

$N = n \times N_0$

$= 0.1 \times 6.022 \times 10^{23}$

$= 6.022 \times 10^{22}$

Sample Problem 4 : How many moles of carbon dioxide are present in 55.5 L ?

Solution : We know that 22.4 L = 1 mol

Therefore, 55.5 L $= \dfrac{55.5 L}{22.4 L}$

$= 2.48$

Thus, 2.48 mol of carbon dioxide are present in 55.5L.

Try Yourself

1. If one mole of carbon atoms weighs 12 grams, what is the mass (in grams) of 1 atom of carbon ?
2. Which has more number of atoms, 100 grams of sodium or 100 grams of iron ? Given, atomic mass of Na = 23 u, Fe = 56 u.
3. Calculate the number of water molecules in 250g of water. [8.364×10^{24} molecules]
4. What is the mass of 1 mole of nitrogen atoms ? Given : Atomic weight N = 14u [14g]
5. What is the mass of 4 moles of aluminium atoms ? Given : Atomic weight Al = 27u [108g]
6. Find the number of moles in 66g of carbon dioxide. Given: Atomic weight C = 12u, O = 16u [1.5 mole]
7. What is the mass of 0.25 mol of water ? Given: Atomic weight H = 1 u, O = 16u [4.5g]
8. Calculate the mass of 3.011×10^{23} number of nitrogen atoms. [7g]
9. Calculate the number of particles in 0.1 moles of carbon atoms. [6.022×10^{22} atoms of C]
10. Calculate the number of particles in 8g of oxygen molecules. Given Atomic weight O = 16u [1.5055×10^{23} molecules of oxygen]

PAPER-PEN TEST : 13

1. Who introduced the word mole ?
2. Give the SI unit of mole.
3. Illustrate the mole concept with an example.
4. Define mole.
5. What is the value of Avogadro's constant ?
6. What is the advantage of mole ?
7. How will you calculate the number of moles in a substance ?
8. Give the relationship between mole, mass and Avogadro number.
9. Relate mass, mole and molar mass.
10. Relate mole and the volume.
11. Relate mole and the number of particles.

COMPENDIUM

- Law of conservation of mass states that mass can neither be created nor be destroyed in a chemical reaction.
- Law of constant proportion or Law of definite proportion states that in a chemical substance, the elements are always present in definite proportion by mass.
- Matter is made of very tiny particles called atoms.
- Atoms are indivisible particles, which cannot be created or destroyed in a chemical reaction.
- Atoms of a given element are identical in mass and chemical properties.
- Atoms of different elements have different masses and chemical properties.
- Atoms combine in the ratio of small whole numbers to form compounds.
- The relative number and kinds of atoms are constant in a given compound.
- Atoms are building blocks of all matter.
- Atomic radius is measured in nanometres (1 nm = 10^{-9}m).
- Individual atoms can be observed using Scanning Tunnelling Microscopes .
- Each element has a name and a unique symbol.
- One atomic mass unit is a mass unit equal to exactly one twelfth(1/12th) of the mass of one atom of carbon-12.
- Relative atomic mass of the atom of an element is defined as the average mass of the atom, as compared to 1/12th the mass of one carbon-12 atom.
- Atoms of most elements are not able to exist independently.
- Atoms form molecules and ions.
- A molecule can be defined as the smallest particle of an element or a compound that is capable of an independent existence and shows all the properties of that substance.
- Molecules of element are formed by the atoms of the same type.
- Atoms of different elements join together in definite proportions to form molecules of compounds.
- Based upon atomicity, we can classify molecules as monoatomic, diatomic, triatomic, tetratomic and polyatomic molecules.
- An ion is a charged particle and can be negatively or positively charged.
- A negatively charged ion is called as an 'anion'.
- A positively charged ion is called as 'cation'.
- Ions may consist of a single charged atom or a group of atoms that have a net charge on them.
- Ionic compounds contain charged species called ions as their smallest unit.
- A group of atoms carrying a fixed charge on them are called polyatomic ions or radicals.
- The chemical formula of a compound is a symbolic representation of its composition.
- Valency is the combining capacity of an element.
- Valency can be used to find out how the atoms of an element will combine with the atom(s) of another element to form a chemical compound.
- The simplest compounds, which are made up of two different elements are called binary compounds.

- Formula of a binary compound is written by criss crossing the valencies of elements present in a molecule of the compound.
- A chemical compound is always electrically neutral, so the positive and negative valencies or charges of the ions in the compound must add up to zero.
- The molecular mass of a substance is the sum of the atomic masses of all the atoms in a molecule of the substance. It is therefore the relative mass of molecule expressed in atomic mass units (u).
- The formula unit mass of a substance is a sum of the atomic masses of all atoms in a formula unit of a compound.
- 1 mole of any substance = 6.022×10^{23} units.
- The mole is the amount of substance that contains the same number of particles (atoms, ions, molecules or formula units etc.) as there are atoms in exactly 12 g of carbon-12.
- Mass of 1 mole of a substance is called its molar mass.
- Atoms of different elements are of different sizes and masses. A mole of one type of atoms will have a different mass from a mole of another type of atoms.
- Molar mass = Mass of one mole of any substance = Gram atomic mass or gram molecular mass or gram formula mass of the substance.
- Number of moles = $\dfrac{\text{Given number of particles}}{\text{Avogadro's number}}$
- Molar mass is expressed in g/mol.
- Atomic mass of an element expressed in grams is called gram atomic mass.
- Molecular mass of a substance expressed in grams is called gram molecular mass.
- Mass of one mole of atoms of any element is equal to gram atomic mass of that element.

EXERCISES (SOLVED)

NCERT INTEXT QUESTIONS

1. In a reaction, 5.3 g of sodium carbonate reacted with 6 g of ethanoic acid. The products were 2.2 g of carbon dioxide, 0.9 g water and 8.2 g of sodium ethanoate. Show that these observations are in agreement with the law of conservation of mass.

Ans : Sodium Carbonate + Ethanoic Acid → Sodium Ethanoate + Carbon Dioxide + Water

In the given reaction, sodium carbonate reacts with ethanoic acid to produce sodium ethanoate, carbon dioxide and water.

Sodium + Ethanoic → Sodium + Carbon + Water
Carbonate   acid   ethanoate dioxide

Mass of sodium carbonate = 5.3 g (given)

Mass of ethanoic acid = 6 g (given)

Mass of sodium ethanoate = 8.2 g (given)

Mass of carbon dioxide = 2.2 g (given)

Mass of water = 0.9 g (given)

Now total mass before the reaction = (5.3 + 6) g
= 11.3 g

Total mass after the reaction = (8.2 + 2.2 + 0.9) g
= 11.3 g

Total mass before reaction = Total mass after the reaction

Hence, the given observations are in agreement with the law of conservation of mass.

2. Hydrogen and oxygen combine in the ratio of 1 : 8 by mass to form water. What mass of oxygen gas would be required to react completely with 3 g of hydrogen gas?

Ans : Given : The ratio of hydrogen and oxygen by mass to form water = 1 : 8

Then, the mass of oxygen gas required to react completely with 1 g of hydrogen gas is 8g.

Therefore, the mass of oxygen gas required to react completely with 3g of hydrogen gas = 8 × 3 = 24g.

3. Which postulate of Dalton's atomic theory is the result of the law of conservation of mass?

Ans : "Atoms are indivisible particles which can neither be created nor be destroyed in a chemical reaction" is the postulate of Dalton's atomic theory as the result of the law of conservation of mass.

4. Which postulate of Dalton's atomic theory can explain the law of definite proportions?

Ans: "The relative number and kind of atoms in a given compound remains constant" is the postulate of Dalton's atomic theory which explains the law of definite proportions.

5. Define atomic mass unit.

Ans: One atomic mass unit is a mass unit equal to exactly one twelfth (1/12th) the mass of one atom of carbon-12.

6. Why it is not possible to see an atom with naked eyes?

Ans: Since the size of the atom is too small, it is not possible to see an atom with naked eyes. Also, the atoms of an element do not exist independently.

7. Write down the formulae of:

(a) Sodium oxide

(b) Aluminium chloride

(c) Sodium sulphide

(d) Magnesium hydroxide

Ans: (a) The formula of sodium oxide = Na_2O

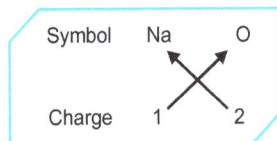

(b) The formula of aluminium chloride = $AlCl_3$

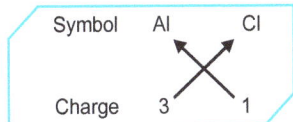

(c) The formula of sodium sulphide = Na_2S

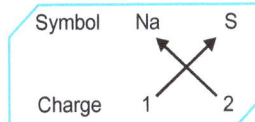

(d) The formula of magnesium hydroxide = $Mg(OH)_2$

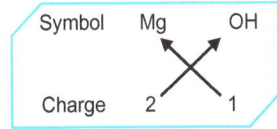

8. Write down the names of compounds represented by the following formulae:

(a) $Al_2(SO_4)_3$

(b) $CaCl_2$

(c) K_2SO_4

(d) KNO_3

(e) $CaCO_3$

Ans: (a) Aluminium sulphate

(b) Calcium chloride

(c) Potassium sulphate

(d) Potassium nitrate

(e) Calcium carbonate

9. What is meant by the term chemical formula?

Ans: The composition of a molecule of the substance in terms of symbols of the elements present in the molecule is known as chemical formulae.

10. How many atoms are present in a:

(a) H_2S molecule,

(b) PO_4^{3-} ion.

Ans: (a) In hydrogen sulphide, there are totally three atoms i.e., two atoms of hydrogen and one atom of sulphur.

(b) In phosphate ion, there are totally five atoms i.e., 1 atom of phosphorus and four atoms of oxygen.

11. Calculate the molecular masses of: (a) H_2, (b) O_2, (c) Cl_2, (d) CO_2, (e) CH_4, (f) C_2H_6, (g) C_2H_4, (h) NH_3, (i) CH_3OH.

Ans: (a) Molecular mass of H_2 = 2× Atomic mass of H

= 2 × 1

= 2u

(b) Molecular mass of O_2 = 2 × Atomic mass of O

= 2 × 16

= 32u

(c) Molecular mass of Cl_2 = 2 × Atomic mass of Cl

= 2 × 35.5

= 71u

(d) Molecular mass of CO_2

= (Atomic mass of C) + (2 × Atomic mass of O)

= 12 + 2 × 16

= 12 + 32

= 44u

(e) Molecular mass of CH_4

= (Atomic mass of C) + (4 × Atomic mass of H)

= 12 + 4 × 1

= 12 + 4

= 16u

(f) Molecular mass of C_2H_6 = (2 × Atomic mass of C) + (6 × Atomic mass of H)
= (2 × 12) + (6 × 1)
= 24 + 6
= 30u

(g) Molecular mass of C_2H_4 = (2 × Atomic mass of C) + (4 × Atomic mass of H)
= 2 × 12 + 4 × 1
= 24 + 4
= 28u

(h) Molecular mass of NH_3 = Atomic mass of nitrogen + (3 × Atomic mass of H)
= 14 + (3 × 1)
= 14 + 3
= 17u

(i) Molecular mass of CH_3OH = Atomic mass of carbon + (4 × Atomic mass of H) + Atomic mass of oxygen
= 12 + (4 × 1) + 16
= 32u

12. Calculate the formula unit masses of : (a) ZnO, (b) Na_2O, (c) K_2CO_3. Given atomic masses of : (a) Zn = 65 u, (b) Na = 23 u, (c) K = 39 u, C = 12 u, O = 16 u.

Ans : (a) Formula unit mass of ZnO = Atomic mass of Zn + Atomic mass of O
= 65 + 16
= 81 u

(b) Formula unit mass of Na_2O = (2 × Atomic mass of Na) + Atomic mass of O
= 2 × 23 + 16
= 46 + 16
= 62 u

(c) Formula unit mass of K_2CO_3 = (2 × Atomic mass of K) + (Atomic mass of carbon) + (3 × Atomic mass of O)
= (2 × 39) + 12 + (3 × 16)
= 78 + 12 + 48
= 138 u

13. If one mole of carbon atoms weighs 12 grams, what is the mass (in grams) of 1 atom of carbon?

Ans : Given : One mole of carbon atoms weighs = 12 g

Hence, mass of 1 mole of carbon atoms = 12 g

Therefore, mass of 6.022×10^{23} number of carbon atoms = 12g

Thus, the mass of 1 atom of carbon = 12/ (6.022×10^{23}) = 1.9962×10^{-23} g

14. Which has more number of atoms, 100 grams of sodium or 100 grams of iron. (Given : atomic mass of Na = 23 u, Fe = 56 u)?

Ans : Given : Atomic mass of Na = 23 u

So, the molar mass of Na = 23g

Atomic mass of Fe = 56 u

So, the molar mass of Fe = 56 g

Therefore,

23g of Na contains 6.022×10^{23} of atoms

100g of Na contains = $6.022 \times 10^{23} \times \dfrac{100}{23}$ = 2.6×10^{24} atoms of Na.

Similarly, molar mass of Fe = 56g

Therefore,

56g of Fe contains 6.022×10^{23} of atoms

100g of Na contains $6.022 \times 10^{23} \times \dfrac{100}{56}$

$= 1.07 \times 10^{24}$ atoms of Na.

NCERT EXERCISES QUESTIONS

1. A 0.24 g sample of compound of oxygen and boron was found by analysis to contain 0.096 g of boron and 0.144 g of oxygen. Calculate the percentage composition of the compound by weight.

Ans : Given : Mass of boron = 0.096 g

Mass of oxygen = 0.144 g

Mass of sample = 0.24 g

Thus, percentage of boron by weight in the compound = $\dfrac{0.096}{0.24} \times 100$ = 40%

Percentage of oxygen by weight in the compound = $\dfrac{0.144}{0.24} \times 100$ = 60%

2. When 3.0 g of carbon is burnt in 8.00 g oxygen, 11.00 g of carbon dioxide is produced. What mass of carbon dioxide will be formed when 3.00 g of carbon is burnt in 50.00 g of oxygen? Which law of chemical combination will govern your answer?

Ans : Carbon + Oxygen → Carbon dioxide

$C + O_2 \to CO_2$

3g of carbon reacts with 8 g of oxygen to give 11 g of carbon dioxide.

Similary, if 3 g of carbon reacts with 50 g of oxygen same mass of carbon dioxide (11g) will be obtained.

The extra oxygen will remain unreacted i.e., 50 − 8 = 42g. The answer will be governed by the law of constant proportions.

3. What are polyatomic ions ? Give examples.

Ans : A polyatomic ion is a group of atoms carrying a net charge (positive or negative). For example, ammonium ion (NH_4^+) , hydroxide ion (OH^-), carbonate ion (CO_3^{2-}).

4. Derive the chemical formulae of the following using valency of the constituent elements or radicals :

(a) Magnesium chloride

(b) Calcium oxide

(c) Copper nitrate

(d) Aluminium chloride

(e) Calcium carbonate

(a) The symbol of the elements present:

Magnesium   Chlorine

Mg   Cl

The valency of the elements

Mg   Cl

2   1

Criss cross the valency of the elements

Thus, the chemical formula of magnesium chloride is $MgCl_2$.

(b) The symbol of the elements present :

Calcium   Oxygen

Ca   O

The valency of the elements

Ca   O

2   2

Criss cross the valency of the elements

Thus, the chemical formula of calcium oxide is CaO.

(c) The symbol of the elements present:

Copper   Nitrate

Cu NO_3

The valency of the elements or radicals

Cu NO_3

2   1

Criss cross the valency of the elements or radicals

Thus, the chemical formula of copper nitrate is $Cu(NO_3)_2$

(d) The symbol of the elements present:

Aluminium   Chlorine

Al   Cl

The valency of the elements

Al   Cl

3   1

Criss cross the valency of the elements

Thus, the chemical formula of aluminium chloride is AlCl$_3$.

(e) The symbol of the elements or radicals present :

    Calcium   Carbonate
    Ca   CO$_3$

The valency of the elements
    Ca   CO$_3$
    2   2

Criss cross the valency of the elements and simplify

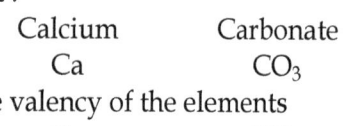

Thus, the chemical formula of calcium carbonate is CaCO$_3$

5. Give the names of the elements present in the following compounds.

(a) Quick lime

(b) Hydrogen bromide

(c) Baking powder

(d) Potassium sulphate.

Ans : (a) It contains calcium and oxygen elements- CaO

(b) It contains hydrogen and bromine elements- HBr

(c) It contains sodium, hydrogen, carbon and oxygen elements –NaHCO$_3$

(d) It contains potassium, sulphur and oxygen elements –K$_2$SO$_4$

6. Calculate the molar mass of the following substances.

(a) Ethyne, C$_2$H$_2$

(b) Sulphur molecule, S$_8$

(c) Phosphorus molecule, P$_4$ (Atomic mass of phosphorus = 31)

(d) Hydrochloric acid, HCl

(e) Nitric acid, HNO$_3$

Ans : (a) The atomic weight of carbon = 12u

The atomic weight of hydrogen = 1u

The molecular mass of ethyne = (2 × at. wt of C) + (2 × at. wt of H)

= (2 × 12)+ (2 × 1)

= 24 + 2 = 26g/mol

(b) The atomic weight of sulphur = 32u

The molecular mass of sulphur molecule = 8 × at. wt of sulphur = 8 × 32 = 256g/mol

(c) The atomic weight of phosphorus = 31u

The molecular mass of phosphorus molecule = 4 × at. wt of phosphorus = 4 × 31 = 124g/mol

(d) The atomic weight of hydrogen = 1u

The atomic weight of chlorine = 35.5u

The molecular mass of hydrogen chloride = at. wt of hydrogen + at. wt of chlorine

= 1 + 35.5

= 36.5 g/mol

(e) The atomic weight of hydrogen = 1u

The atomic weight of nitrogen = 14u

The atomic weight of oxygen = 16u

The molecular mass of nitric acid = at. wt of hydrogen + at. wt of nitrogen + (3 × at. wt of oxygen) = 1 + 14 + (3 × 16) = 15 + 48 = 63g/ mol

ATOMS AND MOLECULES CONCISE CHEMISTRY - IX

7. What is the mass of :
   (a) 1 mole of nitrogen atoms (Atomic mass of nitrogen = 14u)
   (b) 4 moles of aluminium atoms (Atomic mass of aluminium = 27u)
   (c) 10 moles of sodium sulphite (Na_2SO_3)(Atomic mass of sodium = 23u, sulphur = 32u, oxygen = 16u)

Ans : (a) The atomic mass of nitrogen = 14u
   1 mole of nitrogen = The atomic mass of nitrogen = 14u

   (b) The atomic mass of aluminium = 27u
   1 mole of aluminium = The atomic mass of aluminium = 27u
   Therefore, 4 moles of aluminium atoms = 4 × 27 = 108u

   (c) The atomic mass of sodium = 23u
   The atomic mass of sulphur = 32u
   The atomic mass of oxygen = 16u
   1 mole of sodium sulphite = (2 × at. wt of Na) + (1 × at. wt of S) + (3 × at. wt of O)
   = (2 × 23) + (1 × 32) + (3 × 16)
   = 46 + 32 + 48
   = 126u
   Therefore, 10 moles of sodium sulphite = 10 × 126 = 1260 u

8. Convert into mole :
   (a) 12 g of oxygen gas
   (b) 20 g of water
   (c) 22 g of carbon dioxide

Ans : (a) Molecular mass of oxygen = 32u
   1 mole of oxygen = 32g
   Therefore, 12g of oxygen = $\frac{12}{32}$
   = 0.375 mole

   (b) Molecular mass of water (H_2O) = 2 × 1 + 16 = 18u
   1 mole of water = 18g
   Therefore, 20g of water = $\frac{20}{18}$
   = 1.11 mole

   (c) Molecular mass of carbon dioxide (CO_2) = (12) + (16 × 2) = 12 + 32 = 44u
   1 mole of carbon dioxide = 44g
   Therefore, 22g of carbon dioxide = $\frac{22}{44}$
   = 0.5 mole

9. What is the mass of :
   (a) 0.2 mole of oxygen atoms
   (b) 0.5 mole of water molecules

Ans : (a) The atomic weight of oxygen = 16u

$$1 \text{ mole of oxygen} = 16g$$
$$\text{Therefore, } 0.2 \text{ mole of oxygen} = 0.2 \times 16$$
$$= 3.2g$$

(b) Molecular mass of water (H_2O) = (2 × 1) + 16 = 18u

$$1 \text{ mole of water} = 18g$$
$$0.5 \text{ mole of water} = 0.5 \times 18 = 9.0g$$

10. Calculate the number of molecules of sulphur (S_8) present in 16 g of solid sulphur.

Ans : The atomic weight of sulphur = 32u

$$\text{The molecular mass of sulphur molecule} = 8 \times \text{at. wt of sulphur}$$
$$= 8 \times 32$$
$$= 256 \text{ g/mol}$$
$$1 \text{ mol of sulphur molecule} = 256g$$
$$256 \text{ g of sulphur mol} = 6.022 \times 10^{23} \text{ molecules}$$
$$\text{Therefore, 16 g of sulphur molecule} = \frac{16 \times 6.022 \times 10^{23}}{256}$$
$$= 3.76 \times 10^{22} \text{ molecules}$$

11. Calculate the number of aluminium ions present in 0.051 g of aluminium oxide.

(Hint : The mass of an ion is the same as that of an atom of the same element. Atomic mass of Al = 27 u)

Ans : The formula of aluminium oxide = Al_2O_3

$$\text{The molecular mass of aluminium oxide} = 2 \times 27 + 3 \times 16 = 102u$$
$$1 \text{ mol of aluminium oxide} = 102 \text{ g}$$

1 mole of aluminium oxide contain two moles of aluminium ions.

Therefore,

Mass of aluminium in 1 mole of aluminium oxide = Mass of aluminium × 2 = 27 × 2 = 54 g

Thus, mass of aluminium in 102g of aluminium oxide = 54g of aluminium

So, mass of aluminium in 0.051g of aluminium oxide = $\frac{54}{102} \times 0.051$

$$= 0.027 \text{ g}$$
$$\text{Now, 27g of aluminium ions} = 6.022 \times 10^{23} \text{ ions}$$
$$\text{Therefore, 0.051 g of aluminium oxide} = \frac{2 \times 6.022 \times 10^{23} \times 0.051}{102}$$
$$= 6.022 \times 10^{20}$$

NCERT EXEMPLAR QUESTIONS

1. Which of the following correctly represents 360 g of water?
   (i) 2 moles of H_2O
   (ii) 20 moles of water
   (iii) 6.022 × 10²³ molecules of water
   (iv) 1.2044 × 10²⁵ molecules of water
   (a) (i) (b) (i) and (iv)
   (c) (ii) and (iii) (d) (ii) and (iv)

2. Which of the following statements is not true about an atom?
   (a) Atoms are not able to exist independently

(b) Atoms are the basic units from which molecules and ions are formed

(c) Atoms are always neutral in nature

(d) Atoms aggregate in large numbers to form the matter that we can see, feel or touch

3. The chemical symbol for nitrogen gas is :
   (a) Ni
   (b) N_2
   (c) N^+
   (d) N

4. The chemical symbol for sodium is :
   (a) So
   (b) Sd
   (c) NA
   (d) Na

5. Which of the following would weigh the highest?
   (a) 0.2 mole of sucrose ($C_{12}H_{22}O_{11}$)
   (b) 2 moles of CO_2
   (c) 2 moles of $CaCO_3$
   (d) 10 moles of H_2O

6. Which of the following has maximum number of atoms?
   (a) 18g of H_2O
   (b) 18g of O_2
   (c) 18g of CO_2
   (d) 18g of CH_4

7. Which of the following contains maximum number of molecules?
   (a) 1g CO_2
   (b) 1g N_2
   (c) 1g H_2
   (d) 1g CH_4

8. Mass of one atom of oxygen is :
   (a) $\dfrac{16}{6.022 \times 10^{23}} g$
   (b) $\dfrac{32}{6.022 \times 10^{23}} g$
   (c) $\dfrac{1}{6.022 \times 10^{23}} g$
   (d) 8u

9. 3.42 g of sucrose are dissolved in 18g of water in a beaker. The number of oxygen atoms in the solution is :
   (a) 6.68×10^{23}
   (b) 6.09×10^{22}
   (c) 6.022×10^{23}
   (d) 6.022×10^{21}

10. A change in the physical state can be brought about :
    (a) Only when energy is given to the system
    (b) Only when energy is taken out from the system
    (c) When energy is either given to, or taken out from the system
    (d) Without any energy change

ANSWERS

1. (d), 2. (a), 3. (b), 4. (d), 5. (c), 6. (a), 7. (c), 8. (a), 9. (a), 10. (c).

1. **Explanation :** (ii) 20 moles of water = 20 ×18 g = 360 g of water, because mass of 1 mole of water is the same as its molar mass, i.e., 18 g.

   (iv) 1.2044×10^{25} molecules of water contains

   Therefore, $\dfrac{1.2044 \times 10^{25}}{N_A}$

   The number of moles, $N_A = 6.023 \times 10^{23}$

   Therefore, $\dfrac{1.2044 \times 10^{25}}{6.022 \times 10^{23}} = 20$ moles

   20 moles of water = 20 × 18 g = 360 g of water.

2. **Explanation :** Inert gases exist in monoatomic form.

5. **Explanation :** Weight of a sample in gram = number of moles × molar mass
   (a) 0.2 moles of $C_{12}H_{22}O_{11}$ = 0.2 × 342 = 68.4 g
   (b) 2 moles of CO_2 = 2 × 44 = 88 g
   (c) 2 moles of $CaCO_3$ = 2 × 100 = 200 g
   (d) 10 moles of H_2O = 10 × 18 = 180 g

6. **Explanation :**

   $$\text{Number of Atoms} = \dfrac{\text{Mass of substance} \times \text{Number of atoms in the molecule}}{\text{Molar mass}} \times N_A$$

$$18\text{g of water} = \frac{18 \times 3}{18} \times N_A = 3 N_A$$

$$18\text{g of oxygen} = \frac{18 \times 2}{32} \times N_A = 1.12 N_A$$

$$18\text{g of carbon dioxide} = \frac{18 \times 3}{44} \times N_A = 1.23 N_A$$

$$18\text{g of methane} = \frac{18 \times 3}{44} \times N_A = 1.23 N_A$$

7. **Explanation :** $1\text{g of hydrogen} = \frac{1}{2} \times N_A = 0.5 N_A$

$$= 0.5 \times 6.022 \times 10^{23}$$

$$= 3.011 \times 10^{23}$$

8. **Explanation :** Mass of one atom of oxygen $= \dfrac{\text{Atomic Mass}}{N_A}$

9. **Explanation :** Number of moles of sucrose $= \dfrac{\text{Mass of substance}}{\text{Molar mass}}$

   Substituting the values, we get

   $$\text{Number of moles of sucrose} = \frac{3.42\text{ g}}{342\text{ g mol}^{-1}}$$

   $$= 0.01 \text{ mol}$$

   1 mol of sucrose ($C_{12}H_{22}O_{11}$) contains $= 11 \times N_A$ atoms of oxygen

   0.01 mol of sucrose ($C_{12}H_{22}O_{11}$) contains $= 0.01 \times 11 \times N_A$ atoms of oxygen $= 0.11 \times N_A$ atoms of oxygen

   $$\text{Number of moles of water} = \frac{18\text{ g}}{18\text{ g mol}^{-1}}$$

   $$= 1 \text{ mol}$$

   1mol of water (H_2O) contains $1 \times N_A$ atom of oxygen

   Total number of oxygen atoms = Number of oxygen atoms from sucrose + Number of oxygen atoms from water = $0.11\, N_A + 1.0\, N_A = 1.11\, N_A$

   Number of oxygen atoms in solution = $1.11 \times$ Avogadro's number

   $$= 1.11 \times 6.022 \times 10^{23}$$

   $$= 6.68 \times 10^{23}$$

11. Which of the following represents a correct chemical formula? Name it.
    (a) CaCl (b) $BiPO_4$
    (c) $NaSO_4$ (d) NaS

Ans : (b) $BiPO_4$ – Both Bismuth (Bi) and phosphate (PO_4) are trivalent and hence the chemical formula is correct. It is Bismuth phosphate.

12. Write the molecular formulae for the following compounds :
    (a) Copper (II) bromide

(b) Aluminium (III) nitrate
(c) Calcium (II) phosphate
(d) Iron (III) sulphide
(e) Mercury (II) chloride
(f) Magnesium (II) acetate

Ans : (a) $CuBr_2$ (b) $Al(NO_3)_3$
(c) $Ca_3(PO_4)_2$ (d) Fe_2S_3
(e) $HgCl_2$ (f) $Mg(CH_3COO)_2$

13. Write the molecular formulae of all the compounds that can be formed by the combination of following ions :

Ans : $Cu^{2+}, Na^+, Fe^{3+}, Cl^-, SO_4^{2-}, PO_4^{3-}$

Copper (I) chloride($CuCl_2$)
Copper (II) sulphate($CuSO_4$)
Copper(II) phosphate ($Cu_3(PO_4)_2$)
Sodium chloride (NaCl)
Sodium sulphate (Na_2SO_4)
Sodium phosphate (Na_3PO_4)
Iron (III) chloride ($FeCl_3$)
Iron sulphate ($Fe_2(SO_4)_3$)
Iron (III) phosphate ($FePO_4$)

14. Write the cations and anions present (if any) in the following compounds :
(a) CH_3COONa (b) NaCl
(c) H_2 (d) NH_4NO_3

Ans :

	Anions	Cations
(a)	CH_3COO^-	Na^+
(b)	Cl^-	Na^+
(c)	It is a covalent compound	–
(d)	NO_3^-	NH_4^+

15. Give the formulae of the compounds formed from the following sets of elements :
(a) Calcium and fluorine
(b) Hydrogen and sulphur
(c) Nitrogen and hydrogen
(d) Carbon and chlorine
(e) Sodium and oxygen
(f) Carbon and oxygen

Ans : (a) CaF_2 (b) H_2S (c) NH_3
(d) CCl_4 (e) Na_2O (f) CO, CO_2

16. Which of the following symbols of elements are incorrect: Give their correct symbols ?
(a) Cobalt, CO (b) Carbon, C
(c) Aluminium, AL (d) Helium, He
(e) Sodium, So

Ans : (a) Incorrect, the correct symbol of cobalt is Co
(b) Correct, the symbol of carbon is C
(c) Incorrect, the correct symbol of aluminium is Al
(d) Correct the symbol of helium is, He
(e) Incorrect, the correct symbol of sodium is Na

17. Give the chemical formulae for the following compounds and compute the ratio by mass of the combining elements in each one of them.
(a) Ammonia (b) Carbon monoxide
(c) Hydrogen chloride (d) Aluminium fluoride
(e) Magnesium sulphide

Ans : (a) Ammonia (NH_3)
N : H × 3
14 : 1 × 3
14 : 3

(b) Carbon monoxide (CO)
C : O
12 : 16
3 : 4

(c) Hydrogen chloride (HCl)
H : Cl
1 : 35.5
2 : 71

(d) Aluminium fluoride (AlF_3)
Al : F × 3
27 : 19 × 3
9 : 19

(e) Magnesium sulphide (MgS)
Mg : S
24 : 32
3 : 4

18. State the number of atoms present in each of the following chemical species.
(a) CO_3^{2-}
(b) PO_4^{3-}

(c) P_2O_5

(d) CO

Ans : (a) The atoms present in chemical species are carbon and oxygen = 1 + 3 = 4

(b) The atoms present in chemical species are phosphorus and oxygen = 1 + 4 = 5

(c) The atoms present in chemcial species are phosphorus and oxygen = 2 + 5 = 7

(d) The atoms present in chemical species are carbon and oxygen = 1 + 1 = 2

19. What is the fraction of the mass of water due to neutrons?

Ans : Mass of one mole (Avogadro Number) of neutrons ~ 1 g

$$\text{Mass of one neutron} = \frac{1}{\text{Avogadro Number }(N_A)} g$$

$$\text{Mass of one molecule of water} = \frac{\text{Molar mass}}{N_A} g$$

$$= \frac{18}{N_A} g$$

There are 8 neutrons in one atom of oxygen

$$\text{Mass of 8 neutrons} = \frac{8}{N_A}$$

$$\text{Fraction of mass of water due to neutrons} \sim \frac{8}{18} = \frac{4}{9}$$

20. Does the solubility of a substance change with temperature? Explain with the help of an example.

Ans : Yes, solubility is a temperature dependent property. The solubility generally, increases with increase in temperature. For example, you can dissolve more sugar in hot water than in cold water.

21. Classify each of the following on the basis of their atomicity :

(a) F_2 (b) NO_2 (c) N_2O (d) C_2H_6 (e) P_4
(f) H_2O_2 (g) P_4O_{10} (h) O_3 (i) HCl (j) CH_4 (k) He
(l) Ag

Ans : (a) Number of atoms of F in F_2 = 2 (Diatomic)

(b) Number of atoms of N and O in NO_2 = 1 atom of N + 2 atoms of O = 3 (Triatomic)

(c) Number of atoms of N and O in N_2O = 2 atoms of N + 1 atom of O = 3 (Triatomic)

(d) Number of atoms of C and H in C_2H_6 = 2 atoms of C + 6 atoms of H = 8 (Polyatomic)

(e) Number of atoms of P in P_4 = 4 (Tetratomic)

(f) Number of atoms of H and O in H_2O_2 = 2 atoms of H + 2 atoms of O = 4 (Tetratomic)

(g) Number of atoms of P and O in P_4O_{10} = 4 atoms of P + 10 atoms of O = 14 (Polyatomic)

(h) Number of atoms of O in O_3 = 3 (Triatomic)

(i) Number of atoms of H and Cl in HCl = 1 atom of H + 1 atom of Cl = 2 (Diatomic)

(j) Number of atoms of C and H in CH_4 = 1 atom of C + 4 atoms of H = 5 (Polyatomic)

(k) Number of atoms of He in He = 1 (Monoatomic)

(l) Number of atoms of Ag in Ag = 1

22. You are provided with a fine white coloured powder which is either sugar or salt. How would you identify it without tasting?

Ans : On heating the powder, it will char if it is a sugar. The powder may be dissolved in water and checked for its conduction of electricity. If it conducts, it is a salt.

23. Calculate the number of moles of magnesium present in a magnesium ribbon weighing 12 g. Molar atomic mass of magnesium is 24g mol^{-1}.

Ans : Number of moles = $\frac{\text{Given mass}}{\text{Molar mass}} = \frac{12g}{24g/m}$

= 0.5 moles

24. Verify by calculating that :

(a) 5 moles of CO_2 and 5 moles of H_2O do not

have the same mass.

(b) 240 g of calcium and 240 g magnesium elements have a mole ratio of 3 : 5.

Ans : (a) CO_2 has molar mass = 44g mol^{-1}

5 moles of CO_2 have molar mass = 44 × 5
$$= 220 \text{ g}$$

H_2O has molar mass = 18 g mol^{-1}

5 moles of H_2O have mass = 18 × 5 g = 90 g

(b) Number of moles in 240g Ca metal = $\dfrac{240}{40}$
$$= 6$$

Number of moles in 240 g of Mg metal = $\dfrac{240}{24} = 10$

Ratio of calcium to magnesium = 6 : 10 = 3 : 5.

25. Find the ratio by mass of the combining elements in the following compounds :

(a) $CaCO_3$ (d) C_2H_5OH
(b) $MgCl_2$ (e) NH_3
(c) H_2SO_4 (f) $Ca(OH)_2$

Ans : (a) $CaCO_3$

Ca : C : O × 3

40 : 12 : 16 × 3

40 : 12 : 48

10 : 3 : 12

(b) $MgCl_2$

Mg : Cl × 2

24 : 35.5 × 2

24 : 71

(c) H_2SO_4

H × 2 : S : O × 4

1 × 2 : 32 : 16 × 4

2 : 32 : 64

1 : 16 : 32

(d) C_2H_5OH

C × 2 : H × 6 : O

12 × 2 : 1 × 6 : 16

24 : 6 : 16

12 : 3 : 8

(e) NH_3

N : H × 3

14 : 1 × 3

14 : 3

(f) $Ca(OH)_2$

Ca : O × 2 : H × 2

40 : 16 × 2 : 1 × 2

40 : 32 : 2

20 : 16 : 1

26. Calcium chloride when dissolved in water dissociates into its ions according to the following equation:

$$CaCl_2 \text{ (aq)} \rightarrow Ca^{2+} \text{ (aq)} + 2Cl^- \text{ (aq)}$$

Calculate the number of ions obtained from $CaCl_2$ when 222 g of it is dissolved in water.

Ans : 1 mole of calcium chloride = 111g

∴ 222g of $CaCl_2$ is equivalent to 2 moles of $CaCl_2$

Since 1 formula unit $CaCl_2$ gives 3 ions, therefore, 1 mol of $CaCl_2$ will give 3 moles of ions

2 moles of $CaCl_2$ would give 3 × 2 = 6 moles of ions.

No. of ions = No. of moles of ions × Avogadro number
$$= 6 × 6.022 × 10^{23}$$
$$= 36.132 × 10^{23}$$
$$= 3.6132 × 10^{24} \text{ ions}$$

27. The difference in the mass of 100 moles each of sodium atoms and sodium ions is 5.48002 g. Compute the mass of an electron.

Ans : A sodium atom and ion differ by one electron. For 100 moles each of sodium atoms and ions there would be a difference of 100 moles of electrons.

Mass of 100 moles of electrons = 5.48002 g

Mass of 1 mole of electron = $\dfrac{5.48002}{100}$ g

Mass of one electron = $\dfrac{5.48002}{100 × 6.022 × 10^{23}}$

$$= 9.1 × 10^{-26} \text{ g}$$
$$= 9.1 × 10^{-29} \text{ kg}$$

28. Cinnabar (HgS) is a prominent ore of mercury. How many grams of mercury are present in 225 g of pure HgS ? Molar mass of Hg and S are 200.6 g mol^{-1} and 32 g mol^{-1} respectively.

Ans : Molar mass of HgS = 200.6 + 32 = 232.6 g mol^{-1}

Mass of Hg in 232.6 g of HgS = 200.6 g

$$\text{Mass of Hg in 225 g of HgS} = \frac{200.6}{232.6} \times 225 = 194.04 g$$

29. The mass of one steel screw is 4.11g. Find the mass of one mole of these steel screws. Compare this value with the mass of the Earth (5.98 × 10²⁴ kg). Which one of the two is heavier and by how many times?

Ans : One mole of screws weighs = $4.11 \times 6.022 \times 10^{23}$

$= 2.475 \times 10^{24}$ g

$= 2.475 \times 10^{21}$ kg

Mass of earth = 5.98×10^{24} kgs

So the earth is heavier than a mole of screws of mass 4.11g in order to find how many times the earth is heavier than a mole of screws given above.

$$= \frac{\text{Mass of the Earth}}{\text{Mass of 1 mole of screws}} = \frac{5.98 \times 10^{24} \text{kg}}{2.475 \times 10^{21} \text{kg}}$$

$= 2.4 \times 10^3$

Hence, the mass of earth is 2.4 × 10³ times the mass of screws.

The earth is 2400 times heavier than one mole of screws.

30. A sample of vitamin C is known to contain 2.58 × 10²⁴ oxygen atoms. How many moles of oxygen atoms are present in the sample?

Ans : 1 mole of oxygen atoms = 6.022×10^{23} atoms

Number of moles of oxygen atoms in the given sample of vitamin C = $\frac{2.58 \times 10^{24}}{6.022 \times 10^{23}} = \frac{25.8}{6.022} = 4.28$

Thus, 4.28 moles of oxygen atoms are present in the sample.

31. Raunak took 5 moles of carbon atoms in a container and Krish also took 5 moles of sodium atoms in another container of same weight.

    (a) Whose container is heavier?
    (b) Whose container has more number of atoms?

Ans : (a) Mass of sodium atoms carried by Krish = (5 × 23) g = 115 g

While mass of carbon atoms carried by Raunak = (5 ×12) g = 60g

Thus, Krish's container is heavy

(b) Both the bags have same number of atoms as they have same number of moles of atoms

32. Fill in the missing data in the table given below :

Property	H_2O	CO_2	Na Atom	$MgCl_2$
No. of moles	2	-	-	0.5
No. of particles	-	3.011×10^{23}	-	-
Mass	36 g	-	115 g	-

Ans :

Property	H_2O	CO_2	Na Atom	$MgCl_2$
No. of moles	2	0.5	5	0.5
No. of particles	1.2044×10^{24}	3.011×10^{23}	3.011×10^{24}	3.011×10^{23}
Mass	36 g	22 g	115 g	47.5 g

33. The visible universe is estimated to contain 10^{22} stars. How many moles of stars are present in the visible universe?

Ans : Number of moles of stars = $\dfrac{10^{22}}{6.023 \times 10^{23}}$ = 0.0166 moles

Thus, 0.0166 moles of stars are present in the visible universe.

34. What is the SI prefix for each of the following multiples and sub multiples of a unit?

    (a) 10^3 (b) 10^{-1} (c) 10^{-2} (d) 10^{-6} (e) 10^{-9} (f) 10^{-12}

Ans : (a) kilo

(b) deci

(c) centi

(d) micro

(e) nano

(f) pico

35. Express each of the following in kilograms

    (a) 5.84×10^{-3} mg

    (b) 58.34 g

    (c) 0.584g

    (d) 5.873×10^{-21} g

Ans : (a) 5.84×10^{-9} kg

(b) 5.834×10^{-2} kg

(c) 5.84×10^{-4} kg

(d) 5.873×10^{-24} kg

36. Compute the difference in masses of 10^3 moles each of magnesium atoms and magnesium ions. (Mass of an electron = 9.1×10^{-31} kg)

Ans: A Mg^{2+} ion and Mg atom differ by two electrons.

10^3 moles of Mg^{2+} and Mg atoms would differ by $10^3 \times 2$ moles of electrons

$$\text{Mass of } 2 \times 10^3 \text{ moles of electrons} = 2 \times 10^3 \times 6.022 \times 10^{23} \times 9.1 \times 10^{-31} \text{ kg}$$

$$= 2 \times 6.022 \times 9.1 \times 10^{-5} \text{ kg}$$

$$= 109.6004 \times 10^{-5} \text{ kg}$$

$$= 1.096 \times 10^{-3} \text{ kg}$$

37. Which has more number of atoms : (a) 100g of N_2, (b) 100 g of NH_3.

Ans : (a)

$$100 \text{ g of } N_2 = \dfrac{100}{28} \text{moles}$$

$$\text{Number of molecules} = \dfrac{100}{28} \times 6.022 \times 10^{23}$$

$$\text{Number of atoms} = \dfrac{2 \times 100}{28} \times 6.022 \times 10^{23}$$

$$= 43.01 \times 10^{23}$$

(b) $\quad 100 \text{ g of NH}_3 = \dfrac{100}{17}$ moles

$$= \dfrac{100}{17} \times 6.022 \times 10^{23}$$

No. of molecules in 100 g of NH$_3$ = 35.42 × 10^{23} molecules

One molecule of NH$_3$ has 4 atoms (1 N + 3H)

So no. of atoms in 100g of NH$_3$ = 35.42 × 10^{23} × 4 = 141.68 × 10^{23} atoms

Thus, 100 g of ammonia (NH$_3$) would have more atoms.

38. Compute the number of ions present in 5.85 g of sodium chloride.

Ans: 5.85 g of NaCl = $\dfrac{5.85}{58.5}$ = 0.1 moles or 0.1 moles of NaCl molecule

Each NaCl molecule is equivalent to one Na$^+$ and one Cl$^-$ = 2 ions

Total moles of ions = 0.1 × 2 = 0.2 moles

No. of ions = 0.2 × 6.022 × 10^{23}

= 1.2042 × 10^{23} ions

Thus, 1.2042 × 10^{23} ions of NaCl are present in 5.85 g of sodium chloride.

39. A gold sample contains 90% of gold and the rest copper. How many atoms of gold are present in one gram of this sample of gold?

Ans: One gram of gold sample will contain $\dfrac{90}{100}$ = 0.9 g of gold

Number of moles of gold = $\dfrac{\text{Mass of gold}}{\text{Atomic mass of gold}}$

$= \dfrac{0.9}{197}$

= 0.0046

One mole of gold contains N$_A$ atoms = 6.022 × 10^{23}

∴ 0.0046 mole of gold will contain = 0.0046 × 6.022 × 10^{23}

= 2.77 × 10^{21}

40. What are ionic and molecular compounds? Give examples.

Ans: Atoms of different elements join together in definite proportions to form molecular compounds. Examples include water, ammonia and carbon dioxide. Ionic compounds composed of metals and non-metals containing charged species known as ions. An ion can be negatively or positively charged. A negatively charged ion is called an anion and the positively charged ion is called cation. Examples include sodium chloride, calcium oxide.

41. Compute the difference in masses of one mole each of aluminium atoms and one mole of its ions. (Mass of an electron is 9.1×10^{-28} g). Which one is heavier?

Ans: Mass of 1 mole of aluminium atom = the molar mass of aluminium = 27 g mol^{-1}

An aluminium atom needs to lose three electrons to become an ion, Al^{3+}

For one mole of Al^{3+} ion, three moles of electrons are to be lost.

The mass of three moles of electrons = 3 × (9.1 × 10^{-28}) × 6.022 × 10^{23} g = 27.3 × 6.022 × 10^{-5} g

= 164.400 × 10^{-5} g = 0.00164 g

Molar mass of Al^{3+} = (27 − 0.00164) g mol^{-1}

$$= 26.9984 \text{ g mol}^{-1}$$
$$\text{Difference} = 27 - 26.9984 = 0.0016 \text{ g}$$

42. A silver ornament of mass 'm' gram is polished with gold equivalent to 1% of the mass of silver. Compute the ratio of the number of atoms of gold and silver in the ornament.

Ans:
$$\text{Mass of silver} = m \text{ g}$$
$$\text{Mass of gold} = \frac{m}{100} \text{ g}$$
$$\text{Number of atoms of silver} = \frac{\text{Mass}}{\text{Atomic mass}} \times N_A$$
$$\text{Number of atoms of gold} = \frac{m}{108} \times N_A$$

Ratio of number of atoms of gold to silver = Au : Ag
$$= \frac{m}{100 \times 197} \times N_A : \frac{m}{108} \times N_A$$
$$= 108 : 100 \times 197$$
$$= 108 : 19700$$
$$= 1 : 182.41$$

43. A sample of ethane (C_2H_6) gas has the same mass as 1.5×10^{20} molecules of methane (CH_4). How many C_2H_6 molecules does the sample of gas contain?

Ans: Mass of 1 molecule of $CH_4 = \dfrac{16 \text{ g}}{N_A}$

$$\text{Mass of } 1.5 \times 10^{20} \text{ molecules of methane} = \frac{1.5 \times 10^{20} \times 16}{N_A} \text{ g}$$

$$\text{Mass of 1 molecule of } C_2H_6 = \frac{30 \text{ g}}{N_A}$$

$$\text{Mass of molecules of } C_2H_6 \text{ in given sample} = \frac{1.5 \times 10^{20} \times 16}{N_A} \text{ g}$$

$$\text{Number of molecules of ethane} = \frac{1.5 \times 10^{20} \times 16}{N_A} \times \frac{N_A}{30}$$

$$= 0.8 \times 10^{20} \text{ molecules}$$

44. Fill in the blanks
    (a) In a chemical reaction, the sum of the masses of the reactants and products remains unchanged. This is called _____.
    (b) A group of atoms carrying a fixed charge on them is called _____.
    (c) The formula unit mass of $Ca_3(PO_4)_2$ is _____.
    (d) Formula of sodium carbonate is _____ and that of ammonium sulphate is _____.

Ans : (a) Law of conservation of mass
    (b) Polyatomic ion
    (c) (3 × atomic mass of Ca) + (2 × atomic mass of phosphorus) + (8 × atomic mass of oxygen) = 310.
    (d) Na_2CO_3; $(NH_4)_2SO_4$

45. Complete the following crossword puzzle by using the name of the chemical elements. Use the data given on the next page :

Across

2. The element used by Rutherford during his alpha-scattering experiment

3. An element which forms rust on exposure to moist air

5. A very reactive non-metal stored under water

7. Zinc metal when treated with dilute hydrochloric acid produces a gas of this element which when tested with burning splinter produces a pop sound.

Down

1. A white lustrous metal used for making ornaments and which tends to get tarnished black in the presence of moist air

4. Both brass and bronze are alloys of the element

6. The metal which exists in the liquid state at room temperature

8. An element with symbol Pb

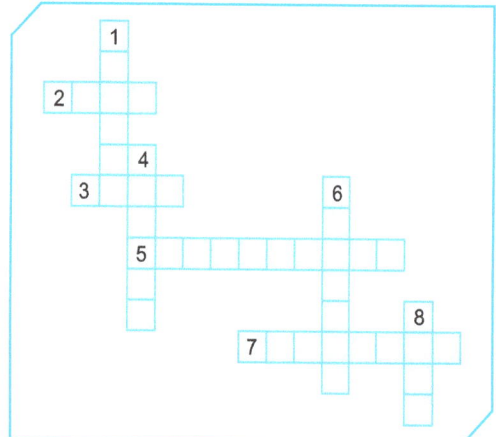

Ans :

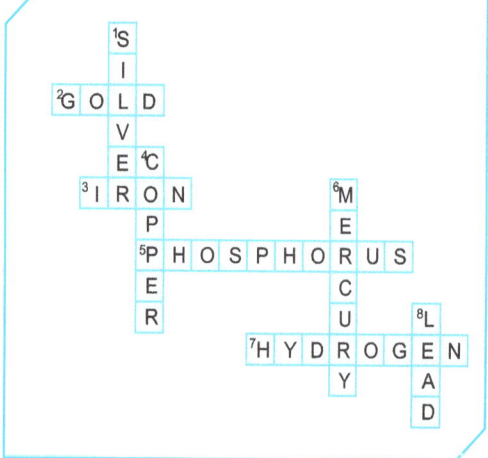

46. (a) In the given crossword puzzle, names of 11 elements are hidden. Symbols of these are given below. Complete the puzzle.

   1. Cl   7. He
   2. H   8. F
   3. Ar   9. Kr
   4. O   10. Rn
   5. Xe   11. Ne
   6. N

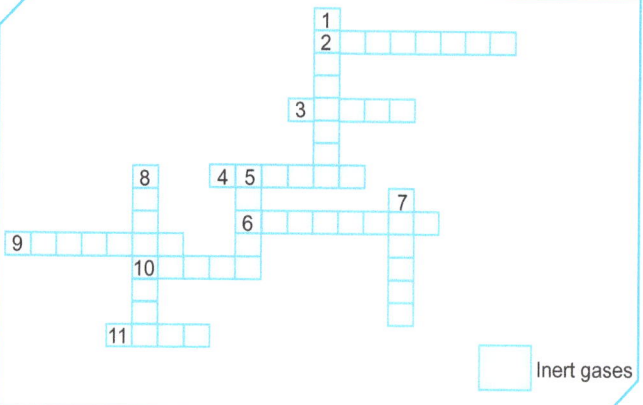

(b) Identify the total number of inert gases, their names and symbols from this cross word puzzle.

Ans :

(a)

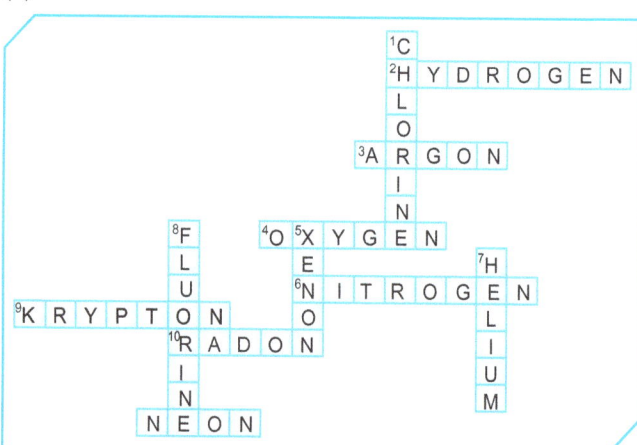

(b) Six : Helium (He); Neon (Ne); Argon (Ar); Krypton (Kr); Xenon (Xe); Radon (Rn).

47. Write the formulae for the following and calculate the molecular mass for each one of them.

   (a) Caustic potash
   (b) Baking powder
   (c) Lime stone
   (d) Caustic soda

(e) Ethanol
(f) Common salt

(d) NaOH = 23 + 16 + 1
= 40 g/mol

Ans :(a) KOH = 39 +16+1
= 56 g/mol

(b) NaHCO$_3$ = 23 + 1 + 12 + (3 × 16)
= 84 g/mol

(c) CaCO$_3$ = 40 + 12 + (3 × 16)
= 100 g/mol

(e) C$_2$H$_5$OH = 2 × 12 + (6 × 1) + 16
= 46 g/mol

(f) NaCl = 23 + 35.5
= 58.5 g/mol

48. In photosynthesis, 6 molecules of carbon dioxide combine with an equal number of water molecules through a complex series of reactions to give a molecule of glucose having a molecular formula C$_6$H$_{12}$O$_6$. How many grams of water would be required to produce 18 g of glucose? Compute the volume of water so consumed assuming the density of water to be 1 g cm^{-3}.

Ans : $6CO_2 + 6H_2O \xrightarrow{Chlorophyll/Sunlight} C_6H_{12}O_6 + 6O_2$

1 mole of glucose needs 6 moles of water

180 g of glucose needs (6×18) g of water

18 g of glucose would need = $\dfrac{108}{180} \times 18\,g$ of water = 10.8 g

Volume of water used = $\dfrac{Mass}{Density}$

= $\dfrac{10.8\,g}{1\,g\,cm^{-3}}$

= 10.8 cm^3

HIGHER ORDER THINKING SKILL QUESTIONS (HOTS)

1. Mala prepared aqueous solution of barium chloride and sodium sulphate. She weighed them separately and then mixed them in a beaker. A white precipitate was immediately formed. She filtered the precipitate, dried it and then weighted it. After reading this narration, answer the following questions :

   (a) Will the weight of the precipitate be the same as that of the reactants before mixing?
   (b) If not, what she should have done ?
   (c) Which law of chemical combination does this support ?

Ans : (a) No, it will not be the same.
   (b) She should have weighed the total contents of the beaker after the reaction and not the precipitate alone.
   (c) It supports the law of conservation of mass.

2. In order to verify the law of conservation of mass, Neelam mixed 6.3 g of sodium carbonate and 15.0 g of ethanoic acid in a conical flask. After the experiment, she weighed the flask again. The weight of the residue in the flask was only 18.0 g. She approached the teacher who guided him to carry the experiment in a closed flask with a cork. There was no difference in weight of the flask before and after the experiment.

   (a) What was the mistake committed by her ?
   (b) Why did not the two weights match earlier ?

Ans :(a) She was carrying the experiment in an open flask.
   (b) Because CO$_2$ gas evolved during the reaction escaped from the flask.

$2CH_3COOH + Na_2CO_3 \rightarrow 2CH_3COONa + H_2O + CO_2$

3. John was asked by his teacher to verify the law of conservation of mass in a laboratory. He prepared 5% aqueous solutions of NaCl and Na$_2$SO$_4$. He mixed 10 ml of both these solution in a conical flask. He weighed the flask on a balance. He then stirred the flask with a rod and weighed it after some time. There was no change in mass.

(a) Was John able to verify the law of conservation of a mass ?

(b) If not, what was the mistake committed by him ?

(c) In your opinion what he should have done ?

Ans : (a) No, he could not verify the law of conservation of mass, inspite of the fact that there was no change in mass.

(b) No chemical reaction must have taken place between NaCl and Na_2SO_4.

(c) He should have performed the experiment by using aqueous solution of $BaCl_2$ and Na_2SO_4 because on mixing these solutions, chemical reaction takes place and a white precipitate of $BaSO_4$ is formed.

4. Dalton was the first scientist to introduce symbols for the known elements. Modern symbols were given by J.J. Berzelius. A symbol in general may be defined as the short hand representation of the name of an element.

(a) How do symbols help in identifying elements ?

(b) Do we use symbols in daily life ?

Ans : (a) All the known elements are identified by their symbols. For example symbol of calcium = Ca; symbol of copper = Cu; symbol of iron = Fe

(b) Yes. These are very common in daily life. For example, all road signs such as diversions, dangerous zones etc., are indicated by symbols. In playground umpires, signify the various happening such as "LBW", OUT etc., in cricket by symbols

5. Mole concept is an important tool for dealing with chemical calculations. The elements have atomic masses while compounds have molecular masses or molar masses. Mole is in fact, a collection of Avogadro's number (N_A) of the particles of a substance whether element or compound. The value of Avogadro's number is 6.022×10^{23}

(a) Why is mole commonly called chemist dozen ?

(b) Give the relation of Mole, Mass and Molar mass.

Ans : (a) Just as a dozen represents 12 articles, a mole represents 6.022×10^{23} or Avogadro's number of particles. Therefore, it has been rightly called chemist's dozen.

(b)

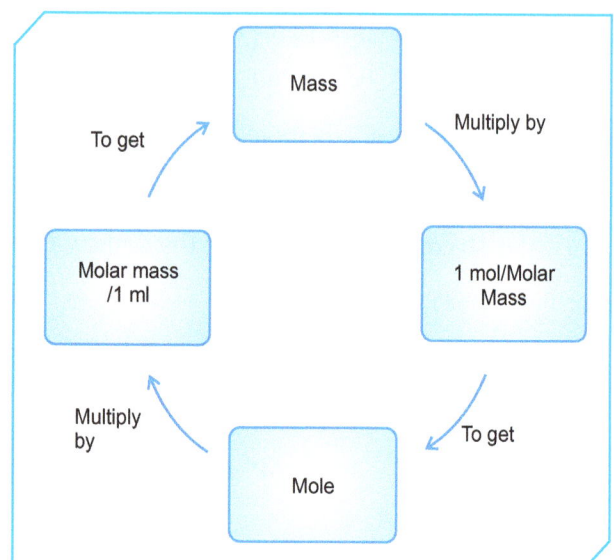

6. If 'X' is a monovalent element, write the formula of its

(a) Sulphate

(b) Phosphate

(c) Hydroxide

Ans : Hint : Try crossing-over method.

(a) X_2SO_4

(b) X_3PO_4

(c) XOH

7. (a) Do atoms in some of the elements have actually fractional mass?

(b) Which can exist independently? Atoms or Molecules

(c) Are the mass of a molecule of a substance and its molar mass the same?

Ans :(a) No, the atoms do not have fractional mass.

(b) Molecules.

(c) No, they are different. Mass of a molecule will be in the order of N 10^{-20} grams. Molar mass is mass of 1 mole of he substance and equals its relative atomic mass in grams.

8. (a) Can we regard sodium as monoatomic element ?

(b) Does CO represent the symbol of the element cobalt ?

(c) What happens to an element if its atom gains two electrons ?

Ans : (a) Yes, sodium is a monoatomic element.

(b) No, the symbol of cobalt is Co.

(c) It changes to divalent anion.

9. (a) An element froms an oxide with formula A_2O_3. What is the Valency of A ?

(b) The valency of an element X is 4. Give the formula of its oxide.

(c) An element A has valency 3 while the element B has valency 2. Give its formula of the compound between A and B.

Ans : Hint : Try crossing-over method.

(a) The valency of A is 3.

(b) The formula of the oxide = X_2O_4 or XO_2.

(c) The formula of the compound formed between A and B = A_2B_3.

10. (a) The formula of the carbonate of a metal M is M_2CO_3. Give its formula of chloride.

(b) What does the following symbol stands for?

(i) 2O

(ii) O_2

(iii) O_3

(iv) H_2O

Ans : (a) Hint : Try crossing-over method.

The valency of M in M_2CO_3 is +1. Therefore, the formula of metal chloride is MCl.

(b) (i) Two atoms of oxygen

(ii) One molecule of oxygen

(iii) One molecule of ozone

(iv) One molecule of water

11. (a) Give the Valency and symbol of :

1. Sodium
2. Potassium
3. Magnesium
4. Aluminium
5. Ammonium ion

(b) Give the atomic number of :

1. Na
2. P
3. Mg
4. 5

Ans : (a)

	Valency	Symbol
1. Sodium	1	Na
2. Potassium	1	K
3. Magnesium	2	Mg
4. Aluminium	3	Al
5. Ammonium ion	1	NH_4^+

(b) 1 - 11

2 - 12

3 - 15

4 - 16

MULTIPLE CHOICE QUESTIONS (MCQs)

1. The quantity of matter present in an object is called its :

(a) Mass (b) Volume

(c) Density (d) Vapour pressure

2. An element A is tetravalent and another element B is divalent. The compound formed by these two elements will be :

(a) AB_4 (b) A_2B

(c) AB_2 (d) AB

3. An example of a triatomic molecule is :

(a) Ozone (b) Nitrogen

(c) Carbon monoxide (d) Hydrogen

4. Which among the following has maximum mass?

(a) 1g of Fe.

(b) 0.1 mole of ammonia.

(c) 10^{22} atoms of carbon

(d) 10^{22} molecules of carbon dioxide

5. Which among the following is not correctly matched?

(a) Copper – Co (b) Cobalt – Co

(c) Calcium – Ca (d) Silver – Ag

6. A sample of ammonia molecule irrespective of source contains 82.35% of nitrogen and 17.65% of hydrogen by mass obeys :

(a) Avogadro's law

(b) Law of conservation of mass

(c) Law of multiple proportions

(d) Law of definite proportions

7. Indivisibility of an atom was proposed by :
   (a) Dalton (b) Rutherford
   (c) Thomson (d) Bohr

8. The value of Avogadro constant is :
   (a) 6.022×10^{24} (b) 6.022×10^{22}
   (c) 6.022×10^{23} (d) 60.22×10^{23}

9. What is the formula of aluminium oxide?
   (a) Al_3O_2 (b) AlO
   (c) AlO_2 (d) Al_2O_3

10. All samples of carbon dioxide contain carbon and oxygen in the mass ratio of 3:8. This is in agreement with the Law of :
    (a) Conservation of mass
    (b) Constant proportion
    (c) Multiple proportion
    (d) Reciprocal proportion

11. What is the formula of magnesium chloride?
    (a) $MgCl_3$ (b) $MgCl$
    (c) $MgCl_2$ (d) Mg_2Cl

12. One amu means :
    (a) Mass of hydrogen molecule
    (b) Mass of C-12 atom
    (c) $1/12^{th}$ mass of C-12 atoms
    (d) Mass of O – 16 atom

13. The molecular formula of potassium nitrate is :
    (a) KNO (b) KNO_3
    (c) KNO_2 (d) KON

14. The value 6.023×10^{23} is also called :
    (a) Mass number (b) Dalton's number
    (c) Avogadro's number (d) Atomic number

15. Kalium is the Latin name of :
    (a) Potassium (b) Krypton
    (c) Calcium (d) Phosphorus

16. The term 'mole' was introduced by :
    (a) Lavoisier (b) Dalton
    (c) Avogadro (d) Ostwald

17. The smallest particle of a substance that is capable of independent existence is :
    (a) Atom (b) Molecule
    (c) Electron (d) Proton

18. The law of definite proportions was proposed by :
    (a) Dalton (b) Proust
    (c) Lavoisier (d) Ostwald

19. In $^{16}_{8}O$, the number 16 stands for :
    (a) Atomic number (b) Atomic mass
    (c) Atomic mass scale (d) Number of electrons

20. The foundation for the law of chemical combination was laid by :
    (a) Dalton (b) Proust
    (c) Democritus (d) Lavoisier

21. The number of atoms in a molecule of the elementary substance is called :
    (a) Atomic number (b) Avogadro number
    (c) Atomic mass (d) Atomicity

22. Avogadro number represents the number of atoms in :
    (a) 12 grams of 12C (b) 320 g of sulphur
    (c) 32g of oxygen (d) 1g of 12C

23. Two molecules of nitrogen are represented by :
    (a) N (b) $2N_2$
    (c) N_2 (d) 2N

24. A sample contains 22 g of carbon dioxide. This is equal to :
    (a) One molar volume of carbon dioxide
    (b) One mole of carbon dioxide
    (c) Half mole of carbon dioxide
    (d) Two moles of carbon dioxide

ANSWER

1. (a), 2. (c), 3. (a), 4. (b), 5. (a), 6. (d), 7. (a), 8. (c), 9. (d), 10. (b), 11. (c), 12. (c), 13. (b), 14. (c), 15. (a), 16. (d), 17. (b), 18. (b), 19. (b), 20. (d), 21. (d), 22. (a), 23. (b), 24. (c).

VERY SHORT ANSWER TYPE QUESTIONS

1. Which postulate of Dalton's atomic theory is the result of law of conservation of mass?

2. Comment: "The molecular mass of oxygen is 32".

3. What are the building blocks of matter?

4. Give the atomicity of :
   (a) Phosphorus
   (b) Sulphur
5. Give a major drawback of Dalton's atomic theory of matter.
6. Name the elements represented by the following symbols: Ag, Au, Sn, Pb and Hg
7. Give the formula of one element and a compound.
8. What are the particles which have more or less electrons than the normal atoms called?
9. Give the name of the particle which has 18 electrons, 17 neutrons and 17 protons in it.
10. What is the mass of 0.2 moles of oxygen atoms ?
11. How will you convert 12g of oxygen gas into moles ?
12. Give the number of molecules in 2.5 moles of ammonia.
13. Give the unit in which molar mass is expressed.
14. How much is the gram atomic mass of oxygen ?
15. Give the relation of mass, molar mass and moles.
16. Give Latin names for sodium and mercury.
17. How many atoms are there in exactly 12 g of carbon ?
18. Name a triatomic gas.
19. How does an atom differ from a molecule?
20. Give one example each of molecule of an element and molecule of a compound.

SHORT ANSWER TYPE-I QUESTIONS

1. Define atomicity. Give two examples.
2. Define chemical formula.
3. Define the law of conservation of mass.
4. Define molecular mass of a substance.
5. Define one atomic mass unit.
6. Differentiate an atom and a molecule.
7. Comment: "The atomic mass of oxygen is 16".
8. Define 'formula mass' of a compound.
9. Differentiate between ionic compounds and molecular compounds.
10. What is the reason for positive charge on a sodium ion and a negative charge on a chloride ion in the formation of sodium chloride?
11. Define formula unit of an ionic compound.
12. Give the formula unit of sodium chloride and magnesium chloride.
13. Define mole.
14. Comment: "A mole of carbon atoms".
15. Define gram molecular mass of a substance.
16. What is meant by gram atomic mass of a substance ?
17. What is the difference between an atom of hydrogen and a molecule of hydrogen ?
18. Name the elements represented by Hg ,Pb, Au.
19. What is the difference between an anion and a cation ?
20. Write down chemical formula of (a) Hydrogen peroxide (b) Tin chloride (c) Barium sulphate (d) Silver chloride (e) Zinc nitrate.
21. Write chemical names of (a) $Ni(NO_3)_2$ (b) $CdCO_3$ (c) $NaOH$ (d) NH_4NO_2 (e) $BaCl_2$.

SHORT ANSWER TYPE-II QUESTIONS

1. Illustrate the law of conservation of mass.
2. Illustrate the law of definite proportions.
3. Mention the significance of the symbol of an element.
4. Give the significance of the formula of a substance.
5. Explain how sodium ion is formed ?
6. Explain how chloride ion is formed ?
7. If 1g of carbon contains 'a' atoms, then what will be the number of atoms in 1g of Magnesium (Mg) ?
8. How many grams of neon (Ne) will have the same number of atoms as 4g of calcium (Ca) ?
9. If the mass of a single atom of an element 'E' is 2.65×10^{-23} g, then find its atomic weight and identify the element.
10. If the ratio by mass of magnesium and sulphur is 3 : 4 in magnesium sulphide, then what is the ratio of the number of magnesium and sulphur atoms ?

LONG ANSWER TYPE QUESTIONS

1. Mention the features of Dalton's atomic theory.
2. With the help of activity, show that there is no change in mass when a chemical reaction takes place.
3. Write the symbols of some common elements.

NUMERICAL BASED QUESTIONS

1. Calculate the ratio of atoms present in 5 g of magnesium and 5 g of iron. (Atomic mass of Mg = 24 u, Fe = 56 u)

2. Write down chemical formula of :
   (a) Hydrogen peroxide (b) Tin chloride
   (c) Barium sulphate   (d) Silver chloride
3. Write chemical names of :
   (a) $Ni(NO_3)_2$ (b) $CdCO_3$
   (c) $NaOH$ (d) NH_4NO_2
4. Calculate molar mass of acetylene (C_2H_2) and ethanoic acid (CH_3COOH).
5. What is the gram atomic mass of : (a) Hydrogen (b) oxygen.
6. Convert 35 g of aluminium (Al) into mole.
7. How many grams of silicon dioxide (SiO_2) are present in 0.8 mol ?
8. Calculate the number of molecules in 200 g of nitrous oxide (N_2O).
9. Calculate the number of aluminium ions present in 0.051 g of aluminium oxide.
10. Calculate the mass of one atom of sodium ?
11. The atomic mass of calcium is 40 u. What will be the number of calcium atoms in 0.4 u of calcium ?
12. How many atoms of oxygen are present in 120 g of nitric acid ?
13. Calculate molar mass of C_2H_2.
14. Calculate formula unit mass of $CaCl_2$.
15. How many atoms are present in H_2SO_4 ?

EXERCISES (UNSOLVED)

VIVA VOCE QUESTIONS

1. Name the law of chemical combination given by Lavoisier.
2. Name the law of chemical combination given by Proust.
3. Who gave atomic theory of matter ?
4. Name the elements present in water molecule.
5. What is the value of Avogadro number ?
6. Name the unit expressed for the radius of an atom.
7. Name the particles which have more electrons than the normal atoms.
8. Name the particles which have fewer electrons than the normal atoms.
9. Name the element used as a standard for atomic mass scale.
10. Name one element formed from the first letter of the elements name.
11. Name a triatomic gas.
12. What is the radius of one atom of hydrogen ?

FILL IN THE BLANKS

1. ---------------- is positively charged.
2. All matter is composed of tiny particles called ---------------.
3. The unit of --------------- is u.
4. A -------------- particle is called an ion.
5. The proportion of hydrogen and oxygen in water is --------- respectively.
6. 0.5 mole of calcium element has a mass of --------.
7. 1 mole contains ----------------- atoms, molecules or ions of a substance.
8. 64g of oxygen gas contains -------------- moles of oxygen atoms.
9. A ------------represents an Avogadro number of particles of a substance.
10. 60 g of carbon element has ----------- moles of carbon atoms.

TRUE OR FALSE

1. Helium is monoatomic.
2. Copper is diatomic.
3. The symbol of sodium is Sd.
4. Atomic mass is measured in nm.
5. The symbol of aluminium is AL.
6. The formula of calcium oxide is Ca_2O_2.
7. The number of particles in a mole is 6.022×10^{23}.
8. A sulphide ion has positive charge.
9. A potassium ion has a positive charge.
10. The combining capacity of an element is called its valency.

MATCH THE FOLLOWING

1.

S. No	English name of the element	Symbols	Correct match
1.	Krypton	Li	
2.	Barium	Br	
3.	Lithium	B	
4.	Bromine	Kr	
5.	Boron	Ba	

ATOMS AND MOLECULES

CONCISE CHEMISTRY - IX

2.

S. No	Latin name of the element	Symbol	Correct match
1.	Hydragyrum	Na	
2.	Kalium	Ag	
3.	Natrium	Hg	
4.	Argentum	Au	
5.	Aurum	K	

3.

S. No	Molecule	Molecular mass	Correct match
1.	CH_3OH	17 u	
2.	C_2H_4	28 u	
3.	NH_3	16 u	
4.	C_2H_6	32 u	
5.	CH_4	30 u	

CHEMICAL FORMULAE OF MOLEULAR COMPOUNDS

Complete the table given below for writing the formula of a chemical compound.

S. No	Identify the valency		Criss cross the valency		Formula of the compound	Name of the compound
1.	NH_4SO_4		NH_4	SO_4		
2.	Zn	NO_3	Zn	NO_3		
3.	Al	S	Al	S		
4.	Na	PO_4	Na	PO_4		
5.	Ca	N	Ca	N		
6.	K	CrO_4	K	CrO_4		
7.	Mg	CO_3	Mg	CO_3		
8.	Cr	SO_4	Cr	SO_4		
9.	Fe	S	Fe	S		
10.	Al	O	Al	O		

205

SYMPOSIUM

Topic 1 : To verify the law of conservation of mass.

Key words :

(a) Introduction

(b) Definition

(c) Concept

(d) Illustrating with examples

(e) Explaining in activity form

(f) Conclusion

Topic 2: Writing the molecular formulae of certain compounds.

Key words:

(a) Introduction

(b) Chemical formulae

(c) Valency

(d) Writing chemical formulae of simple molecular compounds

(e) Illustrating with few examples

(f) Writing chemical formulae of simple ionic compounds.

(g) Illustrating with a few examples

(h) Writing chemical formulae of ionic compounds containing polyatomic ions

(i) Illustrating with a few examples

(j) Conclusion.

GROUP DISCUSSION

Topic 1 : Molecular Mass

Key words:

(a) Introduction

(b) Calculation of molecular mass

(c) Illustrating with examples

(d) Gram molecular mass

(e) Illustrating with examples

(f) Conclusion

Topic 2: Mole Concept

Key words:

(a) Introduction

(b) Different relationship in terms of mole concept

(c) Illustrating each relationship with examples

(d) Conclusion

ANSWERS

VIVA VOCE QUESTIONS

1. Law of conservation of mass
2. Law of definite or constant proportions
3. John Dalton
4. Hydrogen and Oxygen
5. 6.022×10^{23}
6. Nanometre (nm)
7. Anion
8. Cation
9. Carbon (C- 12)
10. Boron (B)
11. Ozone (O_3)
12. 10^{-10} m.

FILL IN THE BLANKS

1. Cation
2. Atom
3. Atomic mass
4. Charged
5. 1 : 8
6. 20 g
7. 6.022×10^{23}
8. 4
9. Mole
10. 5

TRUE OR FALSE

1. True
2. False
3. False
4. False
5. False
6. False
7. True
8. False
9. True
10. True

MATCH THE FOLLOWING

1.

S. No	English name of the element	Symbols	Correct match
1.	Krypton	Li	3

ATOMS AND MOLECULES

CONCISE CHEMISTRY - IX

2.	Barium	Br	4
3.	Lithium	B	5
4.	Bromine	Kr	1
5.	Boron	Ba	2

2.

S. No	Latin name of the element	Symbols	Correct match
1.	Hydragyrum	Na	3
2.	Kalium	Ag	4
3.	Natrium	Hg	1
4.	Argentum	Au	5
5.	Aurum	K	2

3.

S. No	Molecules	Molecular mass	Correct match
1.	CH_3OH	17 u	3
2.	C_2H_4	28 u	2
3.	NH_3	16 u	5
4.	C_2H_6	32 u	1
5.	CH_4	30 u	4

CHEMICAL FORMULAE OF MOLECULAR COMPOUNDS

S. No	Identify the valency		Criss cross the valency		Formula of the compound	Name of the compound
1.	NH_4 [1]	SO_4 [2]	NH_4 [2]	SO_4 [1]	$(NH_4)_2SO_4$	Ammonium sulphate
2.	Zn [2]	NO_3 [1]	Zn [1]	NO_3 [2]	$Zn(NO_3)_2$	Zinc nitrate
3.	Al [3]	S [2]	Al [2]	S [3]	Al_2S_3	Aluminium sulphide
4.	Na [1]	PO_4 [3]	Na [3]	PO_4 [1]	Na_3PO_4	Sodium phosphate
5.	Ca [2]	N [3]	Ca [3]	N [2]	Ca_3N_2	Calcium nitride
6.	K [1]	CrO_4 [2]	K [2]	CrO_4 [1]	K_2CrO_4	Potassium chromate
7.	Mg [2]	CO_3 [2]	Mg [2]	CO_3 [2]	$MgCO_3$	Magnesium carbonate
8.	Cr [3]	SO_4 [2]	Cr [2]	SO_4 [3]	$Cr_2(SO_4)_3$	Chromium sulphate
9.	Fe [2]	S [2]	Fe [2]	S [2]	FeS	Iron (II) sulphide
10.	Al [3]	O [2]	Al [2]	O [3]	Al_2O_3	Aluminium oxide

MOCK TEST-1

Time : 2 Hours
Max. Marks : 50

General Instructions :
- All questions are compulsory.
- There is no overall choice.
- Questions 1 to 5 are one mark questions. These are to be answered in one word or in one sentence.
- Questions 6 to 10 are two marks questions. These are to be answered in about 30 words each.
- Questions 11 to 15 are three marks questions. These are to be answered in about 50 words each.
- Questions 16 to 19 are five marks questions. These are to be answered in about 70 words each.

1. Define molecular mass of a substance
2. What are the building blocks of matter ?
3. What is the name of the particle which contains 10 electrons, 11 protons and 11 neutrons ?
4. What is the mass of 2 moles of nitrogen atoms ?
5. What is the numerical value of Avogadro Number ?
6. What is meant by atomicity? Explain with two examples.
7. Explain difference between 2N and N_2.
8. Calculate the formula masses of the following compounds
   (a) Sodium oxide, Na_2O
   (b) Aluminium oxide, Al_2O_3
9. How many atoms are there in 0.25 mole of hydrogen?
10. Calculate the mass of 3.011×10^{24} atoms of carbon.
11. Name the elements water is made up of. What are the valencies of these elements? Work out the chemical formula for water.
12. Give two drawbacks of Dalton's atomic theory of matter.
13. What is the significance of the formula H_2O?
14. How many moles of oxygen atoms are present in one mole of the following compounds?
    (a) Al_2O_3
    (b) Cl_2O_7
    (c) $Al_2(SO_4)_3$
15. What is the difference between the molecule of an element and the molecule of a compound ? Give one example each.
16. State the law of conservation of mass. Give one example to illustrate this law.
17. What is the difference between cations and anion ? Explain with examples.
18. (a) Define gram molecular mass of a substance.
    (b) How much is the gram molecular mass of sulphur, if sulphur exists as S_8 molecules ?
    (c) Calculate the number of moles in 100 g of sulphur.
19. State various postulates of Dalton's atomic theory of matter.

MOCK TEST-2

Time : 2 Hours
Max. Marks : 50

General Instructions:
- All questions are compulsory.
- There is no overall choice
- Questions 1 to 5 are one mark questions. These are to be answered in one word or in one sentence.
- Questions 6 to 10 are two marks questions. These are to be answered in about 30 words each.

- Questions 11 to 15 are three marks questions. These are to be answered in about 50 words each.
- Questions 16 to 19 are five marks questions. These are to be answered in about 70 words each.

1. Write the relation between nanometer and metre.
2. Define formula mass of a compound.
3. Write down the formula for calcium oxide
4. Convert 12 g of oxygen gas into moles.
5. Name the scientist who gave atomic theory of matter.
6. Which postulate of Dalton's atomic theory can explain the law of definite proportions?
7. Define chemical formula.
8. Give the formulae of the compound :
   (a) magnesium hydroxide (b) sodium sulphide
   (c) aluminium sulphate (d) potassium sulphate
9. What is the mass of 1 mole of the gas, if 5.6 litre of a gas weighs 12g at STP?
10. What is Avogadro's number?
11. Calculate the mole ratio of 240 g of calcium and 240 g of magnesium.
12. Explain the significance of the symbol H.
13. How many moles of calcium carbonate are present in 10 g of the substance ?
14. Calculate the molecular masses of the following compounds
    (a) Hydrogen sulphide, H_2S
    (b) Carbon disuiphide, CS_2
15. An element X has a valency of 4 whereas another element Y has a valency of 1. What will be the formula of the compound formed from X and Y ?
16. Explain how one mole of a substance can be represented ?
17. Give the information conveyed by the chemical formula of water.
18. How is the chemical formula of a compound written based on the valency ? Give any three examples.
19. Explain the law of conservation of mass with the help of an activity.

4

STRUCTURE OF ATOM

CONTENTS

- 4.0 Introduction
- 4.1 Discovery of Electron
- 4.2 Discovery of Proton
- 4.3 Discovery of Neutron
- 4.4 Atomic Models
- 4.5 Thomson's Model of an Atom
- 4.6 Rutherford's Model of an Atom
- 4.7 Bohr's Model of an Atom
- 4.8 Atomic Number
- 4.9 Mass Number
- 4.10 Distribution of Electrons in Different Shells or Orbits in an Atom
- 4.11 Formation of Ions
- 4.12 Valence Electrons and Valency
- 4.13 Inertness of Noble gases
- 4.14 Isotopes
- 4.15 Fractional Atomic Masses of Elements
- 4.16 Radioactive Isotopes
- 4.17 Isobars

4.0 INTRODUCTION

In the previous chapter, we have studied that basic building blocks of matter are atoms and molecules. The presence of different kinds of matter is due to the different types of atoms and molecules present in them. We also know that the atoms are divisible and possess smaller particles in them called the subatomic particles.

Atoms of all the elements except hydrogen are made up of three subatomic particles - electrons, protons and neutrons. This is because, hydrogen atom does not contain neutrons. Thus, it is clear that the atoms of different elements differ in the number of electrons, protons and neutrons.

After the discovery of the fact that the atom is made up of subatomic particles, the scientists were in search of answer for the following questions.

(a) Stability of atoms.

(b) Physical and chemical properties of different elements

(c) Formation of different kinds of molecules.

(d) Radiations emitted or absorbed by the atoms.

Let us now discuss the systematic study of discovery of these subatomic particles, their characteristics and how these helped in forming a structure of an atom.

Subatomic Particles

There are three types of subatomic particles namely,

(a) Electrons

(b) Protons

(c) Neutrons

These subatomic particles are regarded as the fundamental particles. The knowledge of these fundamental particles is necessary to understand the chemical

STRUCTURE OF ATOM

interactions. Protons are the positively charged particles present in the nucleus of the atom. Electrons are the negatively charged particles present in the extra-nuclear part of the atom. Neutrons are the neutrally charged particles present in the nucleus along with the protons.

The electrons are located outside the nucleus of an atom. In other words, they revolve around in the area surrounding the nucleus of an atom in a fixed circular path called *shells or orbit.* An electron is usually represented by the symbol 'e⁻'. An atom on the whole is an electrically neutral entity because electrons have a negative charge that is equal in magnitude to the positive charge of the protons.

Note
- The name 'electron' was suggested by G. Johnstone Stoney in 1874.

Protons and neutrons are located in the nucleus of an atom. A proton is usually represented by the symbol 'p⁺' whereas a neutron is represented by the symbol 'n'. Both protons and neutrons have nearly equal masses. The entire mass of an atom is concentrated in a very small central portion of the atom called *nucleus.* This is because the mass of an electron is very very small compared to the mass of a proton or a neutron. Since the nucleus of an atom consists of positively charged protons and electrically neutral neutrons, the charge on nucleus is positive.

Note
- There are many other smaller particles such as positrons, neutrinos, pions and muons.

Charged Particles in Matter

As early as in 600 BC, the electrical nature of matter was known to ancient Greeks. The electrical nature of matter was indicated by frictional studies by rubbing two objects together. This showed that electricity in one or other way is associated with matter. Many scientists worked on the electrical nature of matter. The production of feeble electricity by rubbing materials was first recorded by **William Gilbert.** He observed that there are two types of electrical charges namely the positive and the negative charges.

However, the experimental evidence of electrical nature of matter was given by **Michael Faraday.** According to him, the flow of electricity is due to the flow of charged particles which are present in the atoms of matter. Let us perform an activity to explain the charged particles in matter.

Activity 4.1– To understand the nature of charged particles in matter.

PROCEDURE
Step 1- Comb your dry hair with a plastic comb.
Step 2- Place the comb immediately near small pieces of paper.
Step 3- Note down your observation.
Step 4- Now rub a glass rod with silk cloth.
Step 5- Bring the rod near an inflated balloon.
Step 6- Note down your observation.

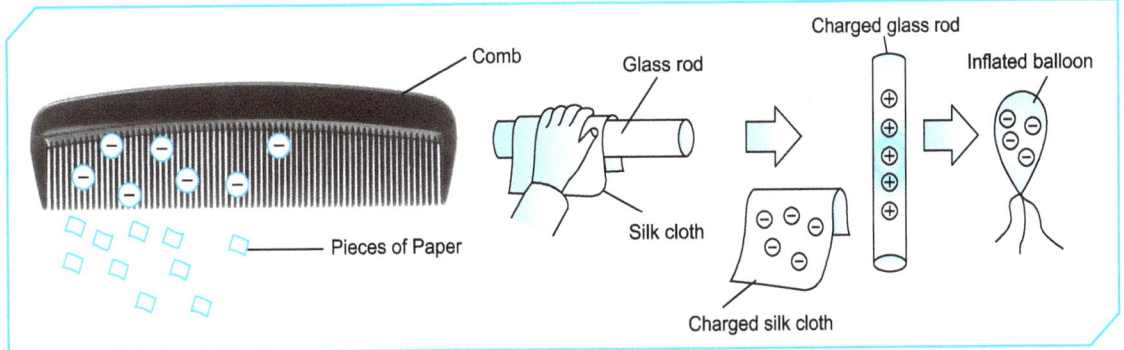

Fig. 4.1 : (a) Combing the dry hair makes the comb electrically charged, which if brought near tiny pieces of paper attracts them.

(b) Rubbing glass rod with silk cloth produces electric charge on the rod. This electrically charged rod attracts the inflated balloon.

OBSERVATION

When a comb is first rubbed with dry hair and then brought near the tiny pieces of paper, the comb attracts the pieces of paper towards itself. But, when the comb is simply brought near the tiny pieces of paper, it has no effect on the comb. When a glass rod is rubbed with silk cloth and then brought close to an inflated balloon, the glass rod attracts the balloon.

CONCLUSION

This shows that when a comb is rubbed with dry hair, it gets electrically charged which exerts an attractive force on the tiny pieces of paper and attracts them. Similarly, when a glass rod is rubbed with a silk cloth, it gets an electric charge which exerts an electric force on the inflated balloon and attracts it. Hence, a substance having electric charge is said to be charged or electrified.

Now, could you guess from where these electric charges come from ? Yes, these are formed within the atoms present in the comb and glass rod. So, the above two observations clearly shows that atoms are divisible.

4.1 DISCOVERY OF ELECTRON

In 1830, **Michael Faraday** proved the electrical structure of matter. He showed that when electricity is passed through a solution of an electrolyte, chemical reactions occurred at the electrodes. However, a closer view into the structure of an atom was obtained from the experiments carried on electrical discharge through gases. In 1850s, many scientists, mainly Faraday, studied the electrical discharge in a partially evacuated tube called *cathode ray discharge tube*.

Fig. 4.2 : J.J. Thomson : The scientist who discovered the existence of the negatively charged particles called electrons in an atom.

But, it was **J. J. Thomson** (Fig. 4.2) who discovered the existence of negatively charged particles called *electrons* in an atom in 1897. He performed experiments on electrical conduction of gases through partially evacuated tubes, known as *cathode ray discharge tube*. A discharge tube is a long glass tube containing metal electrodes fitted on either end, across which high voltage can be applied. The electrode connected to the negative terminal of the battery is called *cathode* while the electrode connected to the positive terminal of the battery is called *anode*. The tube is also connected to a vacuum pump for controlling the pressure of a gas inside the discharge tube (Fig. 4.3).

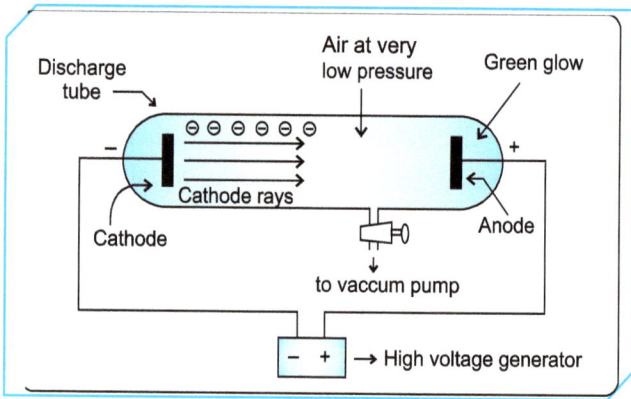

Fig. 4.3 : This figure shows a cathode ray discharge tube.

While performing the experiment, he passed electricity through a gas taken in a discharge tube. The following observations were noted

(a) When a source of high voltage electricity was connected to the electrodes i.e., cathode and anode, no electricity flowed between them.

(b) When the air was partially removed from the discharge tube, the electricity began to flow from one electrode to the other through the air in the partially evacuated discharge tube and the air in the tube gave off a yellowish red light.

(c) When the pressure was slowly decreased to nearly 10^{-4} mm of mercury, the radiations were emitted from cathode to anode in a straight line.

(d) When the emitted cathode rays strike the glass walls of the discharge tube, it started to glow with greenish light called *fluorescence*.

(e) The emission of the radiations of light stopped when the pressure inside the tube was further reduced to about 0.01 mm of mercury.

Later, it was found that fluorescence is caused due to the bombardment of the rays emitted from the cathode with the walls of the discharge tube. Since the rays were coming out from the negative electrode, i.e., cathode, these were called *Cathode Rays* (Fig. 4.4). The nature of these rays does not depend upon the nature of gas or the cathode material used in discharge tube. This means that the charge to mass ratio of an cathode rays was found to be the same as that for an electron (-1.76×10^8 coulomb per gm).

Thus, cathode rays are considered to be a stream of electrons.

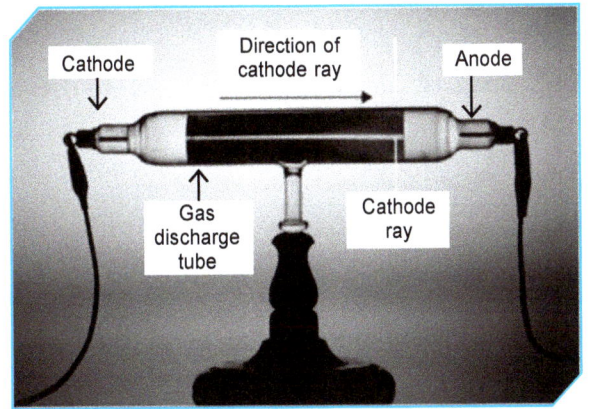

Fig 4.4 : This figure shows the direction of cathode rays (from cathode to anode) in a discharge tube.

Characteristics of Cathode Rays

The cathode rays have following characteristics :

(a) The cathode rays consist of negatively charged particles known as electrons.

(b) The cathode rays always travel in a straight line. When an opaque object is placed in the path of cathode rays, a shadow of the object is formed on the wall opposite to the cathode. The shadow can be formed only if the cathode rays travel in a straight line (Fig. 4.5 a and b).

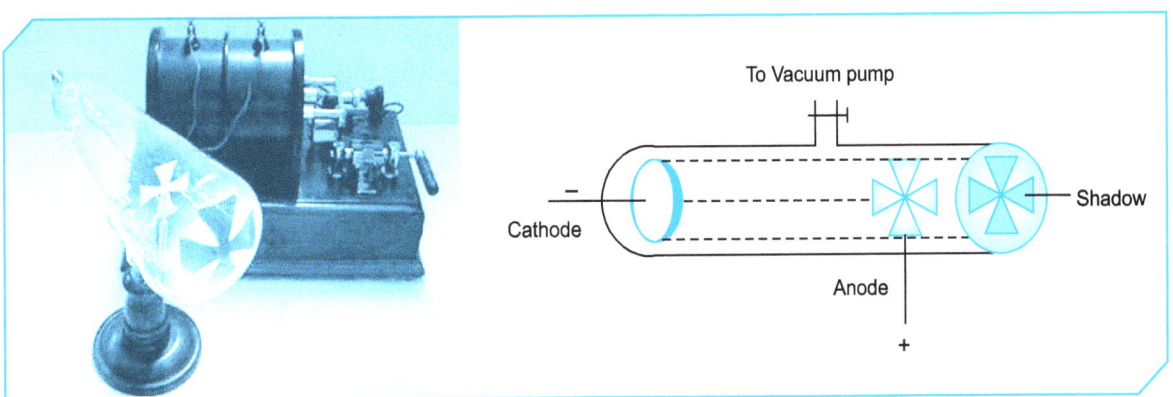

Fig. 4.5 : (a) This figure shows the formation of shadow of an opaque object when placed in the path of cathode rays in a discharge tube.

(b) This figure shows discharge tube in which that cathode rays cast shadow of the object placed in their path.

(c) When the cathode rays strike a solid object, specially a metal of high atomic weight and high melting point such as copper, molybdenum, tungsten etc., they produce X-rays.

(d) When cathode rays strike against a glass surface or screen coated with zinc sulphide, they produce a green glow known as fluorescence (Fig. 4.6).

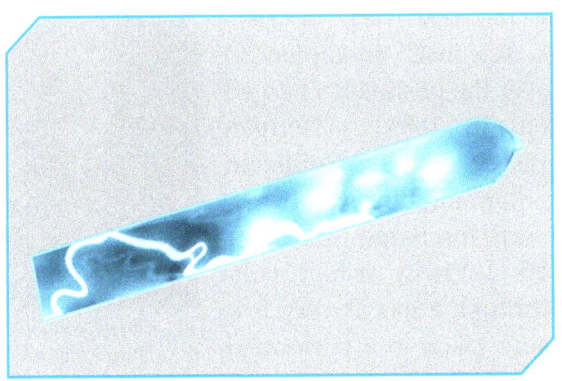

Fig. 4.6 : This figure shows the green glow in the discharge tube.

(e) Cathode rays produce heat when they strike a material surface.

(f) They are deflected from their path by electric and magnetic fields. When cathode rays are passed through a magnetic field, they are deflected towards negatively charged particle which shows that they consists of negatively charged particles. On the other hand, when cathode rays are passed through an electric field, they get deflected in the direction opposite to the deflection caused by the magnetic field i.e., they are deflected towards positively charged particle in their path (Fig. 4.7).

(g) They can cause ionization in gases when gases are exposed to cathode rays. This shows that the cathode rays are negatively charged particles.

(h) They can penetrate through thin metal foils.

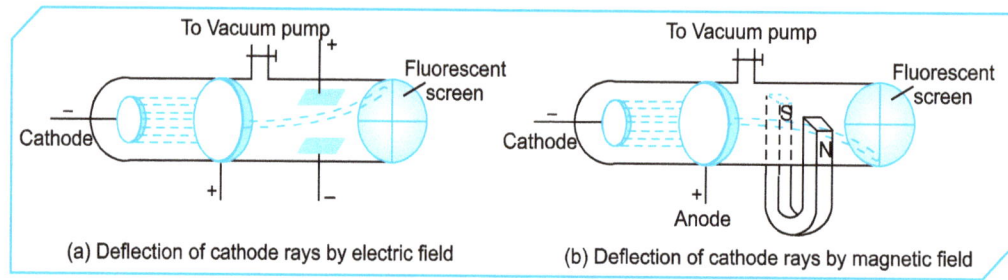

Fig. 4.7 : The figure shows the deflection of cathode rays by electric and magnetic field.

(i) The charge to mass ratio (e/m) for the particles in the cathode is independent of the nature of the gas taken in the discharge tube and the nature of the cathode.

Determination of Charge and Mass on an Electron

It was found that the mass of an electron is about $\frac{1}{1840}$ times the mass of hydrogen atom. Since the mass of a hydrogen atom is 1u, the relative mass of an electron is $\frac{1}{1840}$ u. The absolute mass of the electron was found to be 9.1×10^{-28}g. Since the mass of an electron is too small, it is considered to be negligible.

The charge on the electron was determined by **R.A. Millikan** in 1898 with the help of oil drop experiment. The absolute charge on an electron is 1 coulomb of negative charge. This means that an electron has 1 unit of negative charge i.e., the relative charge of an electron is –1.

PAPER-PEN TEST : 1

1. What are sub-atomic particles ?
2. What are the basic building blocks of matter ?
3. Which sub-atomic particle is not present in hydrogen atom ?
4. The subatomic particles were regarded as the ------------------------.
5. Define shells.
6. How are the electrons represented ?
7. Justify: "An atom on the whole is an electrically neutral entity".
8. Where are protons and neutrons present?
9. How are the protons represented?
10. Define nucleus.
11. Why is the charge on nucleus positive?
12. Why is the entire mass of an atom concentrated on nucleus?
13. The production of feeble electricity by rubbing materials was first recorded by -----------.
14. What are the two types of electric charges?
15. How was the electrical nature of matter indicated?
16. The experimental evidence of electrical nature of matter was show by ------------------.
17. Explain an activity to show charged particles in matter.
18. Who proved the electrical structure of matter ?
19. Describe the discovery of electron by Faraday.
20. Explain the discovery of electron by Thomson.
21. What are the observations made by Thomson?
22. Why are cathode rays considered to be a stream of electrons?
23. Mention the characteristics of cathode rays.
24. How will you determine the charge and mass of an electron?
25. The charge on the electron was determined by ----------------------------.

4.2 DISCOVERY OF PROTON

After the discovery of electrons, scientists attempted to discover the positively charged proton. In 1886, a German scientist **Eugen Goldstein** (Fig. 4.8), modified the cathode ray discharge tube. He passed electricity at high voltage through a gas at very low pressure taken in a perforated discharge tube. Streams of heavy particles were given out by the positive electrode i.e.,

Fig. 4.8 : Eugen Goldstein: The scientist who discovered the existence of positively charged particles called protons in an atom.

anode. These stream of heavy particles are called *anode rays* as these rays were directed away from the anode. These are also called positive rays since, they consist of positively charged particles called protons. Initially, these rays were also called as canal rays as they moved like a stream of water in a canal.

Goldstein explained the formation of protons using hydrogen gas. When a high voltage is applied to hydrogen gas, the electrical energy removes the electrons from the hydrogen atoms. After the removal of negatively charged electron from the hydrogen atom, a positively charged particle called the proton is formed (Fig. 4.9).

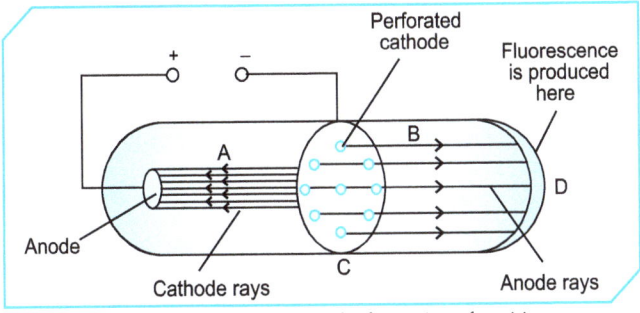

Fig. 4.9 : This figure shows the formation of positive rays called anode rays.

Unlike cathode rays, the formation of anode rays particles depends upon the nature of gas present in the discharge tube. This means that the charge to mass ratio of the positively charged particles is different for different gases.

Characteristics of Anode Rays or Canal Rays

(a) Anode rays consist of a stream of fast moving positively charged particles known as protons.

(b) Anode rays travel in a straight line.

(c) They get deflected from their path by electric and magnetic fields in a direction opposite to the cathode rays.

(d) They can penetrate through thin metal foils and can ionize gases.

(e) The charge to mass ratio of these rays is very low.

(f) They are capable of producing physical and chemical changes.

Determination of Charge and Mass of a Proton

The absolute mass of a proton is found to be 1.6×10^{-24} g. Since the proton is the only constituent of the nucleus of a hydrogen atom, the mass of a proton is equal to the mass of a hydrogen atom. We know that mass of hydrogen atom is 1u, therefore the relative mass of a proton is 1u. The mass of a proton is 1840 times that of an electron.

The charge of a proton is equal and opposite to the charge of an electron. Thus, the absolute charge of a proton is 1.6×10^{-19} coulomb of positive charge. Since the charge of 1.6×10^{-19} coulomb is very very small, therefore the charge carried by a positive particle is taken as the unit of positive charge. Thus, a proton carries one unit positive charge and the relative charge of the proton is +1.

4.3 DISCOVERY OF NEUTRON

After the discovery of protons, a need for the presence of electrically neutral particle as one of the constituent of atom was felt. These particles were discovered by **James Chadwick** in 1932 (Fig. 4.10). When Chadwick bombarded a thin sheet of Beryllium (Be) by alpha particles, electrically neutral particles having a mass slightly greater than that of protons were emitted. He named these particles as *neutrons*. Except hydrogen, atoms of all other elements contain neutral neutron particles (Fig. 4.11).

Fig. 4.10 : James Chadwick : The scientist who discovered the existence of neutral particle called neutron.

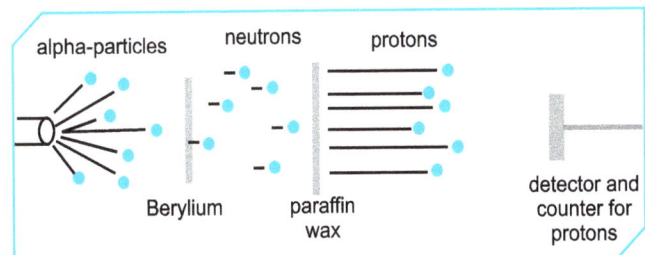

Fig. 4.11 : This figure shows the schematic diagram for the experiment that led to the discovery of neutrons by Chadwick.

Determination of Charge and Mass of a Neutron

The absolute charge of the neutron is zero. It is electrically neutral. The mass of a neutron cannot be determined directly due to lack of charge. Hence, we can obtain the mass of a neutron by subtracting proton mass from deuteron (Deuteron is a positively charged particle consisting of a proton and a neutron equivalent to the nucleus of an atom of deuteron mass. Thus, the absolute mass of a neutron is 1.6×10^{-24} gram and relative mass of a neutron is 1 u.

Let us now summarize the characteristics of the subatomic particles- proton, electron and neutron.

Comparison between Proton, Electron and Neutron.

S. No	Subatomic particles	Symbol	Relative charge	Absolute charge	Relative mass	Absolute mass (in g)	Mass in kg
1.	Proton	p^+	+1	1.6×10^{-19}	1	1.6×10^{-24}	1.672×10^{-27}
2.	Electron	e^-	-1	-1.6×10^{-19}	0	9.1×10^{-28}	9.109×10^{-31}
3.	Neutron	n	0	0	1	1.6×10^{-24}	1.674×10^{-27}

PAPER- PEN TEST : 2

1. Who modified the cathode ray tube to generate anode rays ?
2. Why anode rays are called canal rays?
3. Explain the experiment performed by Goldstein.
4. Describe the formation of protons using hydrogen gas.
5. Mention the characteristics of anode rays.
6. How will you determine the charge and the mass of a proton?
7. The mass of a proton is ------------- times that of an electron.
8. The absolute charge of a proton is ---------------.
9. Who discovered neutron?
10. Explain the experiment performed by Chadwick.
11. How will you determine the charge and the mass of a neutron?
12. Compare the characteristics of proton, electron and neutron.

4.4 ATOMIC MODELS

The discovery of two fundamental particles (electrons and protons) inside the atom led to the failure of Dalton's atomic theory which suggested that the atom was indivisible and indestructible. Thus, it was necessary to know how electrons and protons are arranged within an atom. Different atomic models were proposed to explain the distributions of these charged particles in an atom. Let us discuss a few of these atomic models.

4.5 THOMSON'S MODEL OF AN ATOM

In 1898, **J.J. Thomson** (Fig. 4.12) was the first to propose a detailed model of an atom. He proposed that an atom consists of a uniform sphere of positive charge in which the negatively charged electrons are embedded more or less uniformly. He assumed the mass of the atom to be uniformly distributed over the atom and concluded that the total positive and negative charges are equal in magnitude, due to which an atom is electrically neutral. This model of atom is known as the 'plum-pudding model' or 'raisin pudding model' or 'water-melon model'.

Fig. 4.12 : J.J. Thomson : The scientist who gave Thomson's Model of an atom

Because similar to the plum-pudding or raisin pudding or water melon, electrons are embedded in a sphere of positive charge and resemble the raisins or seeds dispersed in a pudding or water melon respectively (Fig. 4.13). Though this model was able to explain the neutrality or stability of an atom, it failed to explain the observations made by Rutherford in his alpha-scattering experiment.

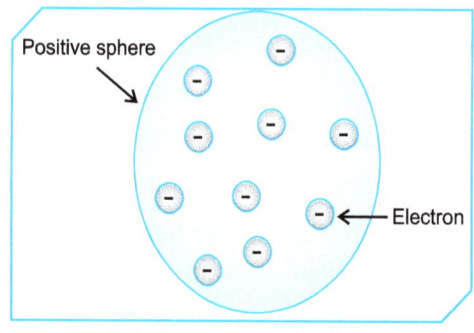

Fig. 4.13 : Thomson's model of an atom.

Drawback of Thomson's Model of an Atom

(a) The Thomson model of an atom did not give the mass of the electron.
(b) He could not explain the results of alpha-particle scattering experiment conducted by Rutherford.

4.6 RUTHERFORD'S MODEL OF AN ATOM

In order to design the structure of atom, **Ernest Rutherford** (Fig. 4.14) in 1910 carried out the famous gold foil experiment in which he bombarded a very thin gold foil with alpha particles. In this experiment, he bombarded a thin sheet of gold foil having thickness of ~100nm or 10^{-5} cm with alpha particles in an evacuated chamber. A circular fluorescent screen coated with zinc sulphide (ZnS) was placed around the foil. When the alpha particles were passed through a slit in a lead plate they struck the zinc sulphide screen and a tiny flash of light was produced at that point. He expected that alpha particles would be deflected by the sub-atomic particles of the gold atoms. But the observations made by Rutherford were unexpected. He observed that :

Fig. 4.14 : Ernest Rutherford: The scientist who discovered the positively charged nucleus in an atom.

(a) Most of the alpha particles passed straight through the gold foil without any deflection from their path.

(b) A small fraction of the alpha particles was deflected at small angles and a few were deflected at large angles.

(c) A very few alpha particles bounced back on hitting the gold foil (Fig. 4.15 a and b).

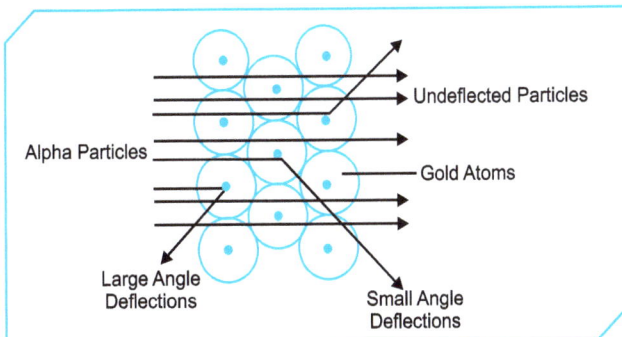

Fig. 4.15 : (a) This figure shows the scattering of alpha particles by the atoms of gold foil.

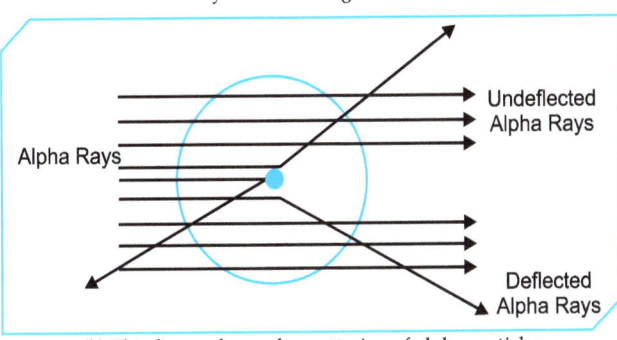

(b) This figure shows the scattering of alpha particles through single atom.

Note

- Alpha particles are positively charged helium ions having high energy. It has +2 charge and mass of 4u.

Results of Rutherford's Experiment

(a) Since, most of the positively charged alpha particles passed through the foil undeflected, it shows that most of the space in an atom is empty.

(b) A few positively charged alpha particles were deflected by small and large angles due to the presence of a heavy positive centre in the atom which repels the positively charged alpha particles and deflect them from their path. He named this positive centre as nucleus.

(c) A very few alpha particles bounced back on hitting the gold foil because nucleus is very hard and dense and it does not allow the alpha particles to pass through it.

(d) The volume occupied by the nucleus is negligibly small compared to the total volume of the atom. This shows that the radius of the atom is about 10^{-10} m while that of a nucleus is 10^{-15} m. In other words, the radius of nucleus has been found to be about 10^5 times smaller than the radius of the atom.

Based on these observations and conclusions of alpha particles scattering experiment, Rutherford proposed the nuclear structure of an atom.

Rutherford's Nuclear Model of an Atom

Based on his experimental findings, Rutherford in 1911 gave a nuclear model of the atom. According to this model,

(a) All the positive charge of the atom and most of the mass of the atom was concentrated in a very small region called nucleus.

(b) The nucleus is the densest part of an atom and contains the positively charged particles, the protons.

(c) The nucleus consists of protons and neutrons called nucleons.

(d) The size of the nucleus an is extremely small as compared to the size of an atom as a whole, as there is a lot of empty space around the nucleus.

(e) The nucleus is surrounded by the electrons which are revolving around it in circular orbits (shells) at very high speed. Electrons and the nucleus are held together by electrostatic force of attraction. This force of attraction between electrons and the nucleus is balanced by the centrifugal force acting on the revolving electrons. This model of atom resembles the model of solar system in which the nucleus plays the role of sun while the electrons act as revolving planets. Hence, this model of atoms is also called the planetary model of atom.

(f) The total negative charge on the electrons is equal to the total positive charge on the nucleus, so that the atom on the whole is electrically neutral.

Drawbacks of Rutherford's Nuclear Model of Atom

(a) The Rutherford's model of atom failed to explain the stability of atom. According to the electromagnetic theory of Maxwell, the charged particles when accelerated should emit electromagnetic radiation. Since, the electrons possess negative charge and are revolving around the positively charged nucleus in a circular path, it would emit radiation and thus orbit will continue to shrink enabling the atom to collapse, but contrary to this explanation, atom is stable (Fig. 4.16).

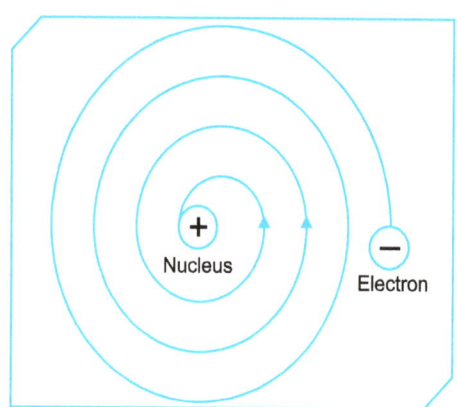

Fig. 4.16 : This figure shows how an energy losing electron get attracted towards nucleus that could lead to the total collapse of an atom.

(b) The Rutherford's model of atom failed to explain the existence of certain definite lines in the hydrogen spectrum.

(c) The Rutherford's model of atom also failed to explain the distribution or the arrangement of electrons around the nucleus.

PAPER-PEN TEST : 3

1. What led to the failure of Dalton's atomic theory?
2. Who was the first to propose a detailed model of the atom?
3. Explain Thomson's model of an atom.
4. What are the drawbacks of Thomson's model of an atom?
5. Describe Rutherford's model of an atom.
6. What were the observations made by Rutherford's model of an atom?
7. What were the results of Rutherford's model of an atom?
8. Illustrate Rutherford's nuclear model of an atom.
9. What are the drawbacks of Rutherford's model of an atom?
10. What was the electromagnetic theory of Maxwell?

4.7 BOHR'S MODEL OF AN ATOM

In order to overcome the drawbacks of Rutherford's model of atom, Neils Bohr (Fig. 4.17) proposed the following postulates about the model of an atom. **Neils Bohr,** a Danish physicist proposed a new model of atom based on Planck's quantum theory. According to him,

Fig. 4.17 : Neils Bohr: The scientist who proposed the concept of the structure of an atom.

(a) An atom consists of a small, heavy positively charged nucleus in the centre.
(b) The negatively charged electrons revolve around the nucleus in definite circular paths called *orbits* or *shells.*
(c) These orbits are arranged concentrically around the nucleus.
(d) The negatively charged electrons revolve only in those orbits which have fixed value of energy. Hence, these orbits are called *energy levels* or *stationary states.*
(e) The different energy levels are numbered as 1, 2, 3, 4 ..... etc., or designated as K, L, M, N...... etc., starting from the shell closest to the nucleus (Fig. 4.18).
(f) The energy of the electron revolving in a particular orbit is fixed and hence does not change with time.
(g) Since the electrons revolve around the orbits of fixed values of energy, the electrons in the atom can have only certain definite or discrete values

of energy. Hence, we can say that the energy of an electron is quantized.

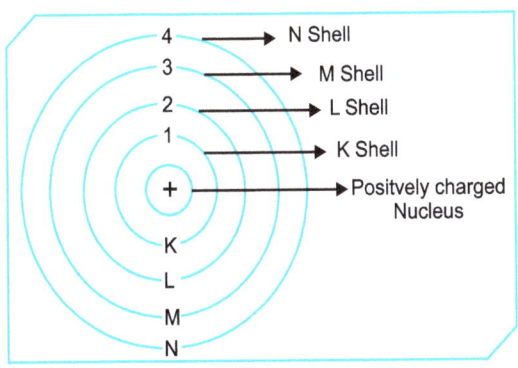

Fig. 4.18 : This figure shows the different energy levels in the Bohr's model of an atom.

(h) While revolving in discrete orbits the electrons do not radiate energy. However, when the electron jumps from lower to higher energy shell, it absorbs definite amount of energy. On the other hand, when the electron jumps from higher to lower energy shell, it emits radiation (Fig. 4.19).

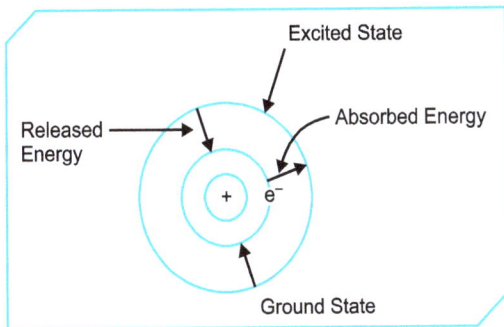

Fig. 4.19 : This figure shows the absorption and emission of energy when electron jumps from lower state to higher or excited state and vice-versa.

4.8 ATOMIC NUMBER

We have already studied that the positively charged protons are present in the nucleus of an atom. The atomic number can be determined by the number of protons present in an atom. Thus, we can say that-

"The atomic number of an element is equal to the number of positively charged protons in the nucleus of an atom."

It is denoted by the letter 'Z'. Hence,

Atomic number of an element (Z) = Number of protons in an atom of the element

Let us discuss the atomic number with a few examples.

Example 1 : An atom of chlorine element has 17 protons in it, so the atomic number of chlorine is 17. Hence, we can say that for chlorine, Z = 17.

Example 2 : An atom of carbon element has 6 protons in it, so the atomic number of carbon is 6. Hence, we can say that for carbon, Z = 6.

Example 3 : An atom of sodium element has 11 protons in it, so the atomic number of sodium is 11. Hence, we can say that for sodium, Z = 11.

The atomic number of an atom of the same element never changes. This means that the number of protons in the nucleus of an atom is always same for same element. No two elements can have the same atomic number. Since, all the atoms of an element have the same number of protons in their nuclei, all possess the same atomic number. However, the atoms of different elements have different number of protons in their nuclei and so possess different atomic numbers.

In a neutral atom, the number of protons is equal to the number of electrons present in it. Hence, we can also say that,

"The atomic number of an element is equal to the number of electrons present in the neutral atom"

It is important to note that atomic number of an element is equal to the number of electrons only in case of neutral atoms. This does not apply to ions, because an ion is formed either by removal or addition of electrons and may contain either less or more electrons than protons. For example, consider the element, sodium (Na) having atomic number 11. Since atomic number is equal to number of protons, therefore, the total number of protons in a sodium atom is also 11. As we know that total number of protons is equal to the total number of electrons, the total number of electrons in sodium atom is also 11. On the other hand, if we consider a sodium (Na) ion, the total number of electrons is not equal to the atomic number. This is because sodium ion is formed by the removal of an electron from the valence shell, hence it possess 10 electrons.

Thus, we can conclude that,

(a) Atomic Number (Z) = Number of Protons.

(b) Atomic Number (Z) = Number of Electrons in a neutral atom.

(c) Atomic number gives us the number of protons present in an atom of the element.

(d) Atomic number gives us the number of electrons present in a neutral atom of the element.

Let us now discuss the mass number of an element.

4.9. MASS NUMBER

We have already studied that an atom consists of protons, neutrons and electrons. The mass of an atom is given by the sum of the masses of protons and neutrons present in the nucleus. Hence, we can define mass number as,

"The total number of protons and neutrons present in an atom of an element"

The mass number is denoted by the letter A. Hence,

Mass number of an element (A) = Number of protons (p^+) + Number of neutrons (n)

The total number of protons and neutrons present in a nucleus are called *nucleons*. So, we can also define mass number as,

"The total number of nucleons present in the nucleus of an atom of an element."

Let us discuss the mass number with a few examples.

Example 1 : A carbon atom consists of 6 protons and 6 neutrons. Therefore, the mass number of carbon is 6 + 6 = 12. Hence, we can say that for carbon, A = 12.

Example 2 : A sodium atom consists of 11 protons and 12 neutrons. Therefore, the mass number of sodium is 11 + 12 = 23. Hence, we can say that for sodium, A = 23.

Example 3 : A hydrogen atom consists of 1 proton and has no neutron. Therefore, the mass number of hydrogen is 1 + 0 = 1. Hence, we can say that for hydrogen, A = 1.

Actually, the mass number of an atom gives us the atomic mass of the element. For instance, if the mass number of an atom is 12, then the atomic mass will be 12 u. Let us now discuss the relationship between atomic number and mass number.

Relationship between Atomic Number and Mass Number

We have studied that,

Mass number = No. of protons + No. of neutrons

But, number of protons is equal to atomic number. Therefore, above equation can be rewritten as :

Mass number = Atomic number + No. of neutrons

Both mass number and atomic number can be indicated on the symbol of an element as follows :

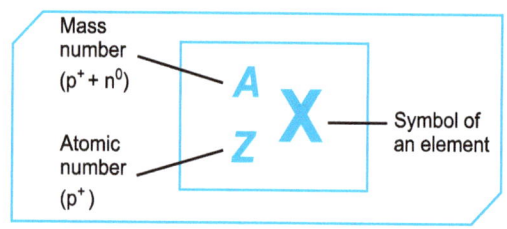

Fig. 4.20 : This figure shows how the atomic number and mass number can be indicated on the symbol of an element.

In the above figure, the alphabet 'X' indicates the symbol of an element, the alphabet 'Z' written on the lower left side of the symbol indicates atomic number and the alphabet 'A' written on the upper left side of the symbol of an element indicates mass number (Fig. 4.20).

For example, sodium atom whose atomic number is 11 and mass number is 23 can be represented as :

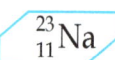

Here, Na indicates the symbol of sodium element, the numerical figure on the upper left side of the symbol (23) indicates the mass number while the numerical figure on the lower left side of the symbol (11) indicates the atomic number.

Let us now discuss how to calculate the number of protons, electrons and neutrons.

Calculation of Protons, Electrons and Neutrons

If we know the atomic number and mass number of an element, it is possible for us to calculate the number of protons, electrons and neutrons.

Number of protons = Atomic number (Z)
Number of electrons in a neutral atom = Atomic number (Z)
Number of neutrons = Mass number (A) − Atomic number (Z)

Let us now solve few problems based on the atomic number and mass number.

STRUCTURE OF ATOM

Solved Sample Problems

Sample Problem 1 : Calculate the atomic number of an element X whose mass number is 31 and number of neutrons is 16. What is the symbol of the element? Indicate the symbol with mass number and atomic number.

Solution : We know that,

$$\text{Mass number} = \text{Atomic number (Z)} + \text{Number of neutrons}$$
$$31 = \text{Atomic number (Z)} + 16$$

Therefore,

$$\text{Atomic number (Z)} = \text{Mass number} - \text{Number of neutrons}$$
$$\text{Atomic number (Z)} = 31 - 16$$
$$= 15$$

The element having atomic number 15 is phosphorus and its symbol is P. Its symbol can be indicated as $^{31}_{15}P$

Sample Problem 2 : The atomic number and the mass number of sodium are 11 and 23, respectively. Calculate the number of protons, electrons and neutrons.

Solution : We know that,

$$\text{No. of protons} = \text{Atomic number (Z)}$$
$$\text{No. of electrons} = \text{Atomic number (Z)}$$

Hence, the number of protons and electrons in an atom of sodium (Na) is 11 and 11 respectively.

Now,

$$\text{No. of neutrons} = \text{Mass number (A)} - \text{Atomic number (Z)}$$
$$= 23 - 11$$
$$= 12$$

Hence, the number of neutrons in an atom of sodium is 12.

Sample Problem 3 : The atomic number and the mass number of magnesium are 12 and 24, respectively. Calculate the number of protons, electrons and neutrons in magnesium atom and magnesium ion.

Solution : We know that,

$$\text{No. of protons} = \text{Atomic number (Z)}$$
$$\text{No. of electrons} = \text{Atomic number (Z)}$$

Thus, for magnesium atom, Mg,

$$\text{No. of protons} = \text{Atomic number} = 12$$
$$\text{No. of electrons} = \text{Atomic number} = 12$$

Now,

$$\text{No. of neutrons} = \text{Mass number} - \text{Atomic number}$$
$$= 24 - 12$$
$$= 12$$

Hence, number of protons, electrons and neutrons in magnesium (Mg) atom is 12, 12 and 12 respectively.

Similarly, for magnesium (Mg^{2+}) ion,

$$\text{No. of protons} = \text{Atomic number} = 12$$
$$\text{No. of electrons} = \text{Atomic number} - \text{Charge}$$
$$= 12 - 2 = 10$$

Now,

No. of neutrons = Mass number − Atomic number
= 24 − 12
= 12

Hence, number of protons, electrons and neutrons in magnesium (Mg^{2+}) ion is 12, 10 and 12 respectively.

Try Yourself

1. The atomic number and the mass number of phosphorus are 15 and 31 respectively. Calculate the number of protons, electrons and neutrons in a neutral atom and ions.

2. Identify the atomic number of each of the following atoms :
   (a) Potassium (p = 19, n =20)
   (b) Argon (p = 20, n = 20)
   (c) Nitrogen (p = 7, n = 7)
   (d) Sulphur (p = 16, n = 16)
   (e) Aluminium (p = 13, n = 14)

3. Give the symbols of the elements from atomic number 1 – 20 with atomic and mass number.

4. If an element has 15 protons and 16 neutrons in the nucleus, find out its atomic number and mass number. Represent the element with atomic and mass number.

PAPER-PEN TEST : 4

1. Bohr model of atom was based on ------------------ theory.
2. Define energy levels.
3. What are the postulates of Bohr's model of an atom ?
4. Define orbits.
5. Draw schematic representation of different energy levels.
6. Justify: "The energy of an electron is quantized".
7. Define atomic number.
8. How is the atomic number determined?
9. What does the statement–"The atomic number of an atom of the same element never changes" mean ?
10. Differentiate between sodium atom and sodium ion.
11. Define mass number.
12. What is mass of an atom?
13. Define nucleons.
14. How does the mass number of an atom help us to calculate the atomic mass of the element?
15. Give the relationship between atomic number and mass number.
16. In the symbol $^{23}_{11}Na$, what does the numerical figure on the upper left side and lower left side represents ?
17. How are the number of protons, electrons and neutrons calculated?

4.10 DISTRIBUTION OF ELECTRONS IN DIFFERENT SHELLS OR ORBITS IN AN ATOM

We have already studied that the electrons are present outside the nucleus. They form a cloud of negative charge which revolves around the nucleus in definite orbits called *'shells'*. These shells are also called as *energy levels*. In order to understand the distribution of electrons, we need to first know about the energy levels.

Let us discuss energy levels in detail.

The shell closest to the nucleus is called K-shell, first shell or 1st shell. The next shell is called the L-shell second shell or 2nd shell. Similarly, M shell, N shells and so on. Generally, the shells are counted from the shell, nearest to the nucleus to the outward. So, we can say that K shell has the minimum energy while the outermost shell of an atom has the highest energy. The energy levels are represented by circles around the nucleus (Fig. 4.21).

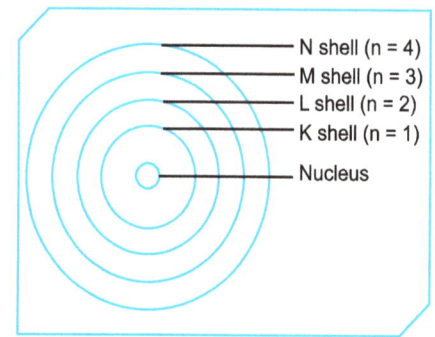

Fig. 4.21 : This figure shows the different electron shells or energy levels (K, L, M, N….) in an atom.

The electrons are distributed in the different shells in a fixed manner. The distribution of electrons in different shells is referred to as *electronic configuration*. Each shell has a limited capacity to hold electrons and each electron tries to occupy a shell which has minimum energy. The problem of distribution of electrons in various shells was solved by **Bohr** and **Bury** and hence, it is called *Bohr-Bury Scheme*. This scheme gives the distribution of electrons in various shells. According to Bohr-Bury scheme, a system is said to be most stable when it has minimum energy. Hence, the electrons occupy the lowest energy level first i.e., K shell which is followed by L shell, M shell and so on.

Let us now discuss the electronic configuration of elements.

Electronic Configuration of Elements

The electronic configuration of elements may be defined as,

"The distribution of electrons in various energy levels or shells of an atom of the element."

However, in order to arrange the electrons in different shells, we should know the following :

(a) The number of electrons in an atom of the element.

(b) The maximum number of electrons that can be accommodated in each shell of the atom.

As discussed earlier, the number of electrons in an atom of the element is equal to the atomic number of the element. Thus, we can find out the number of electrons in an atom of the element, if we know the atomic number of the element. In order to know about the maximum number of electrons that can be accommodated in each shell of the atom, we need to follow Bohr-Bury scheme. According to Bohr-Bury scheme, the distribution of electrons is governed by three main factors,

(a) Maximum number of electrons that can be accommodated in each shell of the atom.

(b) Maximum number of electrons that can be accommodated in the outermost shell.

(c) Formation of a new shell.

Let us discuss these factors one by one in detail.

(a) **Maximum number of electrons that can be accommodated in each shell of the atom**

Bohr-Bury has proposed a formula to find out the maximum number of electrons that can be accommodated in each shell of the atom. According to them, the maximum number of electrons which can be present in any shell of an atom is represented by a formula $2n^2$ where 'n' is the number of the shell as counted from the nucleus. Let us now try to calculate the maximum number of electrons in first four energy levels of the atom.

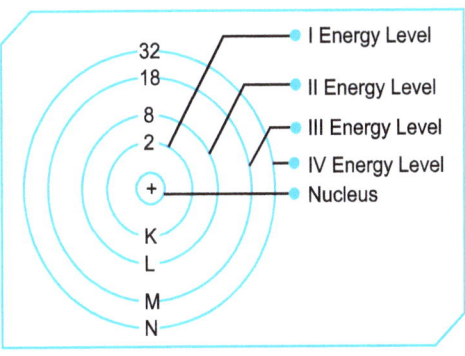

Fig. 4.22 : This figure shows the maximum number of electrons that the first four electron shells or energy levels (K, L, M, N....) in an atom can possess.

(i) For first energy shell i.e., K shell, n = 1

Substituting the value of n in the formula, we get

The maximum no. of electrons = $2n^2$

$= 2 \times (1)^2 = 2$

(ii) For second energy shell i.e., L shell, n = 2

Substituting the value of n in the formula, we get

The maximum no. of electrons = $2n^2$

$= 2 \times (2)^2 = 8$

(iii) For third energy shell i.e., M shell, n = 3

Substituting the value of n in the formula, we get

The maximum no. of electrons = $2n^2$

$= 2 \times (3)^2 = 18$

(iv) For fourth energy shell i.e., N shell, n = 4

Substituting the value of n in the formula, we get

The maximum no. of electrons = $2n^2$

$= 2 \times (4)^2 = 32$

Thus, we can conclude that the maximum number of electrons that can be accommodated in the first energy level is 2, for second energy level is 8, for third energy level is 18 and fourth energy level is 32 (Fig. 4.22). We can also summarize it as follows :

Shell	Shell no. (n)	$2n^2$	Max. no. of electrons in each shell
K shell	1	$2 \times (1)^2$	2 electrons
L shell	2	$2 \times (2)^2$	8 electrons
M shell	3	$2 \times (3)^2$	18 electrons
N shell	4	$2 \times (4)^2$	32 electrons

(b) Maximum number of electrons that can be accommodated in the outermost shell

The outermost shell of an atom cannot have more than eight electrons, even if it has the capacity to accommodate more number of electrons. For instance, if M shell is the outermost shell of an atom, then it can accommodate a maximum of eight electrons only, though it has the capacity to hold 18 electrons. This is because the presence of eight electrons in the outermost shell makes an atom stable. However, if the outermost shell of an atom is the first shell or K shell then it can hold a maximum of 2 electrons only. For instance, in helium atom, K shell is the outermost shell and it can hold a maximum of two electrons only. This is because the presence of two electrons in the outermost shell also makes an atom very stable (Fig. 4.23).

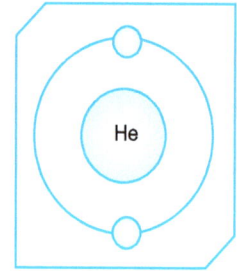

Fig. 4.23 : This figure shows the K-shell or valence shell of Helium atom.

(c) Formation of a new shell

The electrons in an atom do not form a new shell unless all the inner shells are completely filled with electrons. In other words, the electrons are filled in the shells in a systematic way such that first all the electrons are filled in K shell, then L shell, M shell and so on. However, some elements having more than atomic number 18 do not apply this rule. Let us discuss this with an example. In case of calcium having atomic number 20, the maximum number of electrons in each shell can be distributed as 2, 8, 10. Here, M shell is the last shell which has the capacity to hold maximum of 18 electrons. But, according to Bohr Bury scheme, the outermost shell cannot have more than 8 electrons. Hence, the electronic configuration of calcium is 2, 8, 8, 2.

Let us now discuss about the electronic configuration of first twenty elements.

Electronic Configuration of First Twenty Elements

The electronic configurations of the first 20 elements from Hydrogen (H) to Calcium (Ca) having atomic numbers 1 to 20 are given below :

Name of the element	Symbol of the element	Atomic number (Z)	Mass number (A)	No. of protons	No. of electrons	No. of neutrons (A − Z)	Electronic configuration			
							K	L	M	N
Hydrogen	H	1	1	1	1	0	1			
Helium	He	2	4	2	2	2	2			
Lithium	Li	3	7	3	3	4	2	1		
Beryllium	Be	4	9	4	4	5	2	2		
Boron	B	5	11	5	5	6	2	3		
Carbon	C	6	12	6	6	6	2	4		
Nitrogen	N	7	14	7	7	7	2	5		
Oxygen	O	8	16	8	8	8	2	6		
Fluorine	F	9	19	9	9	10	2	7		
Neon	Ne	10	20	10	10	10	2	8		
Sodium	Na	11	23	11	11	12	2	8	1	
Magnesium	Mg	12	24	12	12	12	2	8	2	
Aluminium	Al	13	27	13	13	14	2	8	3	

STRUCTURE OF ATOM   CONCISE CHEMISTRY - IX

Silicon	Si	14	28	14	14	14	2	8	4	
Phosphorus	P	15	31	15	15	16	2	8	5	
Sulphur	S	16	32	16	16	16	2	8	6	
Chlorine	Cl	17	35	17	17	18	2	8	7	
Argon	Ar	18	40	18	18	22	2	8	8	
Potassium	K	19	39	19	19	20	2	8	8	1
Calcium	Ca	20	40	20	20	20	2	8	8	2

Representation of the Atom for First Twenty Elements

Atom of Hydrogen	Atom of Helium	Atom of Lithium	Atom of Beryllium
p = 1, n = 0	p = 2, n = 2	p = 3, n = 4	p = 4, n = 9
$_1^1H$; E.C - 1	$_2^4He$; E.C - 2	$_3^7Li$; E.C - 2,1	$_4^9Be$; E.C - 2, 2
Atom of Boron	**Atom of Carbon**	**Atom of Nitrogen**	**Atom of Oxygen**
p = 5, n = 6	p = 6, n = 6	p = 7, n = 7	p = 8, n = 8
$_5^{11}B$; E.C - 2, 3	$_6^{12}C$; E.C - 2, 4	$_7^{14}N$; E.C - 2, 5	$_8^{16}O$; E.C - 2, 6
Atom of Fluorine	**Atom of Neon**	**Atom of Sodium**	**Atom of Magnesium**
p = 9, n = 10	p = 10, n = 10	p = 11, n = 12	p = 12, n = 12
$_9^{19}F$; E.C - 2, 7	$_{10}^{20}Ne$; E.C - 2, 8	$_{11}^{23}Na$; E.C - 2, 8, 1	$_{12}^{24}Mg$; E.C - 2, 8, 2
Atom of Aluminium	**Atom of Silicon**	**Atom of Phosphorus**	**Atom of Sulphur**
p = 13, n = 14	p = 14, n = 14	p = 15, n = 16	p = 16, n = 16
$_{13}^{27}Al$; E.C - 2, 8, 3	$_{14}^{28}Si$; E.C - 2, 8, 4	$_{15}^{31}P$; E.C - 2, 8, 5	$_{16}^{32}S$; E.C - 2, 8, 6
Atom of Chlorine	**Atom of Argon**	**Atom of Potassium**	**Atom of Calcium**
p = 17, n = 18	p = 18, n = 22	p = 19, n = 20	p = 20, n = 20
$_{17}^{35}Cl$; E.C - 2, 8, 7	$_{18}^{40}Ar$; E.C - 2, 8, 8	$_{19}^{39}K$; E.C - 2, 8, 8, 1	$_{20}^{40}Ca$; E.C - 2, 8, 8, 2

PAPER-PEN TEST: 5

1. Give a schematic representation of distribution of electrons in an atom.
2. How are energy levels represented?
3. Define electronic configuration.
4. Explain Bohr-Bury scheme.
5. What are the conditions for arranging the electrons in different shells?
6. What are the factors that govern the distribution of electrons in Bohr Bury scheme?
7. How will you find out the maximum number of electrons that can be accommodated in each shell of the atom?
8. Give the maximum number of electrons that can be accommodated in all the energy levels.
9. Justify : "The outermost shell of an atom cannot have more than eight electrons, even if it has the capacity to accommodate more number of electrons".
10. How do you represent the following atom?
    (a) Silicon
    (b) Fluorine
    (c) Potassium
11. Give the electronic configuration of the following elements.
    (a) Nitrogen
    (b) Calcium
    (c) Magnesium

4.11 FORMATION OF IONS

We know that the atoms combine with other atoms to achieve the inert gas configuration or to become stable. This is achieved by the atom in three ways:

(a) By sharing one or more electrons with another atom.
(b) By gaining one or more electrons from another atom.
(c) By losing one or more electrons to another atom.

The elements having 1, 2, or 3 electrons in its outermost shell lose electrons to form positively charged ion called cation in order to achieve a stable electronic configuration (Fig. 4.24).

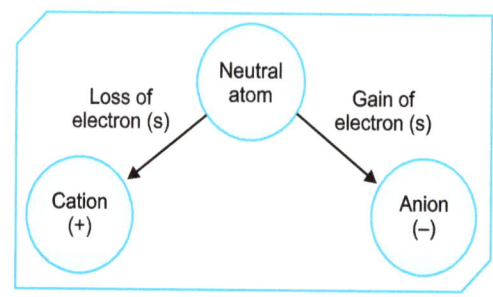

Fig. 4.24 : This figure shows the ways by which a neutral atom can form a positive ion (cation) or a negative ion (anion).

The elements having 5, 6 or 7 electrons in its outermost shell gain electrons to form negatively charged ions called anions in order to achieve a stable electronic configuration (Fig. 4.24).

The element having 4 electrons in its outermost shell neither loses nor gains electrons, and hence share the electrons in order to achieve a stable electronic configuration.

Based on the electronic configuration, let us try to solve few problems.

Solved Sample Problems

Sample Problem 1 : Give the electronic configuration of an element X whose atomic number is 15.

Solution : Atomic number of the element X is 15.

We know that atomic number is equal to the number of electrons. Thus, first shell occupies 2 electrons, second shell occupies 8 electrons, third shell occupies 5 electrons. Hence, the electronic configuration of the element X is 2, 8, 5.

Sample Problem 2 : Give the electronic configuration of a positively charged magnesium (Mg^{2+}) ion. What would be its atomic number?

Solution : The atomic number of magnesium is 12. So, a neutral atom of magnesium has 12 electrons. A positively charged magnesium ion is formed by the removal of two electrons from the magnesium atom. So the number of electrons in the magnesium ions will be 12 – 2 = 10 electrons. Thus, the electronic configuration of magnesium ion is 2, 8.

Since the atomic number of an element is equal to the number of protons in its atom, magnesium atom as well as magnesium ion contain the same number of protons, and hence possess the same atomic number-12.

STRUCTURE OF ATOM

Sample Problem 3 : If an element has 2 electrons in M shell, then what is its atomic number?

Solution : Since there are 2 electrons in M shell, the K shell and L shell must be completely filled with electrons. The maximum number of electrons K shell can hold is 2 that of L shell is 8 and we know that M shell has 2 electrons. So, the total number of electrons are 2 + 8 + 2 = 12. Now, we know that the total number of electrons in a neutral atom is equal to the number of protons, so the atomic number of this element is 12.

Try Yourself

1. If an element has 2 electrons in L shell, then what is its atomic number ?
2. Give the electronic configuration of a positively charged Al^{3+}? What would be its atomic number ?
3. Give the electronic configuration of an element X whose atomic number is 19.

4.12 VALENCE ELECTRONS AND VALENCY

We have already studied that the negatively charged electrons revolve only in those orbits which have fixed value of energy. Hence, these orbits are called *energy levels* or *stationary states*. The outermost electron shell of an atom is called *valence shell* or *valence orbit*, and the electrons present in the outermost shell of an atom are called *valence electrons*. It is important to note that only the valence electrons of an atom take part in chemical reactions. Generally, in a chemical reaction, the valence electrons of an atom are either transferred to the valence shell of another atom or shared with valence electrons of another atom. Let us illustrate the valence electrons with a few examples.

Example 1 : Consider Magnesium (Mg) having atomic number 12, its electronic configuration is 2, 8, 2. So the number of valence electrons in Magnesium is 2.

Example 2 : Consider Sulphur (S) having atomic number 16, its electronic configuration is 2, 8, 6. So the number of valence electrons in Sulphur is 6.

Example 3 : Consider Phosphorus (P) having atomic number 15, its electronic configuration is 2, 8, 5. So, the number of valence electrons in Phosphorus is 5.

Since every atom prefers to be stable, its valence shell should have eight electrons (except the first shell, which can accommodate only two electrons). This stability is achieved by donating, accepting or sharing some or all valence electrons. So, the number of electrons that an atom needs to accept, donate or share so as to achieve stable octet electronic configuration (8 electrons) (except the first shell that forms a duplet) is called *valency*. In other words, we can define valency as,

"The combining capacity of the atom of an element with the atoms of other elements in order to acquire eight electrons (or two electrons in Helium) in its outermost shell."

Relationship between Valency and Valence Electrons

The valency of an element is determined by the number of valence electrons present in the atom of the element. We can calculate the valency of an element by knowing the number of valence electrons because only valence electrons take part in chemical bonding to achieve stable electronic configuration. If we know the number of valence electrons, we can find out how many electrons are lost or gained or shared by an atom of the element to achieve the nearest noble gas electronic configuration. Thus, valency of an element is either equal to the number of valence electrons in its atom or equal to the number of electrons lost or gained by an atom to complete eight electrons in the valence shell.

Valency of a Metal and a Non-metal and Valence Electrons

The valency of an atom is determined by the number of electrons present in the valence shell of that atom. For example, in case of a metal such as sodium and magnesium, the valence electrons are 1 and 2 respectively and so,

The valency of sodium = 1 (No. of valence electrons)

The valency of magnesium = 2 (No. of valence electrons)

Thus, the valency of metal is equal to the number of valence electrons in its atom. We can formulate it as :

The valency of a metal = No. of valence electrons

In case of a non-metal such as sulphur and chlorine, the valence electrons are 6 and 7 respectively but their valencies are not 6 and 7 respectively. Sulphur atom requires 2 electrons to acquire the stable octet electronic configuration whereas chlorine atom requires 1 electron to complete 8 electrons in the valence shell. So,

The valency for sulphur = 8 – 6 = 2

The valency of chlorine = 8 – 7 = 1

Thus, the valency of non-metal is equal to eight minus the number of valence electrons in its atom. We can formulate it as :

> The valency of a non-metal = 8 – No. of valence electrons in its atom

Let us now discuss the valency of certain metals and non-metals.

The metals such as Lithium (Li), Sodium (Na) and Potassium (K) possess 1 valence electron each in their atoms and so their valency is 1. Hence, these elements are called *monovalent*. The arrangement of electrons in the atom of these metals elements can be represented as :

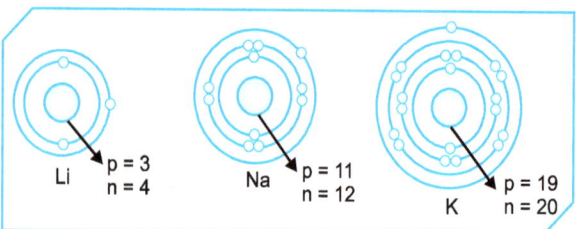

The metal such as Beryllium (Be), Magnesium (Mg) and Calcium (Ca) possess 2 valence electrons each in their atoms and so their valency is 2. Hence, these elements are called *divalent*. The arrangement of electrons in the atom of these metals can be represented as :

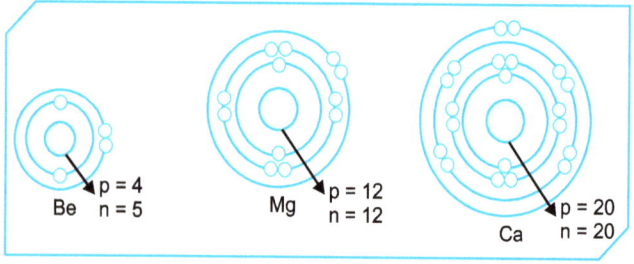

The metals such as Boron (B) and Aluminium (Al) possess 3 valence electrons each in their atoms and so their valency is 3. Hence, these elements are called *trivalent*. The arrangement of electrons in the atom of these metals can be represented as :

The non-metals such as Carbon (C) and Silicon (Si) possess 4 valence electrons each in their atoms and so their valency is 4. Hence, these elements are called *tetravalent*. The arrangement of electrons in the atom of these non-metals can be represented as :

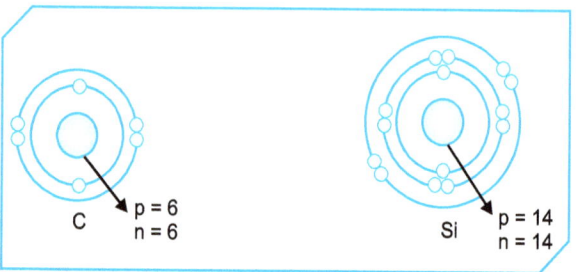

The non-metals such as Nitrogen (N) and Phosphorus (P) possess 5 valence electrons each in their atoms and so their valency is 3. Hence, these elements are called *trivalent*. The arrangement of electrons in the atoms of these non-metals can be represented as :

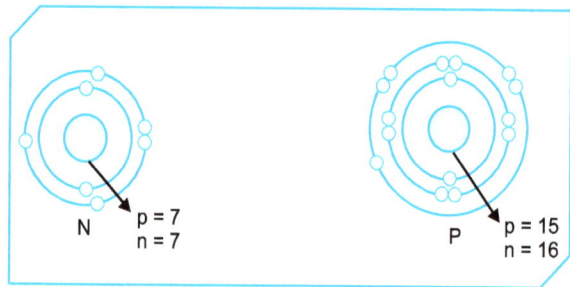

The non-metals such as Oxygen (O) and Sulphur (S) possess 6 valence electrons each in their atoms and so their valency is 2. Hence, these elements are called *divalent*. The arrangement of electrons in the atom of these non-metals can be represented as :

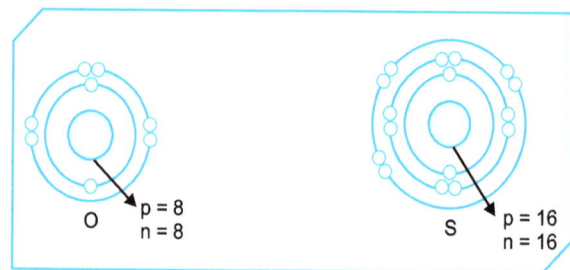

The non-metals such as Fluorine (F), Chlorine (Cl), Bromine (Br) and Iodine (I) possess 7 valence electrons each in their atoms and so their valency is 1. Hence, these elements are called *monovalent*. The arrangement of electrons in the atoms of these non-metals can be represented as :

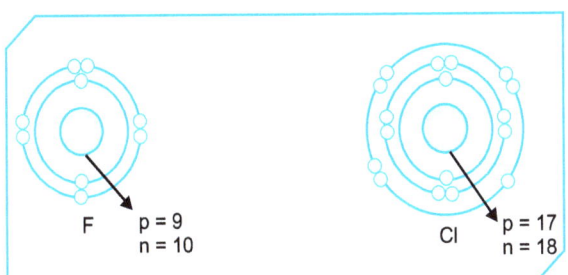

The non-metals such as Helium (He), Neon (Ne) and Argon (Ar) possess 8 valence electrons each in their atoms except Helium which possess 2 valence electrons. Thus, their valency is zero. Hence, these elements are called *zerovalent*. The arrangement of electrons in the atom of these non-metal elements can be represented as :

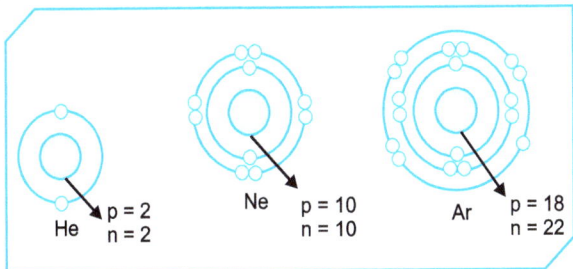

Thus, we can conclude that to find out the valence electrons in an atom, we should write the electronic configuration of the element by using its atomic number. The outermost shell will be the valence shell and the number of electrons in it will be the number of valence electrons.

PAPER-PEN TEST : 6

1. What are the different ways for an atom to attain stability?
2. Differentiate between cation and anion.
3. What is meant by valence shell?
4. Define valence electrons.
5. Illustrate valence electrons with a few examples.
6. Define valency.
7. What is the relationship between valency and valence electrons?
8. How is the valency of an atom determined?
9. Determine the valency of metal and valence electrons with examples.
10. Determine the valency of non-metal and valence electrons with examples.
11. Define the following terms with examples:
    (a) Monovalent
    (b) Divalent
    (c) Trivalent
    (d) Tetravalent
    (e) Zerovalent
12. What is meant by octet and duplet? Give examples.

Types of Valency

The valency is of two types namely,

(a) Electrovalency

(b) Covalency

When an element combines with another element by losing or gaining electrons, then its valency is called *electrovalency*. The compound so formed is called electrovalent or ionic compound. On the other hand, when an element combines with another element by sharing electrons to form a compound, then its valency is called *covalency*. The compound so formed is called covalent compound.

Let us discuss these two types with examples.

Electrovalency

We have discussed earlier that the element either loses or gains electrons in order to achieve the nearest noble gas configuration to become stable. The elements which lose electrons form positive ions and hence have positive electrovalency. The elements which gain electrons form negative ions and hence have negative electrovalency. Thus, electrovalency can be defined as:

When an element combines with another element by the loss or gain of electrons to form a compound, then its valency is called electrovalency.

Let us discuss with a few examples.

Valency of Sodium : We know that the atomic number of sodium is 11, so its electronic configuration is 2, 8, 1. This shows that, it has 1 electron in its valence shell which it can lose to form sodium ion (Na^+) in order to achieve the nearest inert gas (neon) configuration 2, 8. Since the sodium atom loses 1 electron to achieve a stable noble gas configuration, the electrovalency of sodium is +1 (Fig. 4.25).

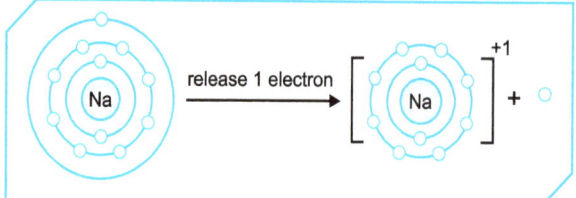

Fig. 4.25 : This figure shows how a neutral sodium (Na) atom releases one electron to achieve stable noble gas configuration.

Valency of Magnesium : We know that the atomic number of magnesium is 12, so its electronic configuration is 2, 8, 2. This shows that, it has 2 electrons in its valence shell which it can lose to form magnesium ion (Mg^{2+}) in order to achieve the nearest inert gas (neon) configuration 2, 8. Since the magnesium atom loses 2 electrons to achieve a stable noble gas configuration, the electrovalency of magnesium is +2 (Fig. 4.26).

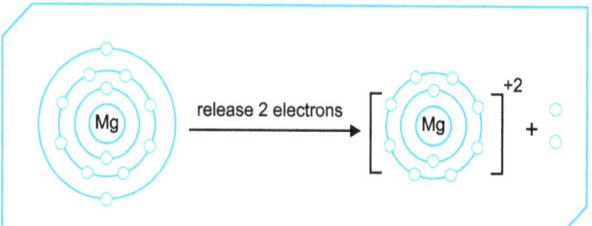

Fig. 4.26 : This figure shows how a neutral magnesium (Mg) atom releases two electrons to achieve stable noble gas configuration.

Valency of Oxygen : We know that the atomic number of oxygen is 8, so its electronic configuration is 2, 6. This shows that, it has 6 electrons in its valence shell and needs two more electrons to form oxide ion (O^{2-}) in order to achieve the nearest inert gas (neon) configuration 2, 8. Since the oxygen atom gains 2 electrons to achieve a stable noble gas configuration, the electrovalency of oxygen is –2 (Fig. 4.27).

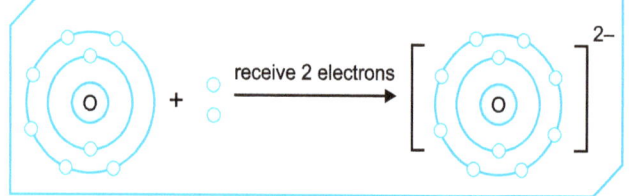

Fig. 4.27 : This figure shows how a neutral oxygen (O) atom acquires two electrons to achieve a stable noble gas configuration.

Covalency

Covalency of an element may be defined as,

"The number of electrons which an atom of the element shares with other atoms during the formation of covalent molecule in order to achieve the nearest inert gas configuration."

Let us discuss covalency with a few examples.

Covalency of Hydrogen : The atomic number of hydrogen is 1, so its electronic configuration is 1. In the formation of hydrogen molecule H_2, two hydrogen atoms share one electron each to achieve the nearest noble gas (Helium) configuration. Since one atom of hydrogen shares one electron to achieve the stable noble gas configuration, the covalency of hydrogen is 1 (Fig. 4.28).

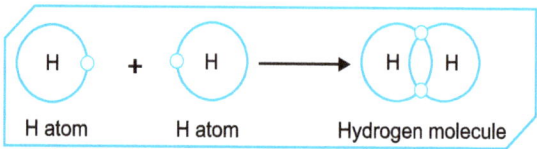

Fig. 4.28 : This figure shows how two atoms of hydrogen share one electron each to achieve a stable noble gas configuration.

Covalency of Chlorine : The atomic number of chlorine is 17, so its electronic configuration is 2, 8, 7. In the formation of chlorine molecule Cl_2, two chlorine atoms share one electron to achieve the nearest noble gas (Argon) configuration. Since one atom of chlorine shares one electron to achieve the stable noble gas configuration, the covalency of chlorine is 1 (Fig. 4.29).

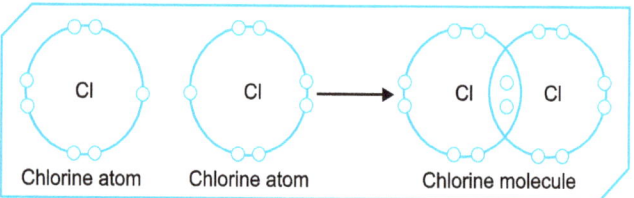

Fig. 4.29 : This figure shows how two atoms of chlorine (Cl) share one electron each to achieve stable noble gas configuration.

Covalency of Oxygen : The atomic number of oxygen is 8, so its electronic configuration is 2, 6. In the formation of oxygen molecule O_2, two oxygen atoms share two electrons each to achieve the nearest noble gas (Neon) configuration. Since one atom of oxygen shares two electrons to achieve the stable noble gas configuration, the covalency of oxygen is 2 (Fig. 4.30).

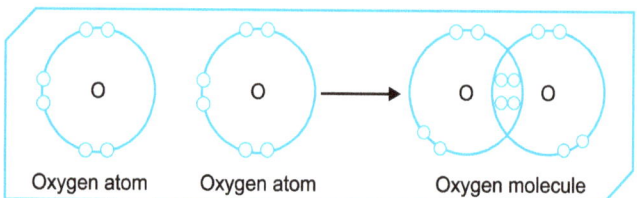

Fig. 4.30 : This figure shows how two atoms of oxygen (O) share two electrons each to achieve a stable noble gas configuration.

Covalency of Carbon : We know that the atomic number of carbon is 6, so its electronic configuration is 2, 4. This shows that it requires four more electrons to attain a stable electronic configuration. Carbon gets these four electrons by mutual sharing. Therefore, carbon atom forms four covalent bonds by sharing its four electrons with the four electrons of other atoms in order to achieve the stable electronic configuration. In other words, carbon is tetravalent (Fig. 4.31). These four valencies are usually represented by drawing four single lines and writing the symbol of carbon at the centre as shown in the figure :

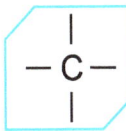

Fig. 4.31 : This figure shows that an atom of carbon (C) is tetravalent.

4.13 INERTNESS OF NOBLE GASES

Earth's atmosphere contains trace amounts of argon, neon, helium and even smaller quantities of krypton, radon and xenon. All these elements such as Helium (He), Neon (Ne), Argon (Ar), Krypton (Kr), Xenon (Xe) and Radon (Rn) are gases at ordinary temperature. They are known as *inert gases* or *noble gases* because of their reluctance to combine or react with other elements to form compounds. These elements are also often called as *'rare elements'* as they occur in nature in trace amounts and are hard to obtain.

The noble gases are generally different from all other elements because all the noble gases have completely filled outermost shells. These completed outer shells of the noble gases make them chemically unreactive.

We shall now discuss the electronic configuration of noble gases.

Electronic Configuration of Noble Gases

As we have studied that the noble gases are chemically unreactive, we can say that the electronic arrangement in their atoms is very stable. The electronic configurations of the noble gases are given in the table below :

Noble gases (Inert gases)	Symbol	Atomic number	Electronic configuration	No. of electrons in the valence shell	Representation of the atom
Helium	He	2	2	2	He
Neon	Ne	10	2, 8	8	Ne
Argon	Ar	18	2, 8, 8	8	Ar
Krypton	Kr	36	2, 8, 18, 8	8	Kr

Xenon	Xe	54	2, 8, 18, 18, 8	8	
Radon	Rn	86	2, 8, 18, 32, 18, 8	8	

The above tabular column shows that the outermost shell of the inert gases are completely filled with electrons. Due to this, the atoms of inert gases having 8 electrons in their valence shell are called as 'octet' of electrons. In other words, we can say that inert gases have octet of electrons in their valence shell and hence are chemically unreactive.

Let us now discuss the reason for the inertness of noble gases in detail.

The noble gases are devoid of all chemical reactions due to the following reasons :

(a) According to electronic theory of valency, except Helium (it accommodates 2 electrons in its outermost shell i.e., K shell) all other inert gases have 8 electrons in their outermost shell. Hence, these atoms do not tend to either gain or lose electrons and does not involve in chemical reactions.

(b) All these elements consist of electrons which are paired. So, it is not possible to either add or remove electrons from the outermost shell of a noble gas atom. Hence, these gases are unreactive as there are no valence shell electrons available for bonding.

Let us now try to solve the problems based on valence electrons and valency.

Solved Sample Problems

Sample Problem 1 : Find out the number of valence electrons in an atom of an element E having atomic number 13. Name the valence shell of this atom.

Solution : First we need to write down the electronic configuration to find out the number of valence electrons. Since, the atomic number of the element is 13, so it contains 13 electrons. The electronic configuration will be 2, 8, 3. Here, the M shell is the outermost shell or valence shell of the atom containing 3 valence electrons.

Sample Problem 2 : An atom of element E has 9 protons, 9 electrons and 10 neutrons. Predict the element name, electronic configuration and valency.

Solution : We know that the atomic number of the element is equal to number of protons. Therefore, the atomic number is 9. The element E is Fluorine. Since, it has 9 electrons, the electronic configuration of F is 2, 7. It needs one more electron to acquire the stable noble gas configuration. Thus, the valency of fluorine is 1.

The valency of flourine = 8 – 7 = 1

Try Yourself

1. If an ion E^{2+} contains 12 neutrons and 10 electrons, then what is the atomic number and mass number of the element? Identify the element.

2. Find out the number of electrons, protons and neutrons present in sodium and chloride ions.

3. The element potassium has atomic number 19 and mass number is 39. Give the number of electrons, protons and neutrons in it. Give the electronic configuration in different energy shells. Mention its valency.

STRUCTURE OF ATOM

4. The element sulphur has atomic number 16 and mass number 32. Calculate the number of electrons, protons and neutrons in the ion formed. Represent the ion. What will be its valency?

5. The atom of an element has 20 protons, 20 neutrons and 20 electrons. Find out
   (a) Its atomic number
   (b) Mass number
   (c) Name of the element
   (d) Its electronic configuration mentioning the shell
   (e) Its valency

PAPER-PEN TEST : 7

1. What are the different types of valency?
2. Define electrovalency.
3. Name a few elements that exhibit electrovalency.
4. Find out the valency and electrovalency shown by the : (a) Sodium atom (b) Magnesium atom (c) Oxygen atom.
5. Define covalency.
6. Name a few elements that exhibit covalency.
7. Find out the valency and covalency shown by the : (a) Hydrogen atom (b) Chlorine atom (c) Carbon atom.
8. Name the noble gases found in traces in the atmosphere.
9. Give any three characteristics of noble gases.
10. Discuss the electronic configuration of noble gases.
11. Why noble gases are called inert gases?
12. Noble gases are devoid of chemical reactions. Why?
13. Why noble gas elements are called rare elements?

4.14 ISOTOPES

We have studied that all atoms of a particular element have the same number of neutrons in their nuclei. However, some elements can have different number of neutrons. Such atoms of an element are called isotopes. Thus, isotopes can be defined as,

"The atoms of the same element having the same atomic number but different mass numbers"

Let us illustrate this with a few examples.

Isotopes of Hydrogen

The hydrogen atom has one proton and one electron. But hydrogen atoms can have 0, 1 or 2 neutrons. In other words, all the hydrogen atoms have the same atomic number 1, but can have mass number 1, 2, or 3. There are three isotopes of hydrogen namely,

(a) Protium

(b) Deuterium

(c) Tritium

Protium is the ordinary hydrogen with mass number 1. It is represented as $_1^1H$. Deuterium is the heavy hydrogen with mass number 2. It is represented as $_1^2H$. Tritium is the heaviest hydrogen isotope with mass number 3. It is represented as $_1^3H$. The diagrammatic representations of the three isotopes of hydrogen are given below (Fig. 4.32) :

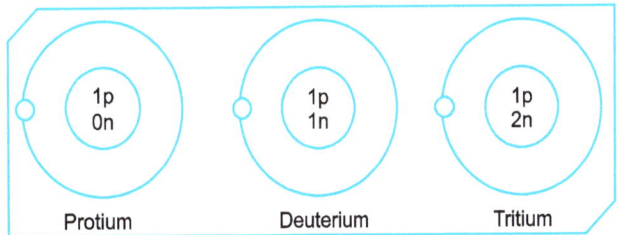

Fig. 4.32 : This figure shows the three isotopes of hydrogen.

Let us now try to write the number of protons, electrons and neutrons present in the isotopes of hydrogen.

Isotope	Symbol	Electrons	Protons	Neutrons
Protium	$_1^1H$	1	1	0
Deuterium	$_1^2H$	1	1	1
Tritium	$_1^3H$	1	1	2

The above table shows that the hydrogen element has three isotopes i.e., protium, deuterium and tritium. All the three isotopes contain 1 proton and 1 electron each but they contain 0, 1 and 2 neutrons respectively. Thus, we can conclude that hydrogen element has three isotopes having the same atomic number of 1 with different mass numbers of 1, 2, and 3 respectively.

Isotopes of Chlorine

There are two isotopes of chlorine namely,

(a) Cl - 35

(b) Cl - 37

These two isotopes of chlorine contain 17 protons and 17 electrons each. But they contain different number of neutrons i.e., 18 and 20 neutrons respectively. In other words, both the isotopes of chlorine have the same atomic number of 17 but have different mass number of 18 and 20 respectively.

The Cl-35 isotope is represented as $^{35}_{17}Cl$ and Cl-37 isotope is represented as $^{37}_{17}Cl$. The diagrammatic representations of the two isotopes of chlorine are given below (Fig. 4.33) :

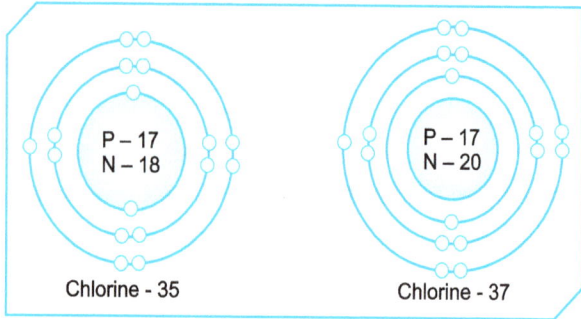

Fig. 4.33 : This figure shows the two isotopes of chlorine.

Let us now try to write the number of protons, electrons and neutrons present in the isotopes of chlorine.

Isotope	Symbol	Electrons	Protons	Neutrons
Cl - 35	$^{35}_{17}Cl$	17	17	18
Cl - 37	$^{37}_{17}Cl$	17	17	20

The table above shows that the chlorine element has two isotopes *i.e.*, Cl - 35 , Cl - 37 . Both the isotopes contain 17 protons and 17 electrons each but they contain 18 and 20 neutrons respectively. Thus, we can conclude that chlorine atom has two isotopes having the same atomic number of 17 with different mass numbers of 35 and 37 respectively.

Isotopes of Carbon

There are three isotopes of carbon namely,

(a) C - 12

(b) C - 13

(c) C - 14

These three isotopes of carbon contain six protons and six electrons each. But they contain an unequal number of neutrons i.e., 6, 7 and 8 neutrons respectively. In other words, all the three isotopes of carbon have the same atomic number of 6 but have different mass number of 12, 13 and 14 respectively.

The C - 12 isotope is represented as $^{12}_{6}C$. The C - 13 isotope is represented as $^{13}_{6}C$ and the C - 14 isotope is represented as $^{14}_{6}C$. The diagrammatic representations of the three isotopes of carbon are given below (Fig. 4.34) :

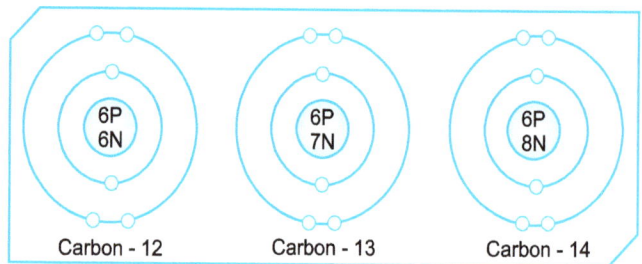

Fig. 4.34 : This figure shows the three isotopes of carbon.

Let us now try to write the number of protons, electrons and neutrons present in the isotopes of carbon.

Isotope	Symbol	Electrons	Protons	Neutrons
C - 12	$^{12}_{6}C$	6	6	6
C - 13	$^{13}_{6}C$	6	6	7
C - 14	$^{14}_{6}C$	6	6	8

The table above shows that the carbon element has three isotopes i.e., C - 12, C - 13 and C - 14. All the three isotopes contain 6 protons and 6 electrons each but they contain 6, 7 and 8 neutrons respectively. Thus, we can conclude that carbon element has three isotopes having the same atomic number of 6 with different mass numbers of 12, 13, and 14 respectively.

Since the chemical properties of the atom of an element depend on the number of protons and electrons, isotopes are chemically alike. In other words, the chemical properties of all the isotopes of an element are identical because they all contain the same number of protons and electrons. This is because all the isotopes of an element have identical electronic configuration. However, the physical properties of an element are different due to difference in their mass. This is because, the physical properties of an element depend on the mass of the atom. The mass of an atom depends on the number of neutrons. Now, since the isotopes of an element have different number of neutrons, the masses of all the isotopes of an element are slightly different and hence the physical properties of the isotopes of an element are different.

Note

- The mass number of an atom is equal to its atomic mass and so the term 'atomic mass' can be used in place of 'mass number'.

Thus, we can conclude the characteristics of isotopes as,

(a) All the isotopes of an element have same atomic number but different mass numbers.

(b) All isotopes of an element have the same number of valence electrons.

(c) All isotopes of an element have identical chemical properties.

(d) The physical properties of the isotopes are different due to the difference in the number of neutrons in their nuclei.

4.15 FRACTIONAL ATOMIC MASSES OF ELEMENTS

The atomic masses of some of the elements such as copper, chlorine etc., are in fractions instead of whole numbers. This does not mean that the mass of each atom is expressed in fractions. The existence of isotopes having different mass number is the reason for the fractional atomic mass. The isotopes of an element have different atomic mass and the percentage of these isotopes vary in nature. The atomic mass of an element is the average relative mass of all the natural isotopes of that element and hence most of the elements have fractional masses. Let us now illustrate an example in order to understand the reason for the fractional atomic masses of elements.

We know that the atomic mass of chlorine is 35.5 u. There are two isotopes of chlorine Cl– 35 and Cl – 37. The mass of chlorine Cl-35 isotopes is 35u and its abundance in nature is 75%, while the mass of chlorine Cl-37 isotope is 37u and its abundance in nature is 25%.

$$\text{Average atomic mass} = \frac{(35 \times 75) + (37 \times 25)}{100} = 35.5 \text{ u}$$

Thus, the average atomic mass of chlorine is 35.5 u.

Since, all the naturally occurring isotopes of an element are present in a fixed proportion, the average atomic mass of an element is also fixed.

Thus, to solve the problem based on isotopes, we can conclude that,

$$\text{Average atomic mass} = \frac{\text{At.mass of isotope 1} \times \% \text{ of occurence} + \text{At. mass of isotope 2} \times \% \text{ of occurence}}{100}$$

Let us now solve some problems based on isotopes.

Solved Sample Problems

Sample Problem 1 : If 80.0% of an element has an atomic mass of 42.0 u and 20.0% has an atomic mass of 43.0 u, what is the average atomic mass of the mixture?

Solution : Given :

80.0% of an element has an atomic mass 42.0 u

20.0% of an element has an atomic mass 43.0 u

So,

$$\text{Average atomic mass} = \frac{\text{At.mass of isotope 1} \times \% \text{ of occurence} + \text{At. mass of isotope 2} \times \% \text{ of occurence}}{100}$$

$$\text{Average atomic mass} = \frac{42 \times 80 + 43 \times 20}{100} = 42.2 \text{ u}$$

Hence, the average atomic mass of the mixture is 42.2 u

Sample Problem 2 : Copper is made up of two isotopes, Cu-63 (62.9296 u) and Cu-65 (64.9278 u). What is the percent abundance of each isotope?

[Given : copper's atomic weight is 63.546]

Solution : Given :

Atomic mass of Cu-63 isotope = 62.9296 u

Atomic mass of Cu-65 isotope = 64.9278 u

Let x represent the abundance of the Cu-63 isotope and (1 - x) represent the abundance of Cu-65 isotope, so,

x% of Cu-63 has an atomic mass = 62.9296 u

(1 - x) % of Cu-65 has an atomic mass = 64.9278 u

Now,

$$\text{Average atomic mass} = \frac{\text{At.mass of isotope 1} \times \% \text{ of occurence} + \text{At. mass of isotope 2} \times \% \text{ of occurence}}{100}$$

(62.9296) (x) + (64.9278) (1 - x) = 63.546

Therefore, x = 0.6915

And, (1 - x) = 0.3085

Hence, the % abundance of Cu-63 isotope is 69.15% and Cu-65 is 30.85 %.

Try Yourself

1. Chlorine is made up of two isotopes, Cl-35 (34.969 u) and Cl-37 (36.966 u). Given chlorine's atomic weight is 35.453 u, what is the percent abundance of each isotope?
2. A sample of naturally occurring silicon consists Si-28 (27.9769 u), Si-29 (28.9765 u) and Si-30 (29.9738 u). If the atomic mass of silicon is 28.0855 and the natural abundance of Si-29 is 4.67%, what are the natural abundances of Si-28 and Si-30?
3. If the relative atomic mass of boron is 10.8, then calculate the percentage of its isotopes $^{10}_{5}B$ and $^{11}_{5}B$ occurring in nature.
4. If 7.4% of an element has an atomic mass 6.015 u and 92.6% of an element has an atomic mass of 7.016 u, then what is the average mass of the element ?
5. The element X has three isotopes with mass numbers 28, 29, 30. The relative atomic mass of element X is 28.09. Which isotope is considered to be most abundant?

3. Differentiate between the properties of isotopes of hydrogen.
4. Draw the structure of isotopes of hydrogen.
5. Explain the isotopes of chlorine.
6. Differentiate between the properties of isotopes of chlorine.
7. Draw the structure of isotopes of chlorine.
8. Differentiate between the properties of isotopes of carbon.
9. Draw the structure of isotopes of carbon.
10. Why are the chemical properties of all the isotopes of an element identical?
11. Why are the physical properties of all the isotopes of an element different?
12. What are the characteristics of isotopes?
13. How will you find out the average atomic mass of the isotopes of an element.
14. Is the average atomic mass of an element fixed ? Why?
15. Calculate the average atomic mass for the isotopes of chlorine.

PAPER-PEN TEST : 8

1. Define isotopes.
2. Name the isotopes of hydrogen?

4.16 RADIO ACTIVE ISOTOPES

The isotopes whose nuclei are unstable (due to the presence of extra neutrons in their nuclei) and dissipate excess energy by spontaneously emitting radiations in the form of alpha, beta and gamma rays are called *radioactive isotopes*. Every chemical element has one or more radioactive isotopes. More than 1,000 radioactive isotopes of the various elements are known. Approximately 50 of these are found in nature; the rest are produced artificially as the direct products of nuclear reactions. The common examples of radioactive isotopes include, Carbon–14, Arsenic–74, Sodium–24, Iodine–131, Cobalt–60, Uranium–235, Plutonium–238 etc. These radioactive isotopes need to be handled very carefully as the high energy radiations emitted by these radioactive isotopes are harmful to human beings and most living beings.

The past one hundred years has brought the incredible field of nuclear chemistry into our lives. We derive numerous benefits from its applications. Let us discuss the applications of various radioactive isotopes in detail.

Applications of Radioactive Isotopes

Radioactive isotopes are effective tracers because their radioactivity is easy to detect. They are useful for establishing the ages of various objects, in the field of medicine to diagnose and treat various ailments, power plants and in various industries.

(a) Radioactive Isotopes in Nuclear Power Plants : Uranium-235 isotope is used as a fuel in nuclear reactors of nuclear power plants for generating electricity. When the heavy nuclei of U- 235 atoms are bombarded with slow moving neutrons, it breaks up into smaller nuclei with the release of tremendous amount of heat energy. This heat energy is used to boil the water in boilers to form steam. The steam turns the turbines to run the generators to produce electricity (Fig. 4.35).

Fig. 4.35 (a) : Radioactive Uranium -235 isotope

(b) Radioactive Uranium-235 isotope which is used as nuclear fuel in nuclear power plants to generate electricity.

(b) Radioactive Isotopes in Medicine :

(i) Iodine-131 has proved effective in locating brain tumors, measuring cardiac output and determining liver and thyroid activity. It acts as a tracer to find out the functioning rate of thyroid gland in our body in the case of goiter (Fig. 4.36).

(ii) Carbon – 14 is useful in studying abnormalities of metabolism that underlie diabetes, gout, anemia and acromegaly.

(iii) Cobalt – 60 is extensively employed as a radiation source to arrest the development of cancer. The treatment of cancer by using radioactive radiations is called *radiotherapy* (Fig. 4.37). In this treatment, high energy gamma radiations from radioactive cobalt-60 isotope are directed on the cancerous cells to burn them.

(iv) Arsenic – 74 tracer is used to detect the presence of tumors.

(v) Sodium – 24 tracer is used to detect the presence of blood clots.

These tracers or low activity radioactive compounds are either given orally or injected into the body of the patient. This radioactive compound accumulates in the area of blood clot or tumor in patient's body which gives the exact position of the tumor or blood clot with the help of a device called *Geiger counter*.

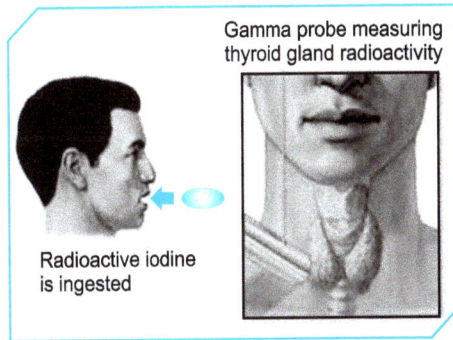

Fig. 4.36 : Radioactive Iodine-131 isotope is used in the treatment of goiter in human body.

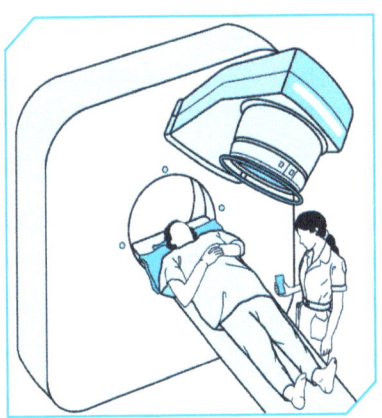

Fig. 4.37 : This figure shows the procedure of radiotherapy.

(c) Radioactive Isotopes in Industries : The leaks in underground water pipes can be identified by a radioactive isotope of hydrogen, tritium. In order to check for the leakage in a metal pipeline, a solution of radioactive substance is introduced. The radioactive solution will leak out from the crack of the metal pipeline, if any. The radioactive detector i.e., Geiger counter indicates the higher level of radiations in the ground around the pipes (Fig. 4.38).

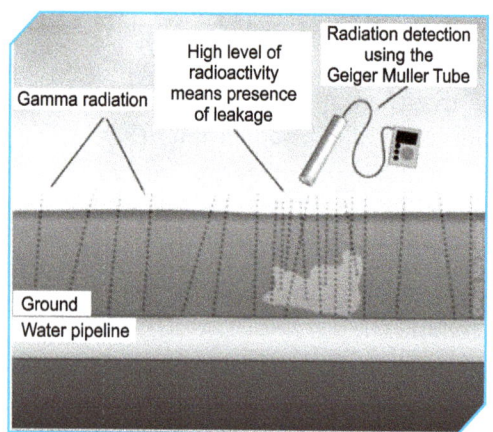

Fig. 4.38 : This figure shows the use of radioactive isotopes for detecting leakage in underground water pipelines.

Radioactive isotopes are used to detect leakage in underground pipes carrying oil or water or gas.

4.17 ISOBARS

We have studied that isotopes are chemically same and physically different. But the isobars are the elements, which are chemically different but physically same. So, we can define isobars as,

"The atoms of different elements having the same mass number (or atomic mass) but different atomic number"

The atoms of isobars possess different number of electrons and hence their chemical properties are different. In other words, isobars have same number of nucleons (protons + neutrons) but different number of protons in their nuclei. Let us discuss isobars with an example.

Note

- When a radioactive isotope is added in small amounts to comparatively large quantities of the stable element, it behaves exactly the same as the ordinary isotope chemically; it can, however, be traced with a Geiger counter or other detection device.

- The process of breaking down of U-235 into smaller nuclei with the release of tremendous amount of heat energy is called nuclear fission.

Calcium and Argon

The elements calcium ($^{40}_{20}Ca$) and argon ($^{40}_{18}Ar$) are isobars. This is because, both possess same mass number of 40. Their complete nuclear composition is shown in the table below :

Isotope	Symbol	Electrons	Protons	Neutrons	Mass Number
Argon	$^{40}_{18}Ar$	18	18	22	18 + 22 = 40
Calcium	$^{40}_{20}Ca$	20	20	20	20 + 20 = 40

Sodium and Magnesium

The radioactive sodium ($^{24}_{11}Na$) and magnesium ($^{24}_{12}Mg$) are isobars. This is because, both possess same mass number of 24. Their complete nuclear composition is shown in the table below :

Isotope	Symbol	Electrons	Protons	Neutrons	Mass Number
Sodium	$^{24}_{11}Na$	11	11	13	11 + 13 = 24
Magnesium	$^{24}_{12}Mg$	12	12	12	12 + 12 = 24

Let us now try to solve the problems based on isobars.

Solved Sample Problems

Sample Problem 1 : Which of the two are isobars?

$^{231}_{90}X$, $^{230}_{91}X$, $^{230}_{90}X$, $^{233}_{91}X$

Solution : We know that, isobars have different atomic numbers but same mass number. The upper

STRUCTURE OF ATOM

figure in the given symbols indicates the mass number. Therefore, $^{230}_{91}X$ and $^{230}_{90}X$ are isobars.

Sample Problem 2 : Give the electronic configuration of a pair of isobars.

Solution : Consider a pair of isobar sodium $^{24}_{11}Na$ and magnesium $^{24}_{12}Mg$. The atomic number of sodium is 11, so its electronic configuration is 2, 8, 1 whereas the atomic number of magnesium is 12, so its electronic configuration is 2, 8, 2.

PAPER-PEN TEST : 9

1. What are radioactive isotopes?
2. Name a few common radioactive isotopes.
3. Comment: The radioactive isotopes need to be handled carefully.
4. How are radioactive isotopes used in nuclear power plants?
5. Match the following :

S. No	Radioactive isotopes	Applications	Correct match
1.	Na - 24	Abnormalities in metabolism	
2.	C - 14	Treatment of cancer	
3.	I - 131	Presence of blood clot	
4.	Co - 60	Presence of tumours	
5.	As - 74	Brain tumours	

6. What is Geiger counter? Mention its significance.
7. What is radiotherapy?
8. How are the underground leakages of water pipes detected?

COMPENDIUM

- Matter is made up of tiny particles called atoms.
- Atom is made of three particles : electron, proton and neutron. These particles are called fundamental particles of an atom or sub-atomic particles.
- Electron is denoted by 'e' and is a negatively charged particle.
- The absolute charge of an electron is equal to 1.6 × 10^{-19} Coulomb of negative charge and is considered equal to 1.
- The relative mass of electron is 1/1840 u.
- Since the mass of an electron is very small, thus it is considered to be equal to 0.
- Electrons revolve around the nucleus of atoms.
- Proton is denoted by 'p' and is a positively charged particle.
- The absolute charge of proton is 1.6×10^{-19} coulomb of positive charge and it is considered to be equal to +1.
- The absolute mass of a proton is equal to 1.6 × 10^{-24} g and is considered to be equal to 1.
- Proton is present in the nucleus of atom.
- Neutron is denoted by 'n' and is a neutral particle.
- The absolute mass of neutron is 1.6 × 10^{-24} g.
- The relative mass of neutron is equal to 1.
- Neutron is present in the nucleus of atom.
- The centre of atom is called nucleus which comprises of neutrons and protons.
- Nucleus of an atom contains the whole mass of an atom.
- In 1897; J. J. Thomson, a British physicist, proposed that atom contains atleast one negatively charged particle. Later, this particle was named as electron. Thomson called those particles as 'corpuscles'.
- Ernest Goldstein in 1886 discovered the presence of new radiation in gas discharge tube even before the identification of electron. He called these rays as canal rays. His experiment led to the discovery of proton.
- In 1932, J. Chadwick discovered another subatomic particle called neutron. Neutron is present in the nucleus of all atoms, except hydrogen $^{1}_{1}H$.

- J. J. Thomson proposed the model of atom similar to a christmas pudding or similar to a water melon. His model of atom is generally called plum and pudding model of atom.
- According to Thomson :
  - An atom consists of positively charged sphere in which electrons are embedded.
  - The quanta of negative and positive charges are equal. The equal number of negative charge and positive charges makes an atom electrically neutral.
- Ernest Rutherford in 1909 bombarded very thin gold foil with alpha particles. He found that:
  - Most of the alpha particles passed without any hindrance.
  - Some of the alpha particles deflected from their original path at a noticeable angle.
  - Only a few of the alpha particles bounced back to their original path.
- The Rutherford's Model of an atom is as follows :
  - Most of the part in an atom is empty.
  - There is a positively charged center in atom, which contains nearly the whole mass of atom. The centre is called nucleus.
  - The size of nucleus is very small compared to an atom.
  - Electrons revolve round the nucleus.
- According to Rutherford's Model, electron revolves around the positively charged nucleus which is not expected to be stable. But a charged particle in an accelerated motion along a circular path would lose energy because of emission of radiations and finally would fall into nucleus. This makes an atom unstable while atoms are quite stable. If atoms were not stable, no matter would exist in nature.
- Rutherford model could not solve the problem of atomic mass of atom as it proposed only the existence of protons in the nucleus. However, the problem of atomic mass was solved after the discovery of neutron.
- Neils Bohr, a Danish physicist, in 1913 proposed model of atom which rectified the problems left by Rutherford's Model. He proposed that :
  - Electrons revolve around the nucleus in a fixed orbit.
  - He called these orbits as 'stationary orbit's.
  - Each stationary orbit is associated with a fixed amount of energy, thus electrons do not radiate energy as long as they keep on revolving around the nucleus in fixed orbit.
- Atomic number is a fundamental property of an atom and is denoted as 'z'.
- Every atom is identified by its unique atomic number.
- Atomic number = Number of protons = Number of electrons
- Mass number of an atom = Number of protons + Number of neutrons
- Mass number is nearly equal to the atomic mass of an atom.
- Since, protons and neutrons reside in the nucleus, thus they are also known as nucleons.
- Rules to write the electronic configuration of an atom:
  - Maximum number of electrons in an orbit is calculated by $2n^2$, where 'n' is number of orbit and may be equal to 1, 2, 3 , ...
  - The maximum number of electrons in K-shell i.e. 1st shell = 2, L-shell = 8, M-shell = 18, N-shell = 32.
  - Electrons occupy the next orbit only after filling the inner orbit completely.
  - The maximum number of electrons in outermost orbit will not be more than 8.
- Valency can be defined as combining capacity of an atom.
- The noble gases have fully filled outermost shell. Due to this, they are stable and they do not react with other elements.
- An element can lose or gain electrons in order to complete its octet. This tendency of losing or gaining electrons imparts valency to an element.
- Elements having same atomic number but different atomic masses are known as isotopes. Carbon-12, Carbon-13, Carbon-14 are three isotopes of carbon atom. Protium, Deuterium, Tritium are three isotopes of hydrogen.
- Uses of Isotopes :

- Carbon 14 (C-14) is used in carbon dating.
- An isotope of uranium (U-235) is used as fuel in nuclear reactor.
- An isotope of cobalt (Co-60) is used in treatment of cancer.
- An isotope of iodine (I-131) is used in treatment of goitre.
- Atoms having same atomic mass and different atomic numbers are known as isobars. Example– Argon and Calcium.

EXERCISES (SOLVED)

NCERT INTEXT QUESTIONS

1. What are canal rays?

Ans: Canal rays are positively charged radiations. These rays consist of positively charged particles known as protons. They were discovered by Goldstein in 1886.

2. If an atom contains one electron and one proton, will it carry any charge or not?

Ans: An electron is a negatively charged particle, whereas a proton is a positively charged particle. The magnitude of their charges is equal. Therefore, an atom containing one electron and one proton will not carry any charge. Thus, it will be a neutral atom.

3. On the basis of Thomson's model of an atom, explain how the atom is neutral as a whole.

Ans: According to Thomson's model of the atom, an atom consists of both negatively and positively charged particles. The negatively charged particles are embedded in the positively charged sphere. These negative and positive charges are equal in magnitude. Thus, by counter balancing each other's effect, they make an atom neutral.

4. On the basis of Rutherford's model of an atom, which sub-atomic particle is present in the nucleus of an atom?

Ans: On the basis of Rutherford's model of an atom, protons (positively-charged particles) are present in the nucleus of an atom.

5. Draw a sketch of Bohr's model of an atom with three shells.

Ans:

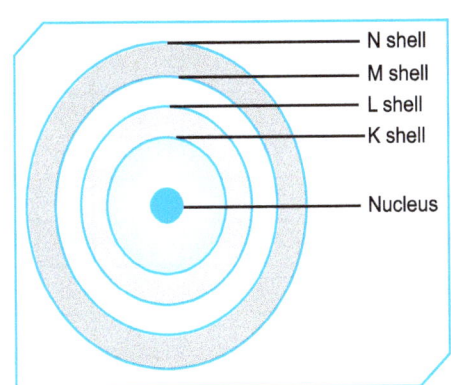

6. What do you think would be the observation if the α-particle scattering experiment is carried out using a foil of a metal other than gold?

Ans: If the α-scattering experiment is carried out using a foil of a metal other than gold, there would be no change in the observation. In the α-scattering experiment, a gold foil was taken because gold is malleable and a thin foil of gold can be easily made. It is difficult to make such foils from other metals.

7. Name the three sub-atomic particles of an atom.

Ans: The three sub-atomic particles of an atom are:

(a) Protons (b) Electrons (c) Neutrons

8. Helium atom has an atomic mass of 4u and two protons in its nucleus. How many neutrons does it have?

Ans: Helium atom has two neutrons. The mass of an atom is the sum of the masses of protons and neutrons present in its nucleus. Since helium atom has two protons, mass contributed by the two protons is (2×1) u = 2 u. Then, the remaining mass $(4 - 2)$ u = 2 u is contributed by

$$\frac{2u}{1u} = 2 \text{ neutrons.}$$

9. Write the distribution of electrons in carbon and sodium atoms?

Ans: The total number of electrons in a carbon atom is 6. The distribution of electrons in carbon atom is given by:

First orbit or K-shell = 2 electrons

Second orbit or L-shell = 4 electrons

Or, we can write the distribution of electrons in a carbon atom as 2, 4.

The total number of electrons in a sodium atom is 11. The distribution of electrons in sodium atom is given by:

First orbit or K-shell = 2 electrons

Second orbit or L-shell = 8 electrons

Third orbit or M-shell = 1 electron

Or, we can write distribution of electrons in a sodium atom as 2, 8, 1.

10. If K and L shells of an atom are full, then what would be the total number of electrons in the atom?

Ans : The maximum number of electrons that can occupy K and L shells of an atom are 2 and 8 respectively. Therefore, if K and L shells of an atom are full, then the total number of electrons in the atom would be (2 + 8) = 10 electrons.

11. How will you find the valency of chlorine, sulphur and magnesium?

Ans : If the number of electrons in the outermost shell of the atom of an element is less than or equal to 4, then the valency of the element is equal to the number of electrons in the outermost shell. On the other hand, if the number of electrons in the outermost shell of the atom of an element is greater than 4, then the valency of that element is determined by subtracting the number of electrons in the outermost shell from 8. The distribution of electrons in chlorine, sulphur, and magnesium atoms are 2, 8, 7; 2, 8, 6 and 2, 8, 2 respectively.

Therefore, the number of electrons in the outer most shell of chlorine, sulphur and magnesium atoms are 7, 6, and 2 respectively.

Thus,

The valency of chlorine = 8 −7 = 1

The valency of sulphur = 8 − 6 = 2

The valency of magnesium = 2

12. If number of electrons in an atom is 8 and number of protons is also 8, then (i) what is the atomic number of the atom and (ii) what is the charge on the atom?

Ans : (a) The atomic number is equal to the number of protons. Therefore, the atomic number of the atom is 8.

(b) Since the number of both electrons and protons is equal, therefore, the charge on the atom is 0.

13. With the help of table given below; find out the mass number of oxygen and sulphur atom.

Composition of Atoms of the First Eighteen Elements with Electron Distribution in various shells

Name of Element	Symbol	Atomic Number	Number of Protons	Number of Neutrons	Number of Electrons	Distribution of Electrons			
Hydrogen	H	1	1	-	1	1	-	-	-
Helium	He	2	2	2	2	2	-	-	-
Lithium	Li	3	3	4	3	2	1	-	-
Beryllium	Be	4	4	5	4	2	2	-	-
Boron	B	5	5	6	5	2	3	-	-
Carbon	C	6	6	6	6	2	4	-	-
Nitrogen	N	7	7	7	7	2	5	-	-
Oxygen	O	8	8	8	8	2	6	-	-
Fluorine	F	9	9	10	9	2	7	-	-
Neon	Ne	10	10	10	10	2	8	-	-
Sodium	Na	11	11	12	11	2	8	1	-
Magnesium	Mg	12	12	12	12	2	8	2	-
Aluminium	Al	13	13	14	13	2	8	3	-
Silicon	Si	14	14	14	14	2	8	4	-
Phosphorus	P	15	15	16	15	2	8	5	-
Sulphur	S	16	16	16	16	2	8	6	-
Chlorine	Cl	17	17	18	17	2	8	7	-
Argon	Ar	18	18	22	18	2	8	8	-

Ans : Mass number of oxygen = Number of protons + Number of neutrons

= 8 + 8

= 16

Mass number of sulphur = Number of protons + Number of neutrons

= 16 + 16

= 32

14. For the symbol H, D and T tabulate three sub-atomic particles found in each of them.

Ans :

Symbol	Proton	Electron	Neutron
Hydrogen, H	1	1	0
Deuterium, D	1	1	1
Tritium, T	1	1	2

15. Write the electronic configuration of any one pair of isotopes and isobars.

Ans : We know that isotopes have the same electronic configuration.

Two isotopes of carbon are $^{12}_{6}C$ and $^{14}_{6}C$

The electronic configuration of $^{12}_{6}C$ is 2, 4.

The electronic configuration of $^{14}_{6}C$ is 2, 4.

$^{40}_{20}Ca$ and $^{40}_{18}Ar$ are a pair of isobars

The electronic configuration of $^{40}_{20}Ca$ is 2, 8, 8, 2.

The electronic configuration of $^{40}_{18}Ar$ is 2, 8, 8.

NCERT EXERCISES QUESTIONS

1. Compare the properties of electrons, protons and neutrons.

Ans :

S. No	Electrons	Protons	Neutrons
1.	Electrons are present outside the nucleus of an atom.	Protons are present in the nucleus of an atom.	Neutrons are present in the nucleus of an atom.
2.	Electrons are negatively charged.	Protons are positively charged.	Neutrons are neutral.
3.	The mass of an electron is considered to be negligible.	The mass of a proton is approximately 2000 times as the mass of an electron.	The mass of neutron is nearly equal to the mass of a proton.

2. What are the limitations of J.J. Thomson's model of an atom?

Ans : According to J.J. Thomson's model of an atom, an atom consists of a positively charged sphere with electrons embedded in it. However, it was later found that the positively charged particles reside at the centre of the atom called the nucleus, and the electrons revolve around the nucleus.

3. What are the limitations of Rutherford's model of the atom?

Ans : According to Rutherford's model of an atom, electrons revolve around the nucleus in fixed orbits. But an electron revolving in circular orbits will not be stable because during revolution, it will experience acceleration. Due to acceleration, the electrons will lose energy in the form of radiations and fall into the nucleus. In such a case, the atom would be highly unstable and collapse.

4. Describe Bohr's model of an atom.

Ans : Niels Bohr proposed the following postulates regarding the model of an atom :

(a) Only certain orbits known as discrete orbits of electrons are allowed inside the atom.

(b) While revolving in these discrete orbits, the electrons do not radiate energy. These discrete orbits or shells are shown in the following diagram :

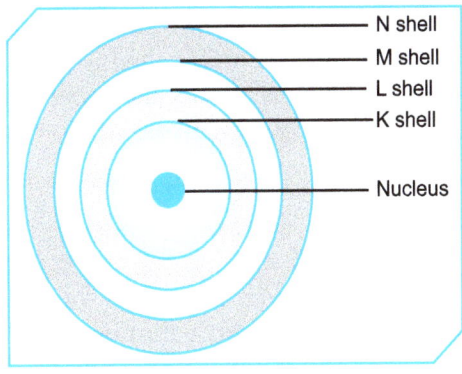

5. Compare all the proposed models of an atom given in this chapter.

Ans : **(a) Thomson's Model :** According to this model, an atom consists of a positively charged sphere with electrons embedded in it.

(b) Rutherford's model : According to this model, an atom consists of positively charged particles concentrated at the centre known as the nucleus. The size of the nucleus is very small as compared to the size of the atom. The electrons revolve around the nucleus in well-defined orbits.

(c) Bohr's model : There are only certain orbits known as discrete orbits inside the atom in which electrons revolve around the nucleus. Electrons do not radiate energy while revolving.

6. Summarize the rules for writing of distribution of electrons in various shells for the first eighteen elements.

Ans : The rules for writing of the distribution of electrons in various shells for the first eighteen elements are given below :

(a) The maximum number of electrons that a shell can accommodate is given by the formula '$2n^2$', where 'n' is the orbit number or energy level index (n = 1, 2, 3...). The maximum number of electrons present in an orbit of n = 1 is given by $2n^2 = 2 \times 1^2 = 2$

Similarly, for second orbit, it is $2n^2 = 2 \times 2^2 = 8$

For third orbit, it is $2n^2 = 2 \times 3^2 = 18$,

and so on…… .

(b) The outermost orbit can accommodate a maximum of 8 electrons.

(c) Shells are filled with electrons in a step-wise manner i.e., the outer shell is not occupied with electrons unless the inner shells are completely filled with electrons.

7. Define valency by taking examples of silicon and oxygen.

Ans : The valency of an element is the combining capacity of that element. The valency of an element is determined by the number of valence electrons present in the atom of that element. If the number of valence electrons of the atom of an element is less than or equal to four, then the valency of that element is equal to the number of valence electrons. For example, the atom of silicon has four valence electrons. Thus, the valency of silicon is four.

On the other hand, if the number of valence electrons of the atom of an element is greater than four, then the valency of that element is obtained by subtracting the number of valence electrons from eight. For example, the atom of oxygen has six valence electrons. Thus, the valency of oxygen is (8 − 6) i.e., two.

8. Explain with examples : (a) Atomic number (b) Mass number (c) Isotopes (d) Isobars. Give any two uses of isotopes.

Ans : **(a) Atomic number :** The atomic number of an element is the total number of protons present in the atom of that element. For example, nitrogen has 7 protons in its atom. Thus, the atomic number of nitrogen is 7.

(b) Mass number : The mass number of an element is the sum of the number of protons and neutrons present in the atom of that element. For example, the atom of boron has 5 protons and 6 neutrons. So, the mass number of boron is 5 + 6 = 11.

(c) Isotopes : Isotopes are atoms of the same element having the same atomic number, but different mass numbers. For example, hydrogen has three isotopes. They are protium $^{1}_{1}H$, deuterium $^{2}_{1}H$ and tritium $^{3}_{1}H$.

(d) Isobars : Isobars are atoms having the same mass number but different atomic numbers i.e., isobars are atoms of different elements having the same mass number. For example, $^{40}_{20}Ca$ and $^{40}_{18}Ar$ are isobars.

Two uses of isotopes are :

(a) Isotope of uranium is used as a fuel in nuclear reactors.

(b) Isotope of cobalt is used in the treatment of cancer.

9. Na^+ has completely filled K and L shells. Explain.

Ans : An atom of Na has a total of 11 electrons. Its electronic configuration is 2, 8, 1. But, Na^+ ion has one electron less than Na atom i.e., it has 10 electrons. Therefore, 2 electrons go to K shell and 8 electrons go to L shell, thereby completely filling K and L shells.

10. If bromine atom is available in the form of, say, two isotopes $^{79}_{35}Br$ (49.7%) and $^{81}_{35}Br$ (50.3%), calculate the average atomic mass of bromine atom.

Ans: It is given that two isotopes of bromine are $^{79}_{35}Br$ (49.7%) and $^{81}_{35}Br$ (50.3%). Then, the average atomic mass of bromine atom is given by:

$$\frac{79 \times 49.7 + 81 \times 50.3}{100} = 80 \text{ u}$$

Hence, the average atomic mass of bromine atom is 80 u

11. The average atomic mass of a sample of an element X is 16.2 u. What are the percentages of isotopes $^{16}_{8}E$ and $^{18}_{8}X$ in the sample?

Ans: Given : Average atomic mass of the sample of element X = 16.2 u.

Let the percentage of isotope $^{18}_{8}X$ be y%. Thus, the percentage of isotope $^{16}_{8}E$ will be (100 − y) %.

Therefore,

$$18 \times \frac{y}{100} + 16 \times \frac{(100-y)}{100} = 16.2$$

$$\frac{18y}{100} + \frac{16(100-y)}{100} = 16.2$$

$$\frac{18y + 1600 - 16y}{100} = 16.2$$

$$18y + 1600 - 16y = 1620$$

$$2y + 1600 = 1620$$

$$2y = 20$$

$$y = 10$$

Hence, the percentage of isotope $^{18}_{8}X$ is 10% and the percentage of isotope $^{16}_{8}E$ is (100 − 10)% = 90%.

12. If Z = 3, what would be the valency of the element? Also, name the element.

Ans: By Z = 3, we mean that the atomic number of the element is 3. Its electronic configuration is 2, 1. Hence, the valency of the element is 1 (since the outer most shell has only one electron).

Therefore, the element with Z = 3 is lithium.

13. Composition of the nuclei of two atomic species X and Y are given as under:

             X   Y

Protons   =   6   6

Neutrons =   6   8

Give the mass numbers of X and Y. What is the relation between the two species?

Ans: Mass number of X = Number of protons + Number of neutrons

= 6 + 6 = 12

Mass number of Y = Number of protons + Number of neutrons

= 6 + 8 = 14

These two atomic species X and Y have the same atomic number but different mass numbers. Hence, they are isotopes.

14. For the following statements, write T for 'True' and F for 'False'.

(a) J.J. Thomson proposed that the nucleus of an atom contains only nucleons.

(b) A neutron is formed by an electron and a proton combining together. Therefore, it is neutral.

(c) The mass of an electron is about $\frac{1}{2000}$ times that of proton.

(d) An isotope of iodine is used for making tincture iodine, which is used as a medicine.

Ans: (a) False   (b) False

(c) True   (d) True

15. Put tick (√) against correct choice and cross (×) against wrong choice in the following questions:

(a) Rutherford's alpha-particle scattering experiment was responsible for the discovery of:

(i) Atomic nucleus

(ii) Electron

(iii) Proton

(iv) Neutron

Ans: Rutherford's alpha-particle scattering experiment was responsible for the discovery of:

(i) Atomic nucleus   (√)

(ii) Electron   (×)

(iii) Proton   (×)

(iv) Neutron   (×)

(b) Isotopes of an element have:

(i) The same physical properties

(ii) Different chemical properties

(iii) Different number of neutrons

(iv) Different atomic numbers

Ans: Isotopes of an element have:

(i) The same physical properties	(×)	
(ii) Different chemical properties	(×)	
(iii) Different number of neutrons	(√)	
(iv) Different atomic numbers	(×)	

(c) Number of valence electrons in Cl⁻ ion are:

(i) 16
(ii) 8
(iii) 17
(iv) 18

Ans : Number of valence electrons in Cl⁻ ion are :

(i) 16	(×)
(ii) 8	(√)
(iii) 17	(×)
(iv) 18	(×)

16. Which one of the following is the correct electronic configuration of sodium?

(i) 2, 8
(ii) 8, 2, 1
(iii) 2, 1, 8
(iv) 2, 8, 1

Ans : (d) The correct electronic configuration of sodium is 2, 8, 1.

17. Complete the following table :

Atomic number	Mass number	Number of neutrons	Number of protons	Number of electrons	Name of the atomic species
9	-	10	-	-	-
16	32	-	-	-	Sulphur
-	24	-	12	-	-
-	2	-	1	-	-
-	1	0	1	1	-

Ans :

Atomic number	Mass number	Number of neutrons	Number of protons	Number of electrons	Name of the atomic species
9	19	10	9	9	Fluorine
16	32	16	16	16	Sulphur
12	24	12	12	12	Magnesium
1	2	1	1	1	Deuterium
1	1	0	1	1	Protium

NCERT EXEMPLAR QUESTIONS

1. Which of the following correctly represent the electronic distribution in the Mg atom?

   (a) 3, 8, 1   (b) 2, 8, 2
   (c) 1, 8, 3   (d) 8, 2, 2

2. Rutherford's alpha particle scattering experiment resulted in the discovery of:

   (a) Electron   (b) Proton
   (c) Nucleus   (d) Atomic mass

3. The number of electrons in an element X is 15 and the number of neutrons is 16. Which of the following is the correct representation of the element?

   (a) $^{31}_{15}X$ (b) $^{31}_{16}X$
   (c) $^{16}_{15}X$ (d) $^{15}_{16}X$

4. Dalton's atomic theory successfully explained :

   (i) Law of conservation of mass
   (ii) Law of constant composition
   (iii) Law of radioactivity
   (iv) Law of multiple proportions

   (a) (i), (ii) and (iii)   (b) (i), (iii) and (iv)
   (c) (ii), (iii) and (iv)   (d) (i), (ii) and (iv)

5. Which of the following statements about Rutherford's model of atom are correct?

   (i) Considered the nucleus as positively charged.
   (ii) Established that the particles are four times as heavy as a hydrogen atom.
   (iii) Can be compared to solar system.

(iv) Was in agreement with Thomson's model
(a) (i) and (iii) (b) (ii) and (iii)
(c) (i) and (iv) (d) only (i)

6. Which of the following are true for an element?
(i) Atomic number = number of protons + number of electrons
(ii) Mass number = number of protons + number of neutrons
(iii) Atomic mass = number of protons = number of neutrons
(iv) Atomic number = number of protons = number of electrons
(a) (i) and (ii) (b) (i) and (iii)
(c) (ii) and (iii) (d) (ii) and (iv)

7. In the Thomson's model of atom, which of the following statements are correct?
(i) The mass of the atom is assumed to be uniformly distributed over the atom.
(ii) The positive charge is assumed to be uniformly distributed over the atom.
(iii) The electrons are uniformly distributed in the positively charged sphere.
(iv) The electrons attract each other to stabilize the atom.
(a) (i), (ii) and (iii) (b) (i) and (iii)
(c) (i) and (iv) (d) (ii), (iii) and (iv)

8. Rutherford's alpha–particle scattering experiment showed that :
(i) Electrons have negative charge.
(ii) The mass and positive charge of the atom is concentrated in the nucleus.
(iii) Neutron exists in the nucleus.
(iv) Most of the space in atom is empty.
Which of the above statements are correct?
(a) (i) and (iii) (b) (ii) and (iv)
(c) (i) and (iv) (d) (iii) and (iv)

9. The ion of an element has 3 positive charges. Mass number of the atom is 27 and the number of neutrons is 14. What is the number of electrons in the ion?
(a) 13 (b) 10
(c) 14 (d) 16

10. Identify the Mg^{2+} ion from the Fig., where, n and p represent the number of neutrons and protons respectively.

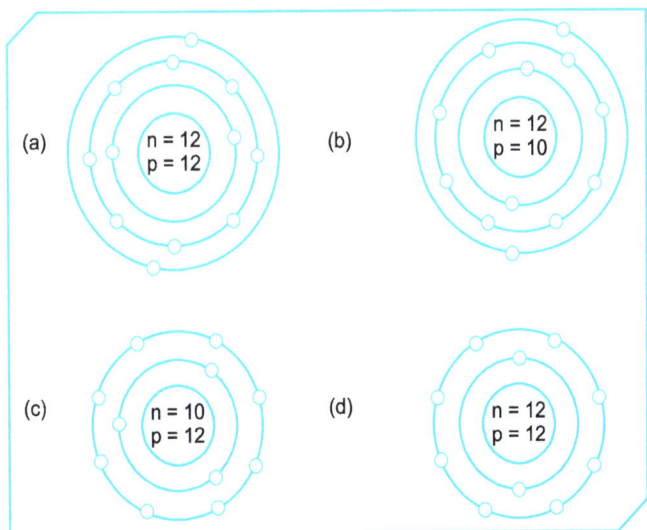

11. In a sample of ethyl ethanoate ($CH_3COOC_2H_5$) the two oxygen atoms have the same number of electrons but different number of neutrons. Which of the following is the correct reason for it?
(a) One of the oxygen atoms has gained electrons.
(b) One of the oxygen atoms has gained two neutrons.
(c) The two oxygen atoms are isotopes
(d) The two oxygen atoms are isobars.

12. Elements with valency 1 are :
(a) Always metals
(b) Always metalloids
(c) Either metals or non-metals
(d) Always non-metals

13. The first model of an atom was given by :
(a) N. Bohr (b) E. Goldstein
(c) Rutherford (d) J.J. Thomson

14. An atom with 3 protons and 4 neutrons will have a valency of :
(a) 3 (b) 7
(c) 1 (d) 4

15. The electron distribution in an aluminium atom is :
(a) 2, 8, 3 (b) 2, 8, 2
(c) 8, 2, 3 (d) 2, 3, 8

16. Which of the following in Fig. do not represent Bohr's model of an atom correctly?

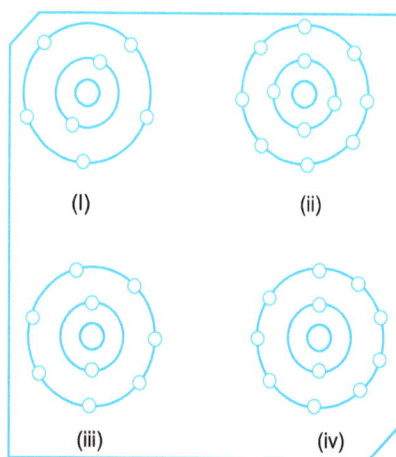

(a) (i) and (ii) (b) (ii) and (iii)
(c) (ii) and (iv) (d) (i) and (iv)

17. Which of the following statement is always correct?

    (a) An atom has equal number of electrons and protons.
    (b) An atom has equal number of electrons and neutrons.
    (c) An atom has equal number of protons and neutrons.
    (d) An atom has equal number of electrons, protons and neutrons.

18. Atomic models have been improved over the years. Arrange the following atomic models in the order of their chronological order :

    (i) Rutherford's atomic model
    (ii) Thomson's atomic model
    (iii) Bohr's atomic model

    (a) (i), (ii) and (iii) (b) (ii), (iii) and (i)
    (c) (ii), (i) and (iii) (d) (iii), (ii) and (i)

ANSWERS

1. (b), 2. (c), 3. (a), 4. (d), 5. (a), 6. (d),
7. (a), 8. (b), 9. (b), 10. (d), 11. (c), 12. (c),
13. (d), 14. (c), 15. (a), 16. (c), 17. (a), 18. (c).

19. Is it possible for the atom of an element to have one electron, one proton and no neutron? If so, name the element.

Ans : Yes, it is true for hydrogen atom which is represented as $_1^1H$.

20. Write any two observations which support the fact that atoms are divisible.

Ans : Discovery of electrons and protons

21. Will ^{35}Cl and ^{37}Cl have different valencies? Justify your answer.

Ans : No, ^{35}Cl and ^{37}Cl are isotopes of an element and so will have the same Valency.

22. Why did Rutherford select a gold foil in his alpha-ray scattering experiment?

Ans : Gold has high malleability.

23. Find out the valency of the atoms represented by the fig.

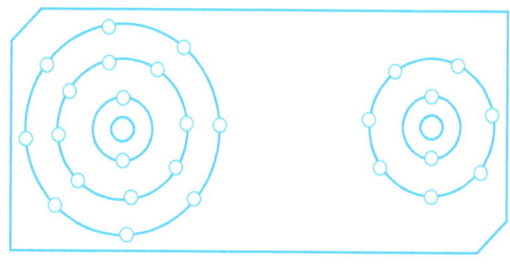

Ans : (a) 0 (b) 1

24. One electron is present in the outer most shell of the atom of an element X. What would be the nature and value of charge on the ion formed if this electron is removed from the outer most shell?

Ans : It is metal as it has only one electron in its outermost shell. The charge is + 1 if this electron is removed from the outer most shell.

25. Write down the electron distribution of chlorine atom. How many electrons are there in the L shell? (Atomic number of chlorine is 17).

Ans : 2, 8, 7. The L shell has eight electrons

26. In the atom of an element X, 6 electrons are present in the outermost shell. If it acquires noble gas configuration by accepting requisite number of electrons, then what would be the charge on the ion so formed?

Ans : In order to attain the noble gas configuration, the element requires two more electrons. Hence, the charge on the ion will be −2.

27. In response to a question, a student stated that in an atom, the number of protons is greater than the number of neutrons, which in turn is greater than the number of electrons. Do you agree with the statement? Justify your answer.

Ans : No, the statement is incorrect. In an atom the number of protons and electrons is always equal.

28. Calculate the number of neutrons present in the nucleus of an element X which is represented as $_{15}^{31}X$.

Ans : Mass number = No. of protons + No. of neutrons
= 31
∴ Number of neutrons = 31 − number of protons
= 31 − 15
= 16

Hence, the number of neutrons in the nucleus of the element X is 16.

29. Match the names of the scientists given in column A with their contributions towards the understanding of the atomic structure as given in column B :

(A)	(B)
(a) Ernest Rutherford	(i) Indivisibility of atoms
(b) J.J.Thomson	(ii) Stationary orbits
(c) Dalton	(iii) Concept of nucleus
(d) Neils Bohr	(iv) Discovery of electrons
(e) James Chadwick	(v) Atomic number
(f) E. Goldstein	(vi) Neutron
(g) Mosley	(vii) Canal rays

Ans : (a) (iii) (b) (iv) (c) (i) (d) (ii) (e) (vi) (f) (vii) (g) (v)

30. The atomic number of calcium and argon are 20 and 18 respectively, but the mass number of both these elements is 40. What is the name given to such a pair of elements?

Ans: Isobars

31. Complete the Table on the basis of information available in the symbols given below:

(a) $_{17}^{35}Cl$ (b) $_{6}^{12}C$ (c) $_{35}^{81}Br$

S.No.	Element	n_p	n_n
(a)			
(b)			
(c)			

Ans :

S. No.	Element	n_p	n_n
(a)	Cl	17	18
(b)	C	6	6
(c)	Br	35	46

32. Helium atom has 2 electrons in its valence shell but its valency is not 2, Explain.

Ans: Helium atom has 2 electrons in its outermost shell and its duplet is complete. Hence, the valency is zero.

33. Fill in the blanks in the following statements :
   (a) Rutherford's alpha-particle scattering experiment led to the discovery of the _____
   (b) Isotopes have same _____ but different _____.
   (c) Neon and chlorine have atomic numbers 10 and 17 respectively. Their valencies will be _____ and _____ respectively.
   (d) The electronic configuration of silicon is _____ and that of sulphur is _____.

Ans: (a) Atomic nucleus
   (b) Atomic number, mass number
   (c) 0 and 1.
   (d) 2, 8, 4; 2, 8, 6

34. An element X has a mass number 4 and atomic number 2. Write the valency of this element?

Ans: Valency is zero as K shell is completely filled.

35. Why do Helium, Neon and Argon have a zero valency?

Ans: Helium has two electrons in its only energy shell, while Argon and Neon have 8 electrons in their valence shells. As these have maximum number of electrons in their valence shells, they do not have any tendency to combine with other elements. Hence, they have a valency equal to zero.

36. The ratio of the radii of hydrogen atom and its nucleus is ~ 10^5. Assuming the atom and the nucleus to be spherical, (a) what will be the ratio of their sizes? (b) If atom is represented by planet earth 'R_e' = 6.4 ×10^6 m, estimate the size of the nucleus.

Ans : (a) Volume of sphere = $\frac{4}{3}\pi r^3$

Let R be the radius of the atom and r be the radius of the nucleus.
Then,
$$R = 10^5 r$$

$$\text{Volume of atom} = \frac{4}{3}\pi r^3 = \frac{4}{3}\pi(10^5 r)^3$$

$$\Rightarrow \frac{4}{3}\pi \times 10^{15}$$

$$\text{Volume of the nucleus} = \frac{4}{3}\pi r^3$$

Ratio of the size of the atom to that of nucleus

$$= \frac{\frac{4}{3} \times 10^{15} \times \pi r^3}{\frac{4}{3}\pi r^3}$$

$$= 10^{15}$$

(b) If the atom is represented by the Earth $R_e = 6.4 \times 10^6$ m, then

Radius of the nucleus, $r_n = \dfrac{R_e}{10^5}$

$r_n = \dfrac{6.4 \times 10^6}{10^5} = 64$ m

37. Enlist the conclusions drawn by Rutherford from his alpha-ray scattering experiment.

Ans : Rutherford concluded from the alpha-particle scattering experiment that :
(a) Most of the space inside the atom is empty because most of the alpha-particles passed through the gold foil without getting deflected.
(b) Very few particles were deflected from their path, indicating that the positive charge of the atom occupies very little space.
(c) A very small fraction of alpha-particles were deflected by 180°, indicating that all the positive charges and mass of the gold atom were concentrated in a very small volume within the atom. From the data, he also calculated that the radius of the nucleus is about 10^5 times less than the radius of the atom.

38. In what way is the Rutherford's atomic model different from that of Thomson's atomic model?

Ans : Rutherford proposed a model in which electrons revolve around the nucleus in well-defined orbits. There is a positively charged centre in an atom called the nucleus. He also proposed that the size of the nucleus is very small as compared to the size of the atom and nearly all the mass of an atom is centred in the nucleus whereas, Thomson proposed the model of an atom to be similar to a Christmas pudding. The electrons are studded like currants in a positively charged sphere like Christmas pudding and the mass of the atom was supposed to be uniformly distributed.

39. What were the drawbacks of Rutherford's model of an atom?

Ans : The orbital revolution of the electron is not expected to be stable. Any particle in a circular orbit would undergo an acceleration and the charged particles would radiate energy. Thus, the revolving electron would lose energy and finally fall into the nucleus. If this were so, the atom should be highly unstable and hence matter would not exist in the form that we know.

40. What are the postulates of Bohr's model of an atom?

Ans : The postulates put forth by Neils Bohr's about the model of an atom :
(a) Only certain orbits known as discrete orbits of electrons are allowed inside the atom.
(b) While revolving in discrete orbits the electrons do not radiate energy. These orbits are called energy levels. Energy levels in an atom are shown by circles. These orbits are represented by the letters K,L,M,N,… or the numbers, n = 1,2,3,4,….

41. Show diagrammatically the electron distribution in a sodium atom and a sodium ion and also give their atomic number.

Ans : Since the atomic number of sodium atom is 11, it has 11 electrons. A positively charged sodium ion (Na^+) is formed by the removal of one electron from a sodium atom. So, a sodium ion has 11−1 = 10 electrons in it. Thus, electronic distribution of sodium ion will be 2, 8. The atomic number of an element is equal to the number of protons in its atom. Since, sodium atom and sodium ion contain the same number of protons, therefore, the atomic number of both is 11.

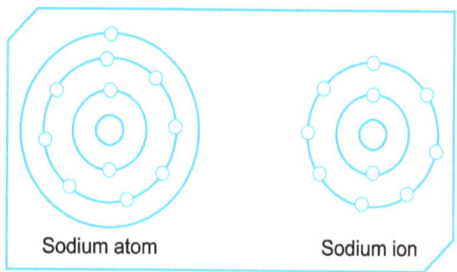

Sodium atom   Sodium ion

43. In the Gold foil experiment of Geiger and Marsden, that paved the way for Rutherford's model of an atom, ~ 1.00% of the alpha-particles were found to deflect at angles > 50°. If one mole of alpha-particles were bombarded on the gold foil, compute the number of alpha-

particles that would deflect at angles less than 50°.

Ans: % of alpha particles deflected more than 50° = 1%

% of alpha particles deflected less than 50° = 100 − 1 = 99%

No. of alpha particles bombarded = 1 mole = 6.022×10^{23} particles

No. of particles that were deflected at an angle less than 50° = $\dfrac{99}{100} \times 6.022 \times 10^{23} = 5.96 \times 10^{23}$

Hence, the number of alpha-particles that would deflect at angles less than 50° is 5.96×10^{23}.

HIGHER ORDER THINKING SKILLS QUESTIONS (HOTS)

1. After explaining Rutherford gold foil experiment to the students, a teacher asked the following questions to the students:

    (a) Why Rutherford choosed the gold foil for his alpha particle scattering experiment?

    (b) This experiment led to the discovery of ---------------------.

Ans : (a) Due to high malleability of gold, Rutherford chose the gold foil for his alpha particle scattering experiment.

    (b) Nucleus.

2. Anil, a science teacher explained the students about the representation of an element as $^{9}_{4}X$. John, a student asked the teacher following questions:

    (a) What does the number 9 indicate?

    (b) What does the number 4 indicate?

    (c) How do you find the number of protons, neutrons and electrons in atom X ?

Ans : (a) The number 9 in the symbol indicates the mass number of the element X.

    (b) The number 4 in the symbol indicates the atomic number of the element X.

    (c) Atomic number of element = Number of protons

    Therefore, the number of protons = 4

    Number of protons = Number of electrons

    Therefore, the number of electrons = 4

    Number of neutrons = Mass number − Atomic number

    Therefore, number of neutrons = 9 − 4 = 5

3. Nirmal who lives in a village has a tumour in his body. He has come to city for treatment. The doctor examined the tumour and then removed some tissue from the tumour and sent it for biopsy to find out the nature of the tumour. The result of biopsy showed that the tumour was malignant and that Nirmal had come to the doctor at an early stage. The doctor recommended for radiotherapy.

    (a) Identify the disease.

    (b) What do you understand by the term 'tumour', 'biopsy' and 'radiotherapy'?

    (c) Which radioactive isotope is used in the treatment of this disease by radiotherapy?

Ans : (a) Nirmal was suffering from cancer.

    (b) **Tumour :** It is the swelling of a part of the body caused by an abnormal growth of tissue.

    Biopsy : It is a method of examining the tissue removed from the tumour.

    Radiotherapy : It is the treatment of cancer disease by using high energy radiations to destroy the cancer cells in the affected area of the body.

    (c) Cobalt-60 (Co-60).

4. What would be the total number of electrons in an atom if K and L shells of an atom are completely filled? Give its valency.

Ans : According to Bohr-Bury scheme, 'K' shell of an atom can have maximum of two electrons and 'L' shell of an atom can have maximum of eight electrons. If these two shells are completely filled, then

    (a) The total number of electrons in an atom = 2 + 8 = 10

    (b) Valency of the atom will be zero.

5. An atom of an element has two electrons in outermost M shell. Find it's (a) Electronic configuration (b) Atomic number (c) Number of protons (d) Valency (e) Name.

Ans : Since the atom of an element has two electrons in outermost M-shell which means that K and L shells are completely filled with electrons of 2 and 8.

    (a) The electronic configuration : 2(K) 8(L) 2(M) : 2, 8, 2

    (b) Atomic number : 2 + 8 + 2 = 12

(c) We know that atomic number is equal to the total number of protons, therefore

Atomic number = 12

(d) Valency of the element is equal to the number of electrons in the outermost shell

Valency = 2

(e) Atomic number 12 belongs to the element Magnesium (Mg).

6. Choose the isotopes from the following nuclei:
(a) 20p + 20n (b) 8p + 8n (c) 8p + 9n (d) 18p + 22n

Ans : For isotopes, the pair of nuclei should possess same atomic number i.e., same number of protons. In the choice given, (b) and (c) possess eight protons. Hence, (b) and (c) are isotopes.

7. The element given is $^{16}_{8}E$: Find (a) Number of protons, electrons and neutrons (b) Valency.

Ans : (a) In the symbol, the subscript represents the atomic number.

We know that,

Atomic number = Number of protons

Therefore,

The number of protons = 8

The total number of protons = Total number of electrons

Therefore,

The total number of electrons = 8

In the symbol, the superscript denotes the mass number.

Number of neutrons = Mass number − Atomic number

Therefore,

The total number of neutrons = 16 − 8 = 8

(b) Since atomic number is equal to 8,

The electronic configuration = 2, 6

Therefore, the valency of element E = 2

8. A particle 'E' has 17 protons, 17 electrons and 18 neutrons. Find out : (a) Mass number of element E (b) Atomic number of element E (c) Valency of element E (d) Name the element E.

Ans : (a) Mass number of element, E = Number of protons + Number of neutrons

Therefore,

Mass number of element, E = 17 + 18 = 35

(b) Atomic number of an element, E = Number of protons

Therefore,

Atomic number of element, E = 17

(c) The atomic number of element E is 17

Therefore, electronic configuration will be 2, 8, 7

Hence, valency is 1

(d) The atomic number 17 belongs to the element Chlorine (Cl).

MULTIPLE CHOICE QUESTIONS (MCQs)

1. Proton was discovered by :
   (a) Rutherford
   (b) Goldstein
   (c) Chadwick
   (d) J.J. Thomson

2. Canal rays are :
   (a) Negative charged particles
   (b) Positive charged particles
   (c) Beam of neutrons
   (d) Gamma radiation

3. α-particles are :
   (a) Negative charged particles
   (b) Positive charged particles
   (c) Beam of neutrons
   (d) Gamma radiation

4. An α-particle is :
   (a) A Hydrogen nucleus
   (b) A Helium nucleus
   (c) A proton
   (d) An electron

5. Rutherford's gold foil experiment showed that most of the α-particles passed through the gold foil without any deflection. It indicates that :
   (a) The nucleus is concentrated at the centre
   (b) The nucleus carries positive charge
   (c) There is lot of empty space in atom
   (d) The nucleus carries the most of the mass

6. Two elements X and Y have the same atomic mass but their atomic numbers are 20 and 21 respectively. X and Y are :
   (a) Isobars
   (b) Isotones
   (c) Isomers
   (d) Isotopes

7. In an atom, the mass number of an atom is equal to the number of :
   (a) Nucleons
   (b) Protons
   (c) Electrons
   (d) Neutrons

STRUCTURE OF ATOM

8. Number of neutrons present in Hydrogen atom is :
   (a) 0 (b) 1
   (c) 2 (d) 3

9. Protium, Deutrium and Tritium are isotopes of:
   (a) Rhodium (b) Sodium
   (c) Hydrogen (d) Helium

10. If Z represents the atomic number and A represents mass number, then the number of neutrons in an atom can be computed as :
    (a) A + Z (b) A – Z
    (c) Z – A (d) Z

11. If Z represents the atomic number and A represents mass number, then the number of electrons in an atom can be computed as :
    (a) A + Z (b) A – Z
    (c) Z – A (d) Z

12. The electronic configuration of an atom is 2,8,3. The number of valence electrons in the atom is:
    (a) 13 (b) 10
    (c) 3 (d) 8

13. The number of electrons in the outermost shell in the atom of an inert element is :
    (a) 0 (b) 1
    (c) 2 (d) 8

14. Which one of the following will have the maximum charge/mass ratio?
    (a) Electron (b) Proton
    (c) Neutron (d) α-particle

15. The maximum number of electrons that can be accommodated in M shell is :
    (a) 2 (b) 8
    (c) 18 (d) 32

ANSWERS
1. (b), 2. (b), 3. (b), 4. (b), 5. (c), 6. (a), 7. (a), 8. (a), 9. (c), 10. (b), 11. (d), 12. (c), 13. (d), 14. (a), 15. (c).

VERY SHORT ANSWER TYPE QUESTIONS

1. Write the names of three elementary particles which constitute an atom.
2. Name the scientist and his experiment to prove that nucleus of an atom is positively charged.
3. Which is heavier, neutron or proton?
4. If an atom contains one electron and one proton, will it carry any charge or not?
5. How many times a proton is heavier than an electron?
6. What was the model of an atom proposed by Thomson?
7. On the basis of Thomson's model of an atom, explain how the atom is neutral as a whole?
8. How many electrons at the maximum can be present in the first shell?
9. Define cathode rays.
10. What type of charge is present on the nucleus of an atom?
11. Give the number of protons in $^{35}_{17}Cl$.
12. Define the mass number of an element.
13. What are isobars?
14. Name the particles which determine the mass of an atom.
15. What are canal rays?
16. Define the term atomic number.
17. Write the relation between mass number and atomic number.

SHORT ANSWER TYPE-I QUESTIONS

1. Define the following terms : (a) Atomic number (b) Mass number
2. What is the mass and charge of an electron?
3. Write the charges on sub atomic particles.
4. Identify the isotopes out of A , B , C and D ?
   $^{33}_{17}A$, $^{40}_{20}B$, $^{37}_{17}C$, $^{38}_{19}D$.
5. Give one achievement and one limitation of J.J Thomson's model of atom?
6. What are valence electrons? Give example.
7. Which kind of elements have tendency to lose electrons? Give example.
8. How many electrons are present in the valence shell of nitrogen and argon?
9. What do you think would be the observation if the alpha-particle scattering experiment is carried out using a foil of a metal other than gold?
10. State the maximum capacity of various shells to accommodate electrons.
11. Helium atom has an atomic mass of 4 units and 2 protons in its nucleus. How many neutrons are present in its nucleus?
12. Give the symbol, relative charge and mass of the three sub atomic particles.

13. Name the scientists who discovered :
    (a) Nucleus of atom.
    (b) Proton.
14. Name the particles which are present in the nucleus and what type of charge is there on them?
15. From the symbol $^{32}_{16}S$ give :
    (a) Atomic number of sulphur.
    (b) Mass number of sulphur.
    (c) Electronic configuration of sulphur.

SHORT ANSWER TYPE-II QUESTIONS

1. Why Helium has zero valency?
2. An atom contains 3 protons, 3 electrons and 4 neutrons. Give its :
    (a) Atomic number
    (b) Mass number
    (c) Valency
3. Find the valency of chlorine, magnesium and sulphur.
4. How are the isotopes of hydrogen represented?
5. Write the complete symbol for the atom with the given atomic number (Z) and mass number (A).
    (a) Z= 17, A = 35
    (b) Z=4, A = 9
    (c) Z= 92, A= 233
6. What would be the electronic configuration of Na^+, Al^{3+}, O^{2-} and Cl^-.
7. What are the similarities and dissimilarities between isotopes of same species? Give example with reasons.
8. Differentiate between canal rays and cathode rays.
9. What is the relation between the valency of an element and the number of valence electrons in its atoms? Explain.
10. Differentiate between the isotopes of hydrogen.

LONG ANSWER TYPE QUESTIONS

1. (a) Give the observations as well as inferences of Rutherford's scattering experiment for determining the structure of an atom.
   (b) On the basis of above experiment write the main features of atomic model.
2. Write the main postulates of Bohr's model of atom.
3. Describe the structure of atom as explained by J.J Thomson.
4. (a) What are cathode rays?
   (b) How cathode rays are formed from the gas taken in the discharge tube?
   (c) What was the result of the cathode ray experiment ?
5. Describe Rutherford's model of an atom.
6. (a) State one drawback of Rutherford's model of an atom.
   (b) How did Bohr explain the stability of the atom?
7. (a) What are radioactive isotopes? Give two examples.
   (b) Mention any three applications of radioactive isotopes.
8. Explain isobars with a few examples.
9. Explain the electrovalency in : (a) Chlorine (b) Nitrogen (c) Magnesium.
10. Describe covalency in : (a) Carbon (b) Hydrogen (c) Nitrogen.

EXERCISES (UNSOLVED)

VIVA VOCE QUESTIONS

1. Which particles are responsible for the mass of the element ? Protons or Neutrons
2. If electrons are more in number than protons in a species, then predict the nature of the ion.
3. Name the metal used by Rutherford in making thin foils.
4. Who discovered neutron for the first time ?
5. What is regarded as universal particle ? Proton or Electron
6. Which isotope of carbon is used for carbon dating ?
7. What is the actual mass of a proton ?
8. Which energy shell is closer to the nucleus of an atom ?
9. What is the number of neutrons present in C – 14 isotope of carbon ?
10. Which one is slightly heavier ? Proton or neutron

NAME THE FOLLOWING

1. The positive particle in the nucleus of an atom.
2. The charge on the proton.
3. The number of neutrons in the hydrogen atom of mass 1.
4. Mass of atom with 12 electrons and 13 neutrons.
5. The neutral particle in an atom.

STRUCTURE OF ATOM

6. The atomic number of fluorine.
7. The charge on the electron.
8. The centre of an atom.
9. The maximum number of electrons in 2nd shell.
10. The charge on the neutron.

COMPLETE THE CHART

Name of the element	Symbol of the element	Atomic number	Mass number	No. of protons	No. of electrons	No. of neutrons	Electronic configuration			
							K	L	M	N
Hydrogen	H	1	1				1			
Helium		2	4			2	2			
Lithium		3								
Beryllium	Be		9	4						
Boron		6		5	5	6	2	3		
Carbon		6		6		6				
Nitrogen		7	14							
Oxygen	O		16			8	2	6		
Fluorine	F	9		9	9	10	2	7		
Neon		10					2	8		
Sodium	Na	11	23		11					
Magnesium	Mg	12		12		12				
Aluminium		13		13		14	2	8	3	
Silicon			28		14		2	8	4	
Phosphorus	P	15	31		15					
Sulphur	S	16			16					
Chlorine	Cl	17	35			18	2	8	7	
Argon			40		18		2	8	8	
Potassium			39							
Calcium	Ca	20			20					

TRUE OR FALSE

1. Electrons lose energy of its own while revolving around the nucleus.
2. Electrons are stationary in different energy shells.
3. The nucleus of an atom contains neutrons only.
4. All atoms exist independently.
5. Mass of an alpha particle is twice than that of proton.
6. The outermost shells in an atom have more than 8 electrons.
7. A cation contains more protons than electrons.
8. Deuterium is also called heavy hydrogen.
9. I-131 is effective in the treatment of cancer.
10. Protium has 1 neutron.
11. Isotopes of an element are chemically similar.
12. Isotopes of an element have always the same number of protons.

FILL IN THE BLANKS

1. _____ rays are negatively charged.
2. The fundamental particle not present in hydrogen atom is _____.
3. Rutherford's scattering experiment is related to the size of _____.
4. The fundamental sub-atomic particle called neutron was discovered by _____.
5. The _____ fundamental sub-atomic particles are negatively charged.

6. The _____ of an atom is dense, small in size and is positively charged.
7. The total number of protons and neutrons in the nucleus of an atom is called its _____.
8. Atomic number is equal to _____.
9. _____ electrons are located in the outermost shell of an atom.
10. The mass number of an atom is equal to the number of _____ in its nucleus.
11. The maximum number of electrons that can be accommodated in L shell are _____.
12. _____ are atoms of the same element, which have same number of protons but different mass numbers.
13. The ------------ are fundamental sub-atomic particles that have no charge.
14. Co-60 a radioisotope is used in treatment of _____.
15. The fundamental sub-atomic particles _____ are positively charged.
16. Mass of a proton is _____ times the mass of an electron.
17. _____ are atoms of different elements which have same number of nnucleons but different atomic numbers.
18. Anode _____ rays are also called.
19. _____ is regarded as a universal particle.
20. _____ isotope is the source of nuclear energy.

MATCH THE FOLLOWING

1. Match the column 1 and column 2.

S. No	Column 1	Column 2	Correct match
1.	Discovery of electron	Chadwick	
2.	Discovery of proton	Rutherford	
3.	Discovery of neutron	Goldstein	
4.	Discovery of nucleus	J. J. Thomson	

2. Match the element with electronic configuration.

S. No	Column 1	Column 2	Correct match
1.	Chlorine	2,8,8,1	
2.	Nitrogen	2,8,8	
3.	Phosphorus	2,8,7	
4.	Potassium	2,8,5	
5.	Argon	2,5	

3. Match the element with their valency.

S. No	Column 1	Column 2	Correct match
1.	Aluminium	–3	
2.	Nitrogen	–2	
3.	Magnesium	+3	
4.	Oxygen	+1	
5.	Sodium	+2	

DATA BASED QUESTIONS

1. From the table given below, find a pair of isotopes.

Particle	Protons	Electrons	Neutrons
A	17	17	18
B	3	2	4
C	18	18	22
D	17	17	20
E	9	10	10

2. From the table given below, find out the relation between the two species. Which element or elements they represent.

Element	Protons	Neutrons
X	18	20
Y	20	20

3. From the table given below, find out :

Particle	Protons	Electrons	Neutrons
A	8	8	8
B	8	8	9

(a) The mass number of A and B.
(b) The relation between A and B.
(c) Identify the element A and B.

STRUCTURE OF ATOM

4. Complete the table.

Protons	Neutrons	Mass number	Atomic number	Electrons	Valency
11	12	-------------	-------------	-------------	-------------

5. Complete the table.

Atomic number	Mass number	Protons	Electrons	Neutrons	Symbol
10	22	----------	----------	----------	----------

SYMPOSIUM

Topic 1 : Electronic configuration of elements from 1 – 20.

Key words :

(a) Introduction.

(b) Aligning of elements.

(c) Protons, electrons and neutrons.

(d) Formulae to find out the fundamental particles.

(e) Explaining each element with diagram.

(f) Conclusion.

Topic 2 : Model of atoms

Key words :

(a) Introduction.

(b) Thomson's model of an atom.

(c) Rutherford's model of an atom.

(d) Bohr's model of an atom.

(e) Conclusion.

GROUP DISCUSSION

Topic 1 : Isotopes

(a) Introduction.

(b) Illustrating with examples.

(c) Conclusion

Topic 2 : Application of isotopes

Key words :

(a) Introduction

(b) Medicine

(c) Leakage detection

(d) Nuclear power plant

(e) Conclusion

ANSWERS

VIVA VOCE QUESTIONS

1. Neutrons
2. Anion
3. Gold
4. Chadwick
5. Electron
6. C- 14
7. 1.67×10^{-27} kg
8. K shell
9. 8 neutrons
10. Neutron

NAME THE FOLLOWING

1. Proton
2. +1
3. Zero
4. 25
5. Neutron
6. 9
7. –1
8. Nucleus
9. 8
10. Zero

CONCISE CHEMISTRY - IX   STRUCTURE OF ATOM

COMPLETE THE CHART

1.

Name of the element	Symbol of the element	Atomic number	Mass number	No. of protons	No. of electrons	No. of neutrons	Electronic configuration			
							K	L	M	N
Hydrogen	H	1	1	1	1	-	1	-	-	-
Helium	He	2	4	2	2	2	2			
Lithium	Li	3	7	3	3	4	2	1		
Beryllium	Be	4	9	4	4	5	2	2		
Boron	B	5	11	5	5	6	2	3		
Carbon	C	6	12	6	6	6	2	4		
Nitrogen	N	7	14	7	7	7	2	5		
Oxygen	O	8	16	8	8	8	2	6		
Fluorine	F	9	19	9	9	10	2	7		
Neon	Ne	10	20	10	10	10	2	8		
Sodium	Na	11	23	11	11	12	2	8	1	
Magnesium	Mg	12	24	12	12	12	2	8	2	
Aluminium	Al	13	27	13	13	14	2	8	4	
Silicon	Si	14	28	14	14	14	2	8	4	
Phosphorus	P	15	31	15	15	16	2	8	5	
Sulphur	S	16	32	16	16	16	2	8	6	
Chlorine	Cl	17	35	17	17	18	2	8	7	
Argon	Ar	18	40	18	18	22	2	8	8	
Potassium	K	19	39	19	19	20	2	8	8	1
Calcium	Ca	20	40	20	20	20	2	8	8	2

TRUE OR FALSE

1. False
2. False
3. False
4. False
5. False
6. False
7. True
8. True
9. False
10. False
11. True
12. True

FILL IN THE BLANKS

1. Cathode rays
2. Neutron
3. Nucleus
4. Chadwick
5. Electrons
6. Nucleus
7. Mass number
8. Number of protons or electrons
9. Valence
10. Nucleons
11. Eight
12. Isotopes
13. Neutrons
14. Cancer
15. Protons
16. 1836
17. Isobars
18. Canal rays
19. Electrons
20. U-235

STRUCTURE OF ATOM

MATCH THE FOLLOWING

1.

S. No	Column 1	Column 2	Correct match
1.	Discovery of electron	Chadwick	3
2.	Discovery of proton	Rutherford	4
3.	Discovery of neutron	Goldstein	2
4.	Discovery of nucleus	J. J. Thomson	1

2.

S. No	Column 1	Column 2	Correct Match
1.	Chlorine	2,8,8,1	4
2.	Nitrogen	2,8,8	5
3.	Phosphorus	2,8,7	1
4.	Potassium	2,8,5	3
5.	Argon	2,5	2

3.

S. No	Column 1	Column 2	Correct match
1.	Aluminium	-3	2
2.	Nitrogen	-2	4
3.	Magnesium	+3	1
4.	Oxygen	+1	5
5.	Sodium	+2	3

DATA BASED QUESTIONS

1. The elements consisting of same number of protons and different number of neutrons are called isotopes. In the particles A and D, there are same numbers of protons but different number of neutrons. Hence, these particles are called isotopes.

2. The mass number of X and Y are 40. The atoms belonging to the different elements with same mass numbers, but different atomic numbers are called isobars. Hence, these are isobars.

   The element X has 18 protons. Hence, the atomic number is also 18. The element with atomic number 18 is Argon (Ar). The element Y has 20 protons. Hence, the atomic number is also 20. The element with atomic number 20 is Calcium (Ca).

3. (a) Mass number of A = Protons + Neutrons = 8 + 8 = 16,

   Mass number of B = Protons + Neutrons = 8 + 9 = 17

   (b) The elements consisting of same number of protons and different number of neutrons are called isotopes. Thus, A and B are isotopes.

   (c) The atomic number is equal to the number of protons. The element with atomic number 8 is oxygen (O).

4.

Protons	Neutrons	Mass number	Atomic number	Electrons	Valency
11	12	P + N 23	At. No = P 11	P = E 11	E. C = 2, 8, 1 1

5.

Atomic number	Mass number	Protons	Electrons	Neutrons	Symbol
10	22	10	10	12	Element 10 is Ne

MOCK TEST-1

Time : 2 Hours   Max. Marks : 50

General Instructions :
- All questions are compulsory.
- There is no overall choice.
- Questions 1 to 5 are one mark questions. These are to be answered in one word or in one sentence.
- Questions 6 to 10 are two marks questions. These are to be answered in about 30 words each.

- Questions 11 to 15 are three marks questions. These are to be answered in about 50 words each.
- Questions 16 to 19 are five marks questions. These are to be answered in about 70 words each.

1. Which sub-atomic particles are same in number in atoms of isobars?
2. Name the particles which determine the mass of an atom.
3. Name two elements which are isobars.
4. Name the particles which are present in the nucleus of an atom.
5. Name the isotope used in the treatment of cancer.
6. Find out the number of valence electrons in : (a) Sodium ion (b) Chloride ion
7. Why neon, helium and argon have zero valencies ?
8. What are the isotopes of carbon ? Give their symbols.
9. Compare a proton and a neutron w.r.t mass and charge.
10. What are the results of alpha-particle scattering experiment ?
11. What are radioactive isotopes ? Mention its applications.
12. Explain why the atomic masses of many elements are in fractions and not in whole numbers ?
13. Describe Thomson's model of an atom.
14. How was it shown that an atom has a lot of empty space within it ?
15. Explain the electrovalency with two examples.
16. Describe Rutherford's scattering experiment.
17. Explain the cause of inertness of noble gases.
18. Explain the arrangement of electrons in an atom by giving examples.
19. Explain the characteristics of cathode rays.

MOCK TEST-2

Time : 2 Hours
Max. Marks : 50

General Instructions :
- All questions are compulsory.
- There is no overall choice.
- Questions 1 to 5 are one mark questions. These are to be answered in one word or in one sentence.
- Questions 6 to 10 are two marks questions. These are to be answered in about 30 words each.
- Questions 11 to 15 are three marks questions. These are to be answered in about 50 words each.
- Questions 16 to 19 are five marks questions. These are to be answered in about 70 words each.

1. What is the mass of a proton ?
2. What are shells ?
3. Name a species which has only $1p^+$ and $1e^-$.
4. Which is heavier ? Proton or Neutron.
5. What is the number of electrons in the valence shell of chlorine (Z = 17) ?
6. Name the elements which have the following electronic configurations : (a) 2,8,1 (b) 2,6 (c) 2,8,8 (d) 2,8,4
7. What are the isotopes of hydrogen ? Give their symbol and name.
8. Compare a proton and an electron w.r.t mass and charge.
9. Mention two observations which show that the atom is not indivisible.
10. Define valency of an element. Give the relation between the valency of an element and the number of valence electrons in its atoms ?
11. Explain isobars with examples.
12. Describe Rutherford's model of an atom.
13. Explain electronic configuration by giving examples.
14. Explain covalency of two elements.
15. Describe Bohr's model of an atom.
16. How are mass and charge of an electron determined ?
17. Compare the characteristics of anode rays.
18. Explain the role of radioactive isotopes in the field of medicine.
19. A sample of an element E contains two isotopes $^{16}_{8}E$ and $^{18}_{8}E$. If the average atomic mass of this sample of the element be 16.2 u, calculate the percentage of the two isotopes in this sample.